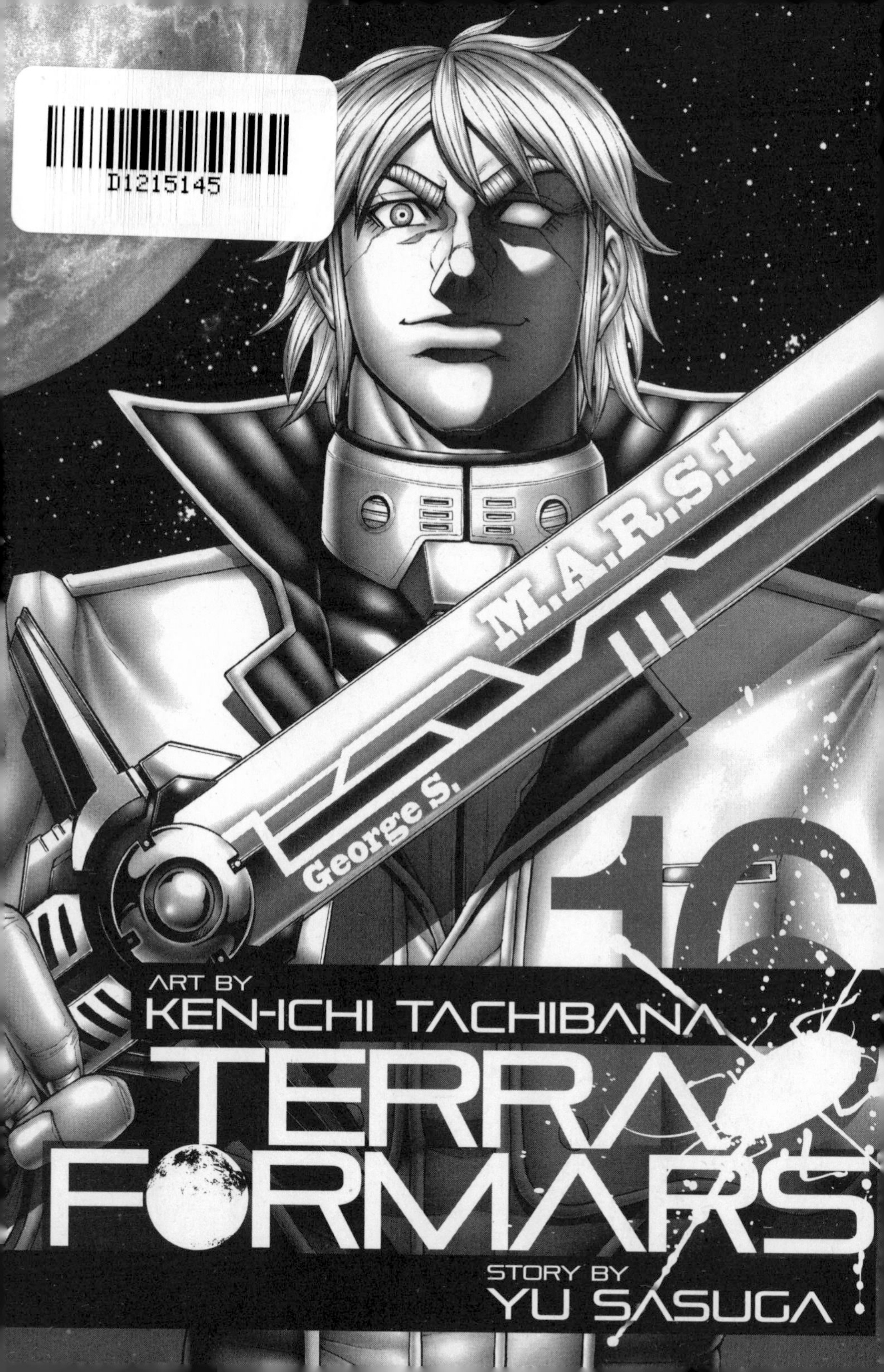
M.A.R.S.1
George S.
ART BY
KEN-ICHI TACHIBANA
TERRA FORMARS
STORY BY
YU SASUGA

TERRA FORMARS 16

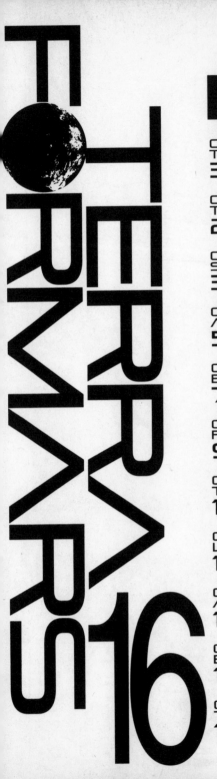

CONTENTS

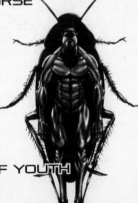

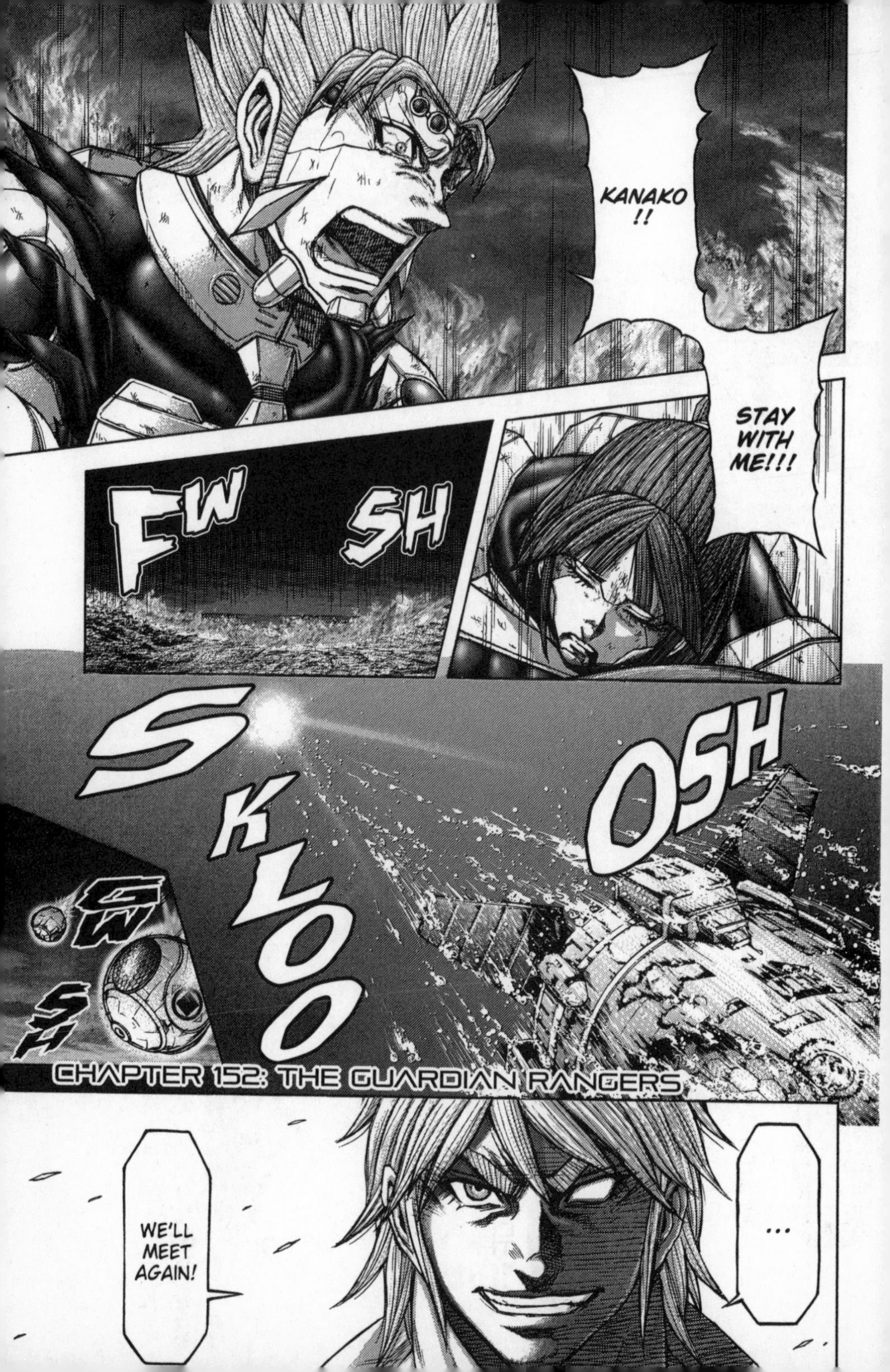
KANAKO !!
STAY WITH ME!!!
FWSH
SKLOOSH
GWSH
...
WE'LL MEET AGAIN!

CHAPTER 152: THE GUARDIAN RANGERS

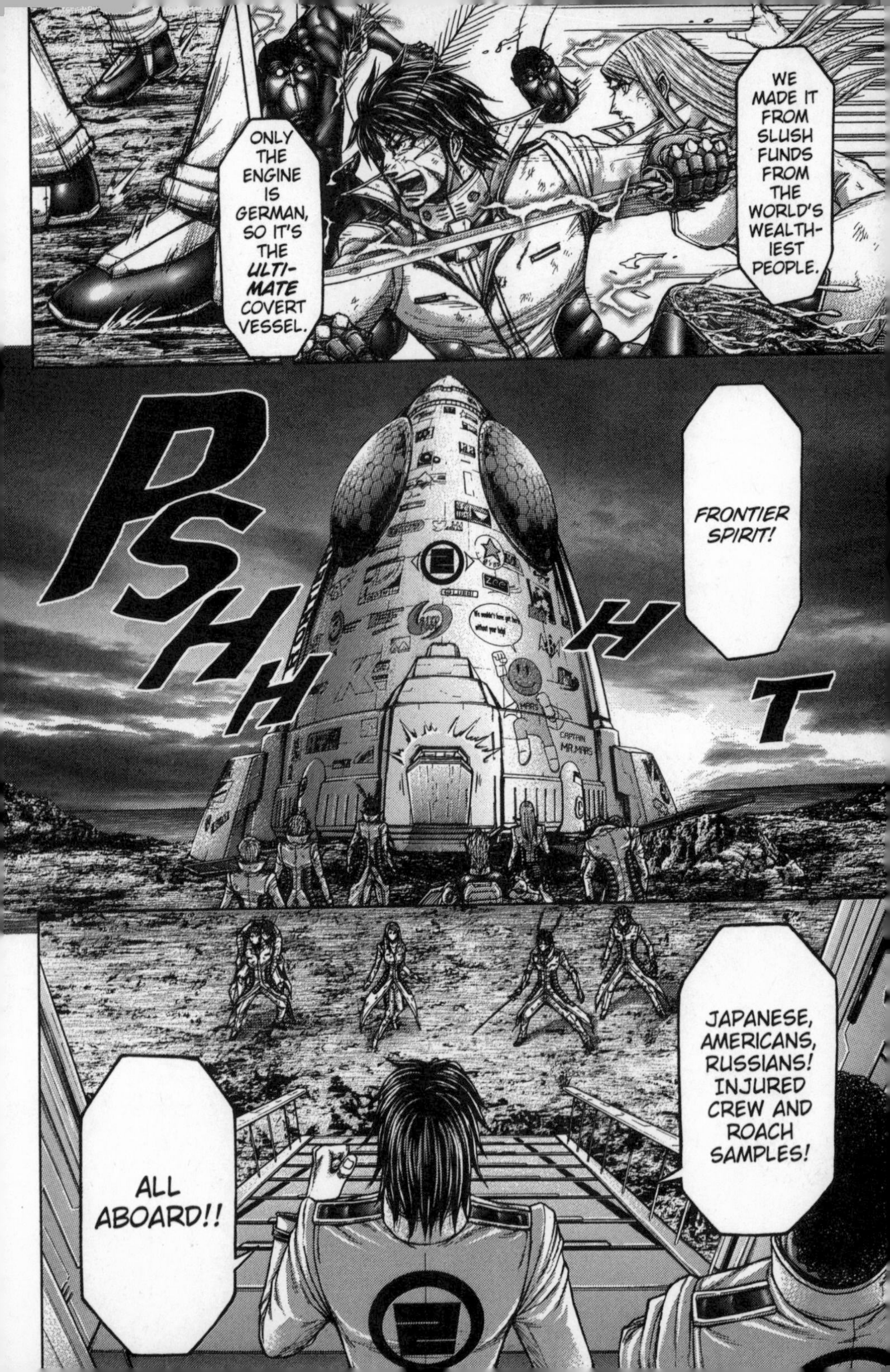

WE MADE IT FROM SLUSH FUNDS FROM THE WORLD'S WEALTHIEST PEOPLE.
ONLY THE ENGINE IS GERMAN, SO IT'S THE *ULTIMATE* COVERT VESSEL.
PSHHHT
FRONTIER SPIRIT!
CAPTAIN MR.MARS
JAPANESE, AMERICANS, RUSSIANS! INJURED CREW AND ROACH SAMPLES!
ALL ABOARD!!

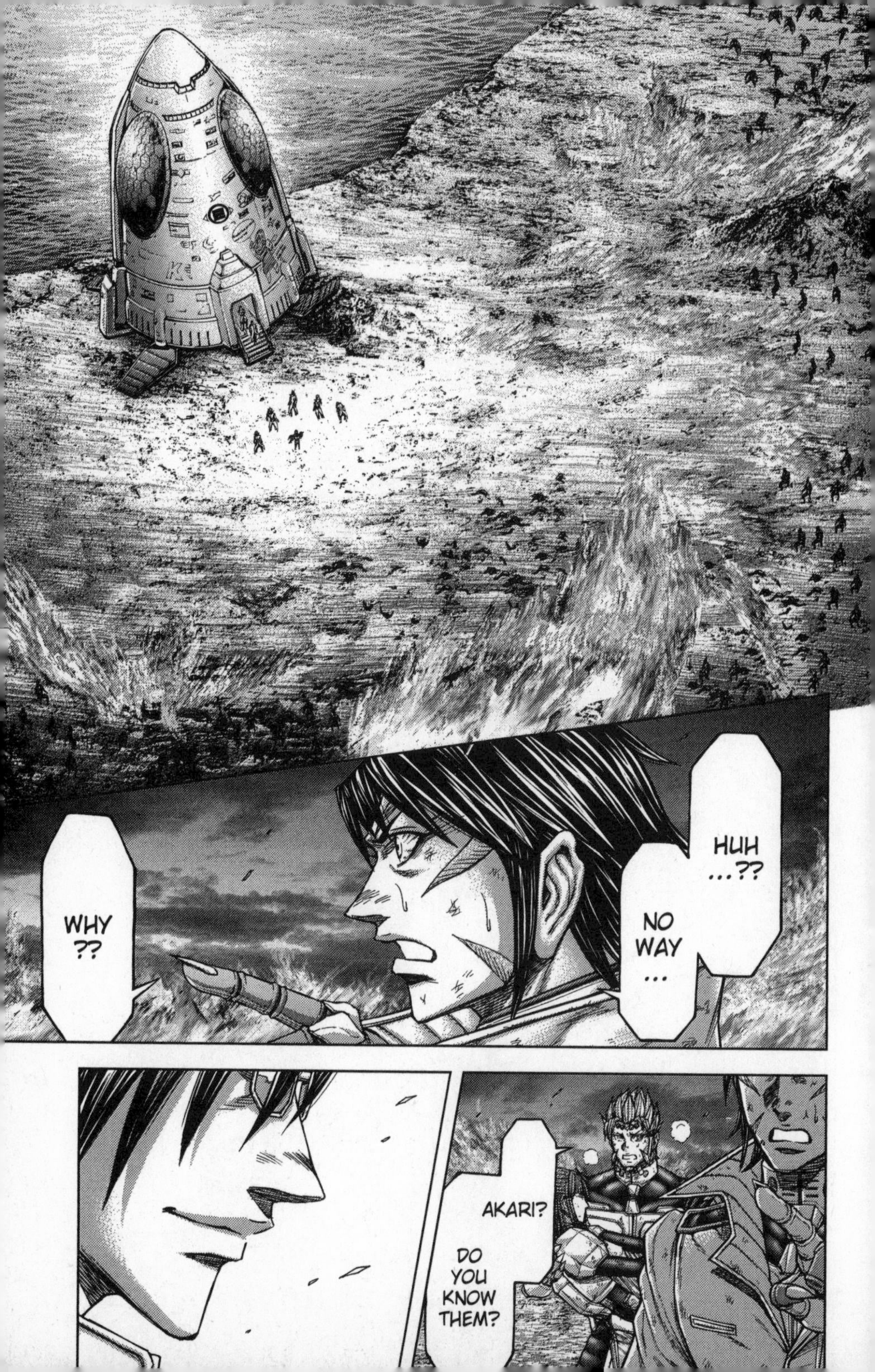
HUH ...??
NO WAY ...
WHY ??
AKARI?
DO YOU KNOW THEM?

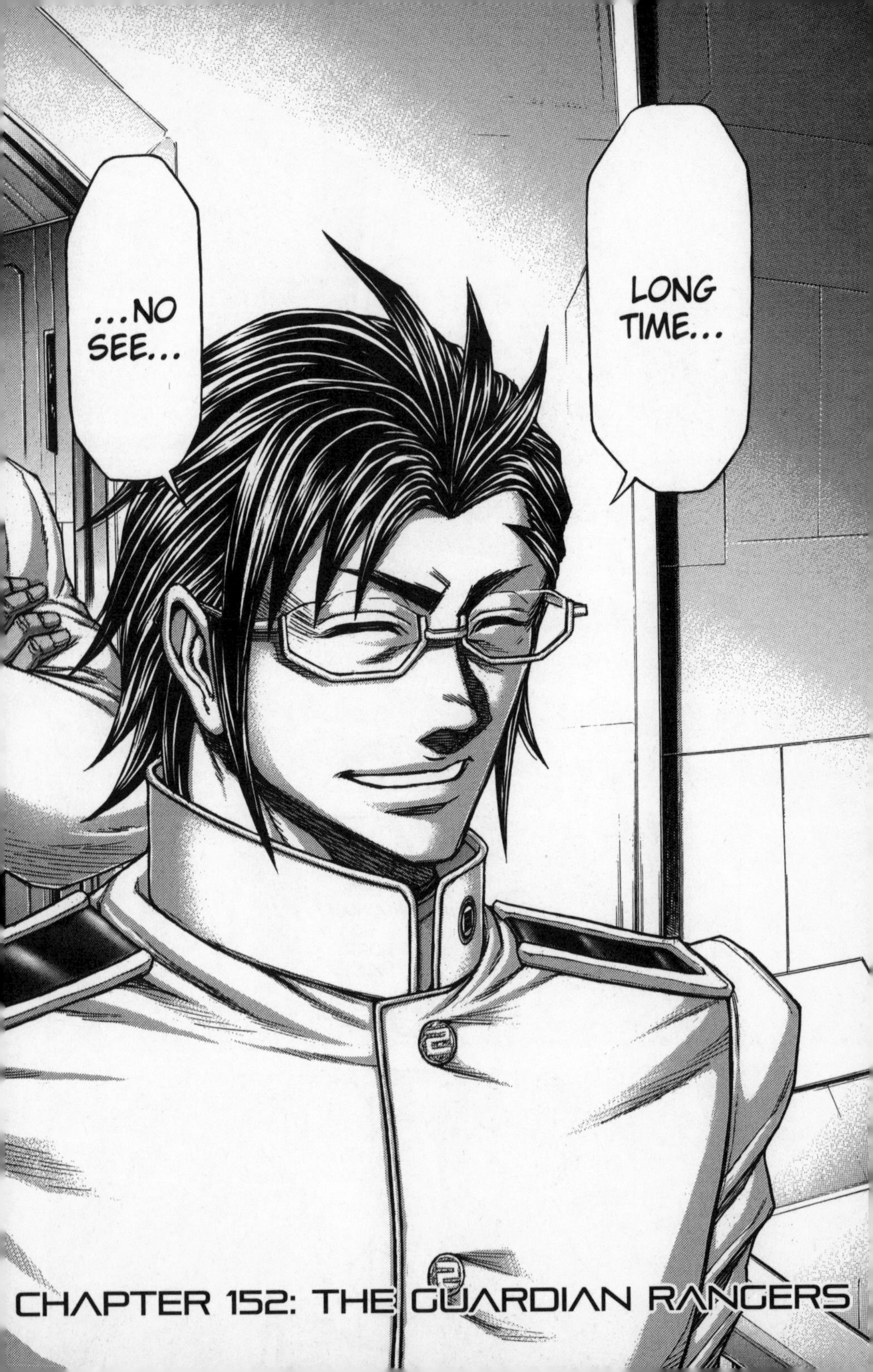
LONG TIME...
...NO SEE...

CHAPTER 152: THE GUARDIAN RANGERS

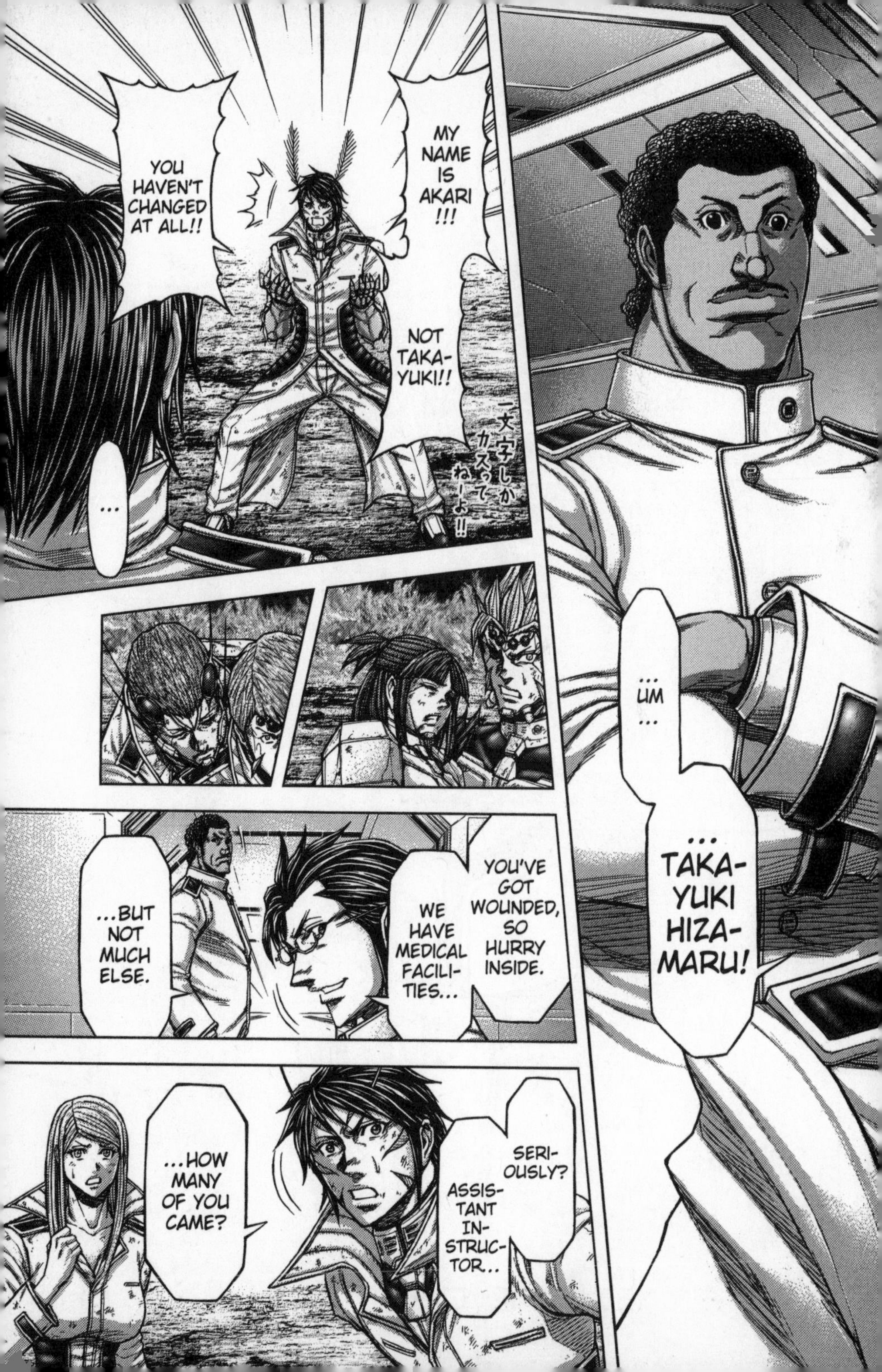
...UM...
...TAKA-YUKI HIZA-MARU!
MY NAME IS AKARI!!!
YOU HAVEN'T CHANGED AT ALL!!
NOT TAKA-YUKI!!
一文字しかカスってねーよ!!
...
YOU'VE GOT WOUNDED, SO HURRY INSIDE.
WE HAVE MEDICAL FACILI-TIES...
...BUT NOT MUCH ELSE.
SERI-OUSLY?
ASSIS-TANT IN-STRUC-TOR...
...HOW MANY OF YOU CAME?

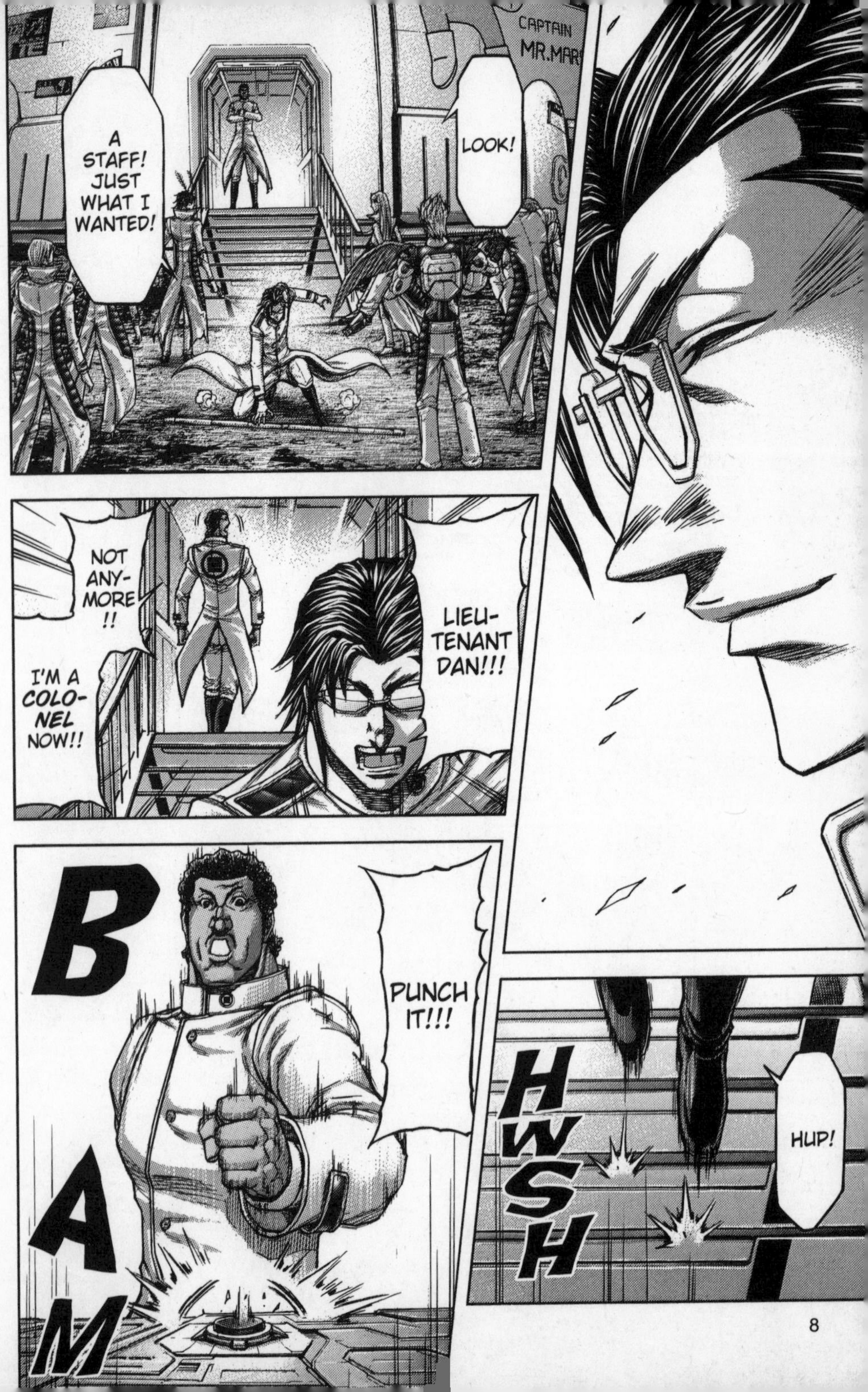
CAPTAIN
LOOK!
A STAFF! JUST WHAT I WANTED!
LIEUTENANT DAN!!!
NOT ANYMORE!!
I'M A COLONEL NOW!!
HUP!
HWSH
PUNCH IT!!!
BAM

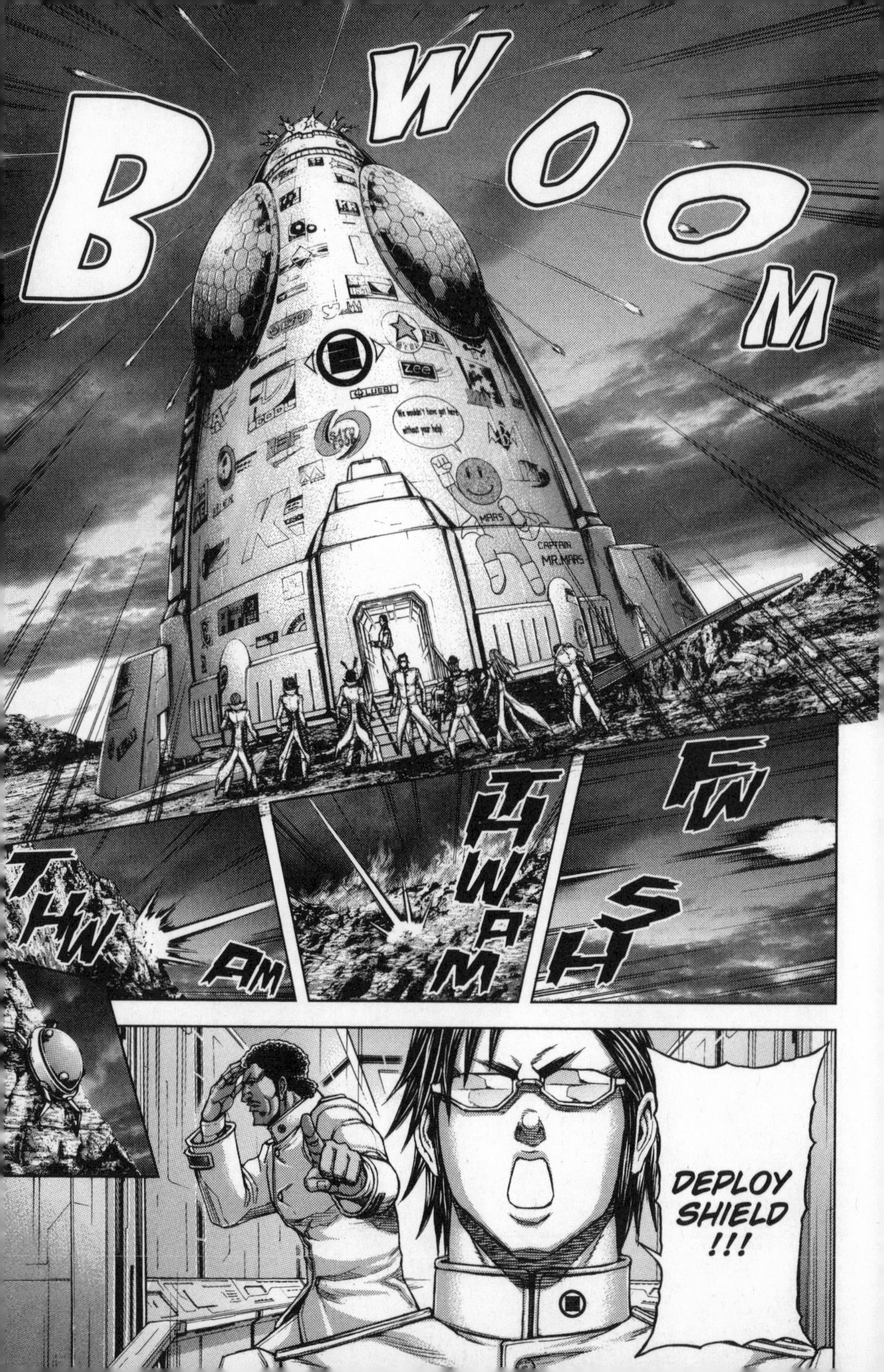
BWOOOM
We wouldn't have got here without your help!
MARS
CAPTAIN MR.MARS
FWSH
THWAM
THWAM
DEPLOY SHIELD !!!

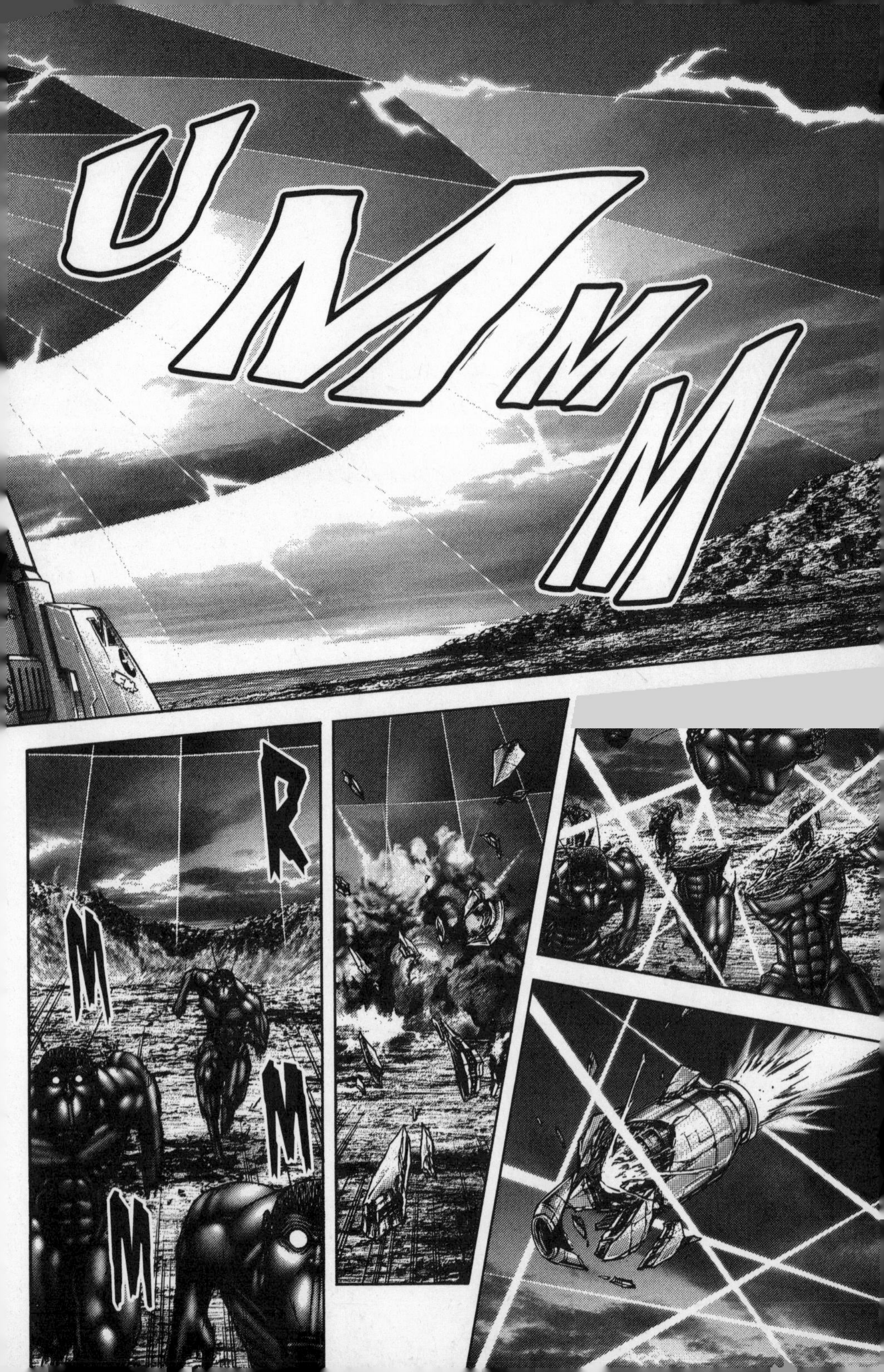
UMMM
RMMM

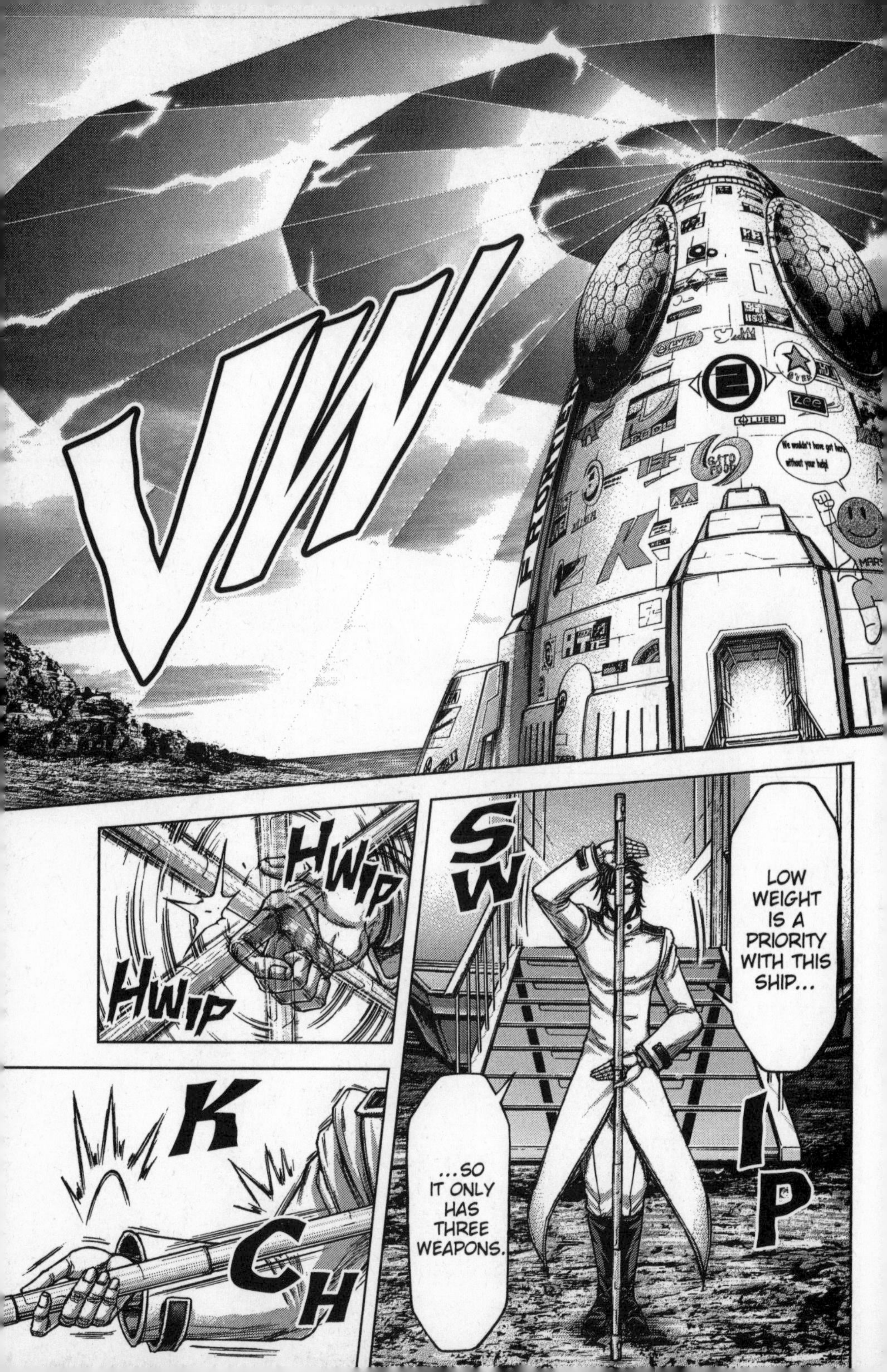
VW
FRONTIER
We wouldn't have got here without your help!
SW
LOW WEIGHT IS A PRIORITY WITH THIS SHIP...
...SO IT ONLY HAS THREE WEAPONS.
IP
HWIP
HWIP
K
CH

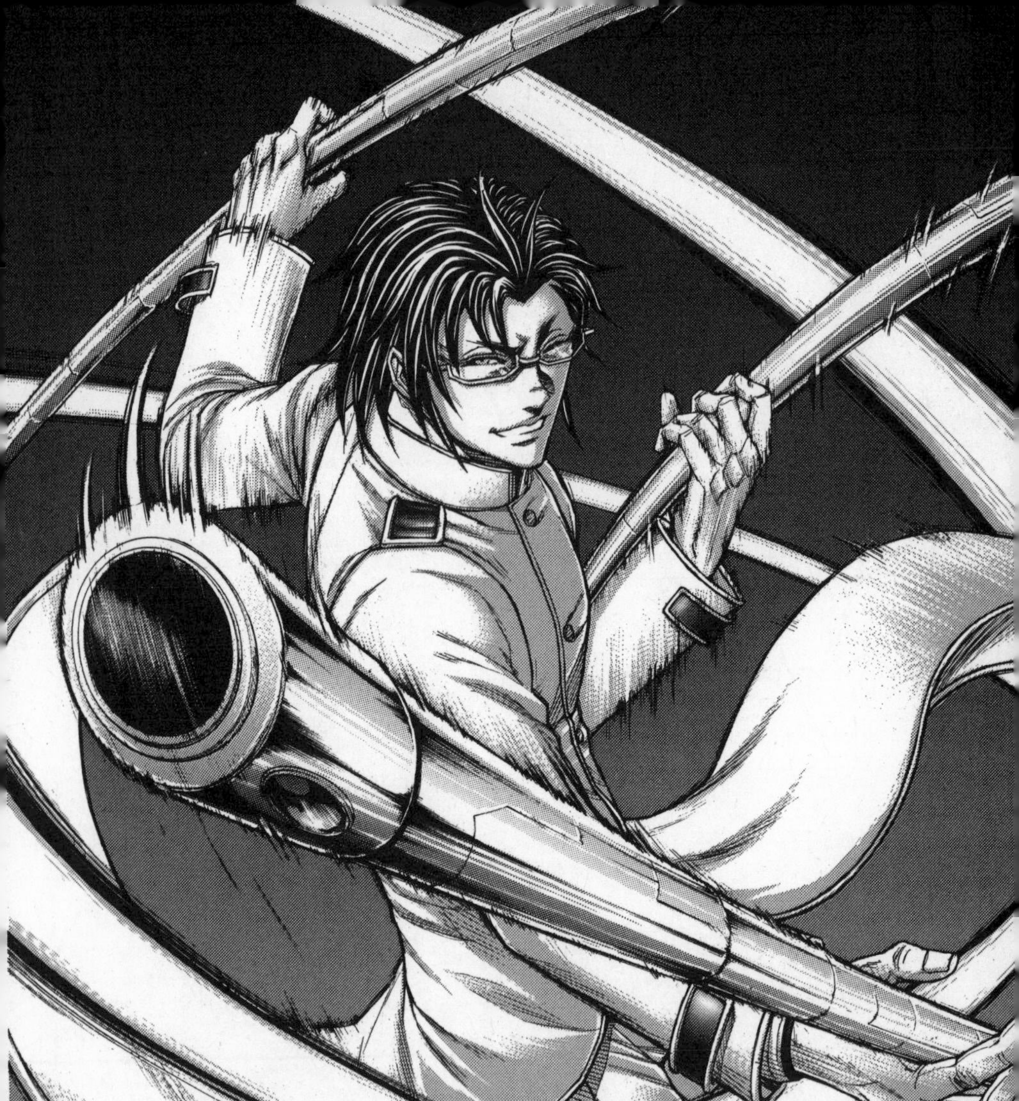

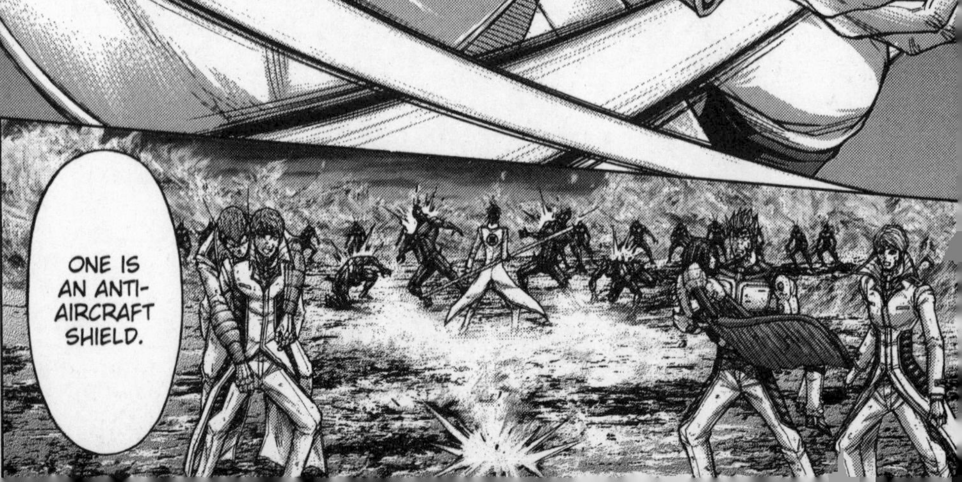
ONE IS AN ANTI-AIRCRAFT SHIELD.

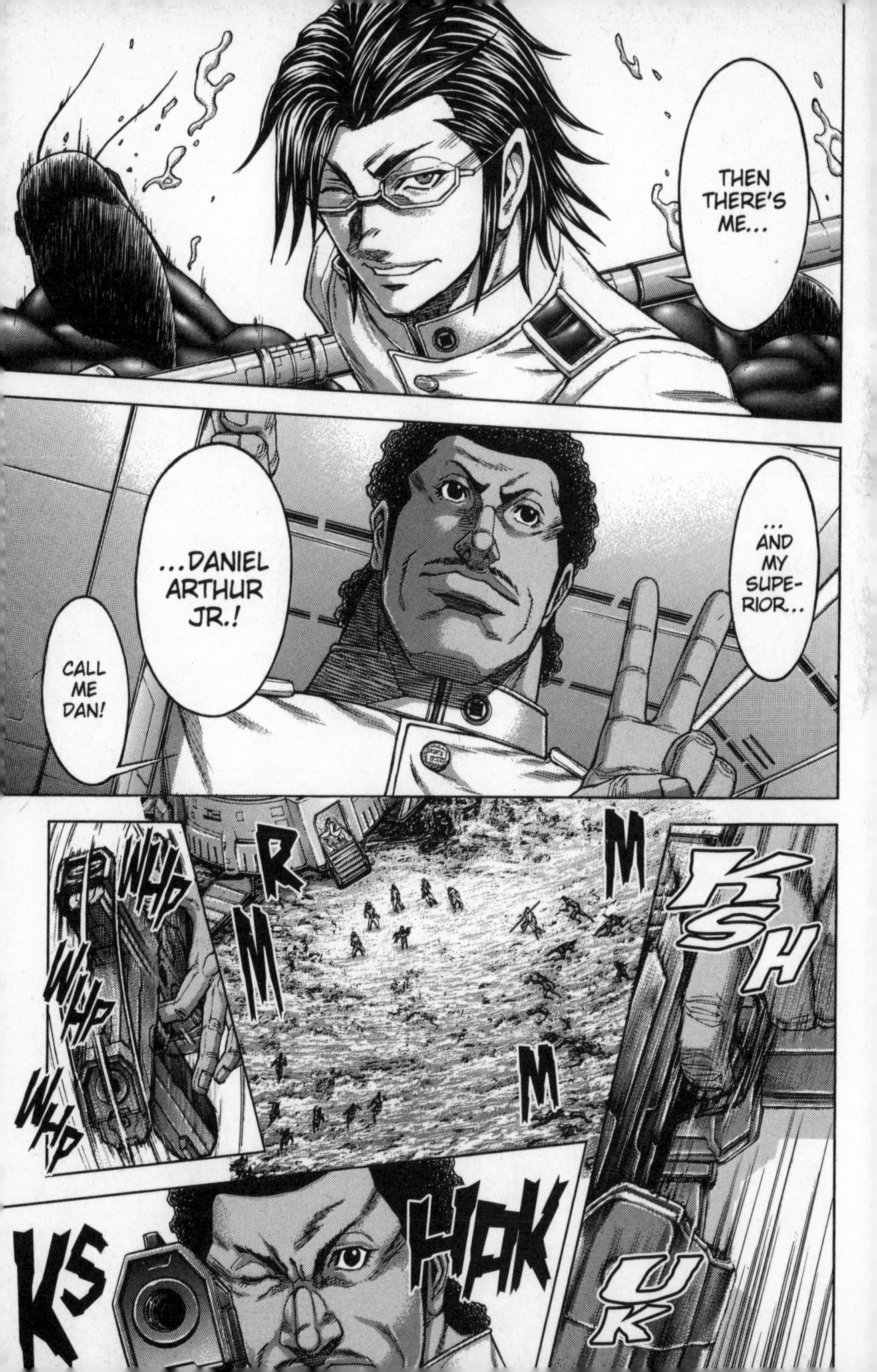
THEN THERE'S ME...
... AND MY SUPER-IOR...
...DANIEL ARTHUR JR.!
CALL ME DAN!
KSH
M
R
M
M
WHP
WHP
WHP
UK
HAK
KS

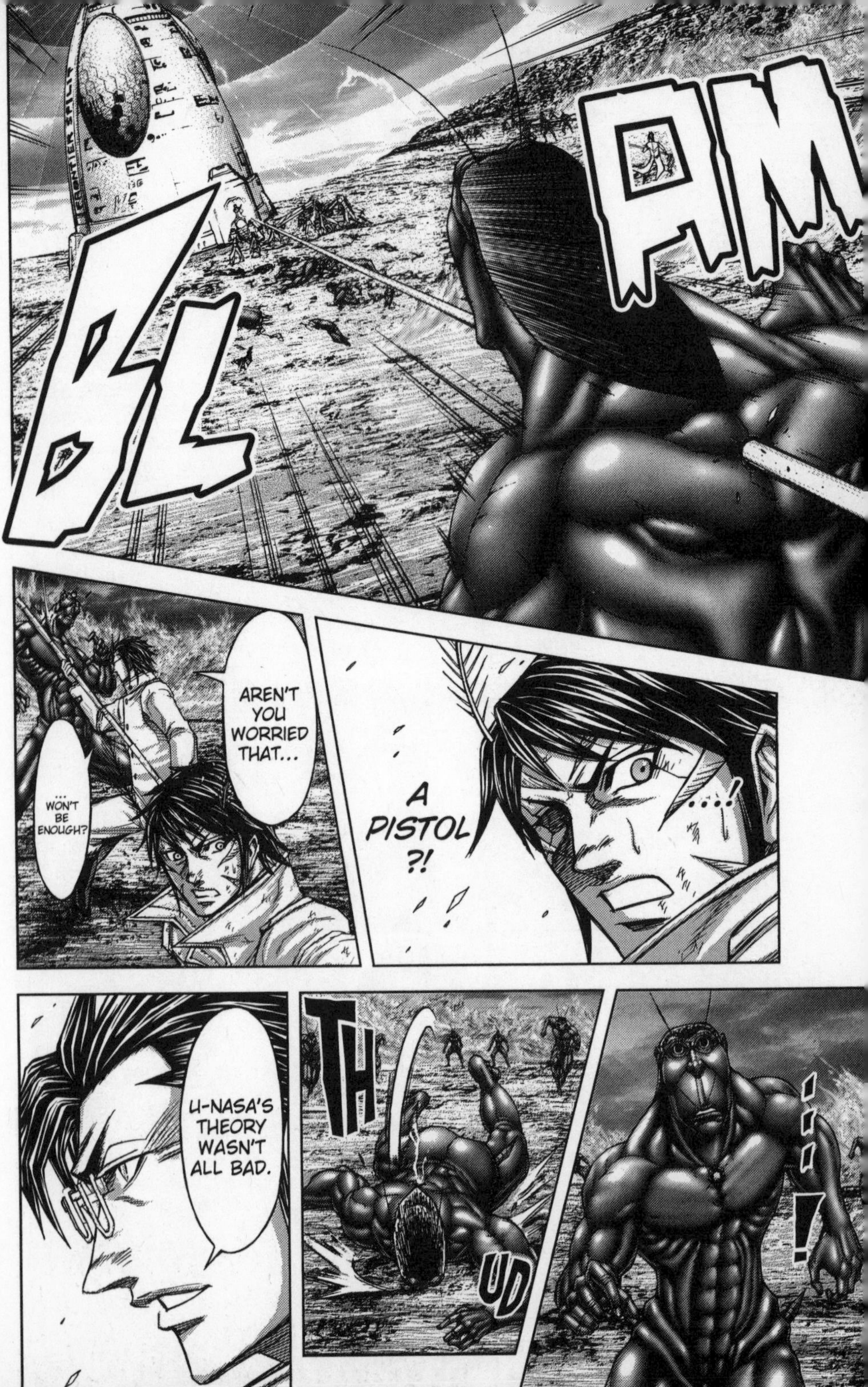
BLAM
...!
A PISTOL ?!
AREN'T YOU WORRIED THAT...
... WON'T BE ENOUGH?
...!
THUD
U-NASA'S THEORY WASN'T ALL BAD.

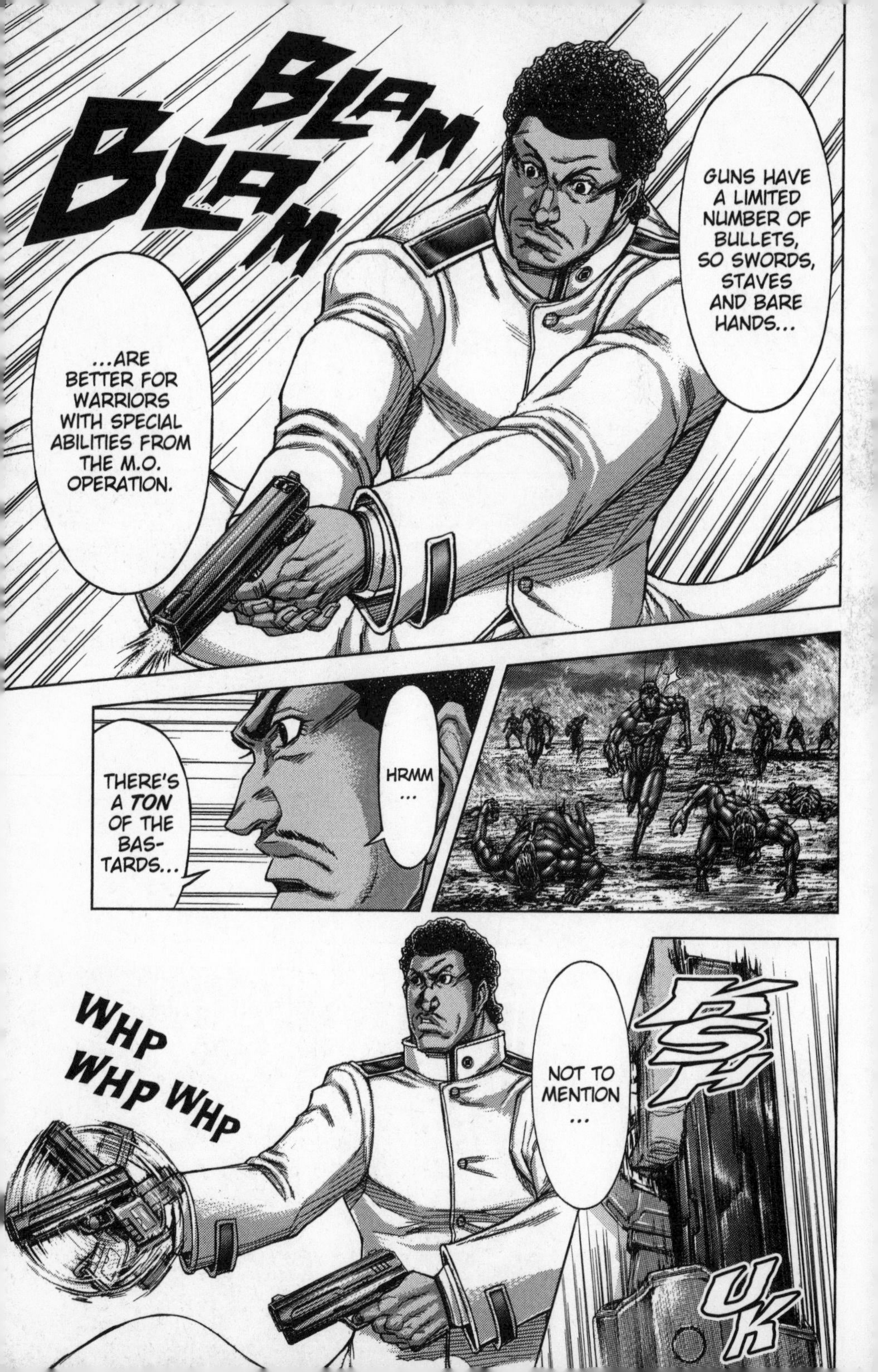
BLAM BLAM
GUNS HAVE A LIMITED NUMBER OF BULLETS, SO SWORDS, STAVES AND BARE HANDS...
...ARE BETTER FOR WARRIORS WITH SPECIAL ABILITIES FROM THE M.O. OPERATION.
HRMM ...
THERE'S A *TON* OF THE BAS-TARDS...
NOT TO MENTION ...
WHP WHP WHP

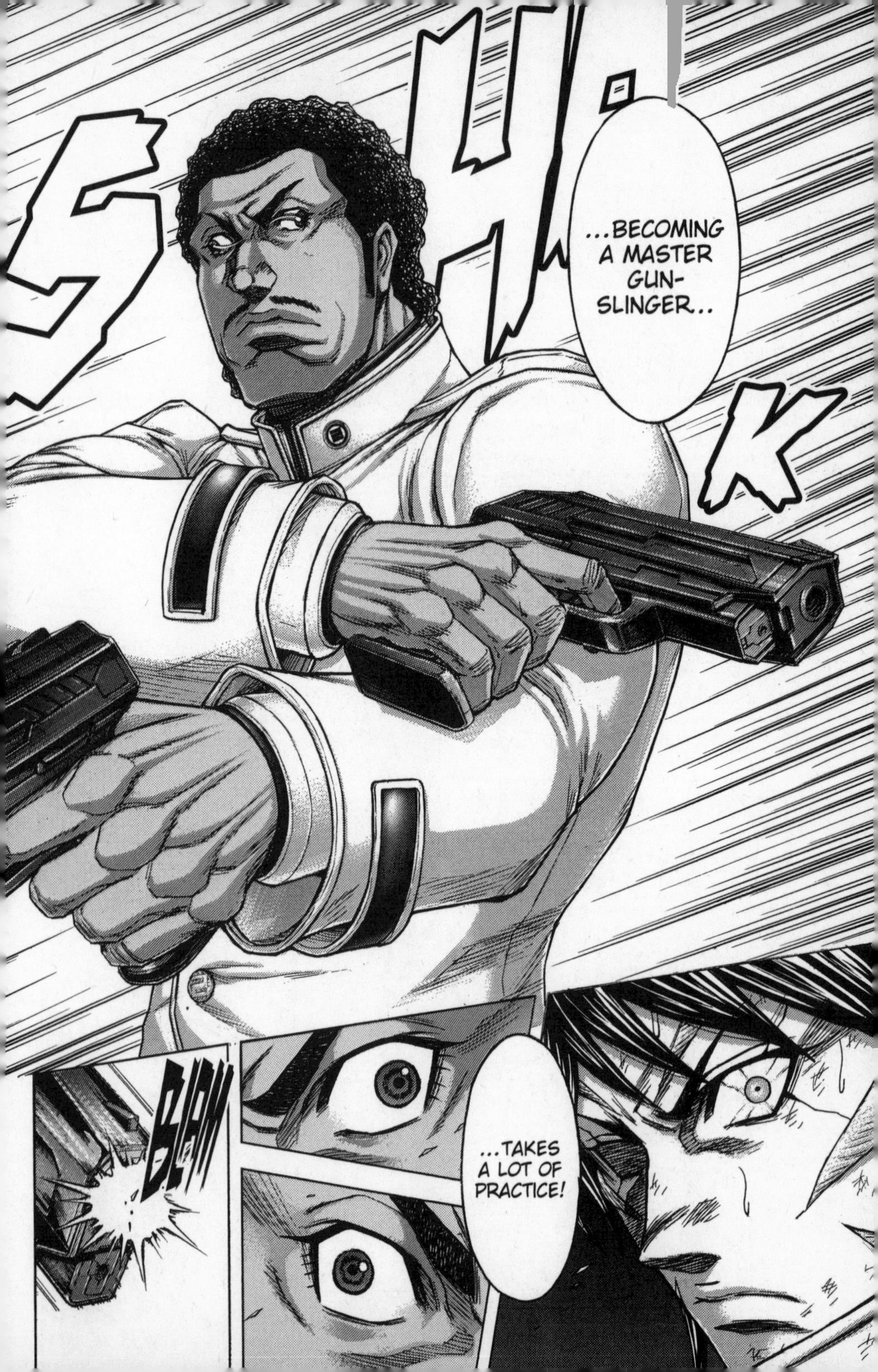
SHHK
...BECOMING A MASTER GUN-SLINGER...
BLAM
...TAKES A LOT OF PRACTICE!

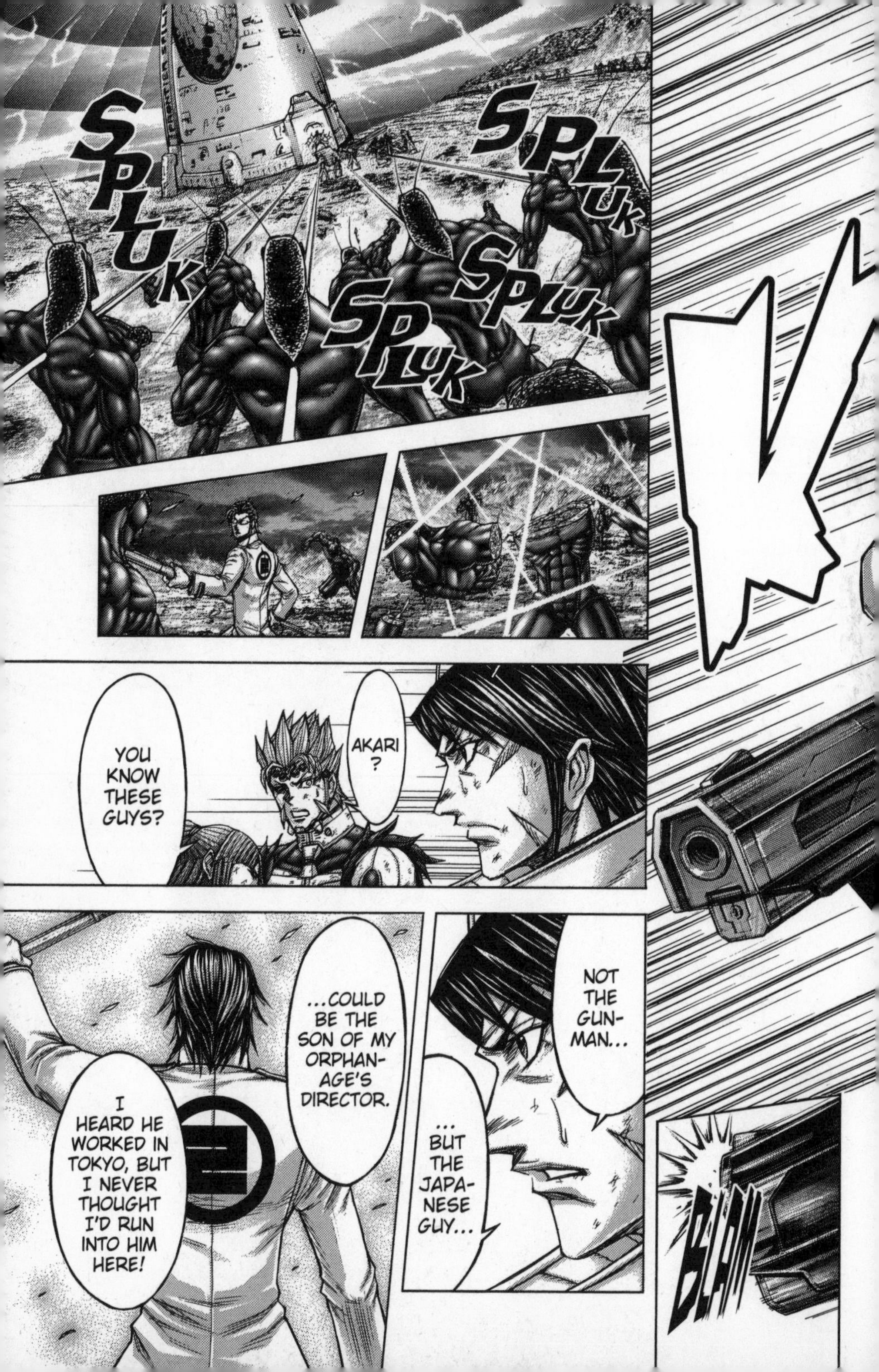
SPLUK
SPLUK
SPLUK
SPLUK
AKARI?
YOU KNOW THESE GUYS?
NOT THE GUN-MAN...
...BUT THE JAPA-NESE GUY...
...COULD BE THE SON OF MY ORPHAN-AGE'S DIRECTOR.
I HEARD HE WORKED IN TOKYO, BUT I NEVER THOUGHT I'D RUN INTO HIM HERE!
BLAM

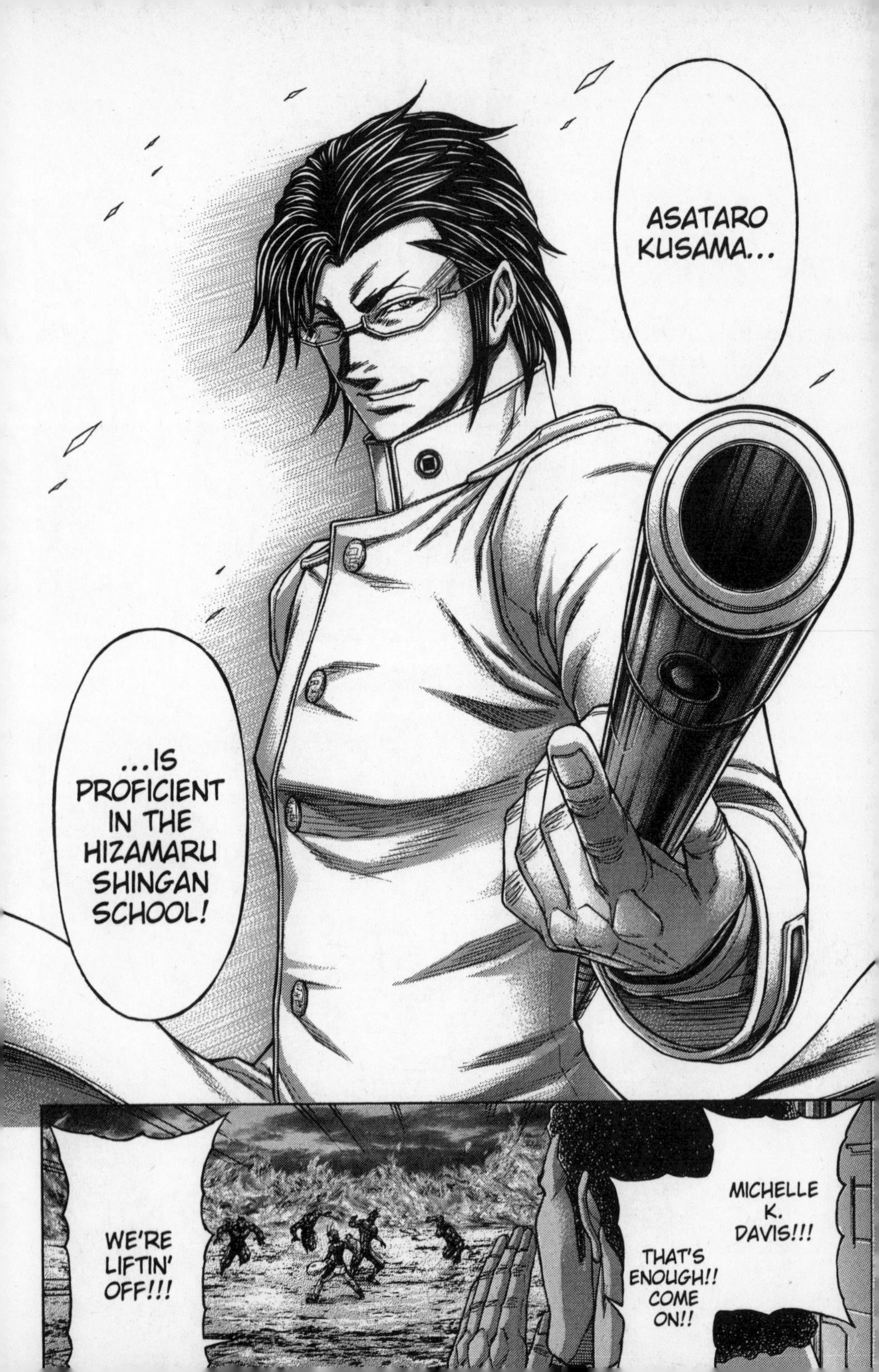
ASATARO KUSAMA...
...IS PROFICIENT IN THE HIZAMARU SHINGAN SCHOOL!
MICHELLE K. DAVIS!!!
THAT'S ENOUGH!! COME ON!!
WE'RE LIFTIN' OFF!!!

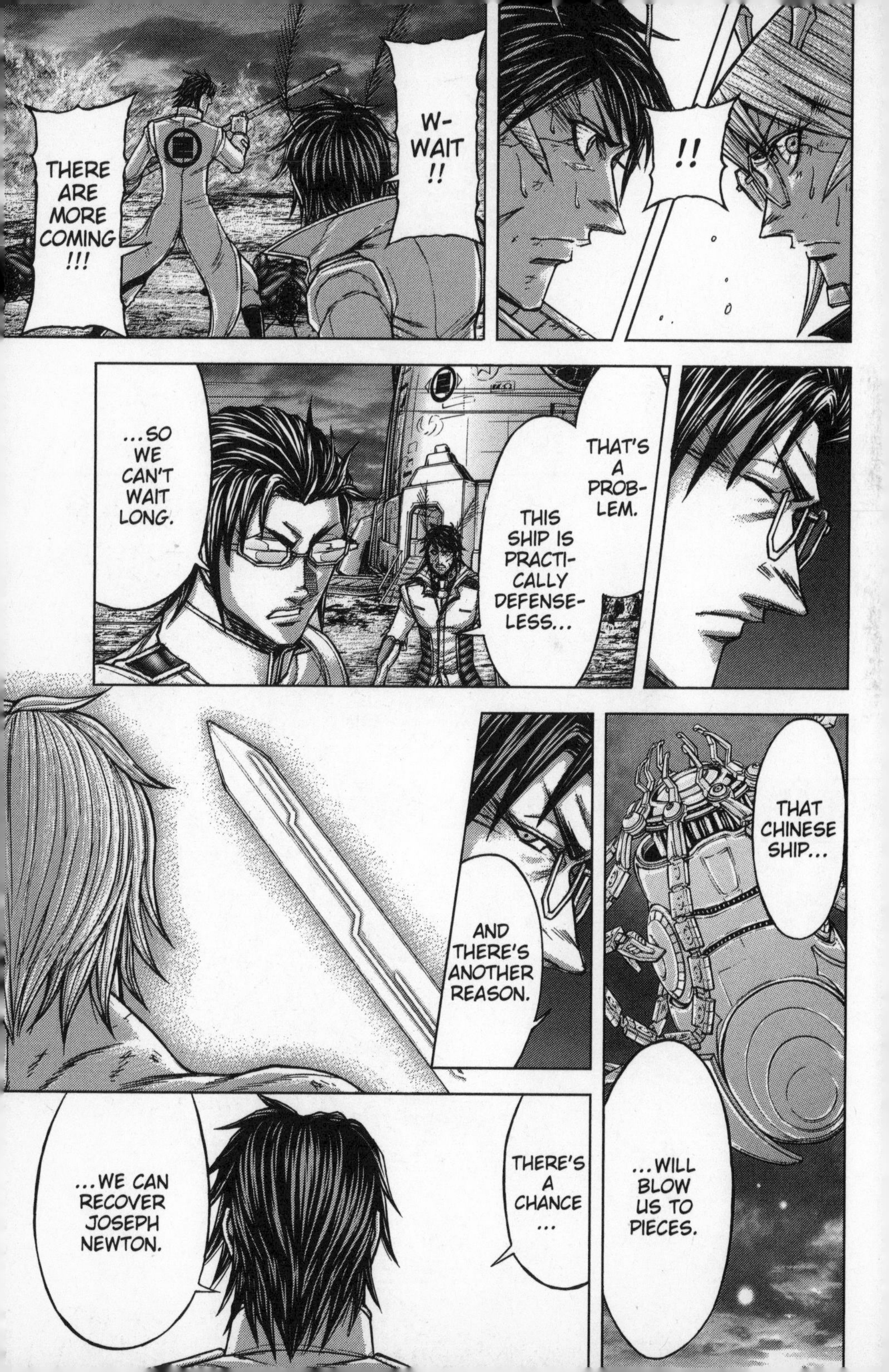
!!
W-WAIT!!
THERE ARE MORE COMING!!!
THAT'S A PROBLEM.
THIS SHIP IS PRACTICALLY DEFENSELESS...
...SO WE CAN'T WAIT LONG.
THAT CHINESE SHIP...
...WILL BLOW US TO PIECES.
AND THERE'S ANOTHER REASON.
THERE'S A CHANCE...
...WE CAN RECOVER JOSEPH NEWTON.

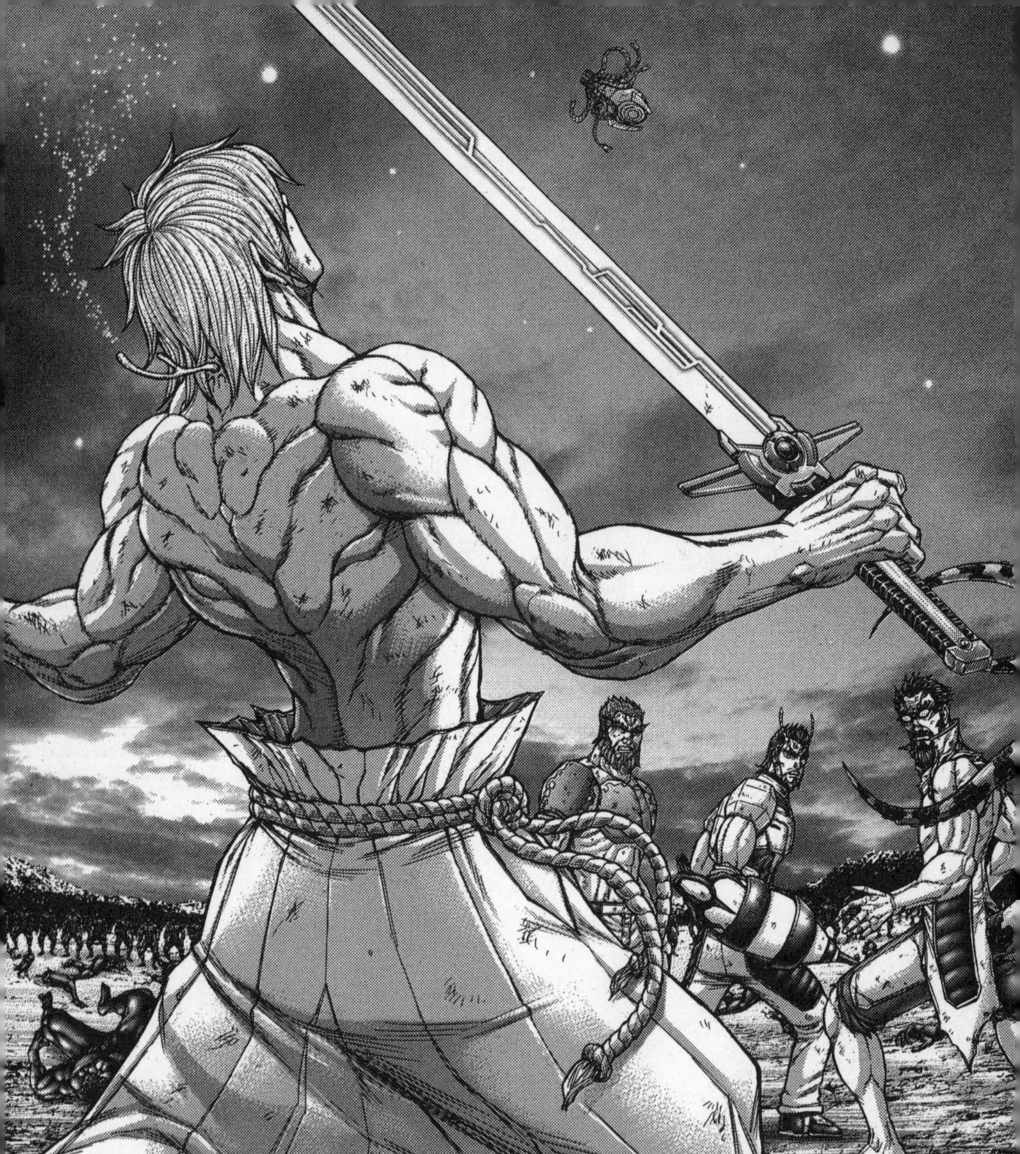

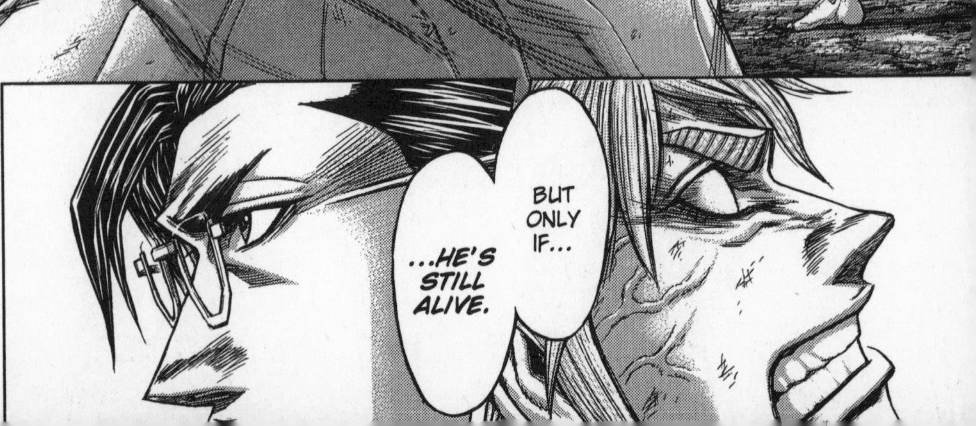
BUT ONLY IF...
...HE'S STILL ALIVE.

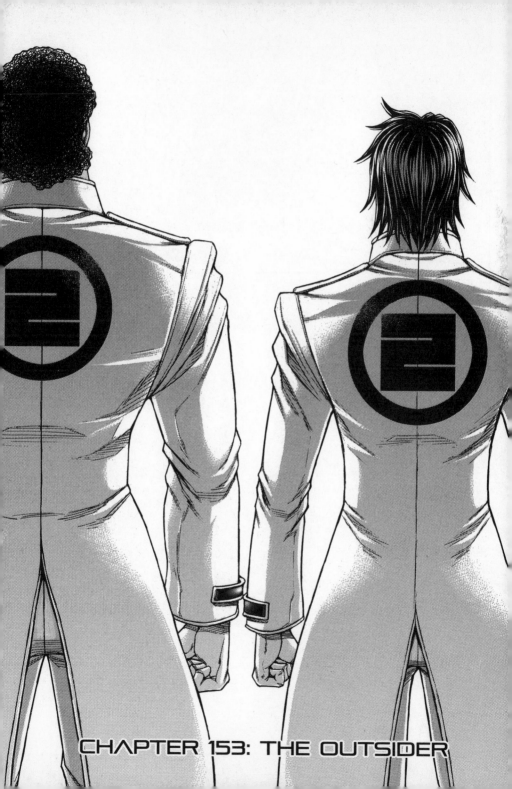

CHAPTER 153: THE OUTSIDER

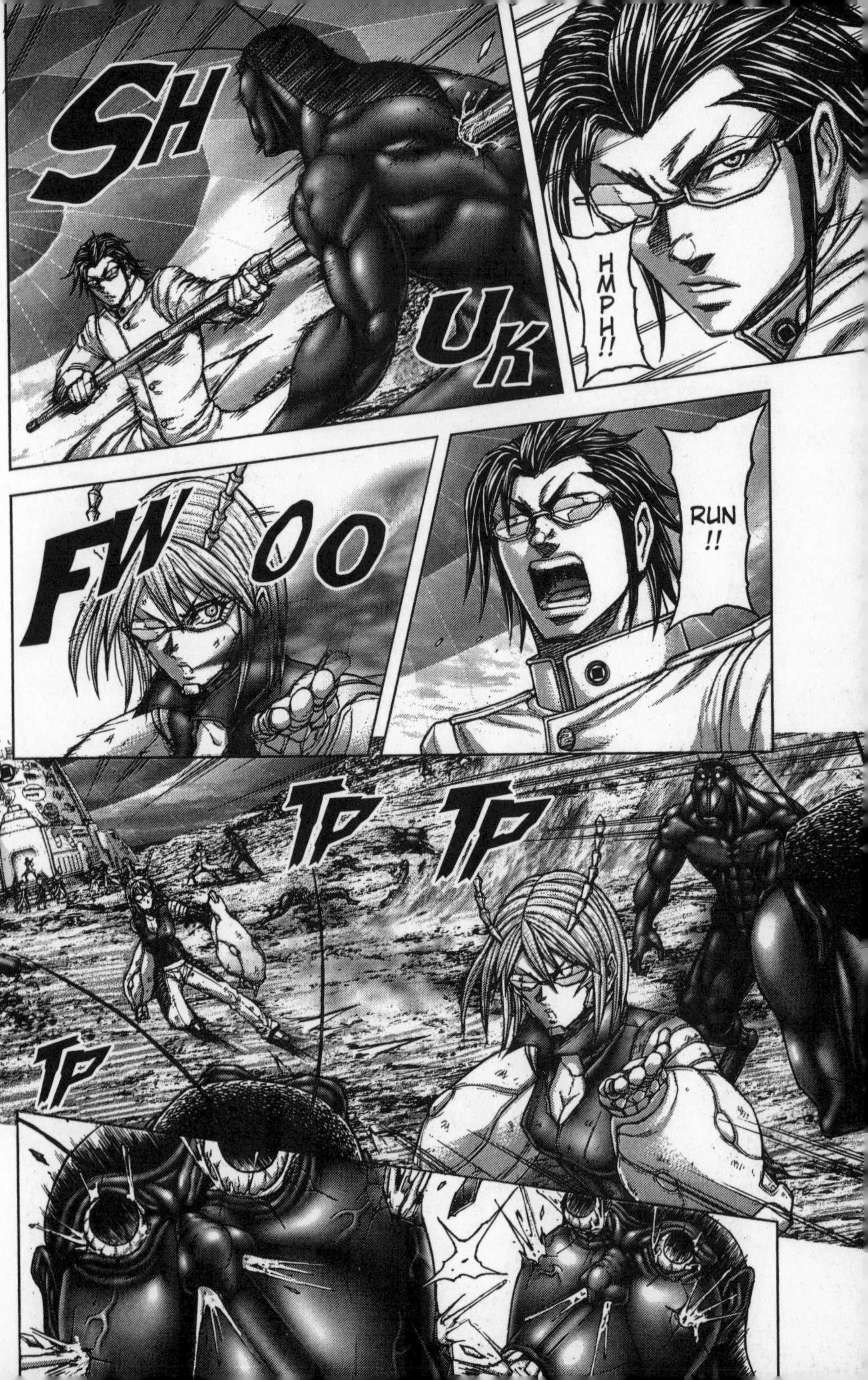
HMPH!!
SH
UK
RUN!!
FWOO
TP
TP
TP

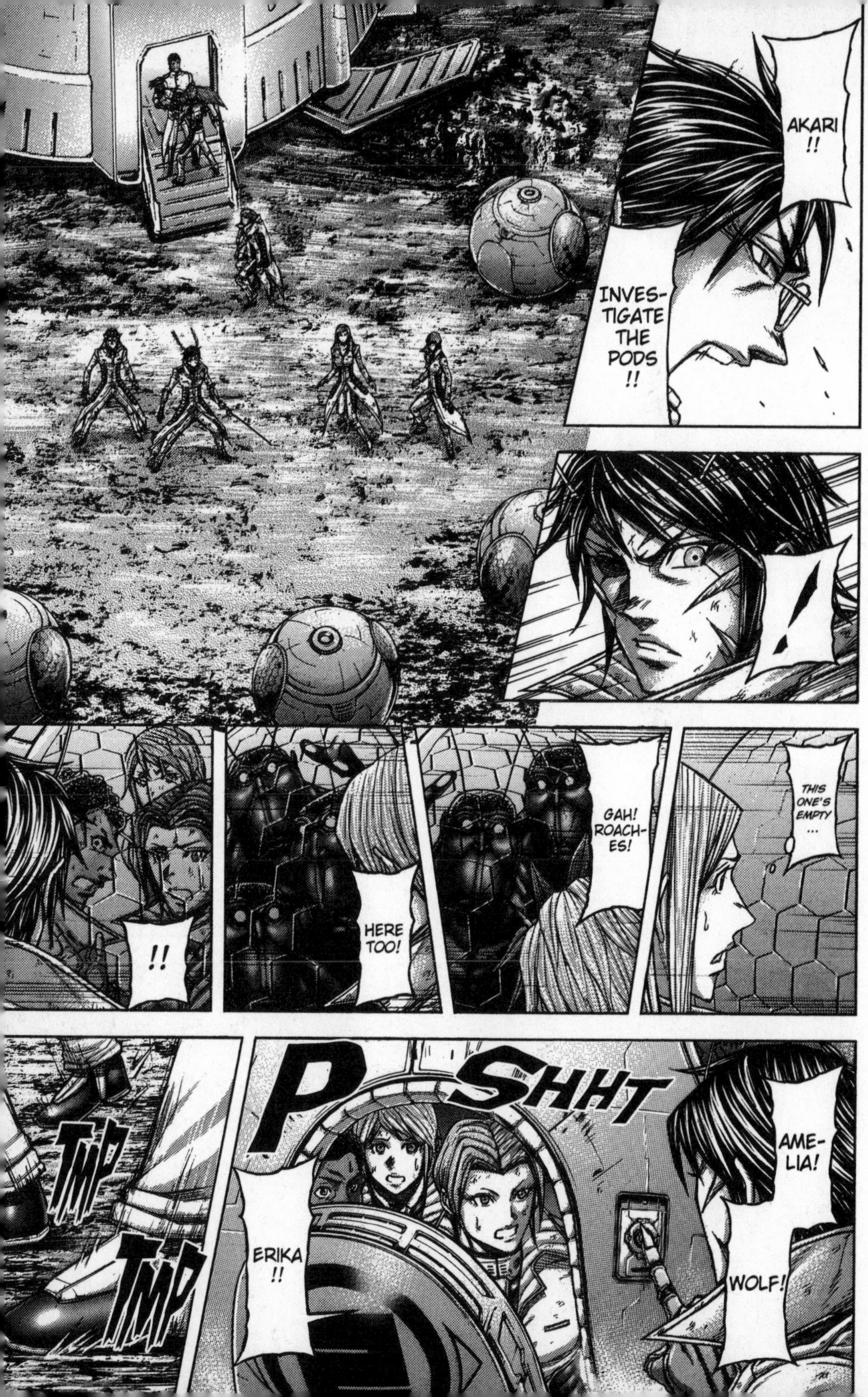
AKARI !!
INVESTIGATE THE PODS !!
!
THIS ONE'S EMPTY ...
GAH! ROACHES!
HERE TOO!
!!
AMELIA!
WOLF!
PSHHT
ERIKA !!
TMP
TMP

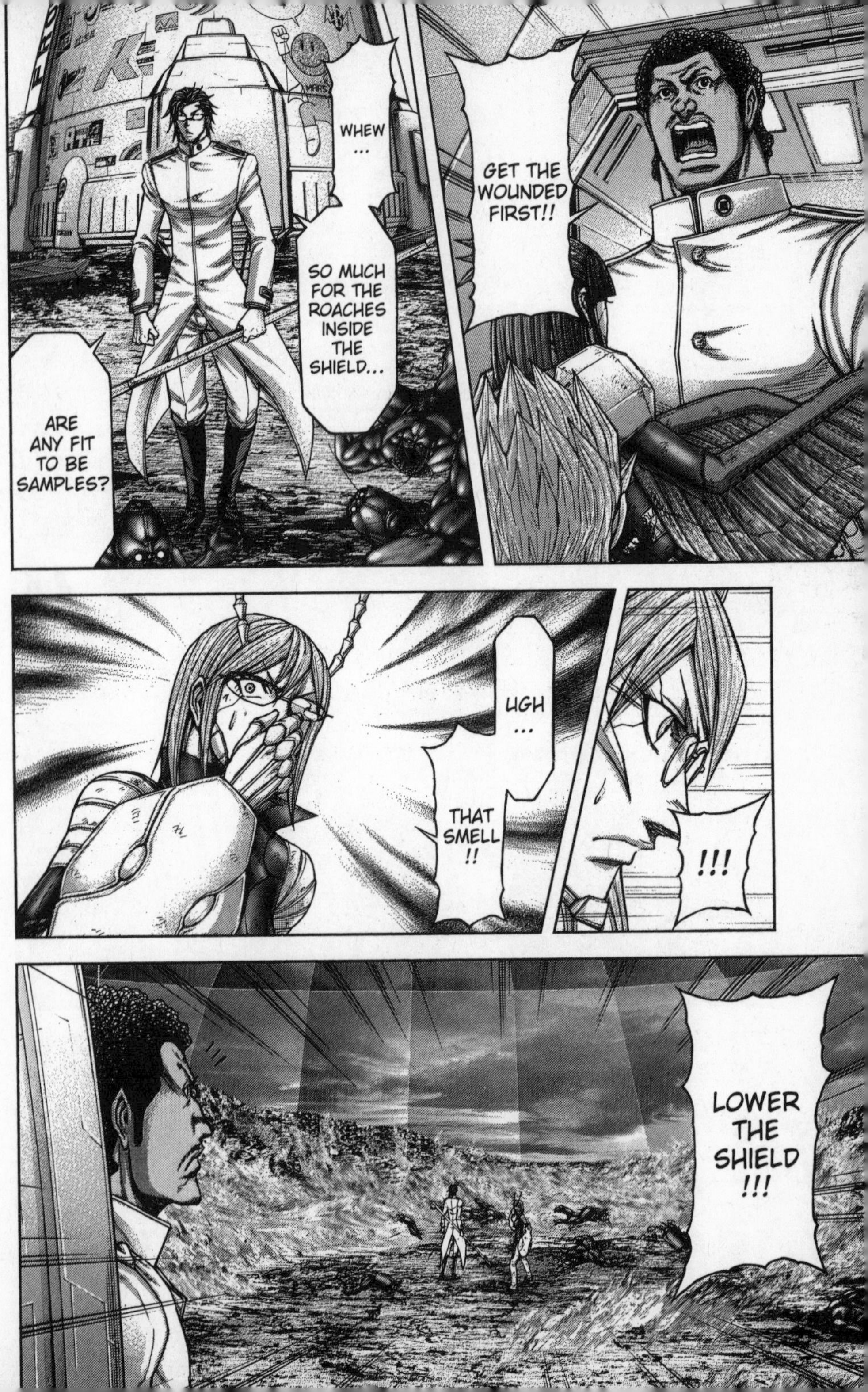
GET THE WOUNDED FIRST!!
WHEW ...
SO MUCH FOR THE ROACHES INSIDE THE SHIELD...
ARE ANY FIT TO BE SAMPLES?
!!!
UGH ...
THAT SMELL !!
LOWER THE SHIELD !!!

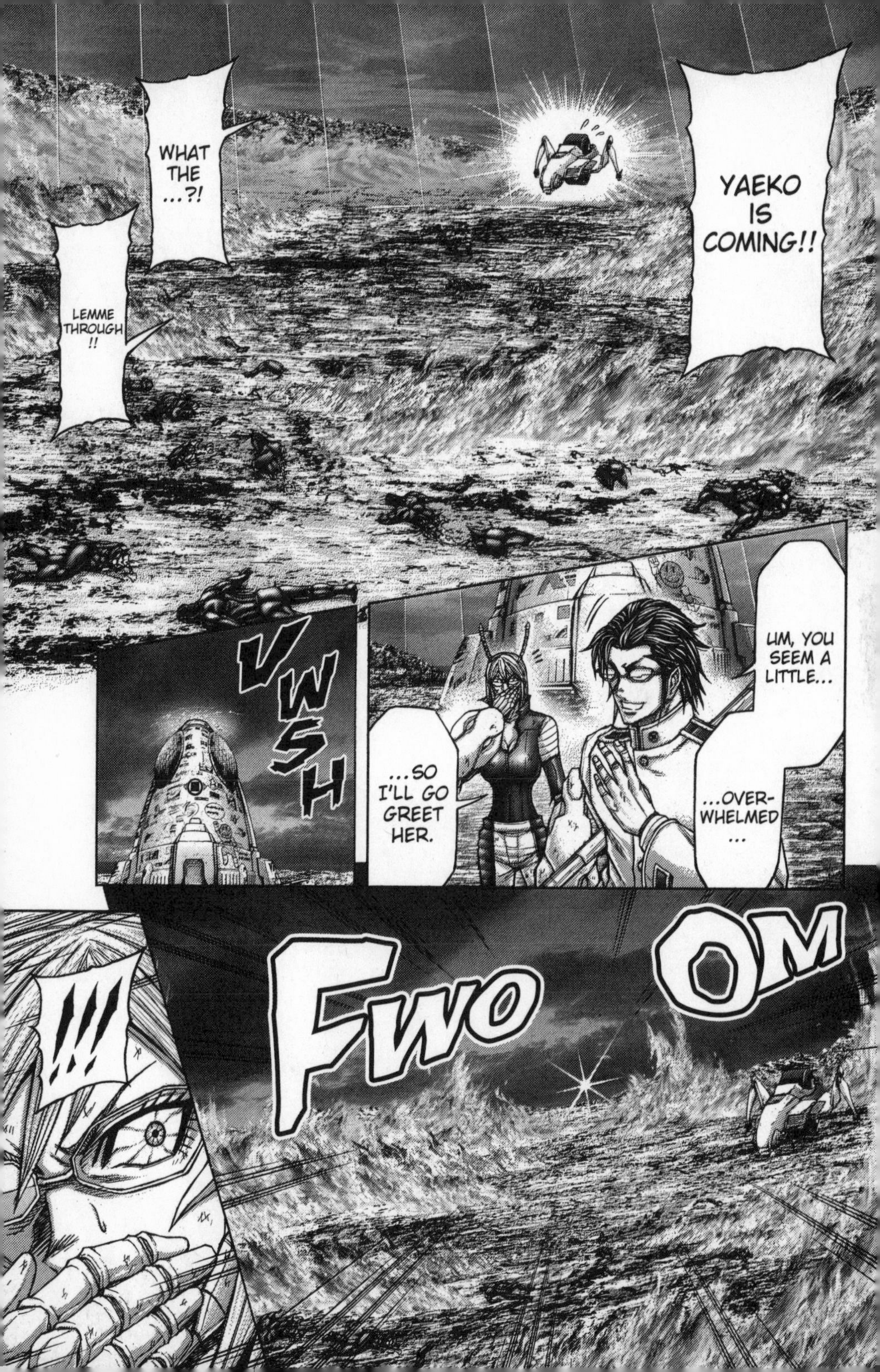
YAEKO IS COMING!!
WHAT THE ...?!
LEMME THROUGH !!
UM, YOU SEEM A LITTLE...
...OVER-WHELMED ...
...SO I'LL GO GREET HER.
VWSH
FWO OM
!!!

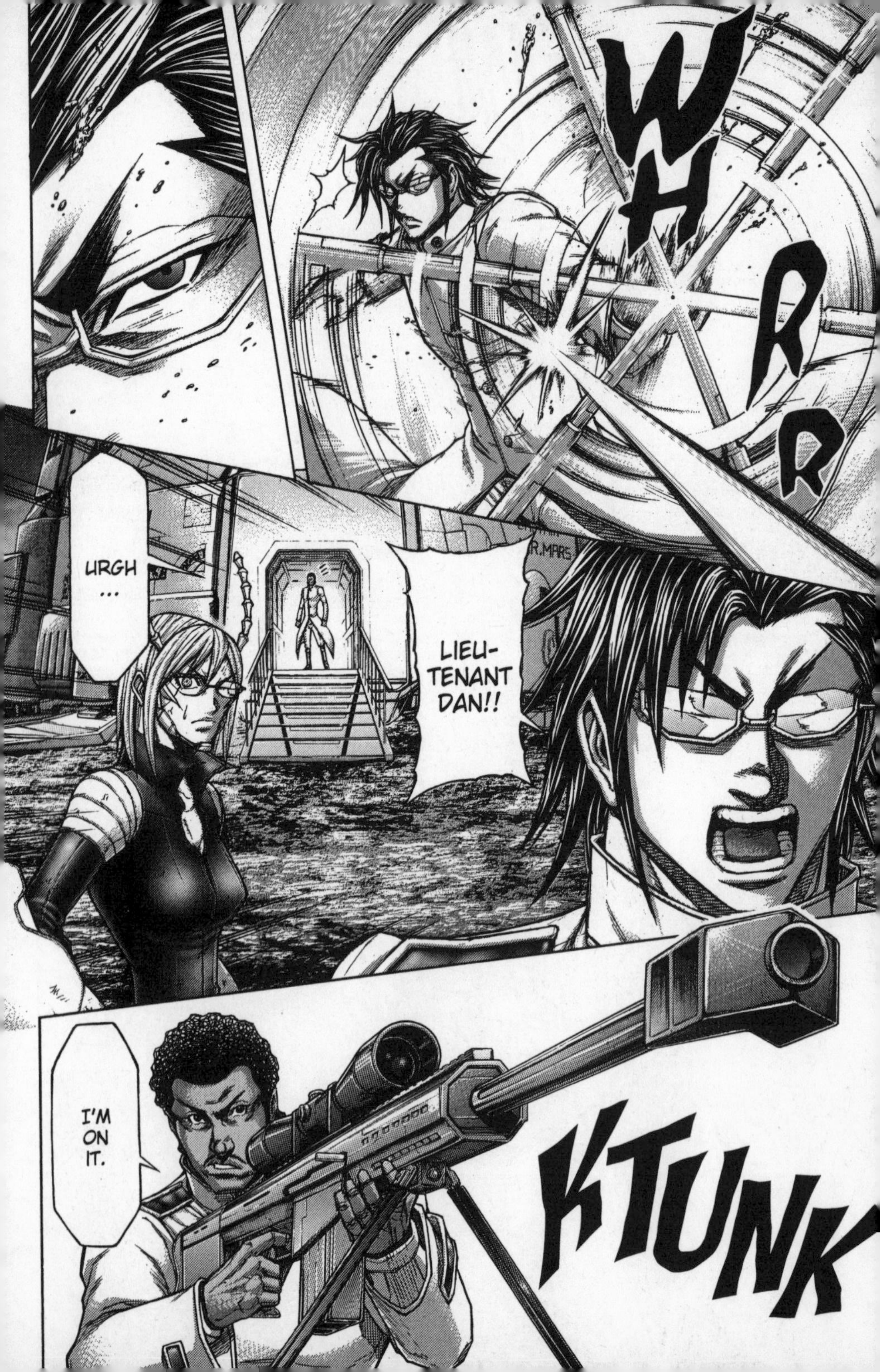
WHRR
LIEU-TENANT DAN!!
URGH ...
I'M ON IT.
KTUNK

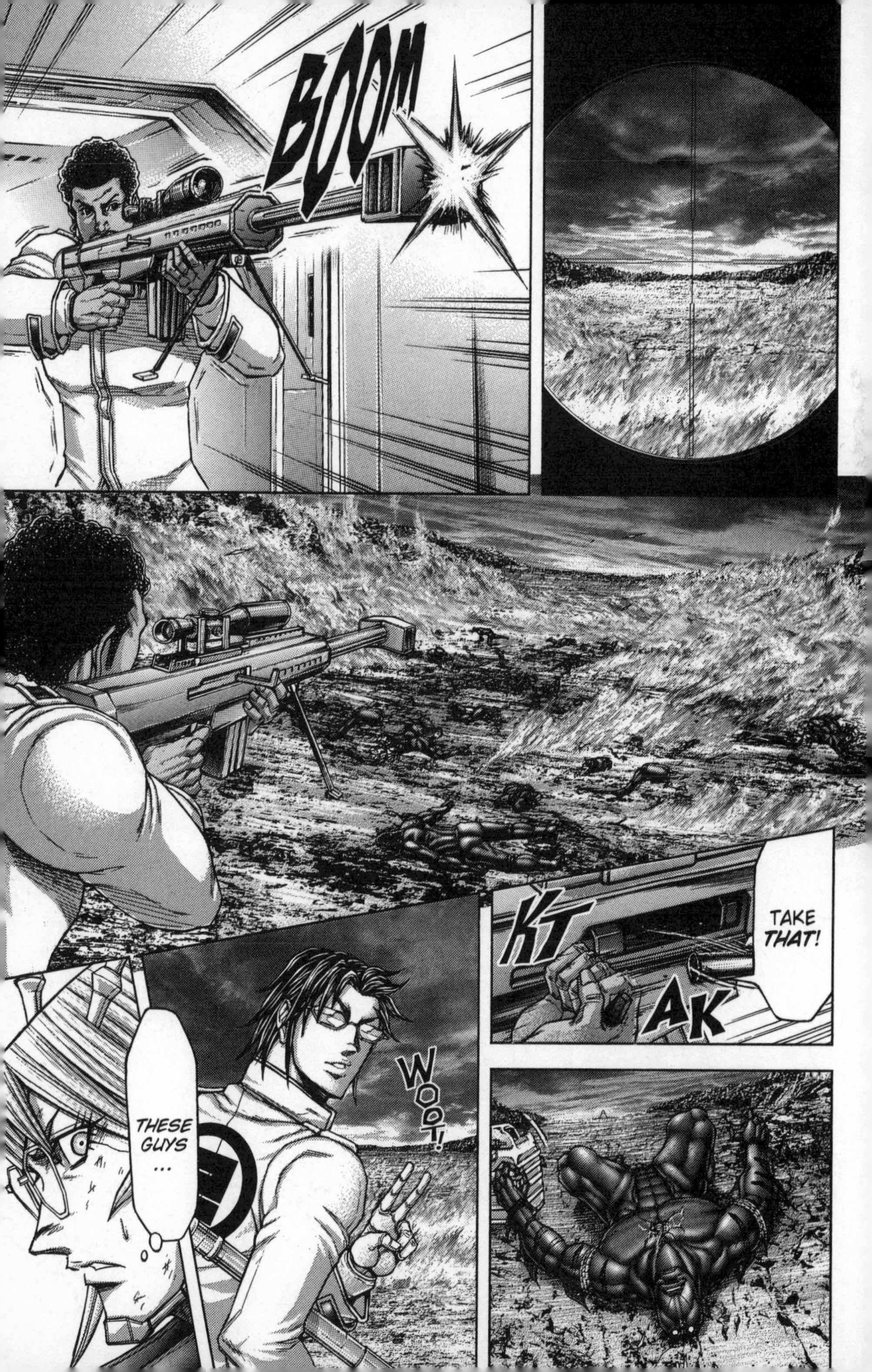
BOOM
KT
AK
TAKE THAT!
WOOT!
THESE GUYS ...

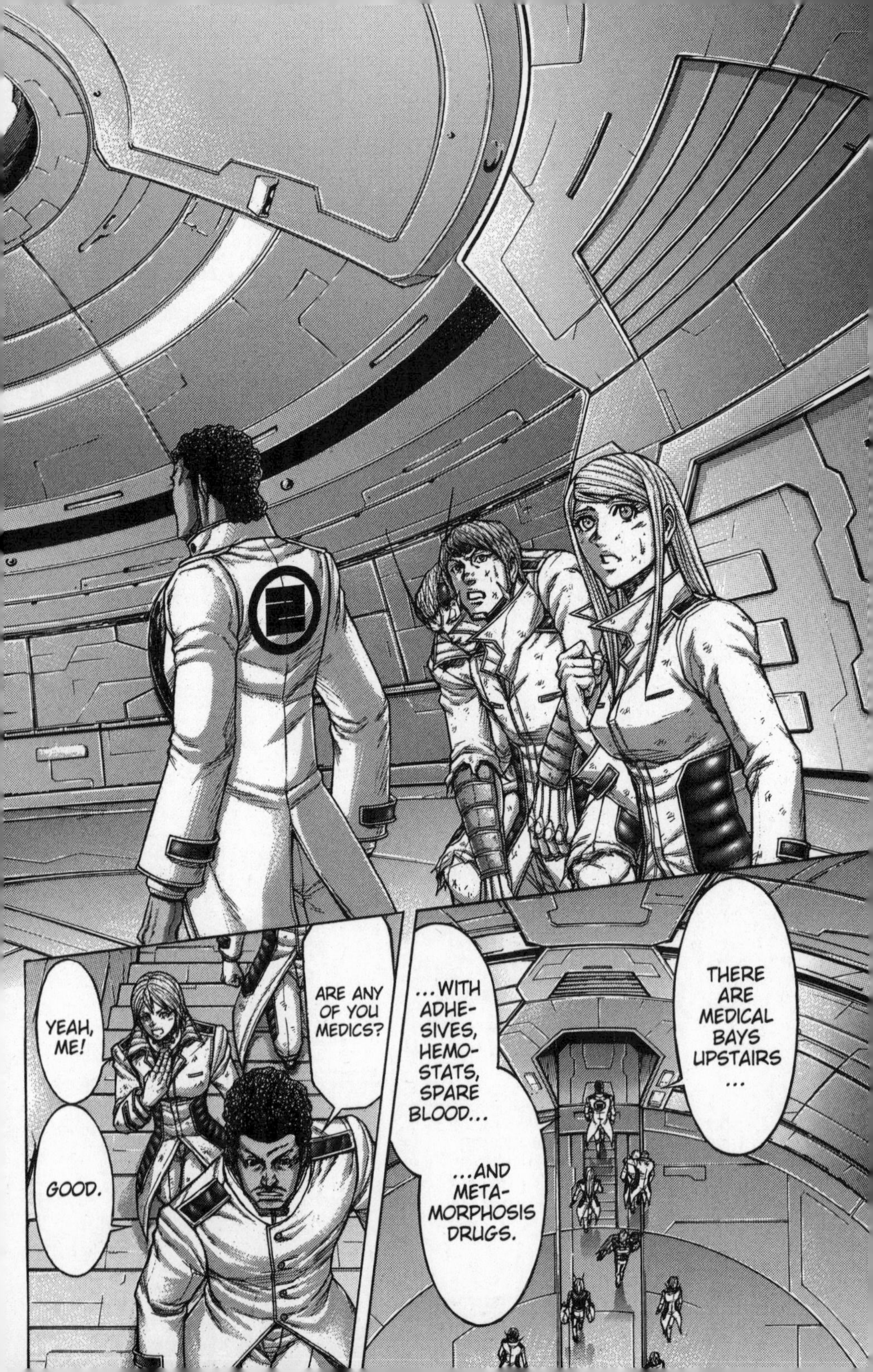
THERE ARE MEDICAL BAYS UPSTAIRS...
...WITH ADHESIVES, HEMOSTATS, SPARE BLOOD...
...AND METAMORPHOSIS DRUGS.
ARE ANY OF YOU MEDICS?
YEAH, ME!
GOOD.

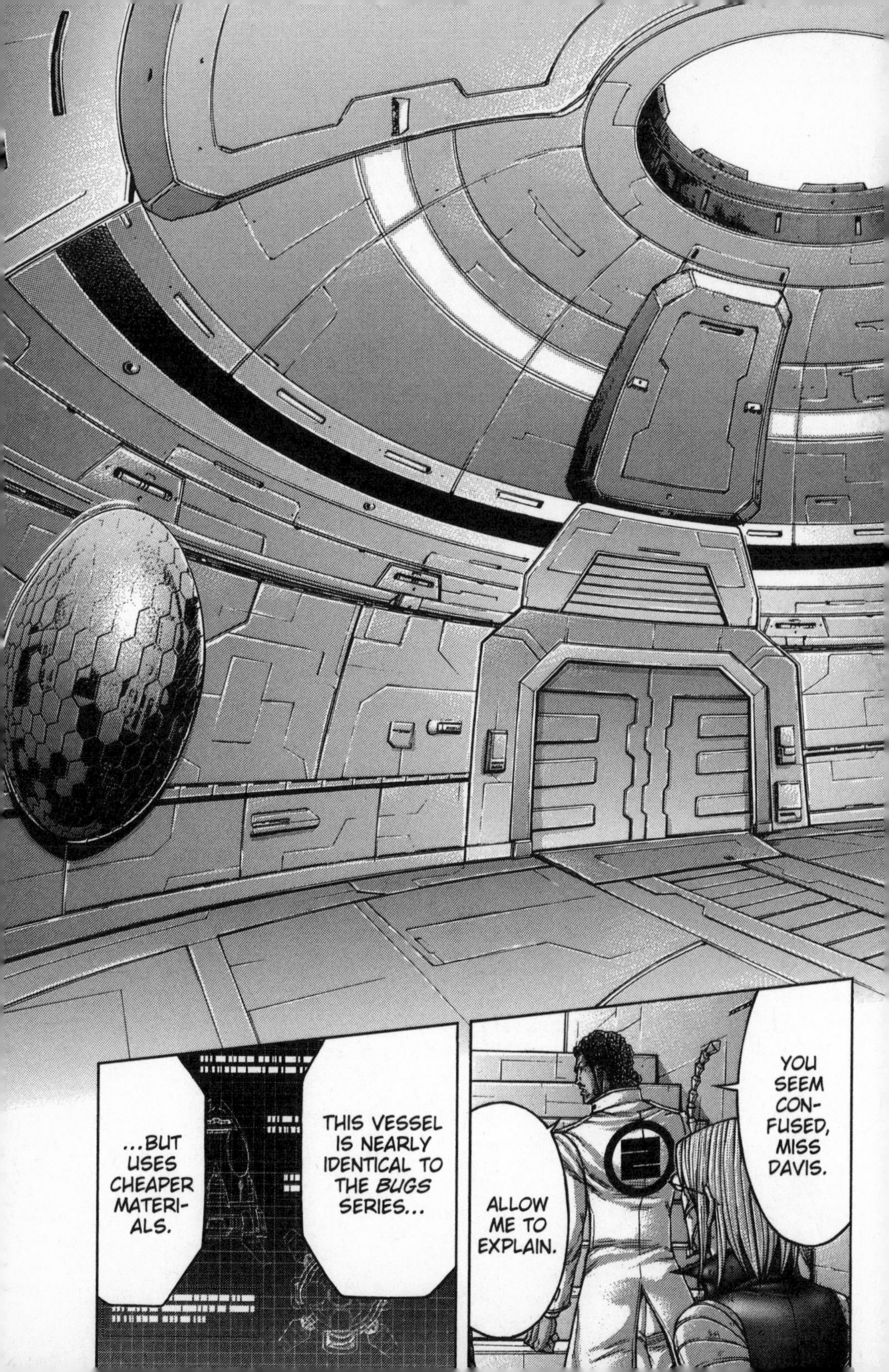
YOU SEEM CON-FUSED, MISS DAVIS.
ALLOW ME TO EXPLAIN.
THIS VESSEL IS NEARLY IDENTICAL TO THE *BUGS* SERIES…
…BUT USES CHEAPER MATERI-ALS.

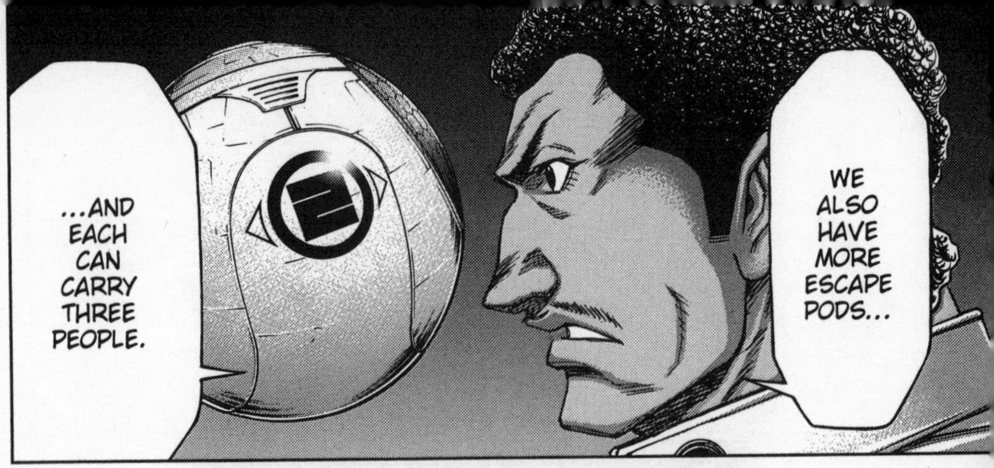
WE ALSO HAVE MORE ESCAPE PODS...
...AND EACH CAN CARRY THREE PEOPLE.

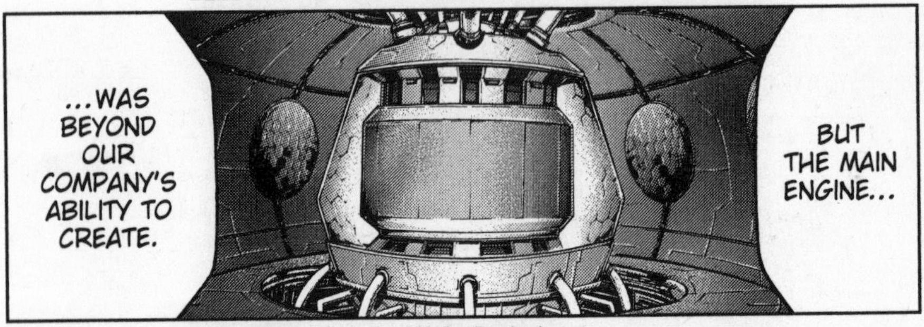
BUT THE MAIN ENGINE...
...WAS BEYOND OUR COMPANY'S ABILITY TO CREATE.

*Variable Specific Impulse Magnetoplasma Rocket. As of 2015, still in development.

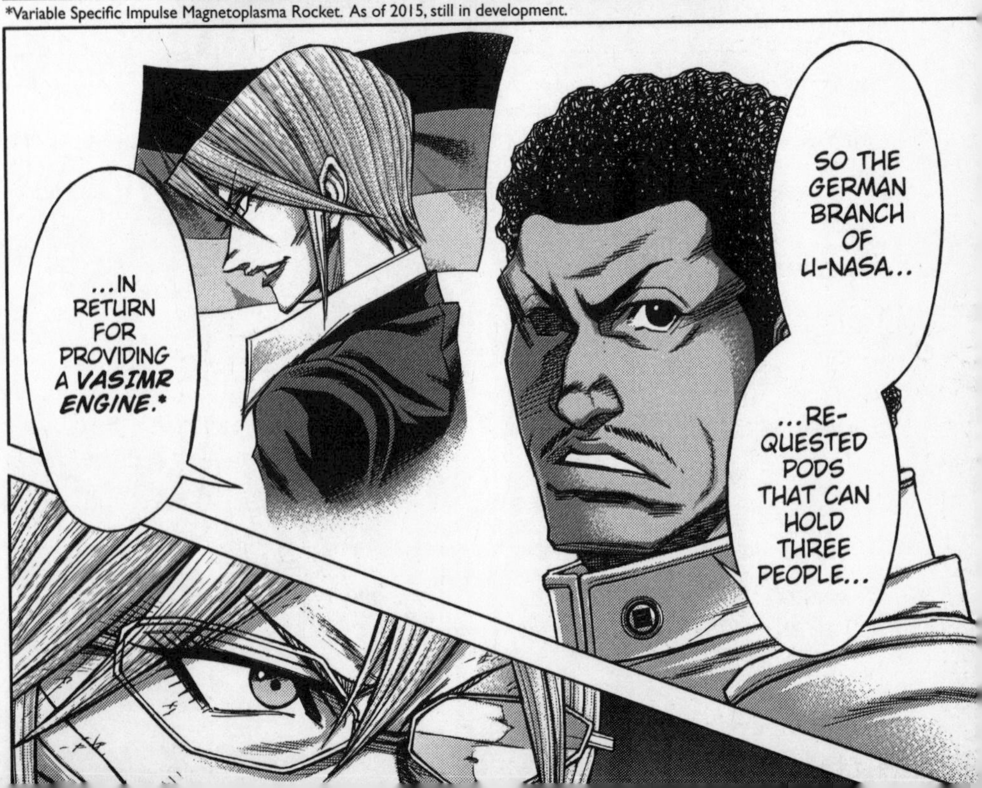
SO THE GERMAN BRANCH OF U-NASA...
...RE-QUESTED PODS THAT CAN HOLD THREE PEOPLE...
...IN RETURN FOR PROVIDING A VASIMR ENGINE.*

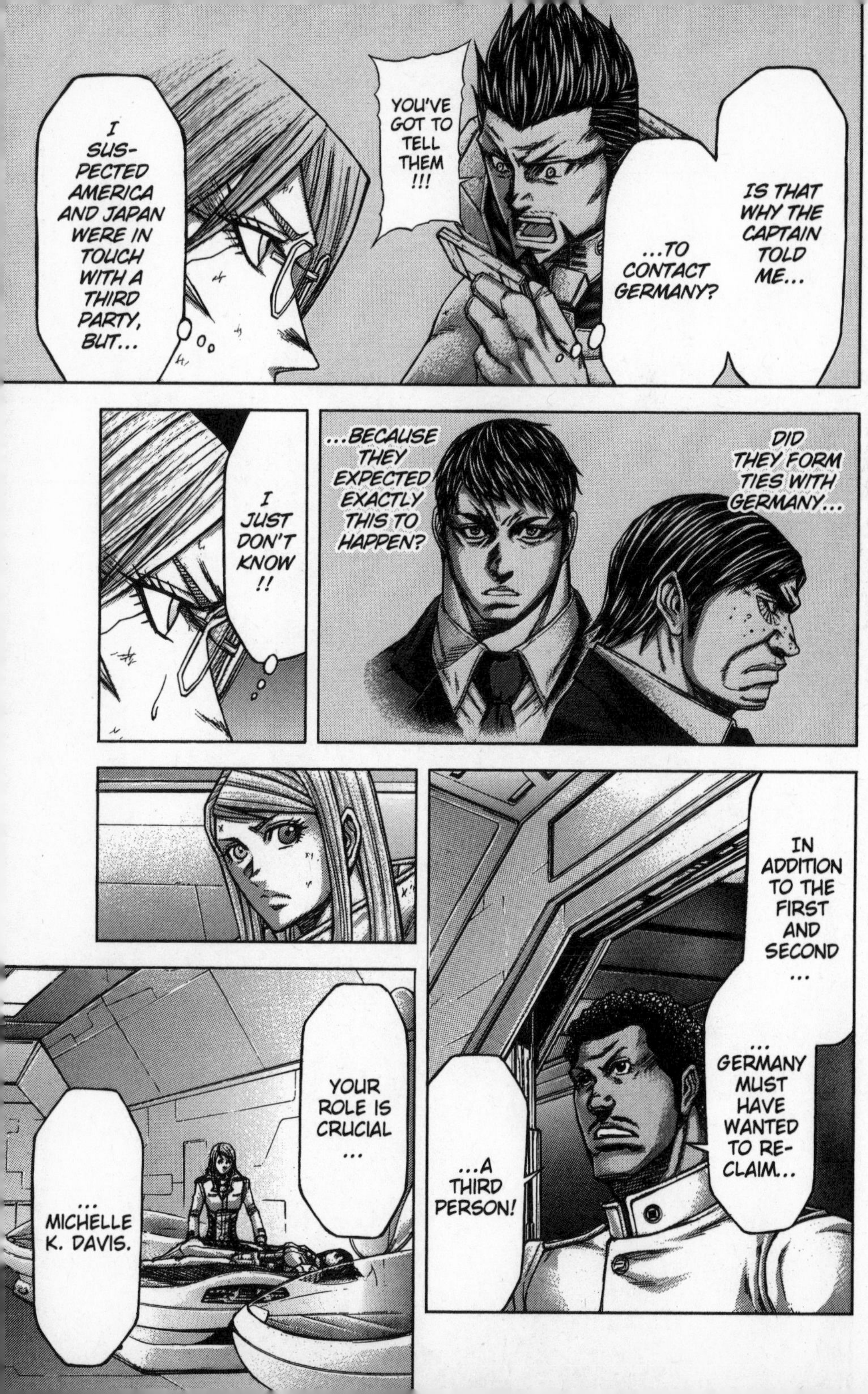
IS THAT WHY THE CAPTAIN TOLD ME...
...TO CONTACT GERMANY?
YOU'VE GOT TO TELL THEM!!!
I SUSPECTED AMERICA AND JAPAN WERE IN TOUCH WITH A THIRD PARTY, BUT...
DID THEY FORM TIES WITH GERMANY...
...BECAUSE THEY EXPECTED EXACTLY THIS TO HAPPEN?
I JUST DON'T KNOW!!
IN ADDITION TO THE FIRST AND SECOND...
...GERMANY MUST HAVE WANTED TO RECLAIM...
...A THIRD PERSON!
YOUR ROLE IS CRUCIAL...
...MICHELLE K. DAVIS.

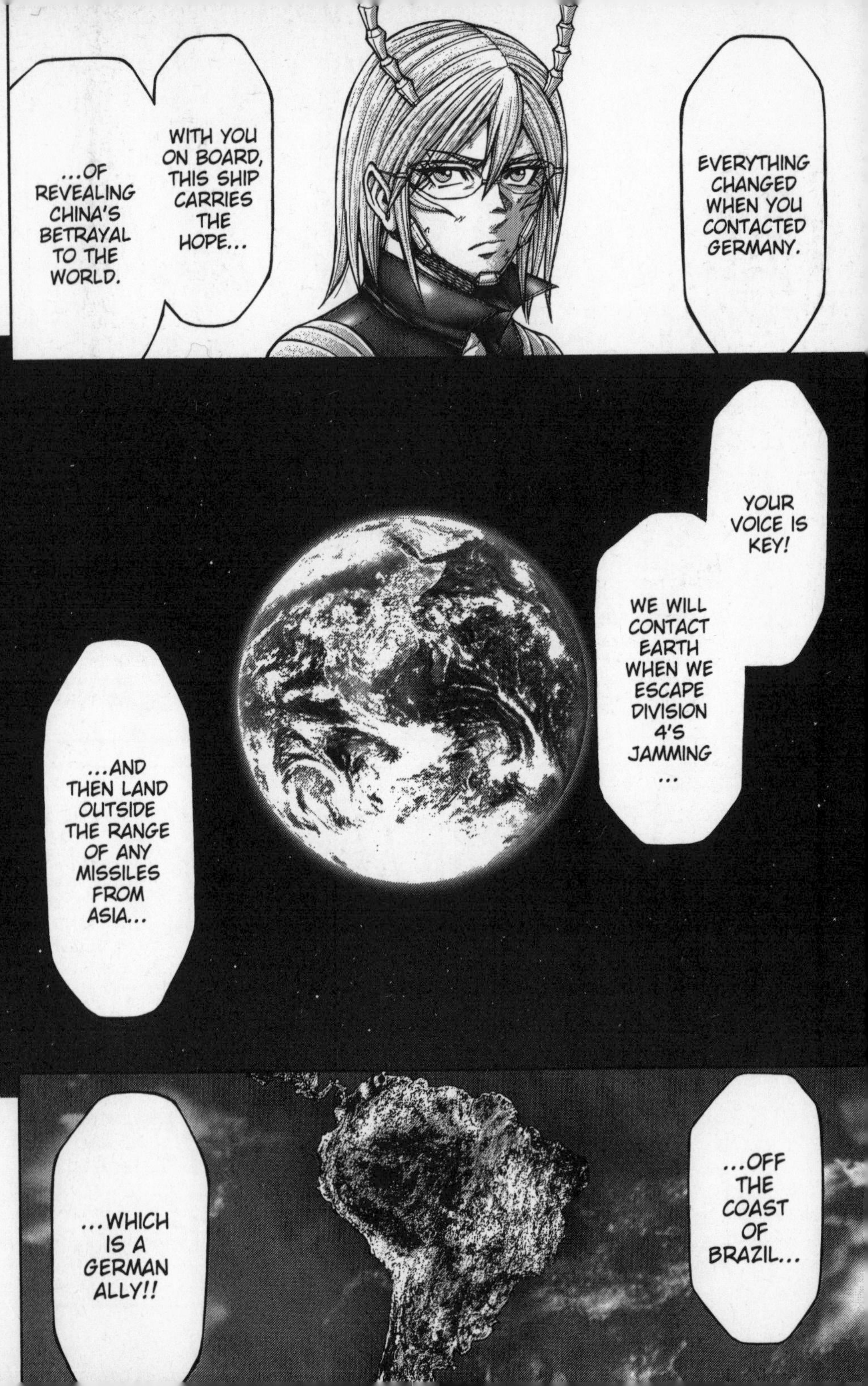
EVERYTHING CHANGED WHEN YOU CONTACTED GERMANY.
WITH YOU ON BOARD, THIS SHIP CARRIES THE HOPE...
...OF REVEALING CHINA'S BETRAYAL TO THE WORLD.
YOUR VOICE IS KEY!
WE WILL CONTACT EARTH WHEN WE ESCAPE DIVISION 4'S JAMMING...
...AND THEN LAND OUTSIDE THE RANGE OF ANY MISSILES FROM ASIA...
...OFF THE COAST OF BRAZIL...
...WHICH IS A GERMAN ALLY!!

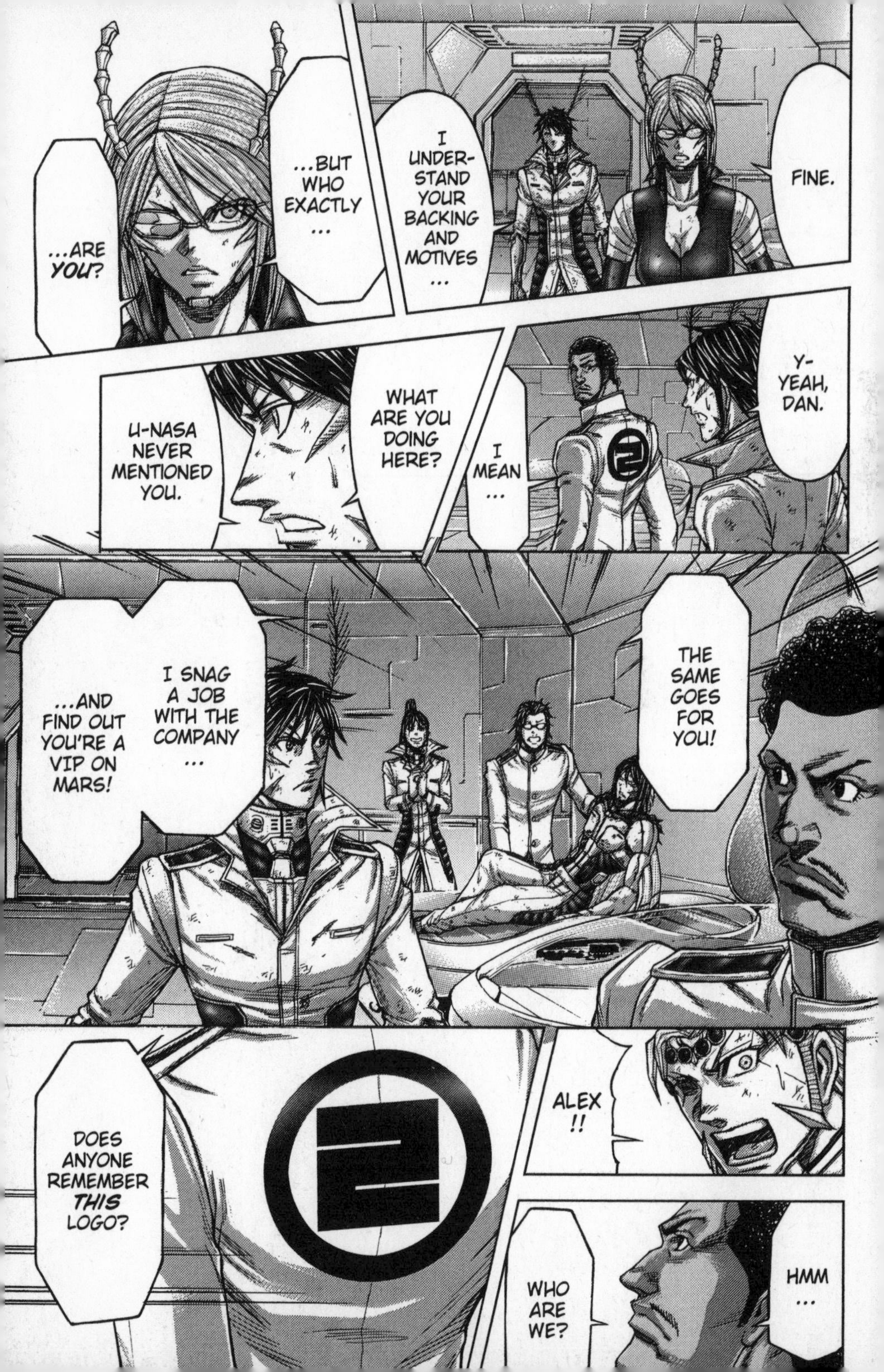
FINE.
I UNDER-STAND YOUR BACKING AND MOTIVES ...
...BUT WHO EXACTLY ...
...ARE *YOU*?
Y-YEAH, DAN.
I MEAN ...
WHAT ARE YOU DOING HERE?
U-NASA NEVER MENTIONED YOU.
THE SAME GOES FOR YOU!
I SNAG A JOB WITH THE COMPANY ...
...AND FIND OUT YOU'RE A VIP ON MARS!
ALEX !!
HMM ...
WHO ARE WE?
DOES ANYONE REMEMBER *THIS* LOGO?

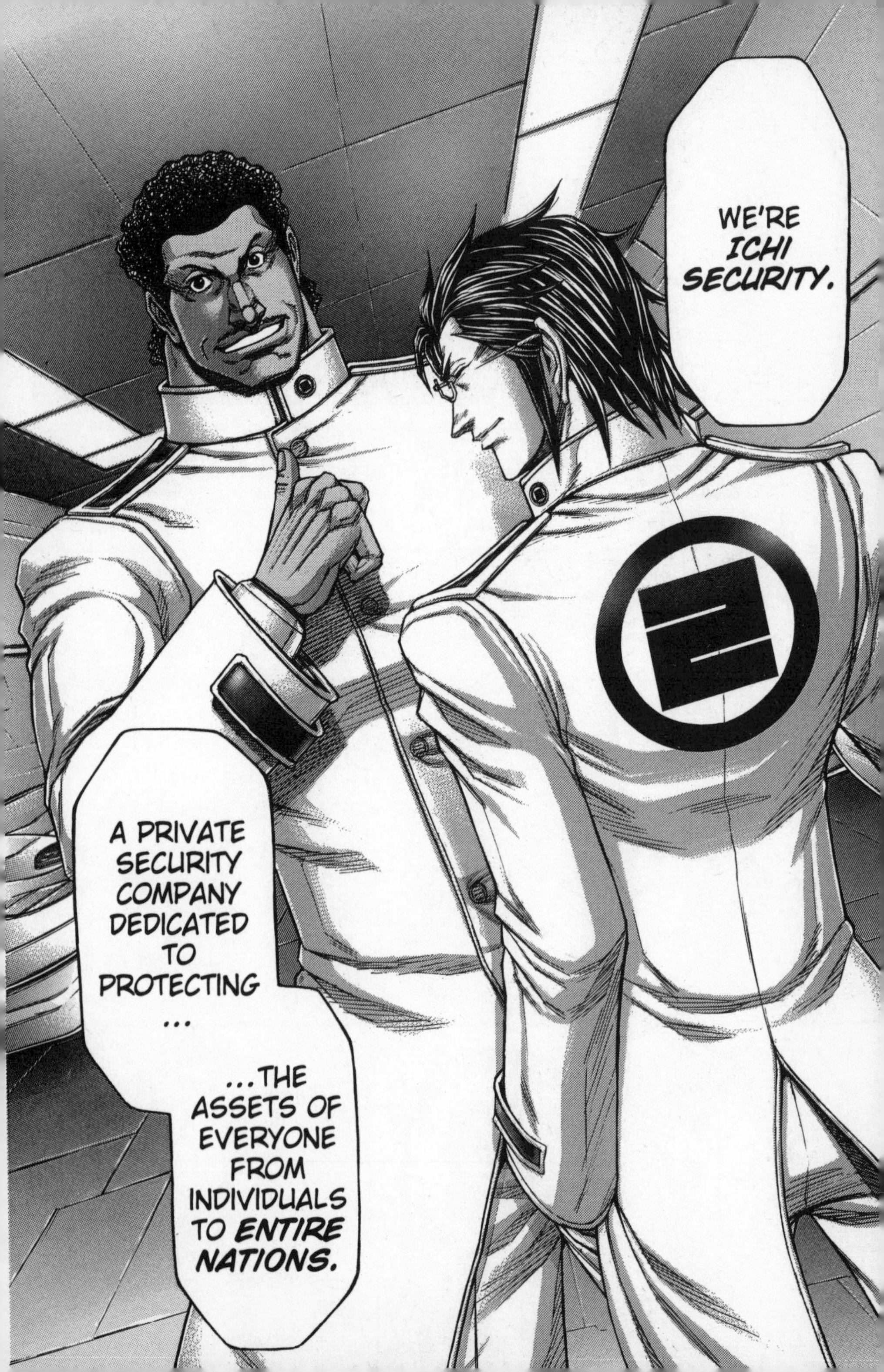
WE'RE *ICHI* SECURITY.
A PRIVATE SECURITY COMPANY DEDICATED TO PROTECTING...
...THE ASSETS OF EVERYONE FROM INDIVIDUALS TO *ENTIRE NATIONS.*

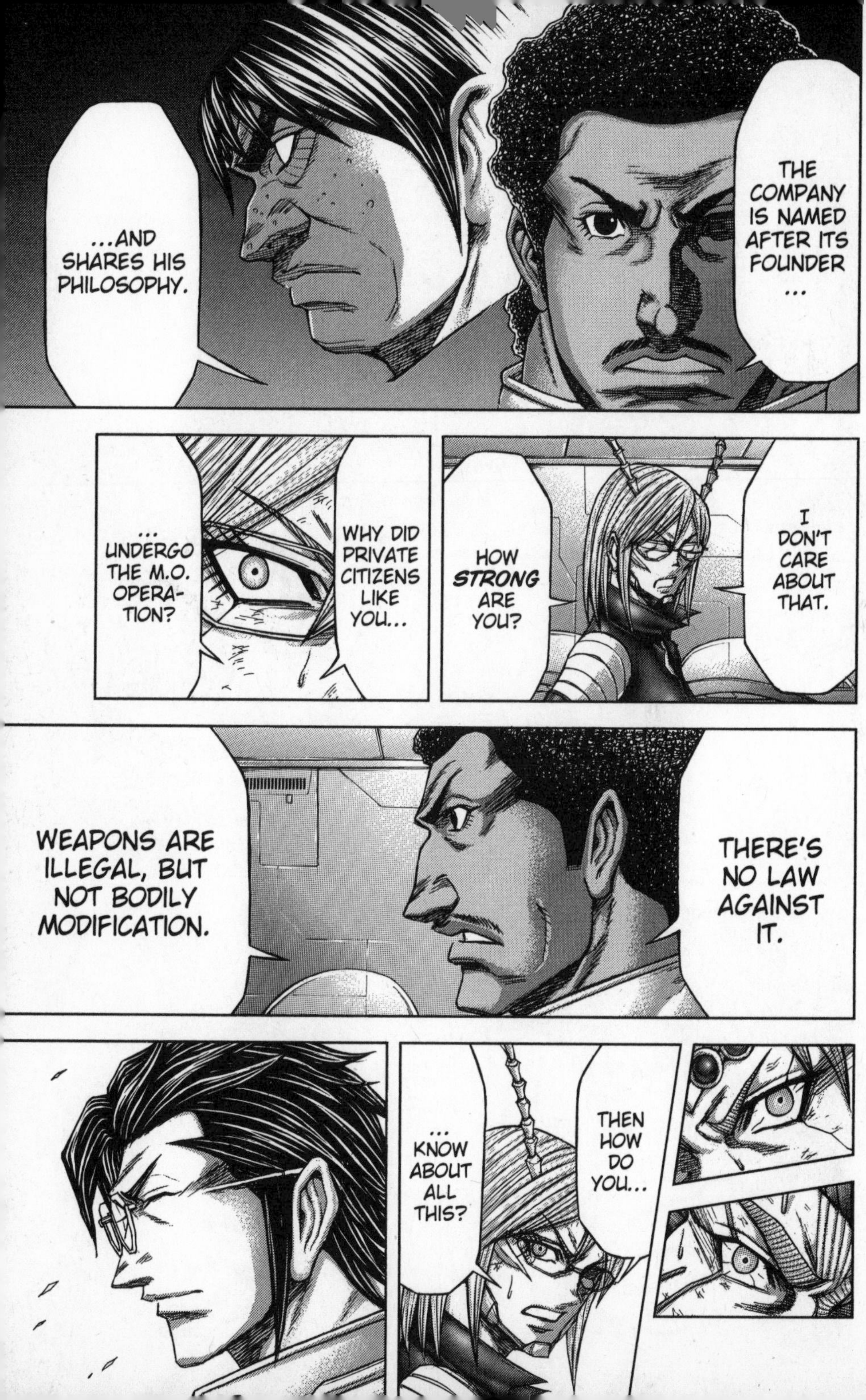
THE COMPANY IS NAMED AFTER ITS FOUNDER ...
...AND SHARES HIS PHILOSOPHY.
I DON'T CARE ABOUT THAT.
HOW STRONG ARE YOU?
WHY DID PRIVATE CITIZENS LIKE YOU...
... UNDERGO THE M.O. OPERATION?
THERE'S NO LAW AGAINST IT.
WEAPONS ARE ILLEGAL, BUT NOT BODILY MODIFICATION.
THEN HOW DO YOU...
... KNOW ABOUT ALL THIS?

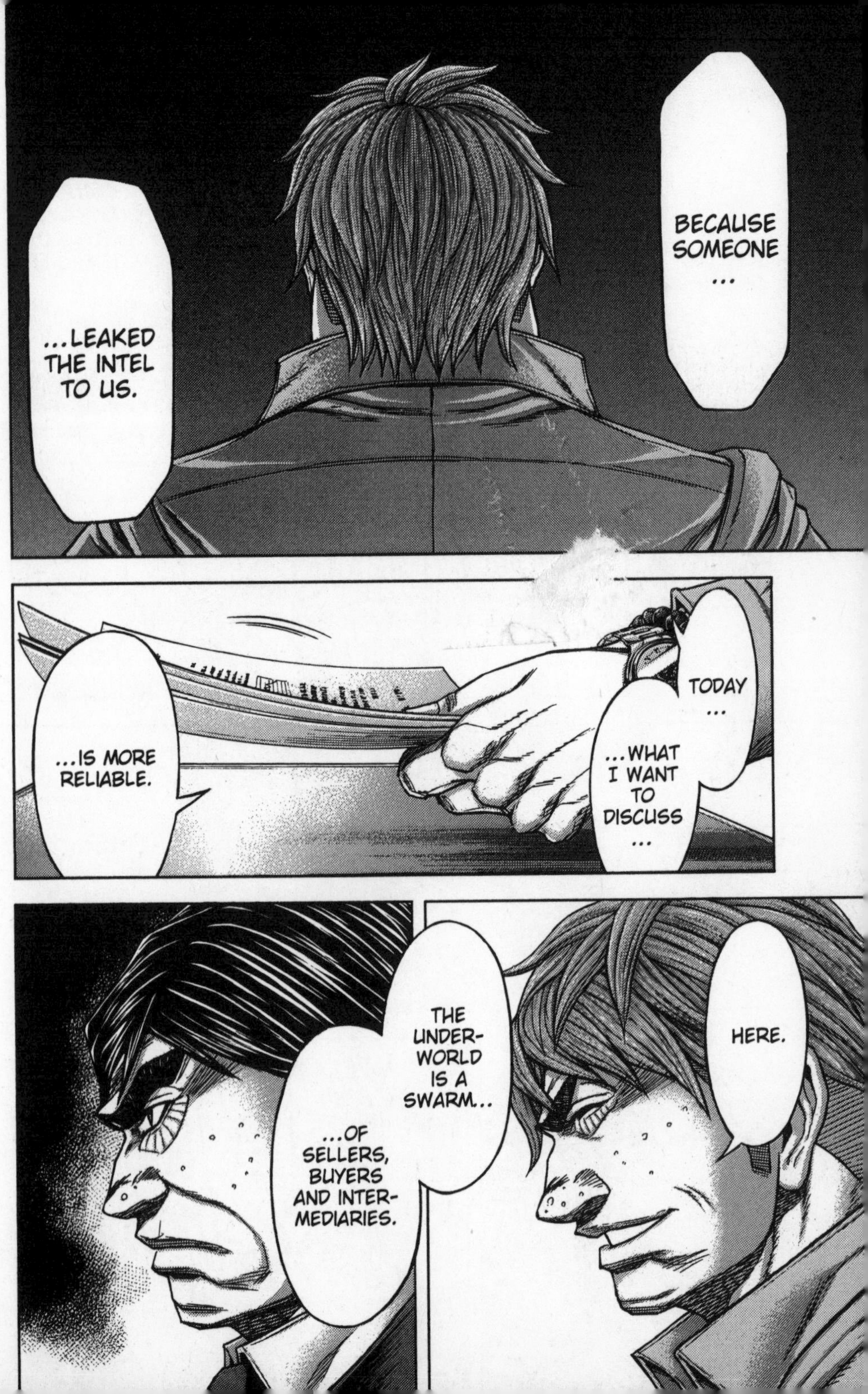
BECAUSE SOMEONE ...
...LEAKED THE INTEL TO US.
TODAY ...
...WHAT I WANT TO DISCUSS ...
...IS MORE RELIABLE.
HERE.
THE UNDER-WORLD IS A SWARM...
...OF SELLERS, BUYERS AND INTER-MEDIARIES.

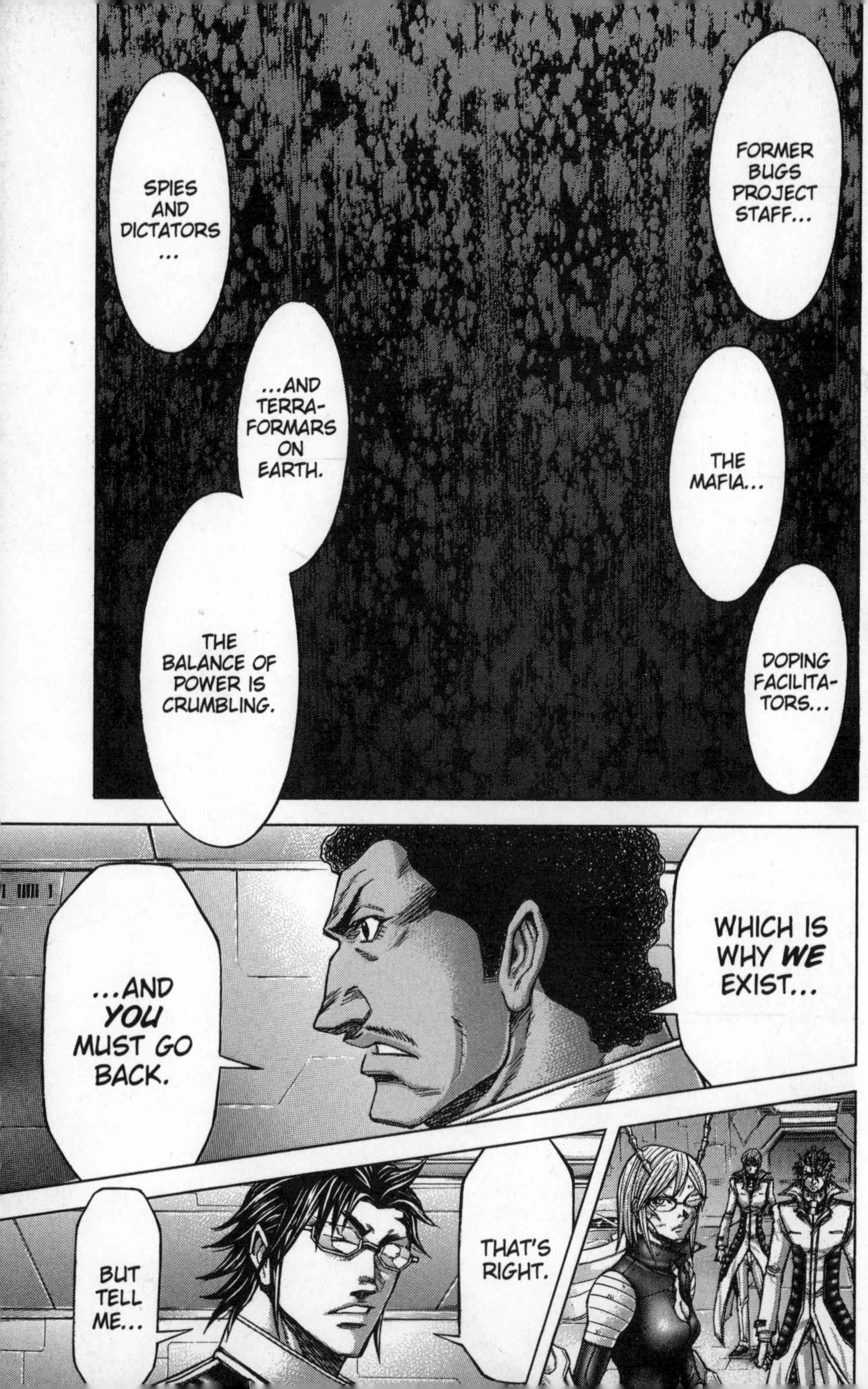
FORMER BUGS PROJECT STAFF...
THE MAFIA...
DOPING FACILITATORS...
SPIES AND DICTATORS...
...AND TERRAFORMARS ON EARTH.
THE BALANCE OF POWER IS CRUMBLING.
WHICH IS WHY WE EXIST...
...AND YOU MUST GO BACK.
THAT'S RIGHT.
BUT TELL ME...

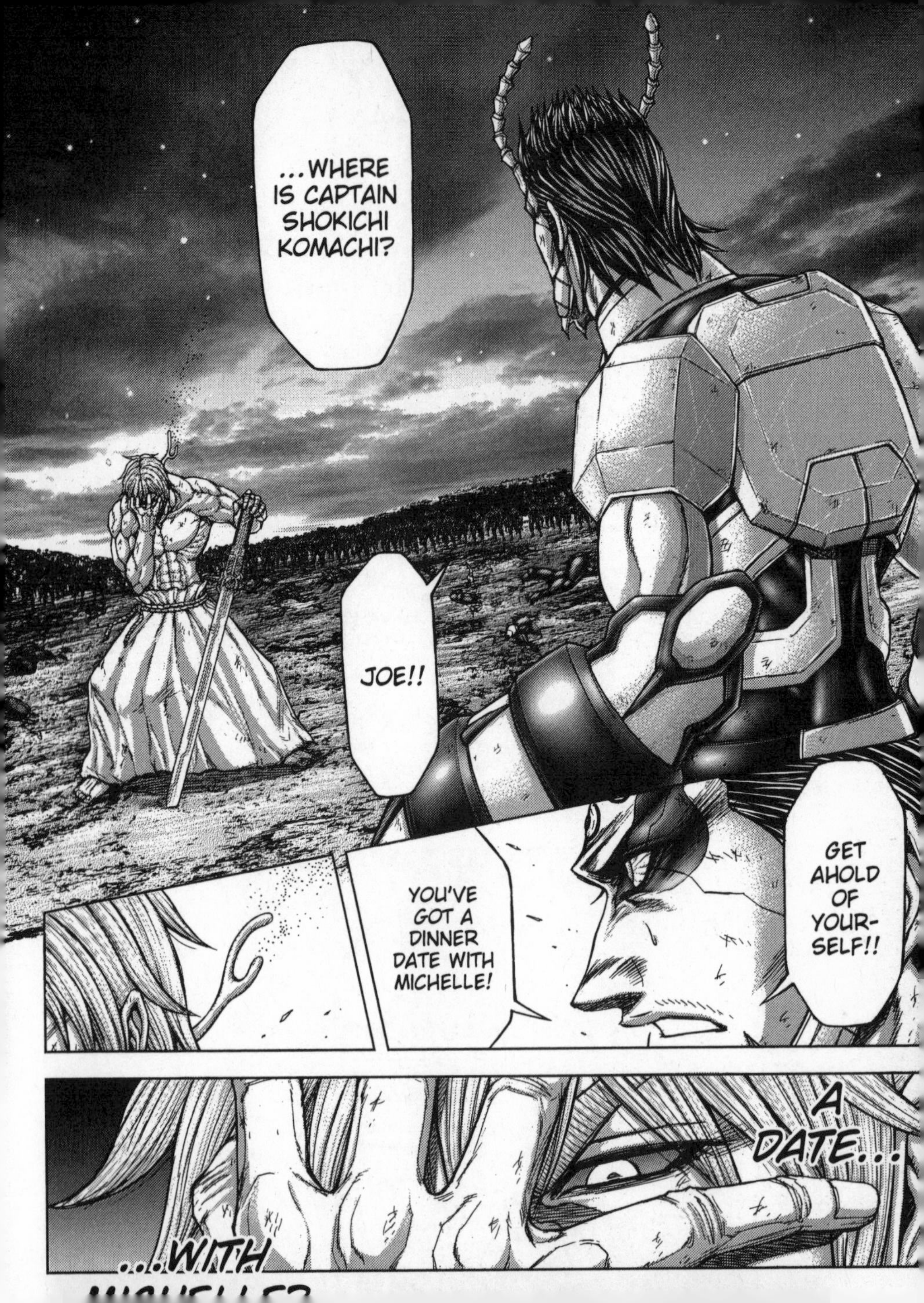
...WHERE IS CAPTAIN SHOKICHI KOMACHI?
JOE!!
GET AHOLD OF YOURSELF!!
YOU'VE GOT A DINNER DATE WITH MICHELLE!
A DATE...
...WITH

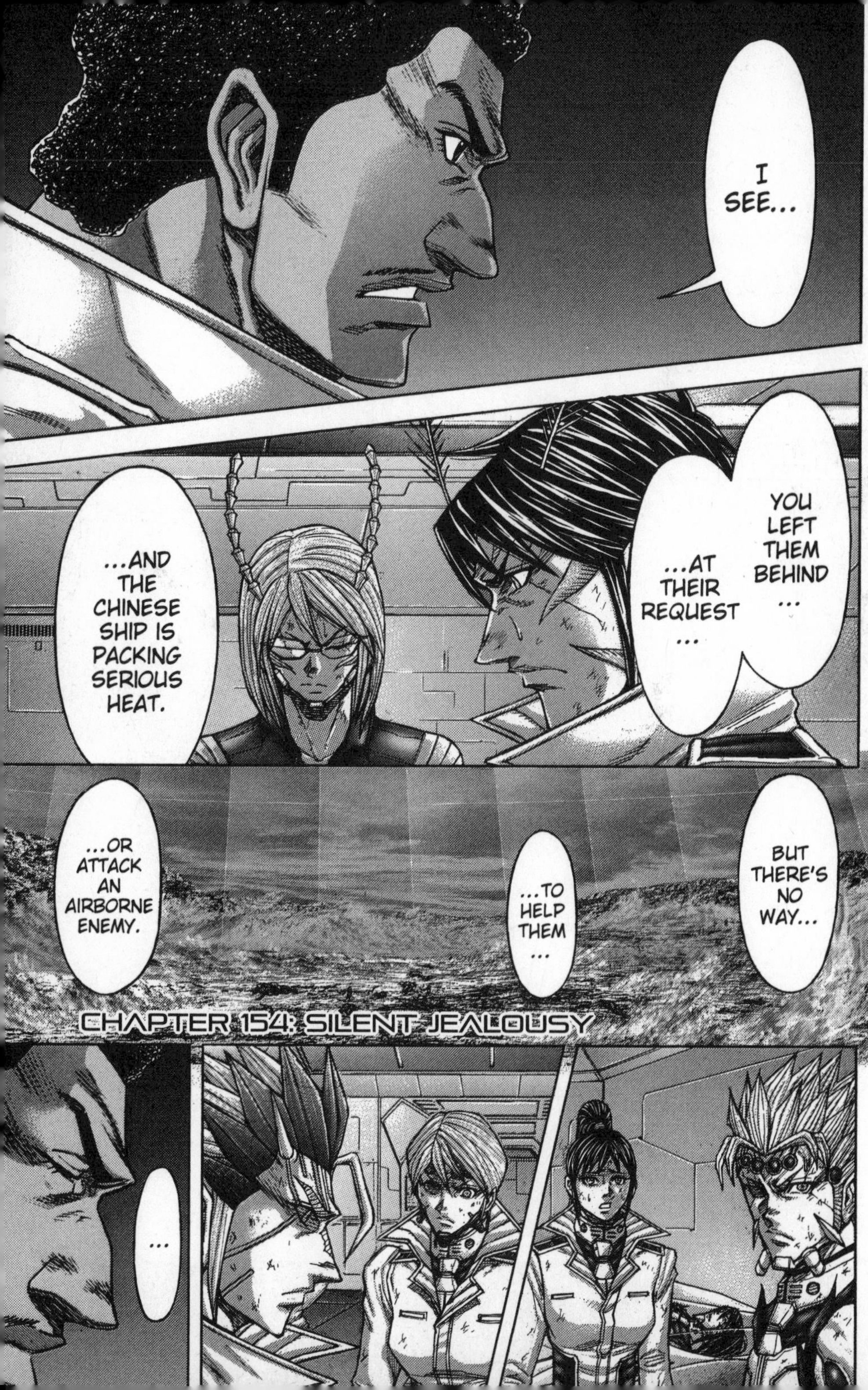
I SEE...
YOU LEFT THEM BEHIND...
...AT THEIR REQUEST...
...AND THE CHINESE SHIP IS PACKING SERIOUS HEAT.
BUT THERE'S NO WAY...
...TO HELP THEM...
...OR ATTACK AN AIRBORNE ENEMY.
CHAPTER 154: SILENT JEALOUSY
...

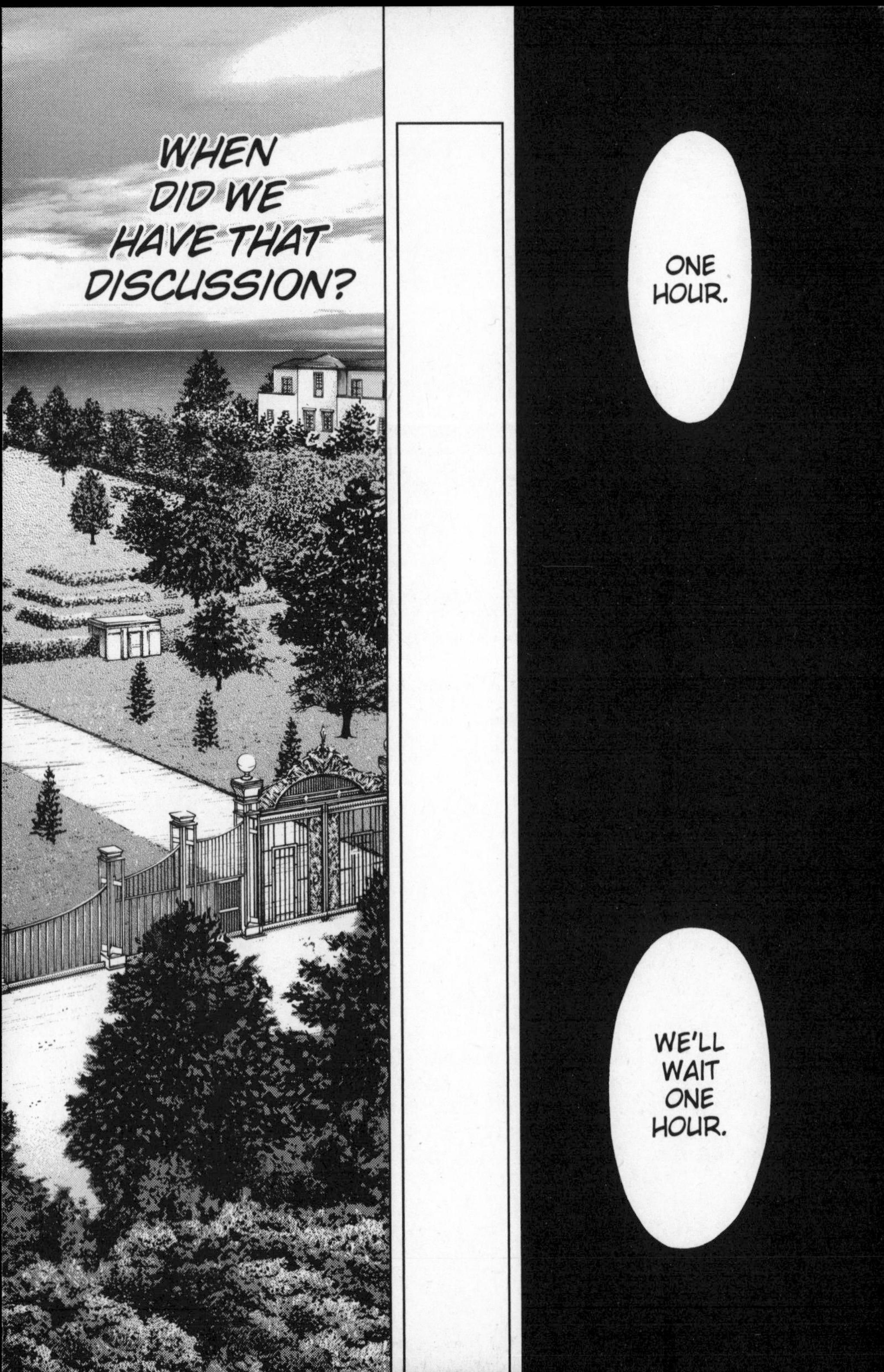
ONE HOUR.
WE'LL WAIT ONE HOUR.
WHEN DID WE HAVE THAT DISCUSSION?

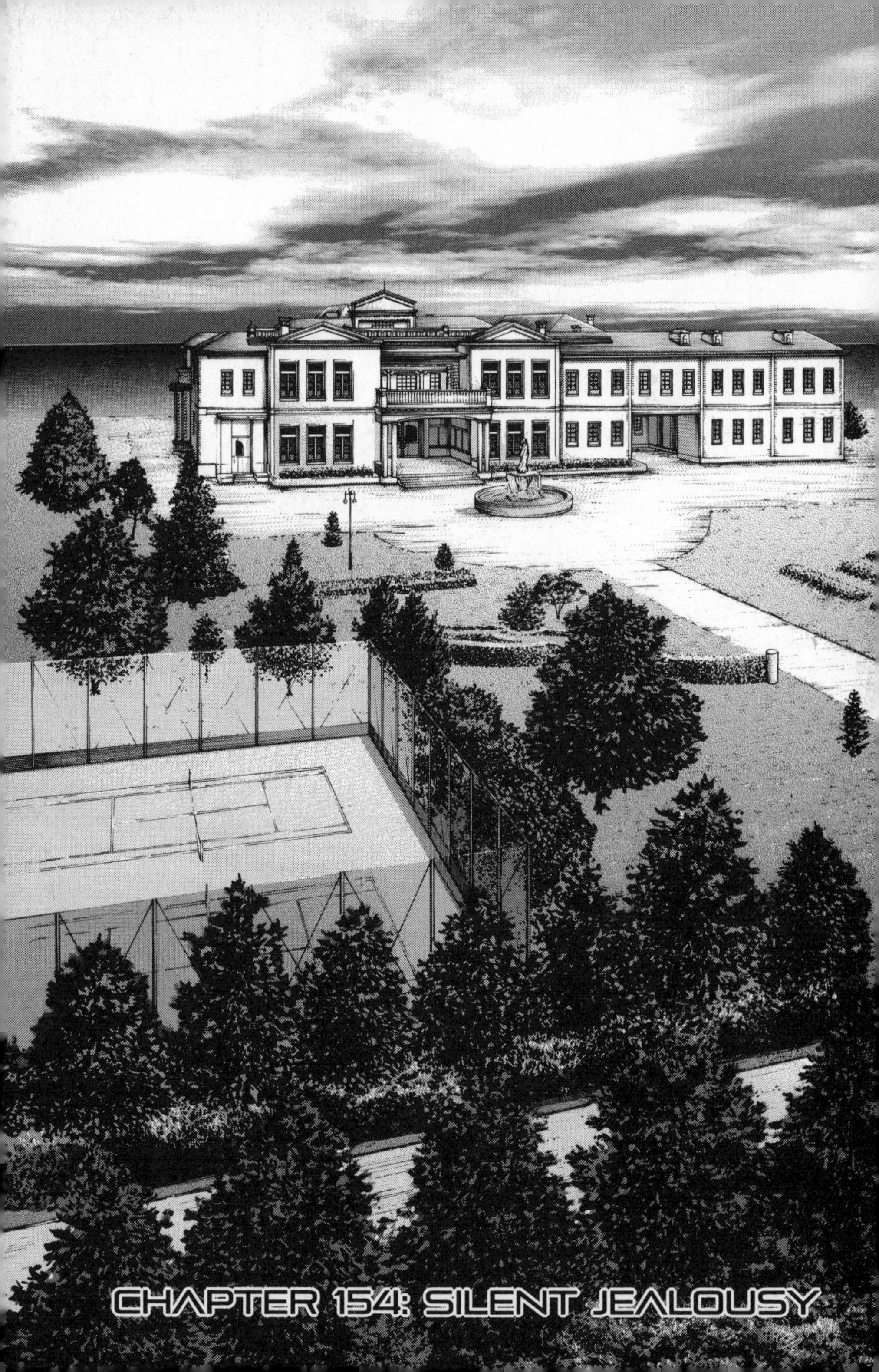

CHAPTER 154: SILENT JEALOUSY

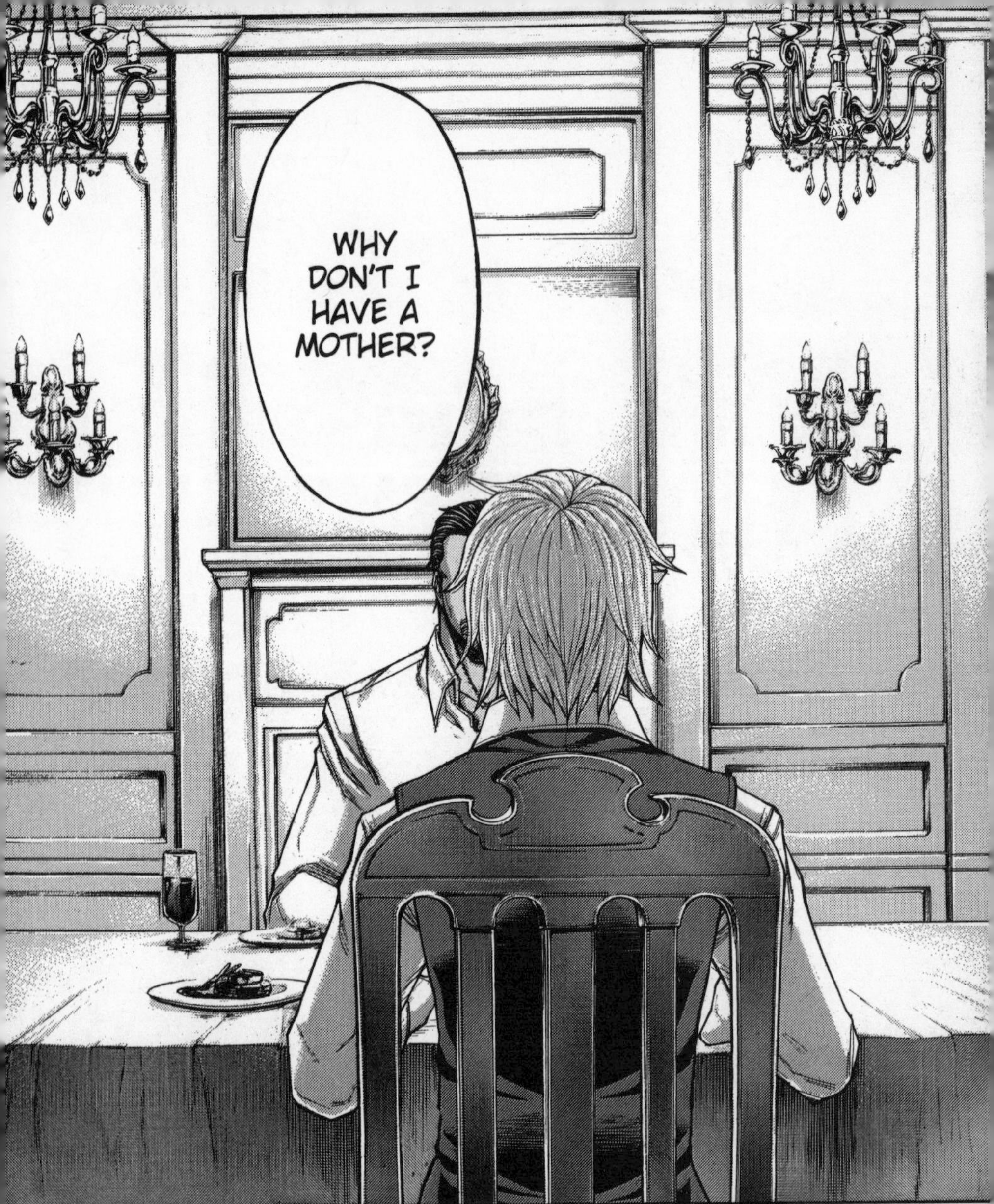
WHY DON'T I HAVE A MOTHER?
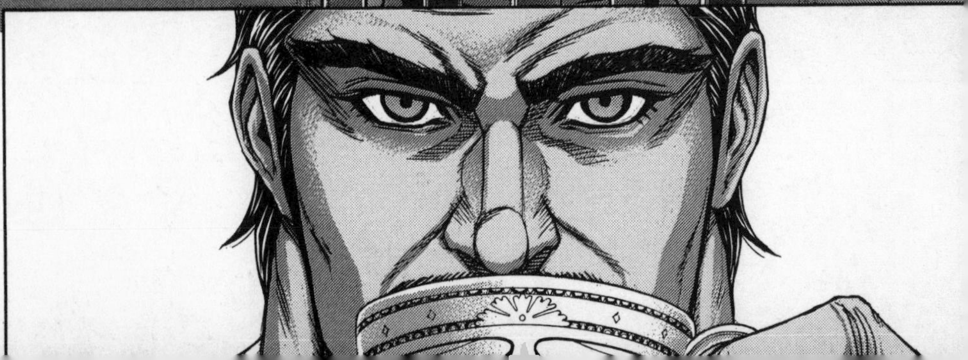

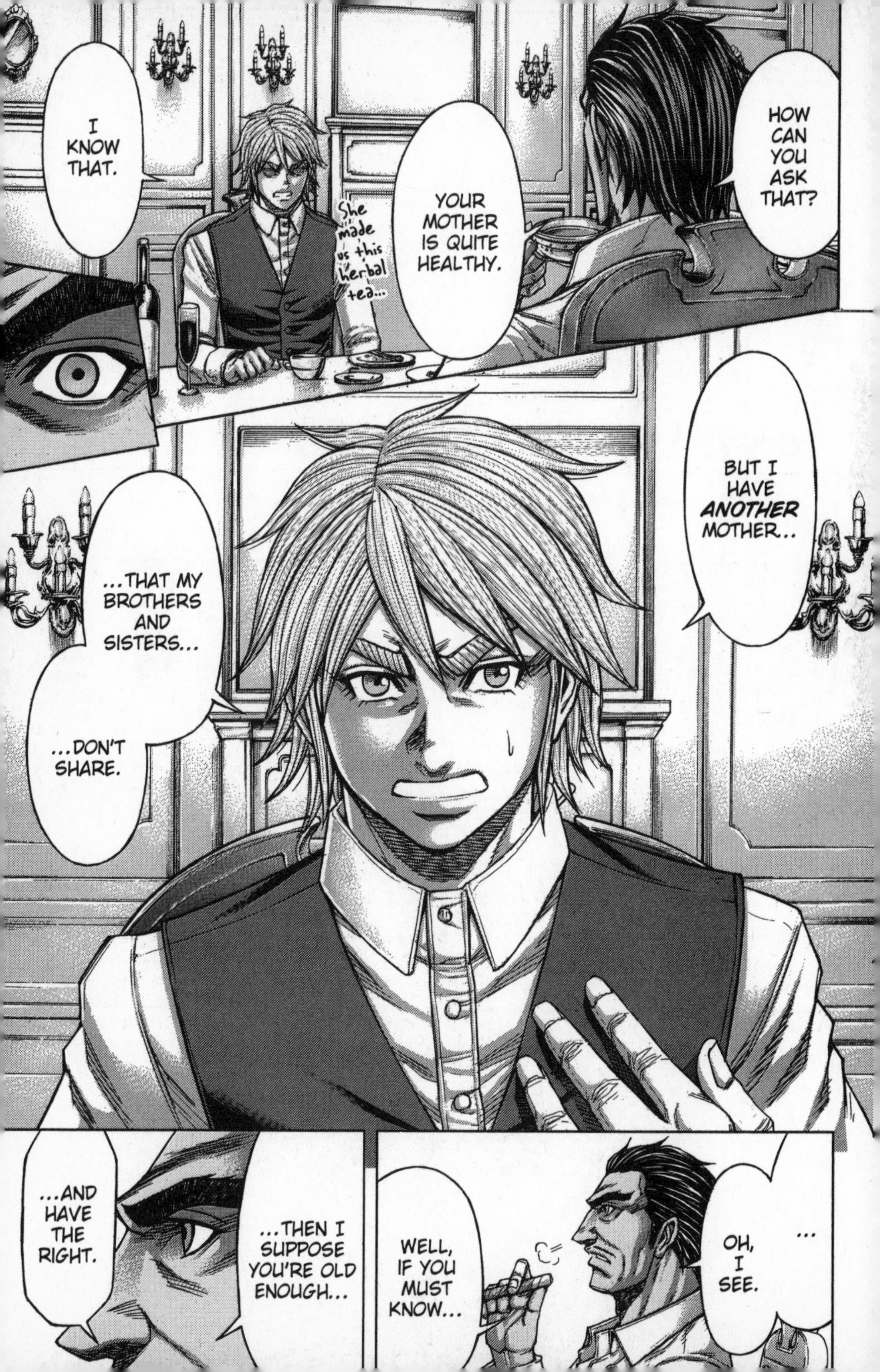
HOW CAN YOU ASK THAT?
YOUR MOTHER IS QUITE HEALTHY.
She made us this herbal tea...
I KNOW THAT.
BUT I HAVE *ANOTHER* MOTHER...
...THAT MY BROTHERS AND SISTERS...
...DON'T SHARE.
...
OH, I SEE.
WELL, IF YOU MUST KNOW...
...THEN I SUPPOSE YOU'RE OLD ENOUGH...
...AND HAVE THE RIGHT.

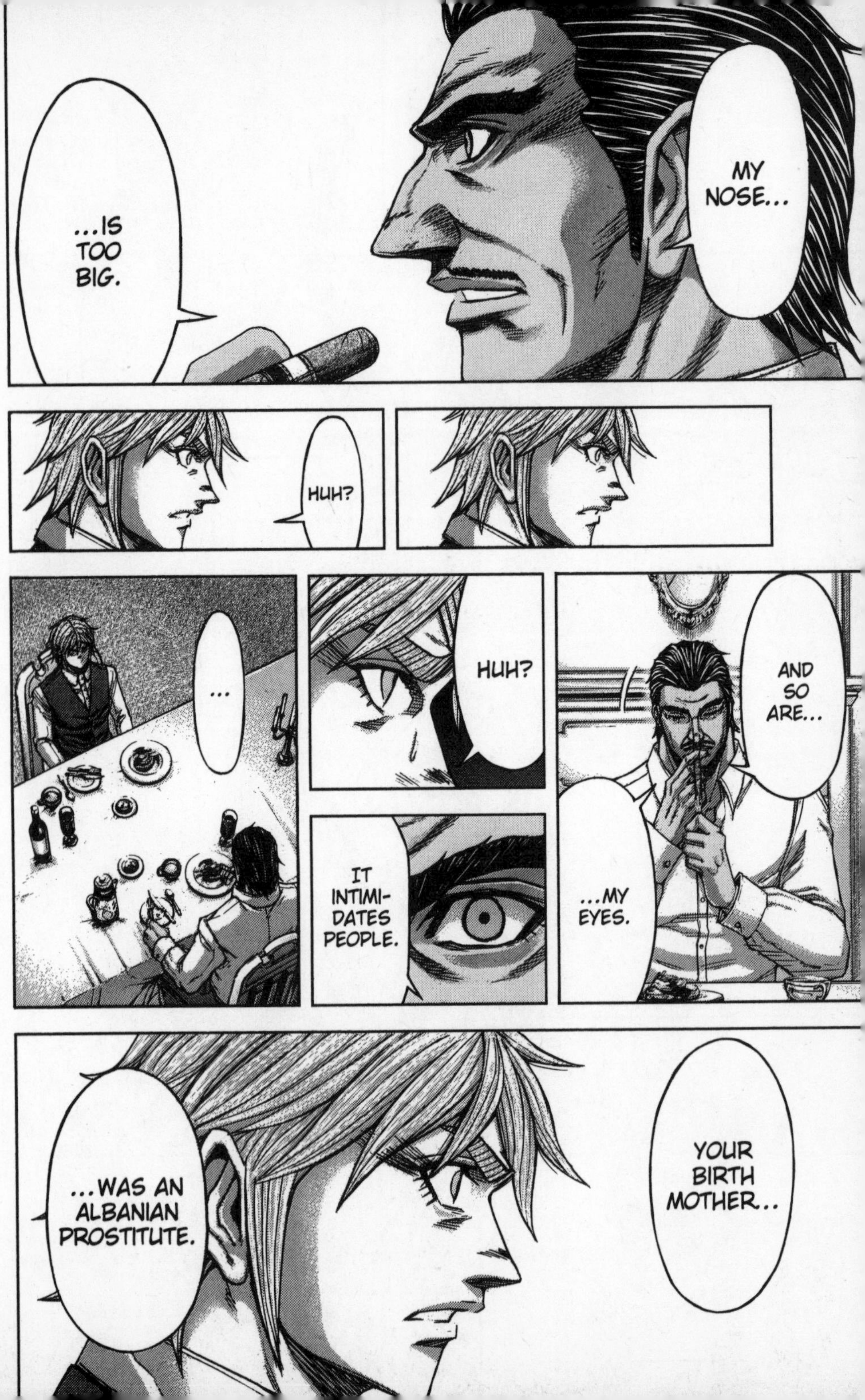
MY NOSE...
...IS TOO BIG.
HUH?
AND SO ARE...
...MY EYES.
HUH?
IT INTIMIDATES PEOPLE.
...
YOUR BIRTH MOTHER...
...WAS AN ALBANIAN PROSTITUTE.

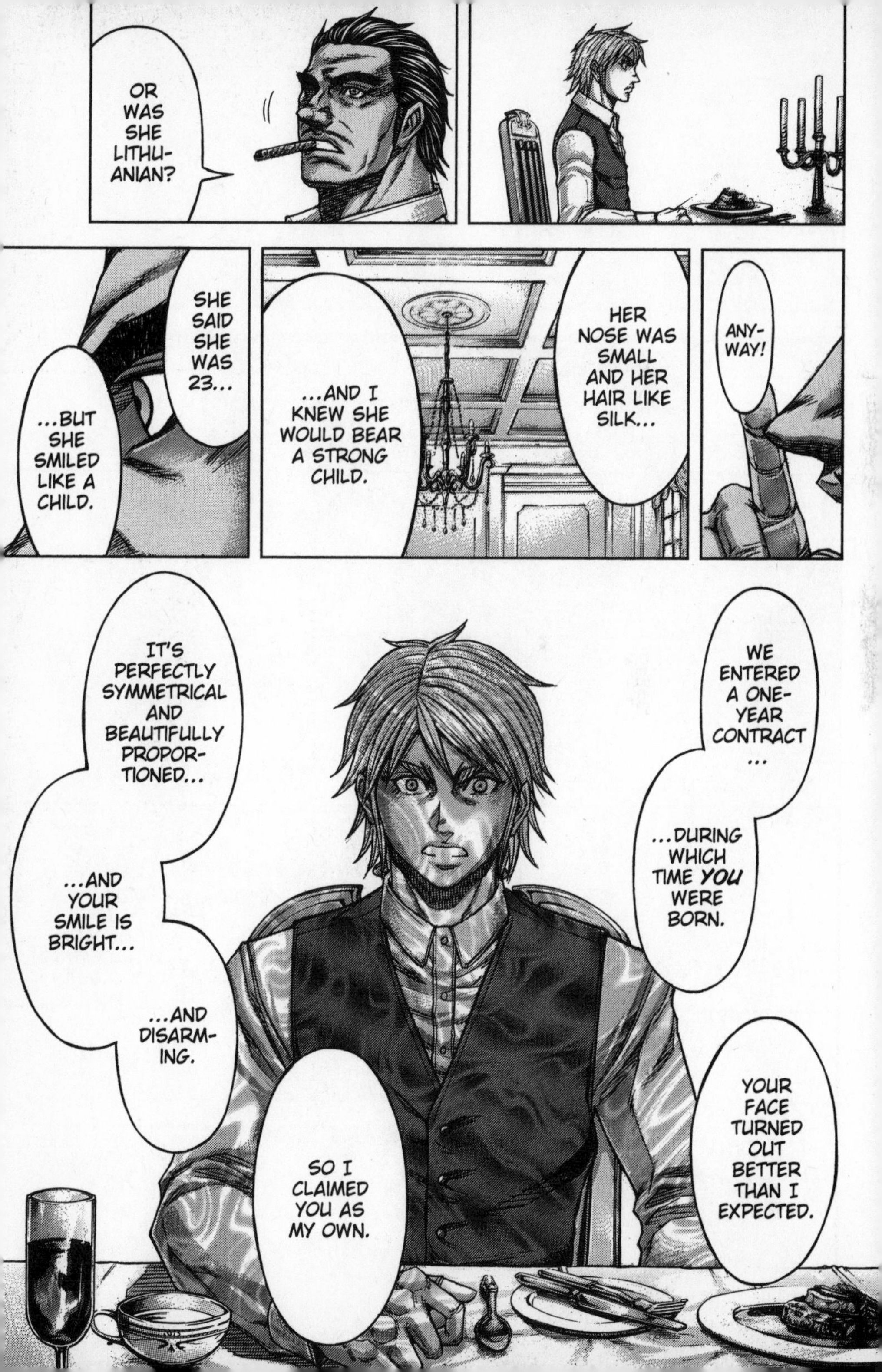
OR WAS SHE LITHUANIAN?
ANYWAY!
HER NOSE WAS SMALL AND HER HAIR LIKE SILK...
...AND I KNEW SHE WOULD BEAR A STRONG CHILD.
SHE SAID SHE WAS 23...
...BUT SHE SMILED LIKE A CHILD.
WE ENTERED A ONE-YEAR CONTRACT...
...DURING WHICH TIME *YOU* WERE BORN.
YOUR FACE TURNED OUT BETTER THAN I EXPECTED.
IT'S PERFECTLY SYMMETRICAL AND BEAUTIFULLY PROPORTIONED...
...AND YOUR SMILE IS BRIGHT...
...AND DISARMING.
SO I CLAIMED YOU AS MY OWN.

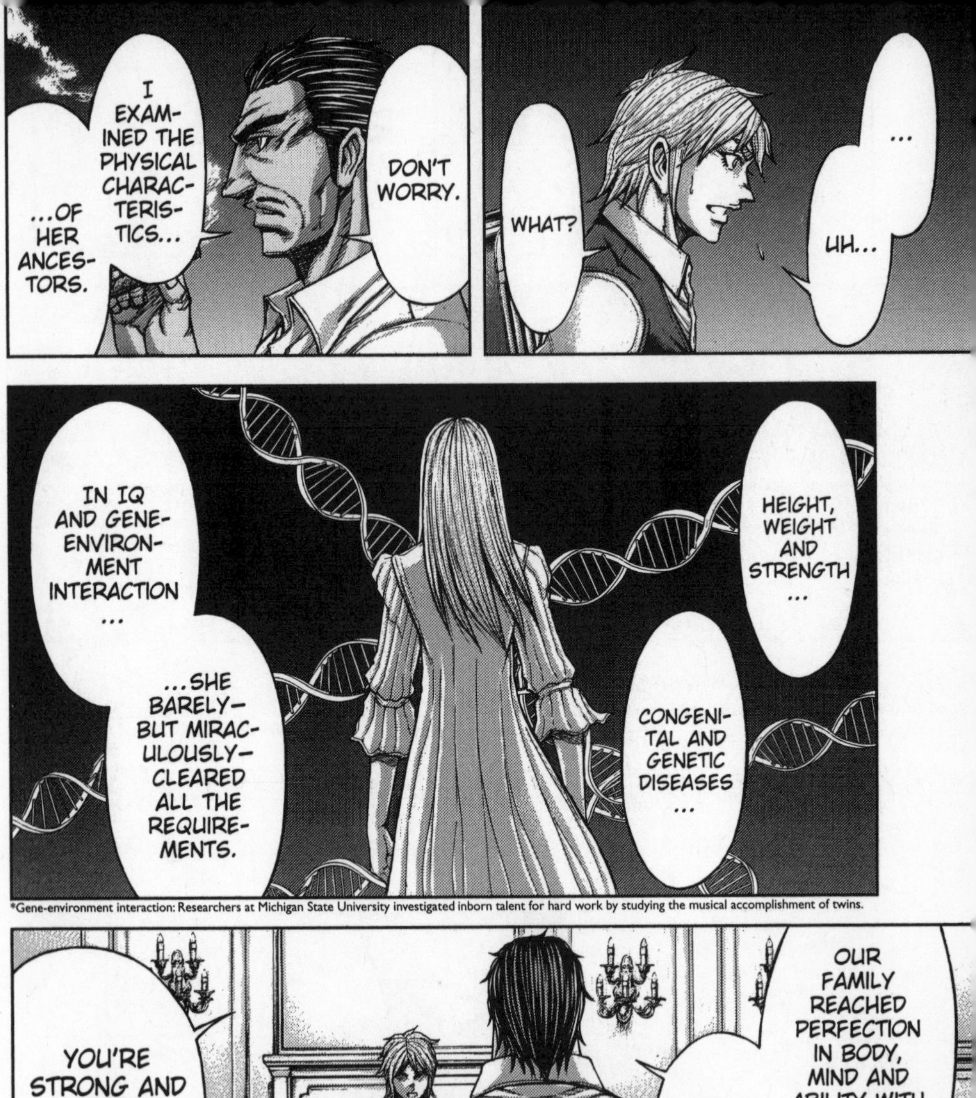
...
UH...
WHAT?
DON'T WORRY.
I EXAMINED THE PHYSICAL CHARACTERISTICS...
...OF HER ANCESTORS.
HEIGHT, WEIGHT AND STRENGTH...
CONGENITAL AND GENETIC DISEASES...
IN IQ AND GENE-ENVIRONMENT INTERACTION...
...SHE BARELY—BUT MIRACULOUSLY—CLEARED ALL THE REQUIREMENTS.

*Gene-environment interaction: Researchers at Michigan State University investigated inborn talent for hard work by studying the musical accomplishment of twins.

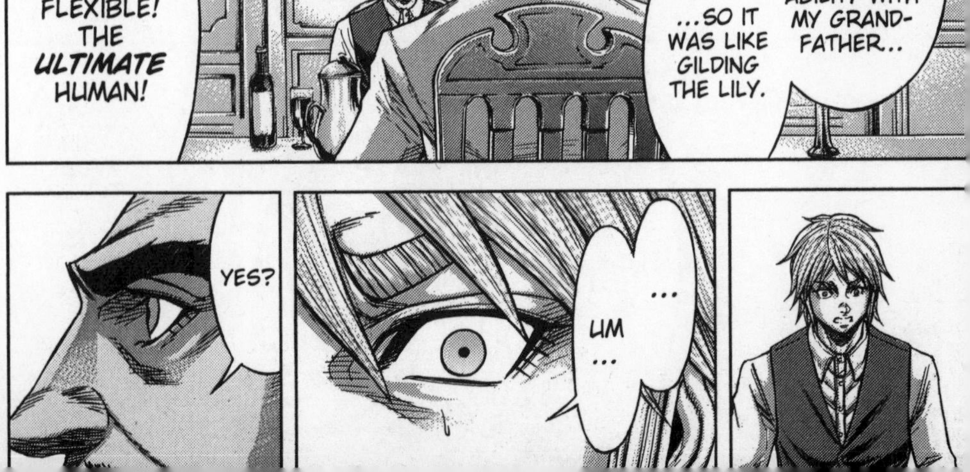
OUR FAMILY REACHED PERFECTION IN BODY, MIND AND ABILITY WITH MY GRANDFATHER...
...SO IT WAS LIKE GILDING THE LILY.
YOU'RE STRONG AND FLEXIBLE! THE *ULTIMATE* HUMAN!
...
UM ...
YES?

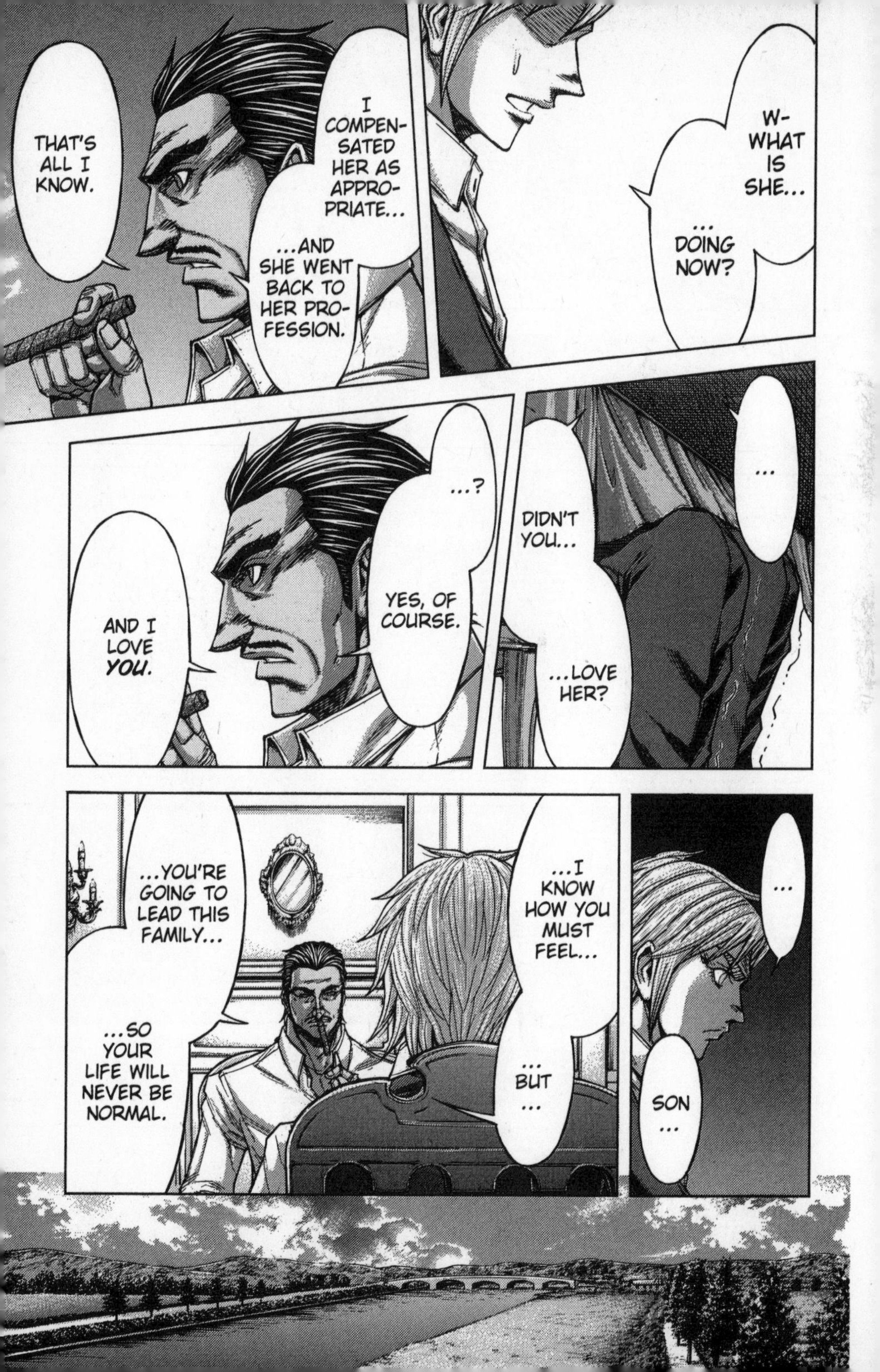
W-WHAT IS SHE...
...DOING NOW?
I COMPENSATED HER AS APPROPRIATE...
...AND SHE WENT BACK TO HER PROFESSION.
THAT'S ALL I KNOW.
...
DIDN'T YOU...
...LOVE HER?
...?
YES, OF COURSE.
AND I LOVE *YOU*.
...
SON...
...I KNOW HOW YOU MUST FEEL...
...BUT...
...YOU'RE GOING TO LEAD THIS FAMILY...
...SO YOUR LIFE WILL NEVER BE NORMAL.

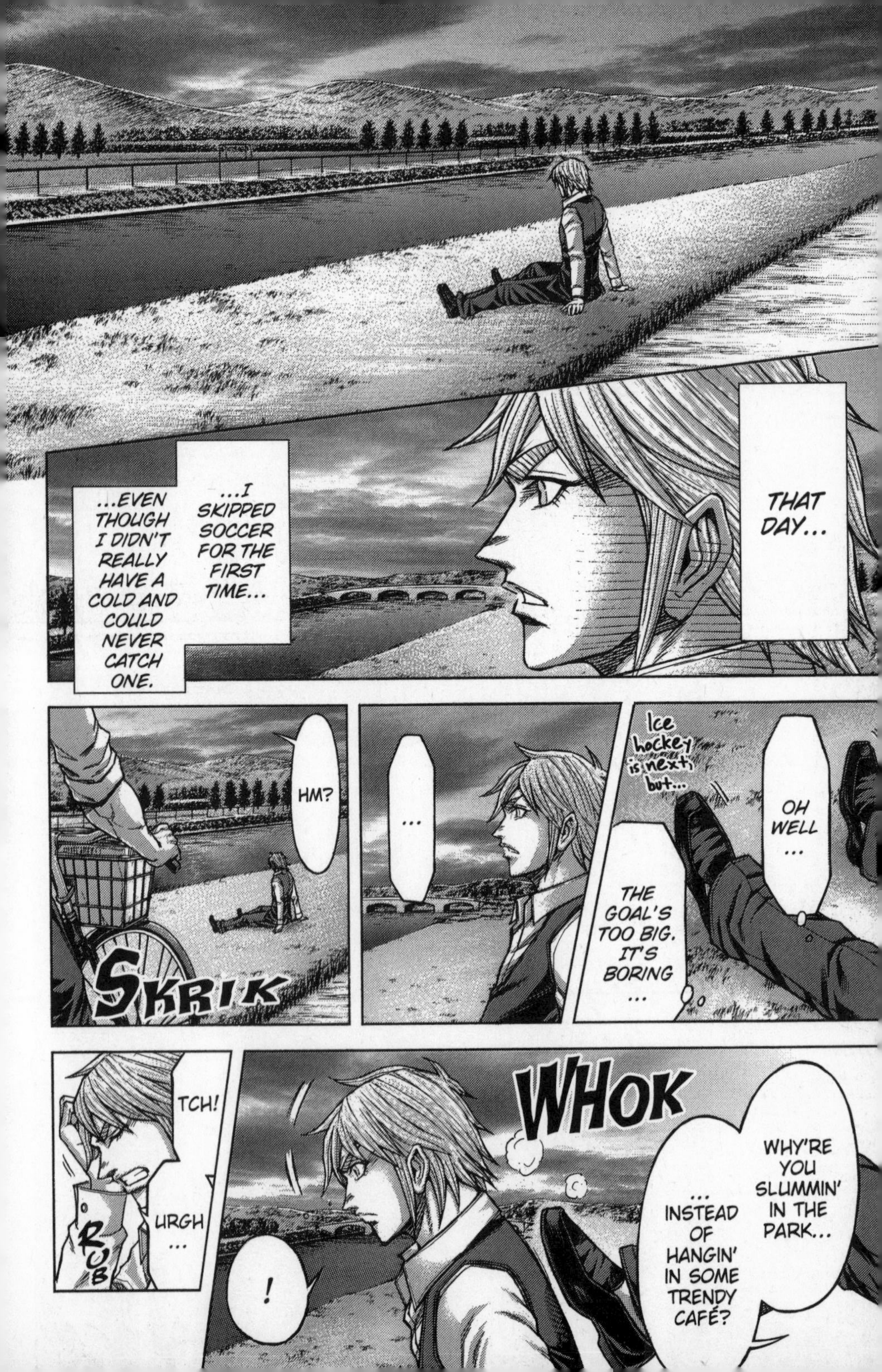
THAT DAY...
...I SKIPPED SOCCER FOR THE FIRST TIME...
...EVEN THOUGH I DIDN'T REALLY HAVE A COLD AND COULD NEVER CATCH ONE.
OH WELL...
Ice hockey is next, but...
THE GOAL'S TOO BIG. IT'S BORING...
...
HM?
SKRIK
WHY'RE YOU SLUMMIN' IN THE PARK...
...INSTEAD OF HANGIN' IN SOME TRENDY CAFÉ?
WHOK
!
TCH!
URGH...
RUB

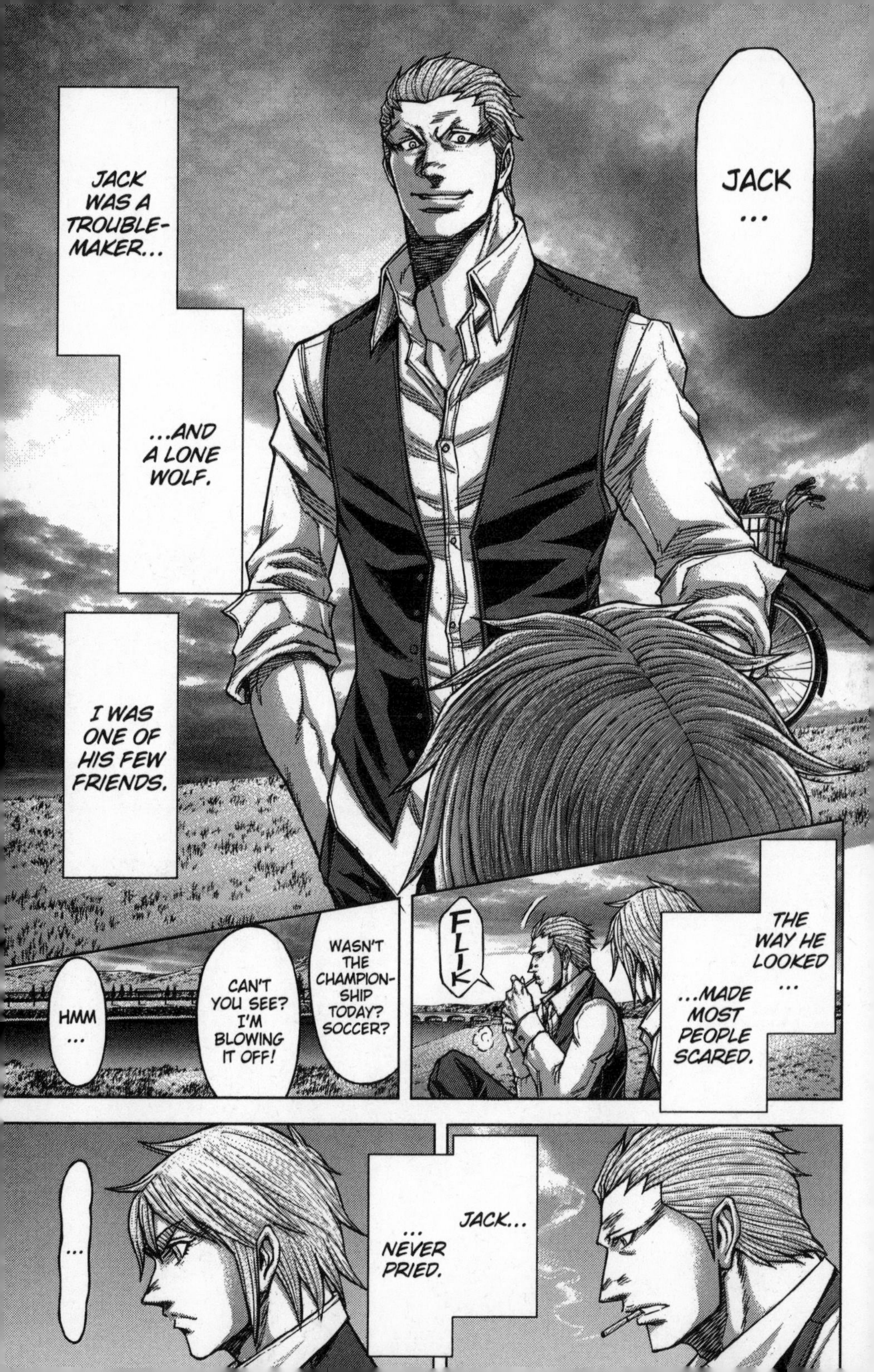
JACK ...
JACK WAS A TROUBLE-MAKER...
...AND A LONE WOLF.
I WAS ONE OF HIS FEW FRIENDS.
THE WAY HE LOOKED ...
...MADE MOST PEOPLE SCARED.
FLIK
WASN'T THE CHAMPION-SHIP TODAY? SOCCER?
CAN'T YOU SEE? I'M BLOWING IT OFF!
HMM ...
JACK...
... NEVER PRIED.
...

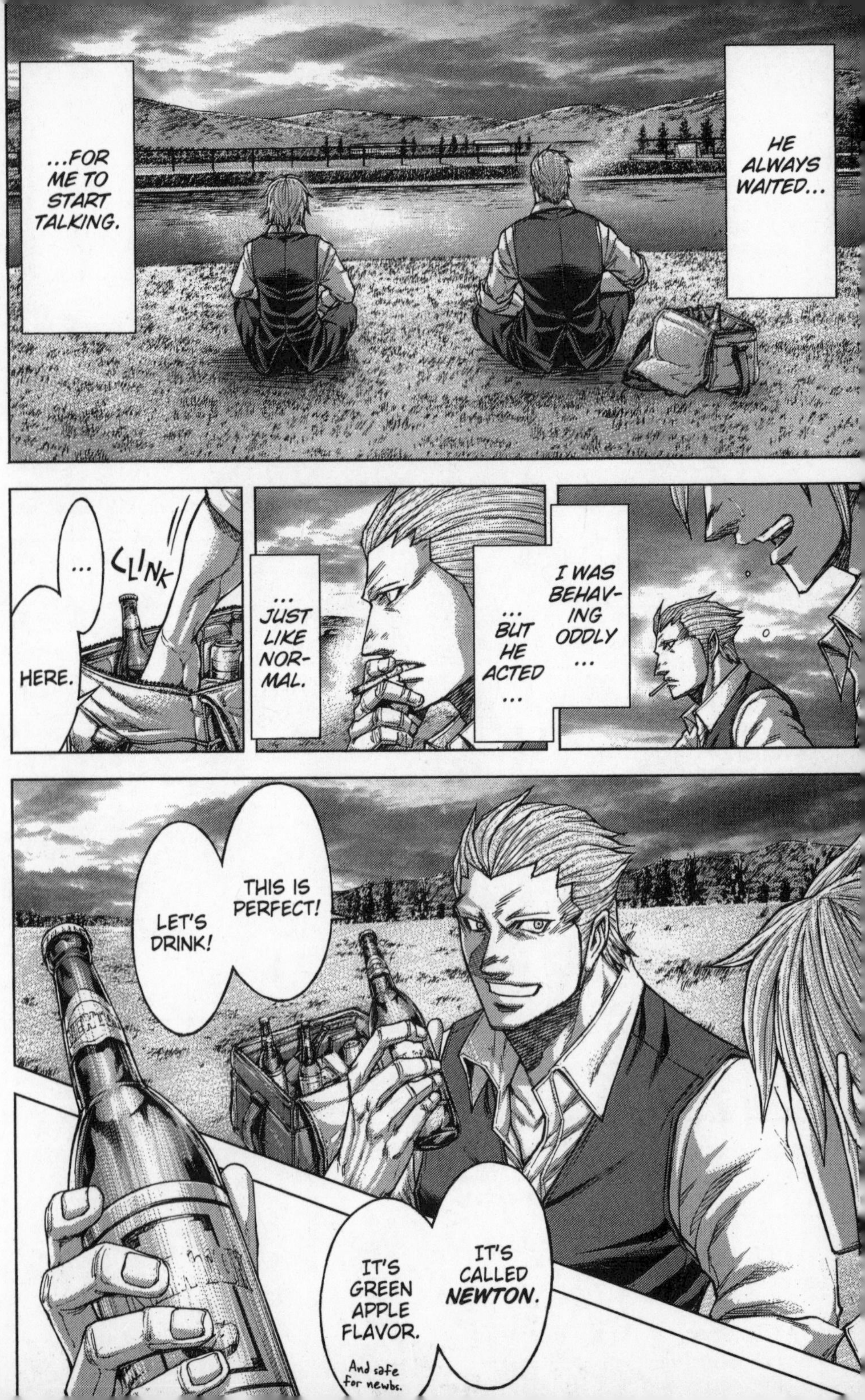
HE ALWAYS WAITED...
...FOR ME TO START TALKING.
I WAS BEHAV-ING ODDLY ...
... BUT HE ACTED ...
... JUST LIKE NOR-MAL.
...
CLINK
HERE.
THIS IS PERFECT!
LET'S DRINK!
IT'S CALLED **NEWTON**.
IT'S GREEN APPLE FLAVOR.
And safe for newbs.

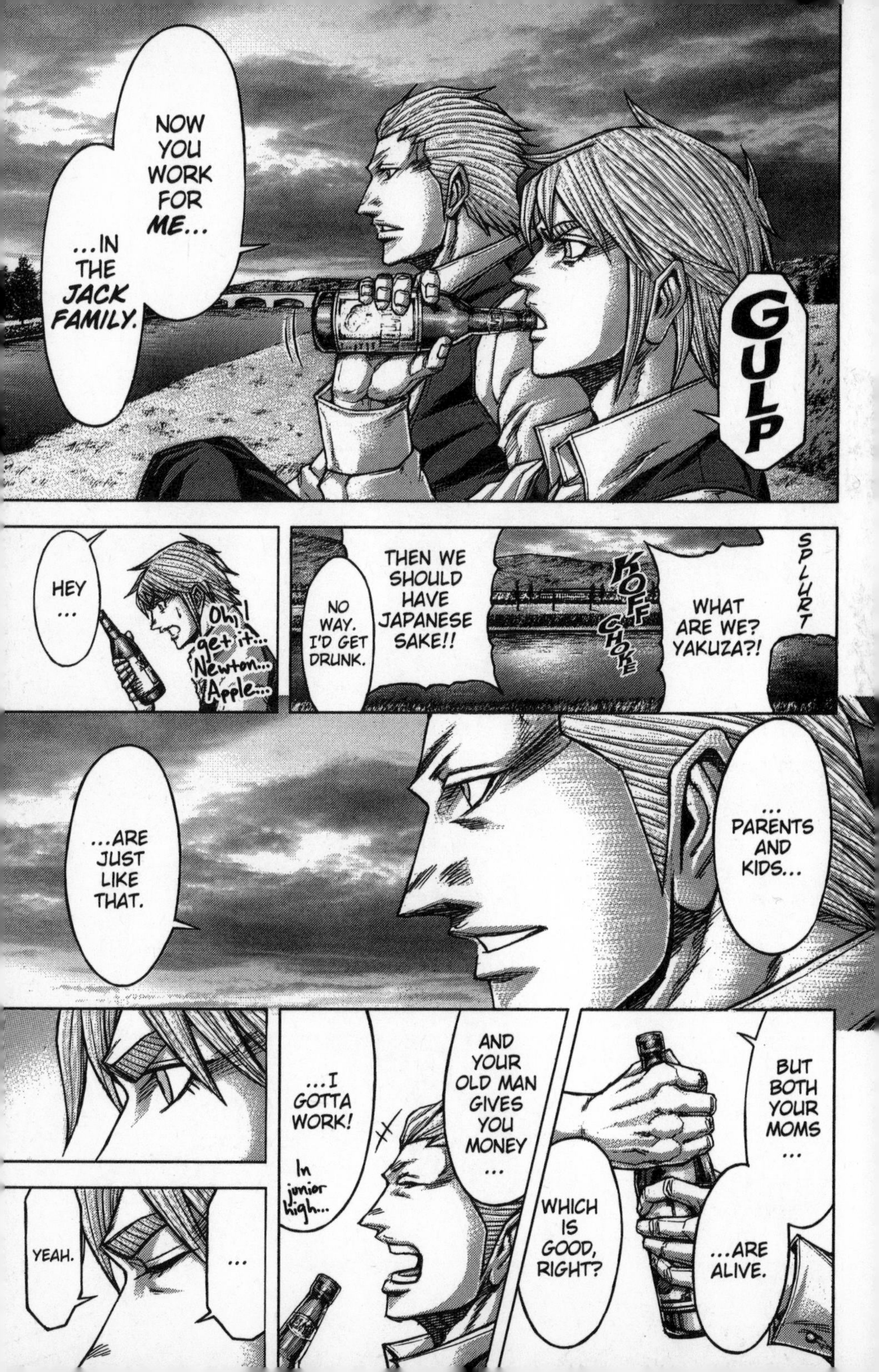
NOW YOU WORK FOR ME...
...IN THE JACK FAMILY.
GULP
SPLURT
WHAT ARE WE? YAKUZA?!
KOFF CHOKE
THEN WE SHOULD HAVE JAPANESE SAKE!!
NO WAY. I'D GET DRUNK.
HEY ...
Oh, I get it... Newton... Apple...
...PARENTS AND KIDS...
...ARE JUST LIKE THAT.
BUT BOTH YOUR MOMS ...
...ARE ALIVE.
AND YOUR OLD MAN GIVES YOU MONEY ...
WHICH IS GOOD, RIGHT?
...I GOTTA WORK!
In junior high...
...
YEAH.

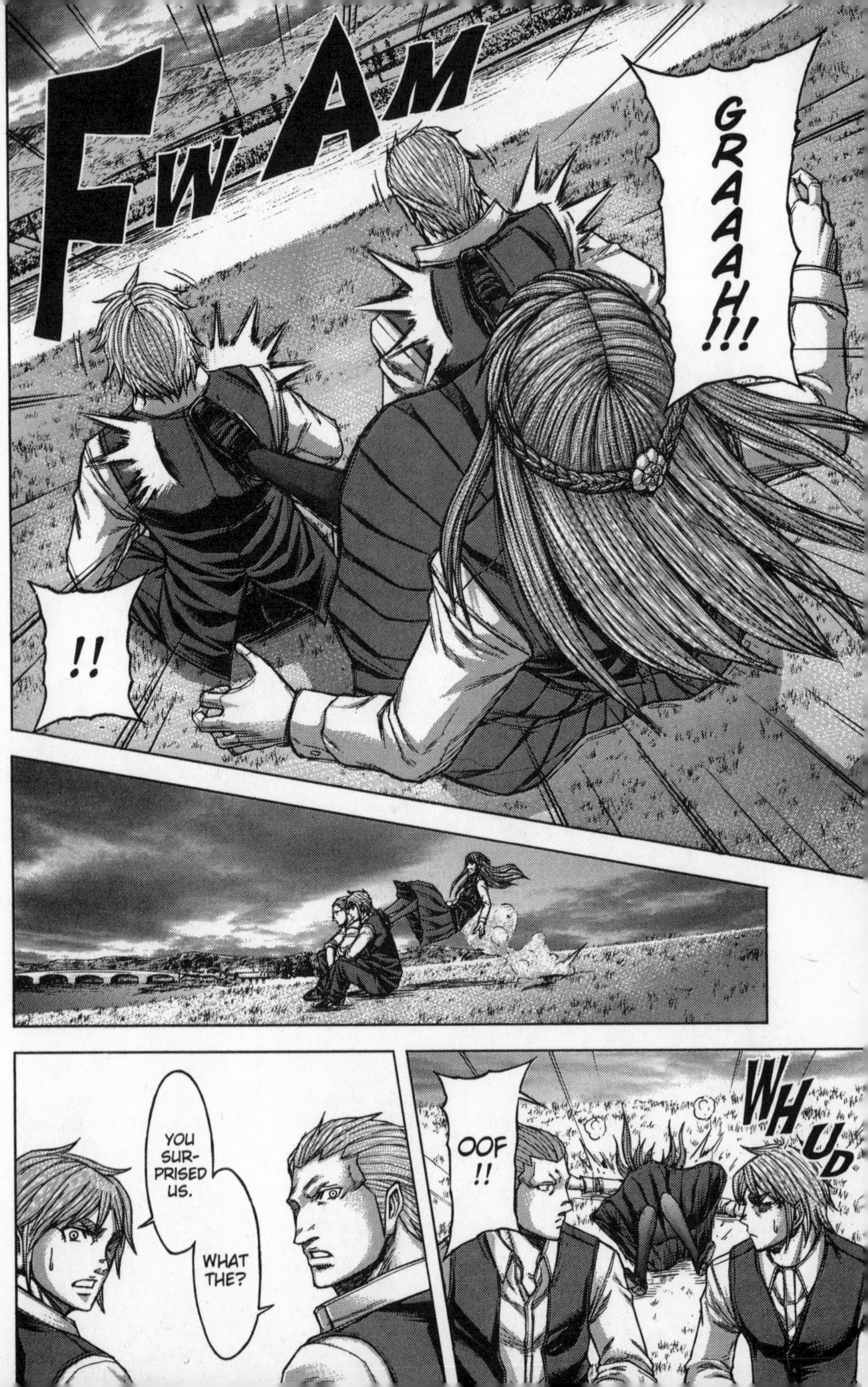
GRAAAAH!!!
FWAM
!!
WHUD
OOF!!
YOU SURPRISED US.
WHAT THE?

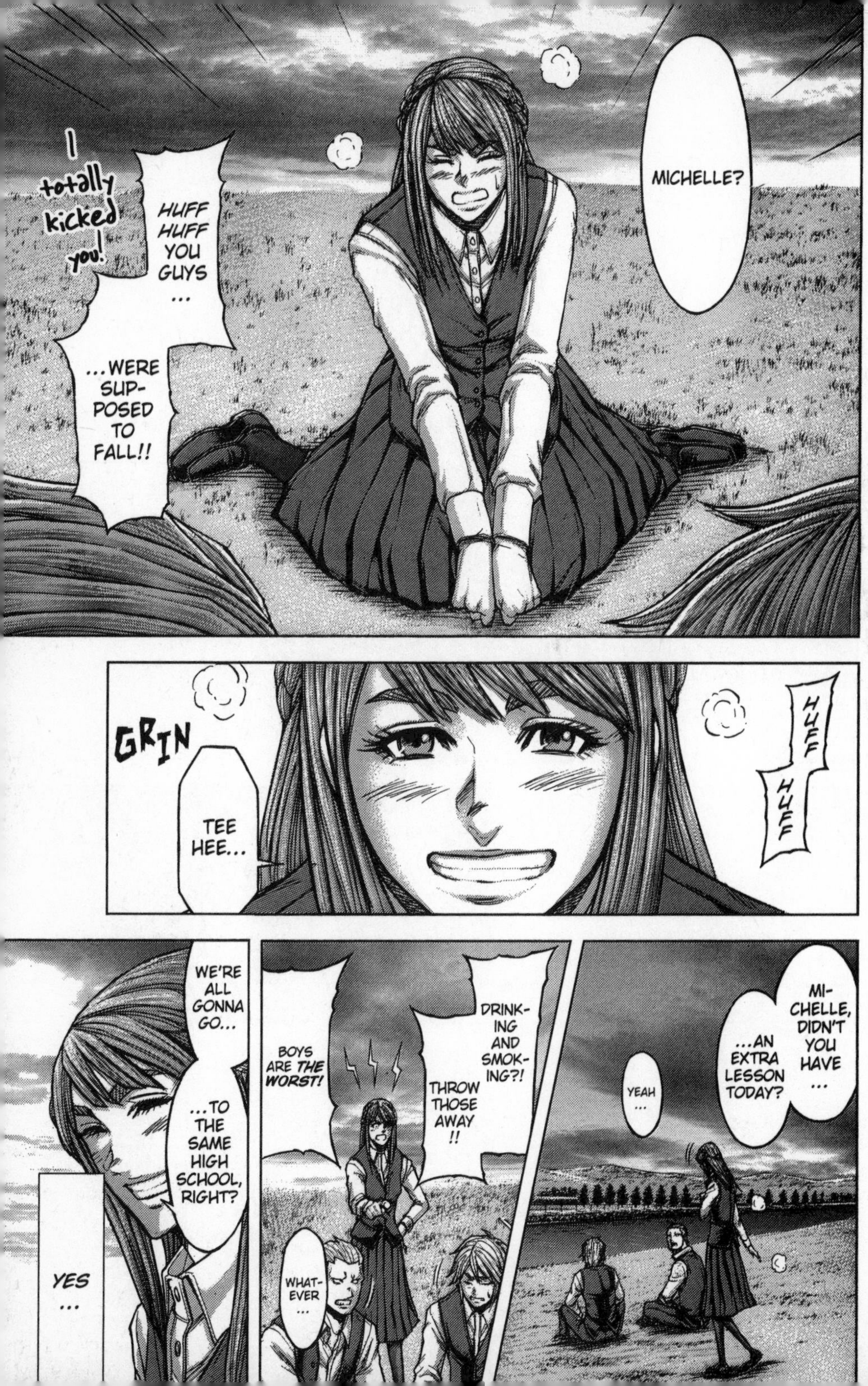
MICHELLE?
HUFF HUFF YOU GUYS ...
...WERE SUPPOSED TO FALL!!
I totally kicked you!
HUFF HUFF
GRIN
TEE HEE...
MICHELLE, DIDN'T YOU HAVE ...
...AN EXTRA LESSON TODAY?
YEAH ...
DRINKING AND SMOKING?!
THROW THOSE AWAY!!
BOYS ARE THE WORST!
WHATEVER ...
WE'RE ALL GONNA GO...
...TO THE SAME HIGH SCHOOL, RIGHT?
YES ...

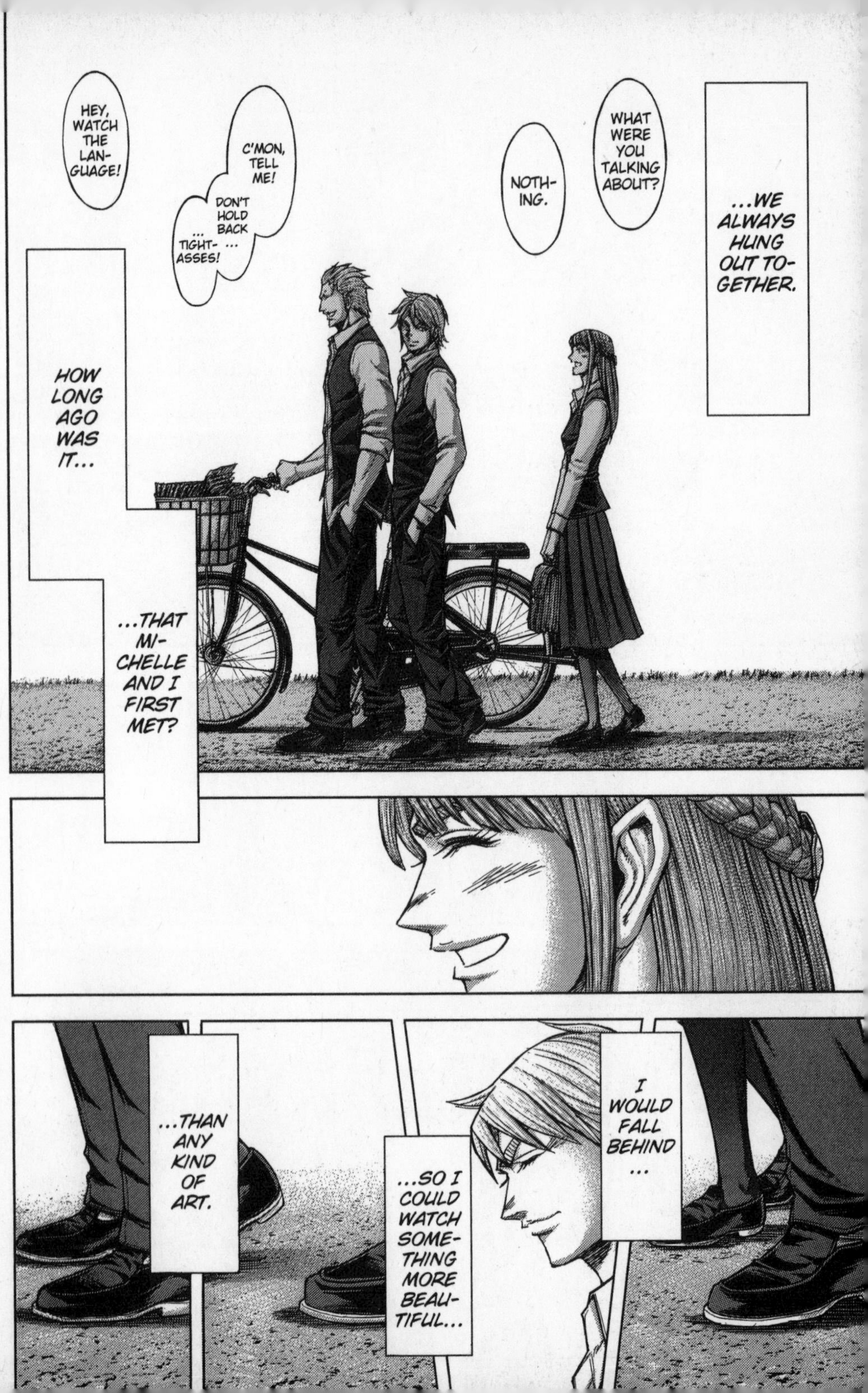
...WE ALWAYS HUNG OUT TOGETHER.
WHAT WERE YOU TALKING ABOUT?
NOTHING.
C'MON, TELL ME!
DON'T HOLD BACK... ...TIGHT-ASSES!
HEY, WATCH THE LANGUAGE!
HOW LONG AGO WAS IT...
...THAT MICHELLE AND I FIRST MET?
I WOULD FALL BEHIND...
...SO I COULD WATCH SOMETHING MORE BEAUTIFUL...
...THAN ANY KIND OF ART.

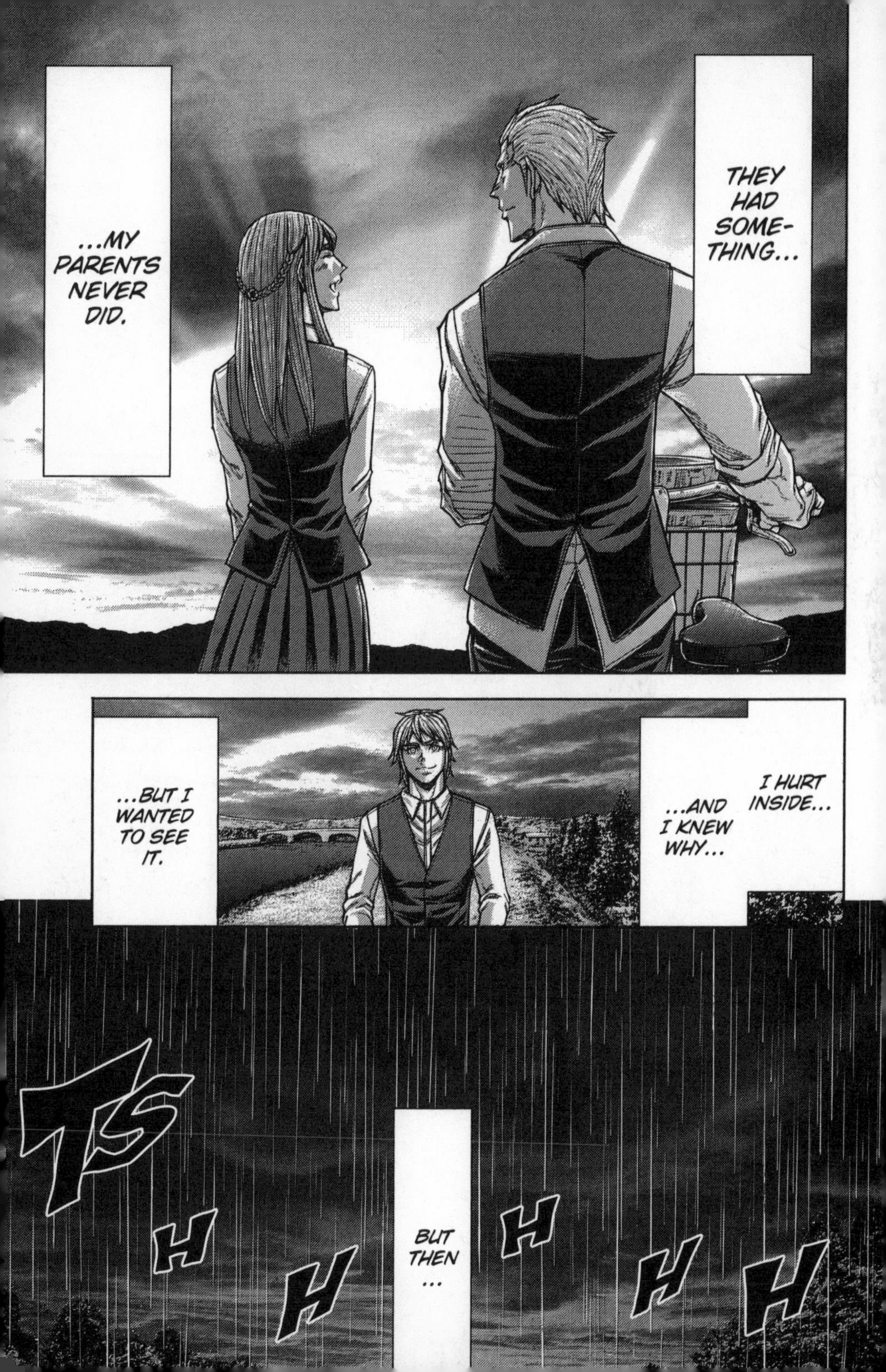
THEY HAD SOMETHING...
...MY PARENTS NEVER DID.
I HURT INSIDE...
...AND I KNEW WHY...
...BUT I WANTED TO SEE IT.
BUT THEN ...
TSHHHHHH

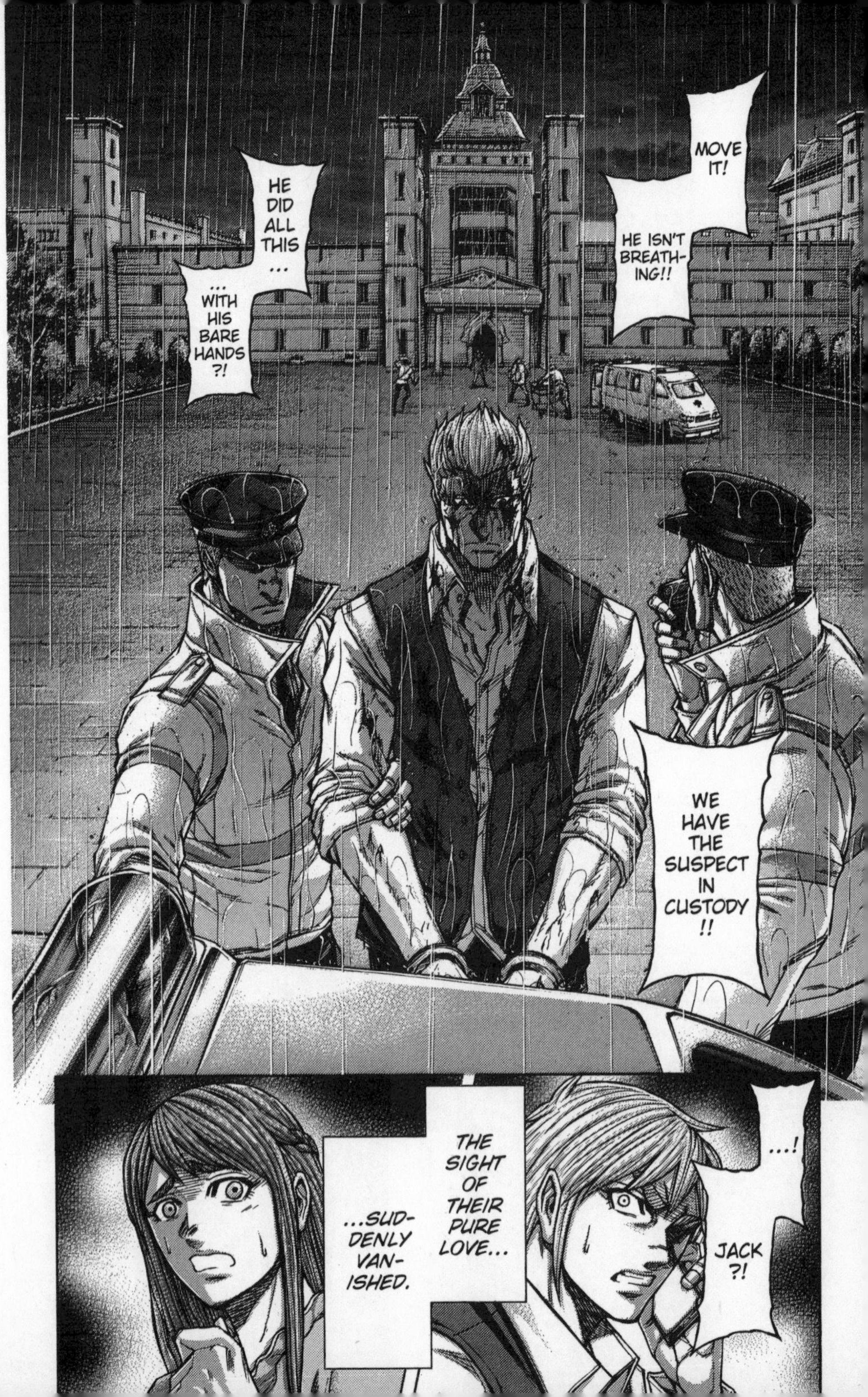
MOVE IT!
HE ISN'T BREATHING!!
HE DID ALL THIS...
...WITH HIS BARE HANDS?!
WE HAVE THE SUSPECT IN CUSTODY!!
...!
JACK?!
THE SIGHT OF THEIR PURE LOVE...
...SUDDENLY VANISHED.

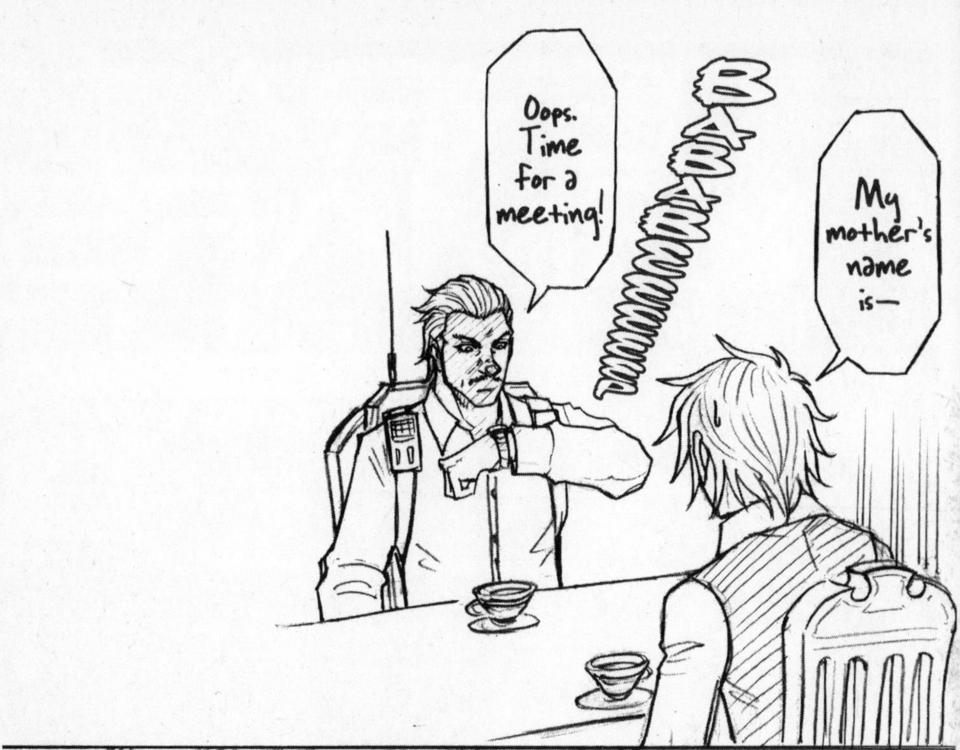
My mother's name is—
Oops. Time for a meeting!

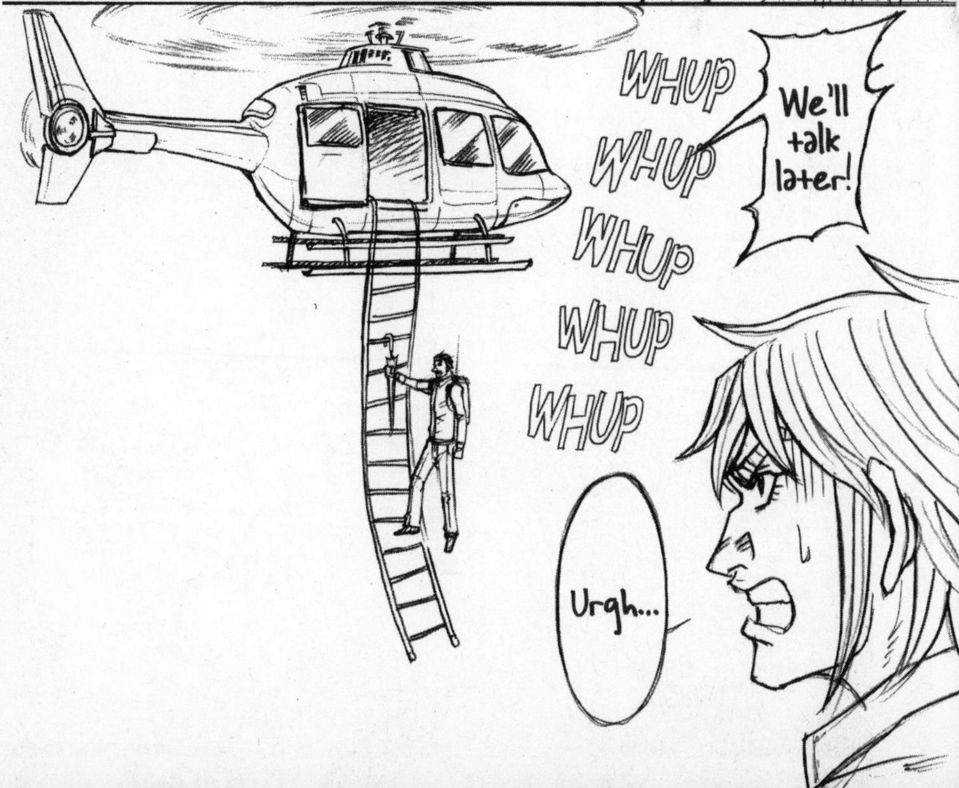
We'll talk later!
WHUP
WHUP
WHUP
WHUP
WHUP
Urgh...

TERRA FORMARS

Character

Asataro Kusama ♂

Japan 38 yrs. 183 cm 91 kg

Favorite Foods: Beef pho
Dislikes: Mysterious occupations such as answering
questions online as a professional love adviser.
Eye Color: Black Blood Type: AB
DOB: January 25 (Aquarius)
Skills: Seven to eight languages, including African languages

The son of Akari's master and the assistant instructor of the Hizamaru Shingan School. However, he remained somewhat uninvolved with the dojo and thus only taught Akari for a short time. In his college days, he began wandering around the world and eventually put his knack for languages to use in jobs overseas.

He joined Ichi Security a few years ago and only recently learned the secrets of the trade to become fully proficient.

Shigure Kusama ♂

Japan 66 yrs. 172 cm 57 kg

Favorite Foods: Salt, sake, mochi
Dislikes: Bar restrooms with lots of
political posters.
Eye Color: Black Blood Type: B
DOB: July 11 (Cancer)
Skills: In addition to Shingan School, he knows judo, ninja arts, and more. He's also a train nerd.

Director of the orphanage where Akari and Yuriko grew up and the head of the Hizamaru Shingan School.

When he was young, he was the worst hooligan in town and people called him Hiroshima Space Junk. Later, he went to Tokyo to learn judo. He experienced much hardship, but he eventually became the leader of an orphanage and dojo in Kanagawa.

The Shingan School recruits students from a few locations in the capital region but is having trouble finding a successor due to a lack of popularity. Loves riding trains.

CHAPTER 155: AN ORDINARY ABNORMALITY

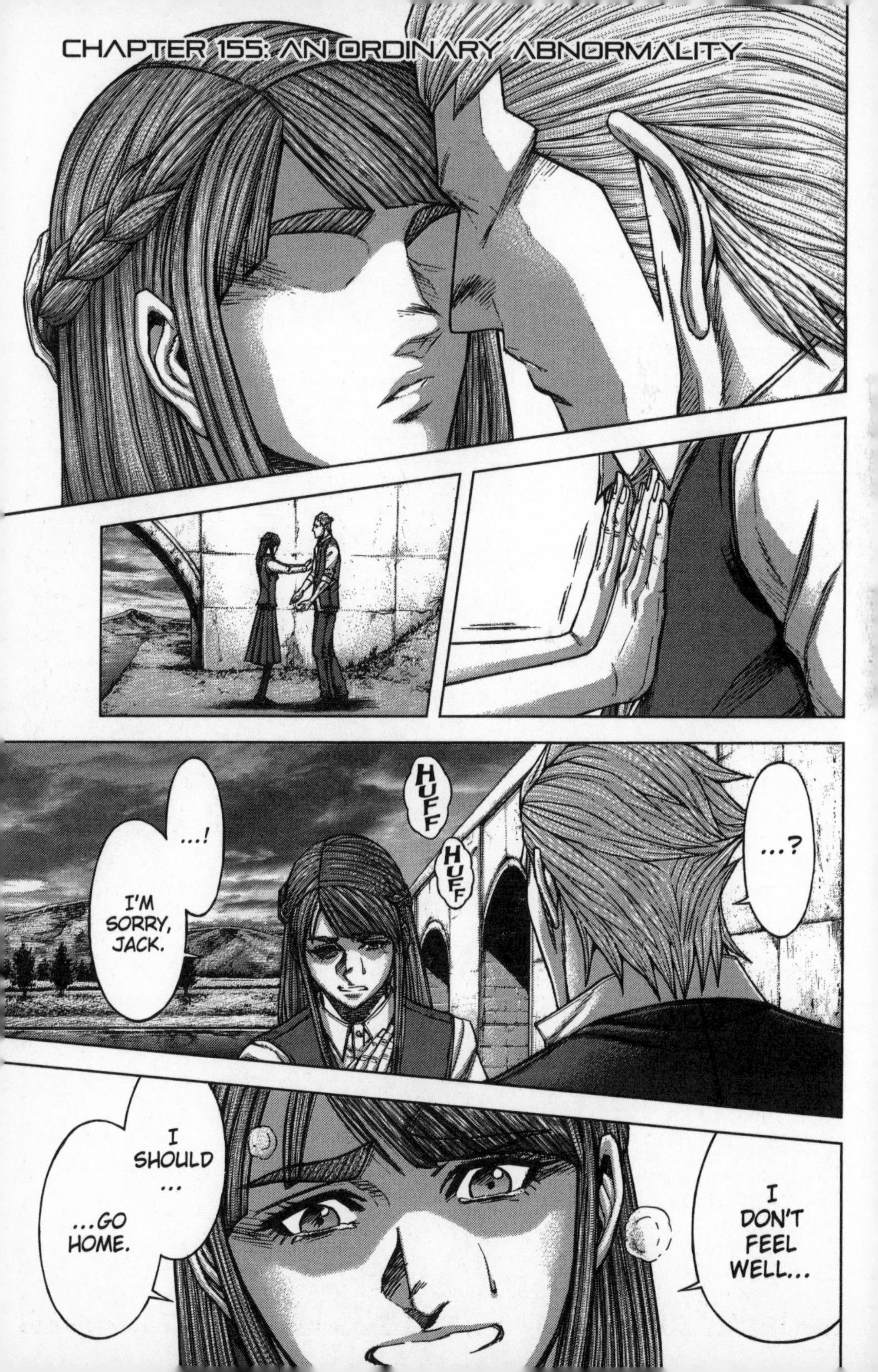
...?
HUFF
HUFF
...!
I'M SORRY, JACK.
I DON'T FEEL WELL...
I SHOULD ...
...GO HOME.

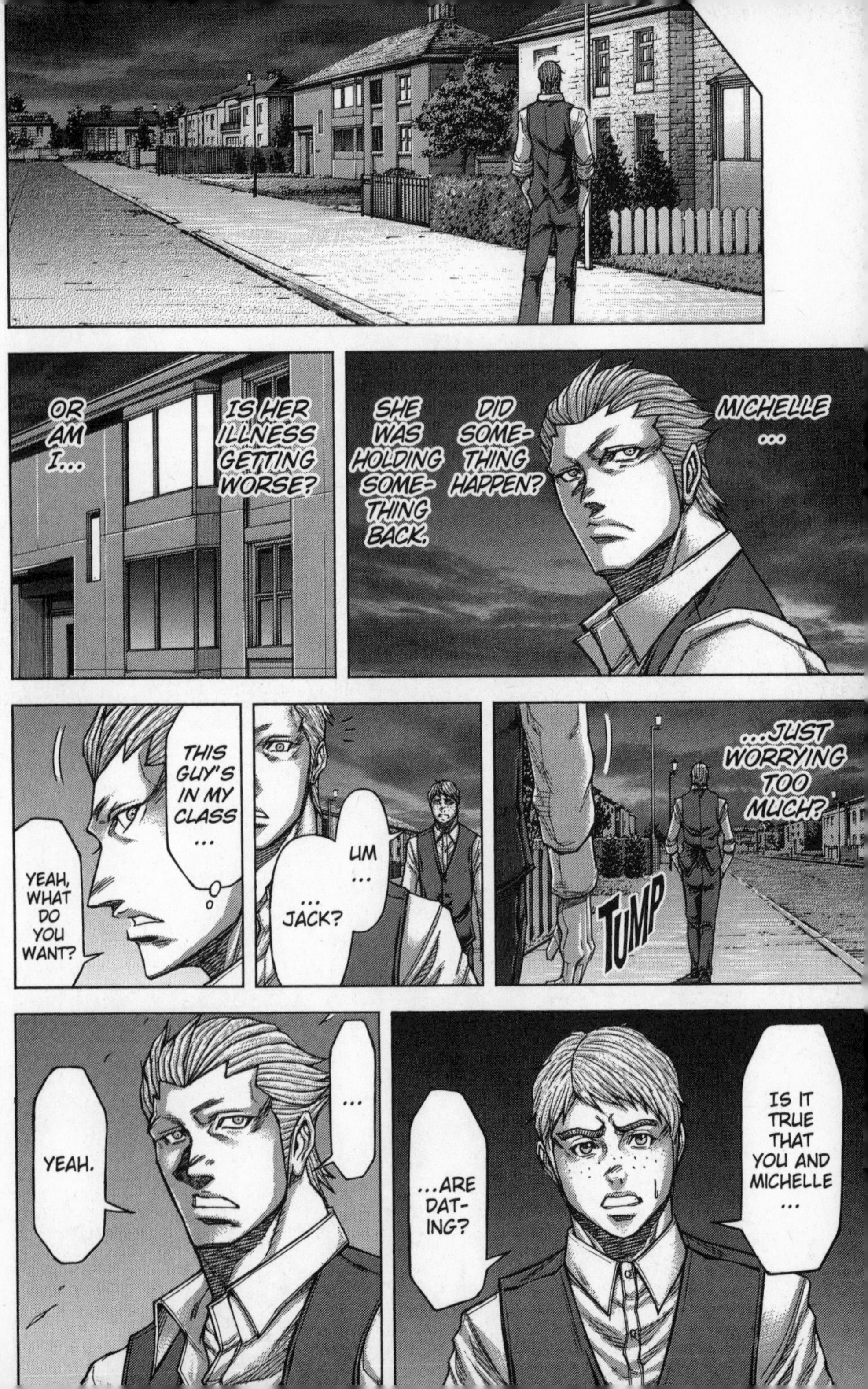
MICHELLE ...
DID SOMETHING HAPPEN?
SHE WAS HOLDING SOMETHING BACK.
IS HER ILLNESS GETTING WORSE?
OR AM I...
...JUST WORRYING TOO MUCH?
TUMP
UM ...
... JACK?
THIS GUY'S IN MY CLASS ...
YEAH, WHAT DO YOU WANT?
IS IT TRUE THAT YOU AND MICHELLE ...
...ARE DATING?
...
YEAH.

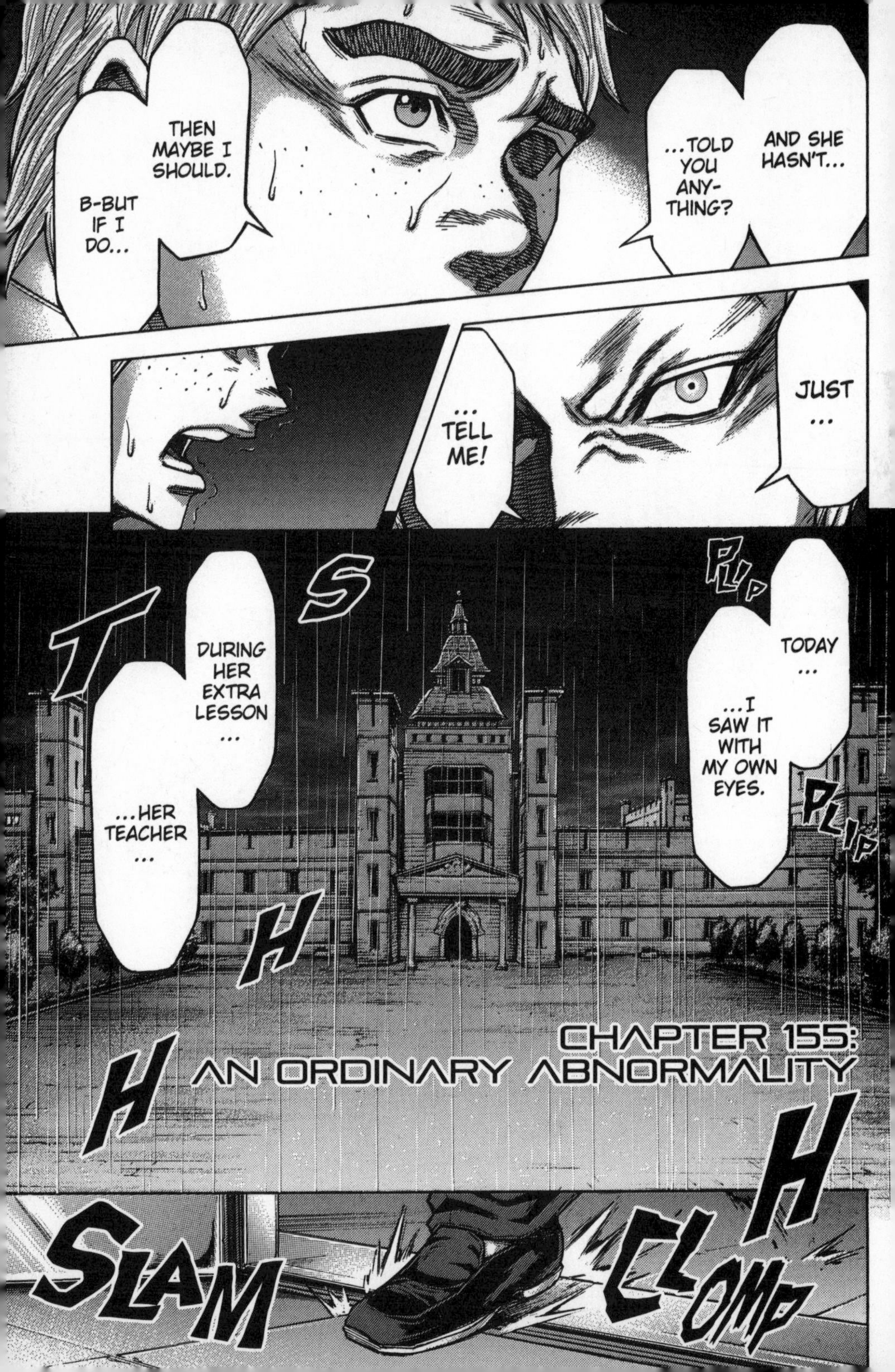
AND SHE HASN'T...
...TOLD YOU ANYTHING?
THEN MAYBE I SHOULD.
B-BUT IF I DO...
JUST ...
... TELL ME!
PLIP
TODAY ...
...I SAW IT WITH MY OWN EYES.
PLIP
S
T
DURING HER EXTRA LESSON ...
...HER TEACHER ...
H
H
CHAPTER 155:
AN ORDINARY ABNORMALITY
H
CLOMP
SLAM

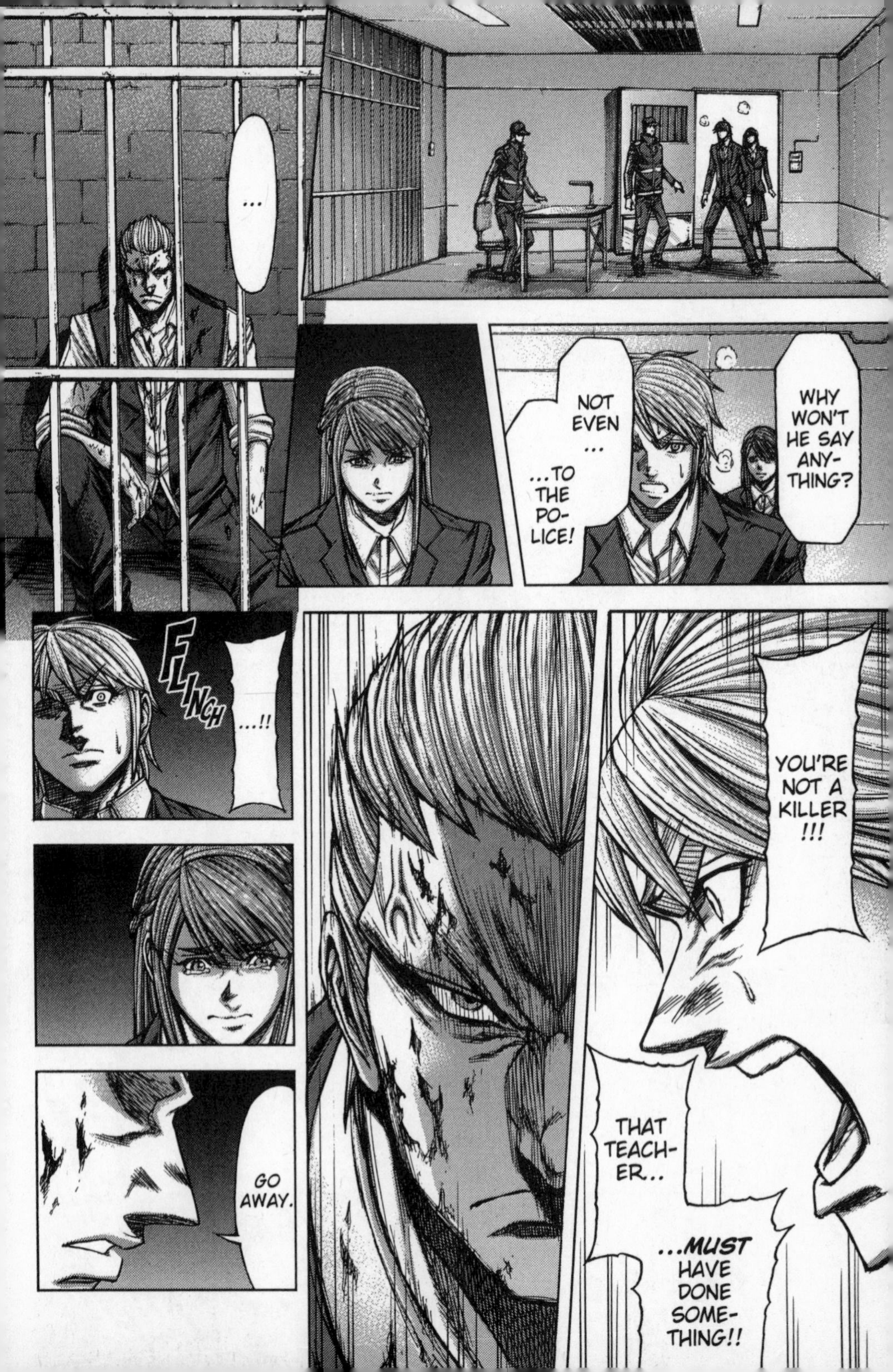
WHY WON'T HE SAY ANY-THING?
NOT EVEN ...
...TO THE PO-LICE!
...
YOU'RE NOT A KILLER !!!
THAT TEACH-ER...
...MUST HAVE DONE SOME-THING!!
FLINCH
...!!
GO AWAY.

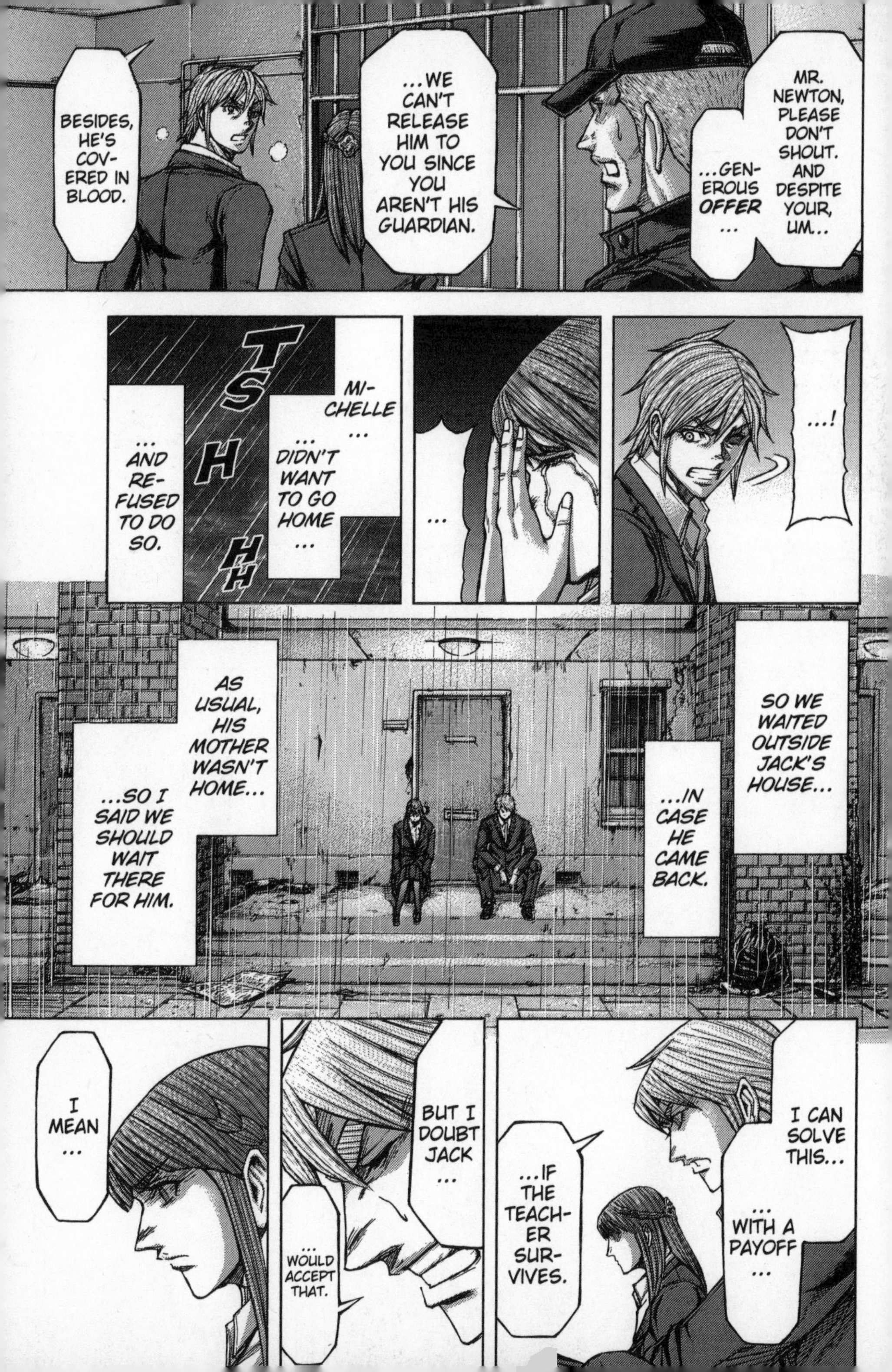
MR. NEWTON, PLEASE DON'T SHOUT. AND DESPITE YOUR, UM...
...GENEROUS OFFER...
...WE CAN'T RELEASE HIM TO YOU SINCE YOU AREN'T HIS GUARDIAN.
BESIDES, HE'S COVERED IN BLOOD.
...!
...
MICHELLE... DIDN'T WANT TO GO HOME...
TSHHH
...AND REFUSED TO DO SO.
SO WE WAITED OUTSIDE JACK'S HOUSE...
...IN CASE HE CAME BACK.
AS USUAL, HIS MOTHER WASN'T HOME...
...SO I SAID WE SHOULD WAIT THERE FOR HIM.
I CAN SOLVE THIS...
...WITH A PAYOFF...
...IF THE TEACHER SURVIVES.
BUT I DOUBT JACK...
...WOULD ACCEPT THAT.
I MEAN...

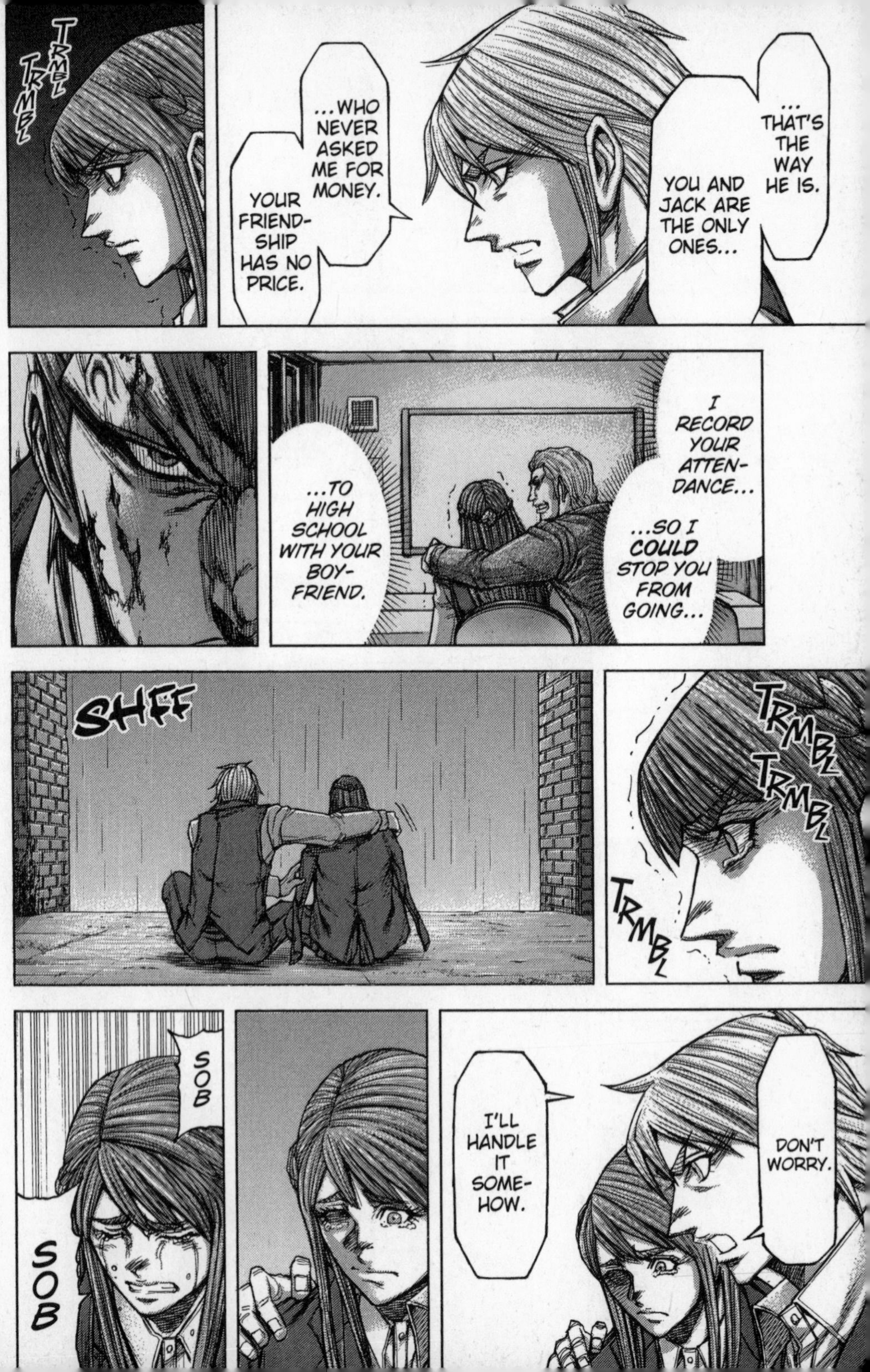
... THAT'S THE WAY HE IS.
YOU AND JACK ARE THE ONLY ONES...
...WHO NEVER ASKED ME FOR MONEY.
YOUR FRIEND-SHIP HAS NO PRICE.
TRMBL
TRMBL
I RECORD YOUR ATTEN-DANCE...
...SO I COULD STOP YOU FROM GOING...
...TO HIGH SCHOOL WITH YOUR BOY-FRIEND.
TRMBL
TRMBL
TRMBL
SHFF
DON'T WORRY.
I'LL HANDLE IT SOME-HOW.
SOB
SOB

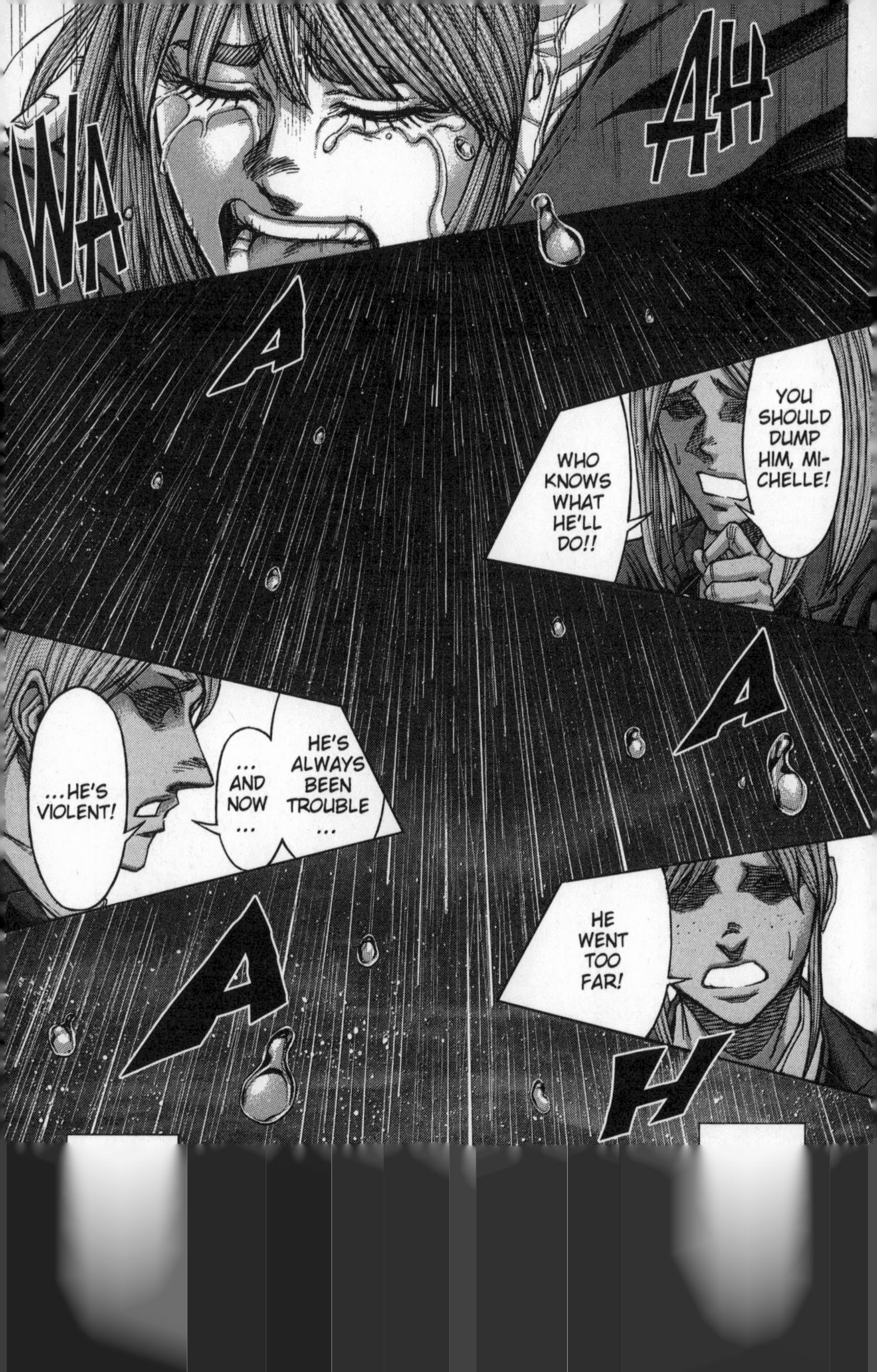
WA
AH
A
YOU SHOULD DUMP HIM, MI-CHELLE!
WHO KNOWS WHAT HE'LL DO!!
A
HE'S ALWAYS BEEN TROUBLE ...
... AND NOW ...
...HE'S VIOLENT!
HE WENT TOO FAR!
A
H

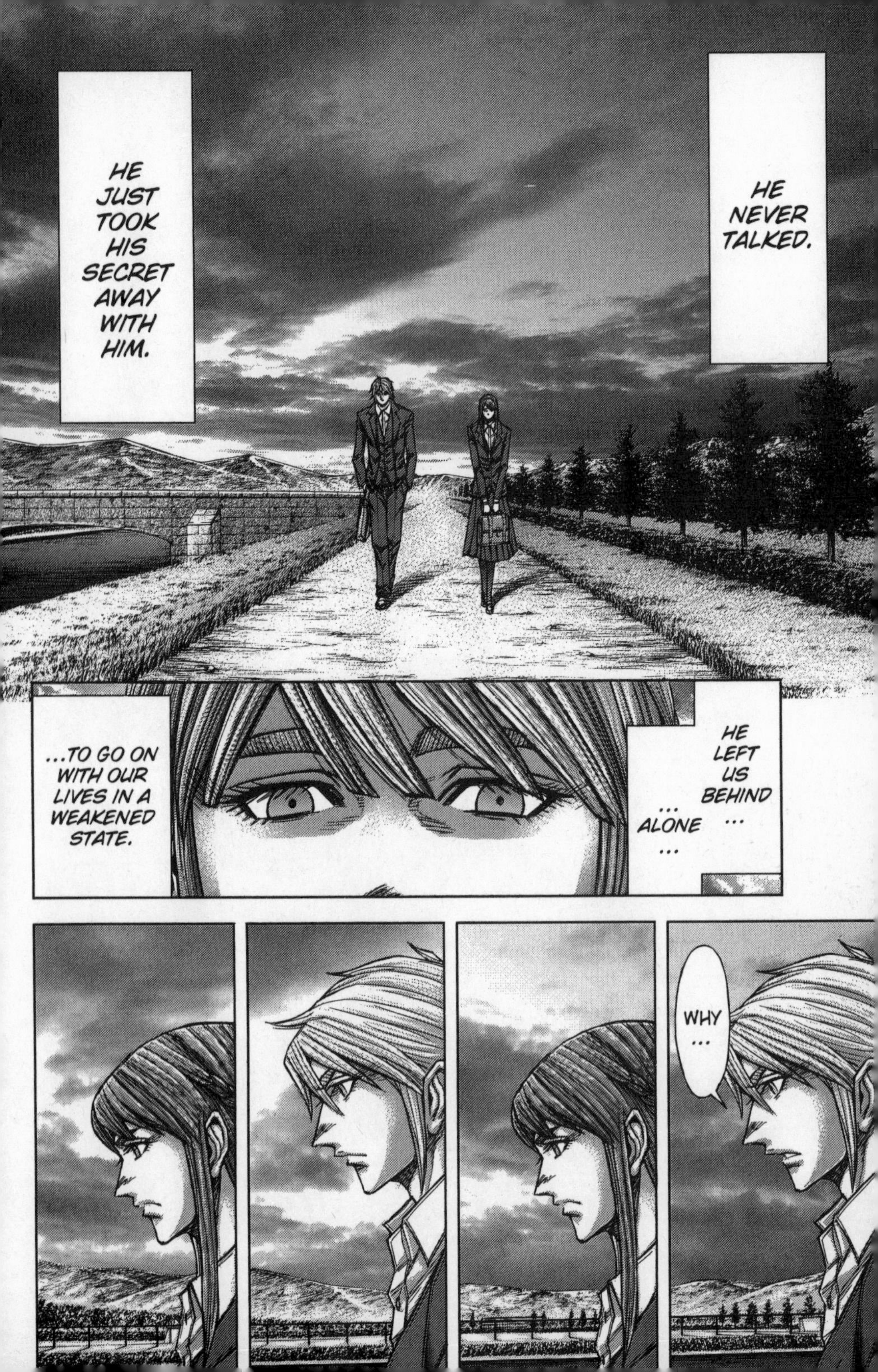
HE NEVER TALKED.
HE JUST TOOK HIS SECRET AWAY WITH HIM.
HE LEFT US BEHIND ... ... ALONE ...
...TO GO ON WITH OUR LIVES IN A WEAKENED STATE.
WHY ...

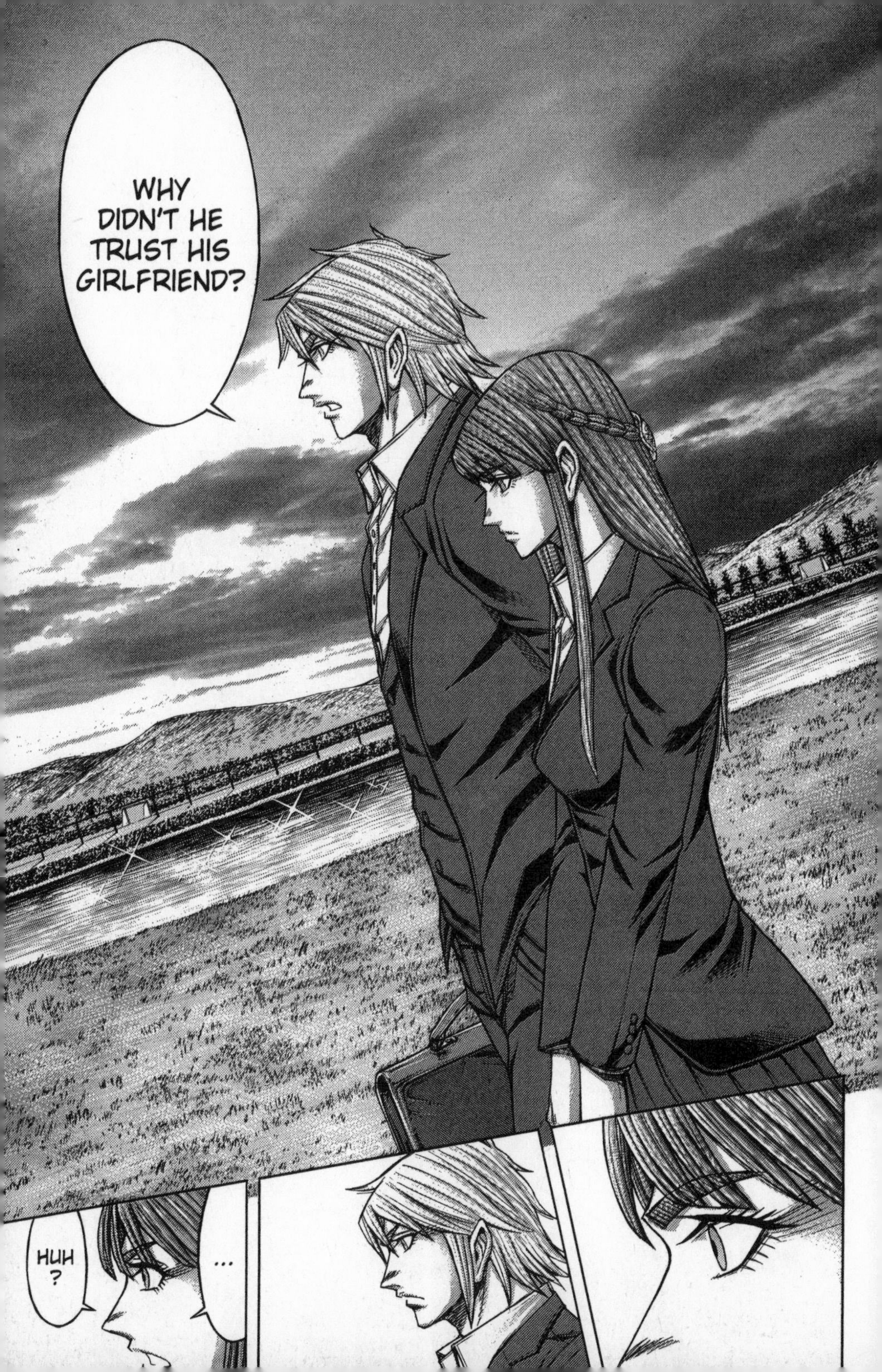
WHY DIDN'T HE TRUST HIS GIRLFRIEND?
...
HUH ?

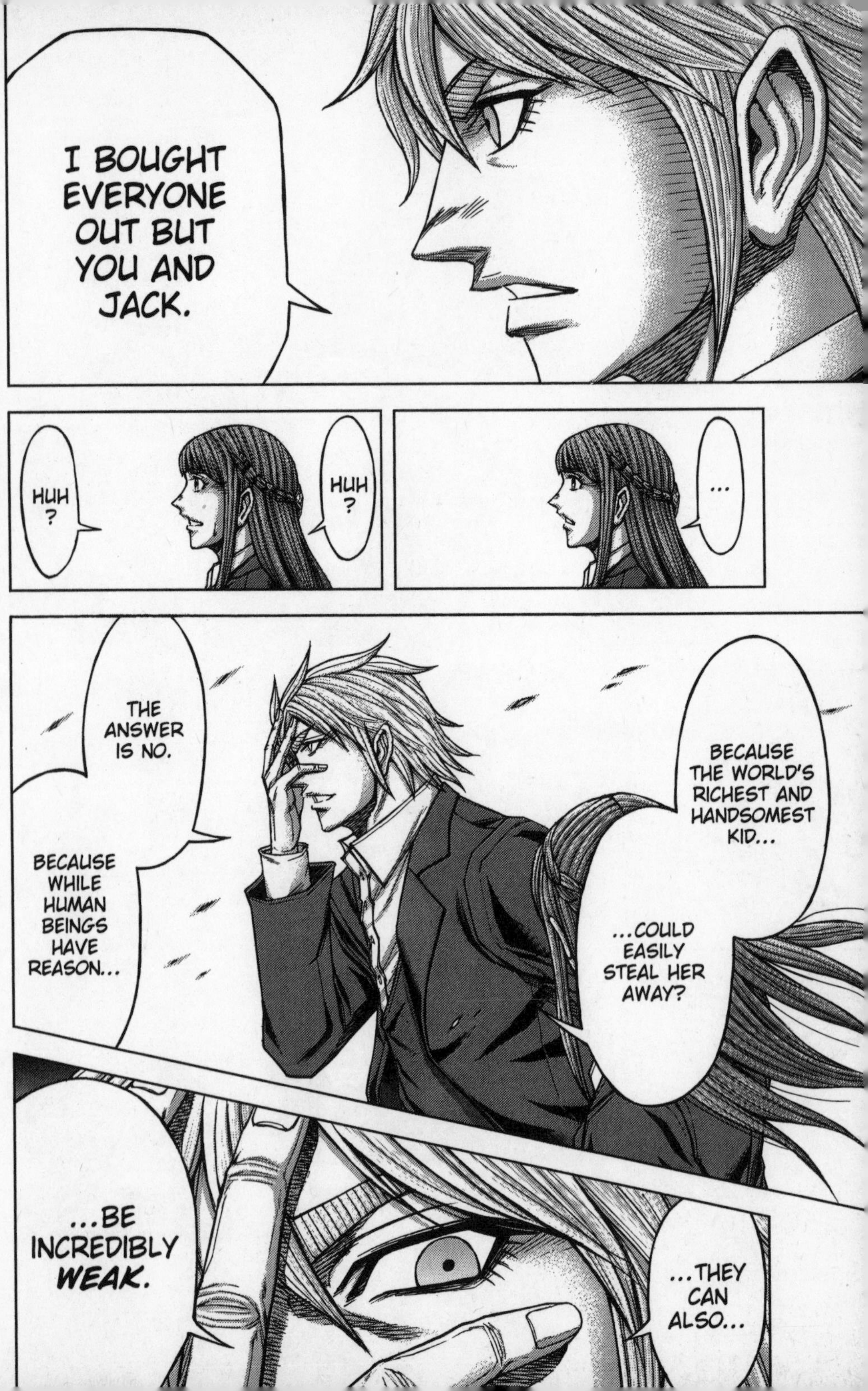
I BOUGHT EVERYONE OUT BUT YOU AND JACK.
...
HUH ?
HUH ?
BECAUSE THE WORLD'S RICHEST AND HANDSOMEST KID...
...COULD EASILY STEAL HER AWAY?
THE ANSWER IS NO.
BECAUSE WHILE HUMAN BEINGS HAVE REASON...
...THEY CAN ALSO...
...BE INCREDIBLY *WEAK*.

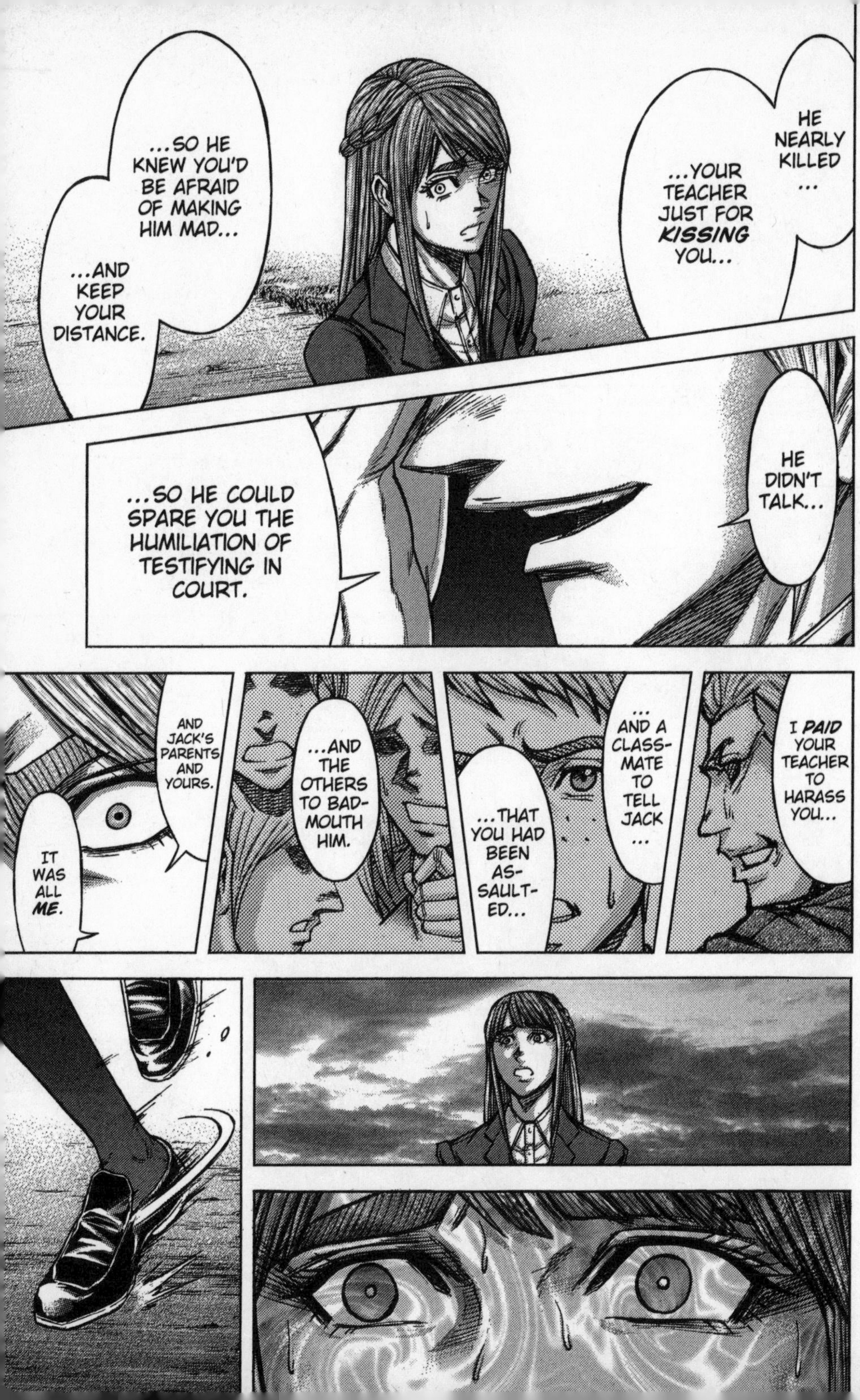
HE NEARLY KILLED ...
...YOUR TEACHER JUST FOR *KISSING* YOU...
...SO HE KNEW YOU'D BE AFRAID OF MAKING HIM MAD...
...AND KEEP YOUR DISTANCE.
HE DIDN'T TALK...
...SO HE COULD SPARE YOU THE HUMILIATION OF TESTIFYING IN COURT.
I *PAID* YOUR TEACHER TO HARASS YOU...
... AND A CLASS-MATE TO TELL JACK ...
...THAT YOU HAD BEEN AS-SAULT-ED...
...AND THE OTHERS TO BAD-MOUTH HIM.
AND JACK'S PARENTS AND YOURS.
IT WAS ALL *ME*.

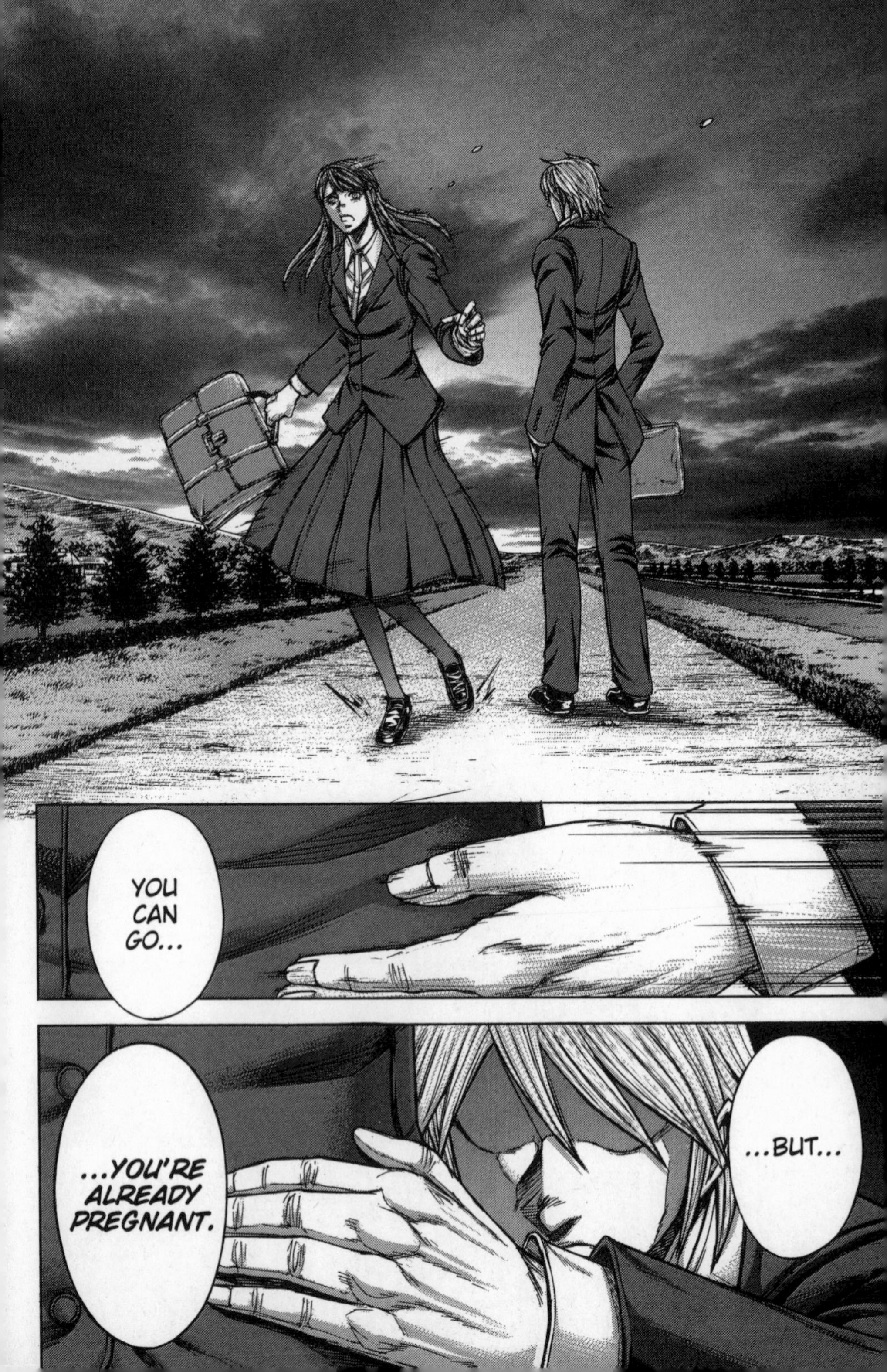
YOU CAN GO...
...BUT...
...YOU'RE ALREADY PREGNANT.

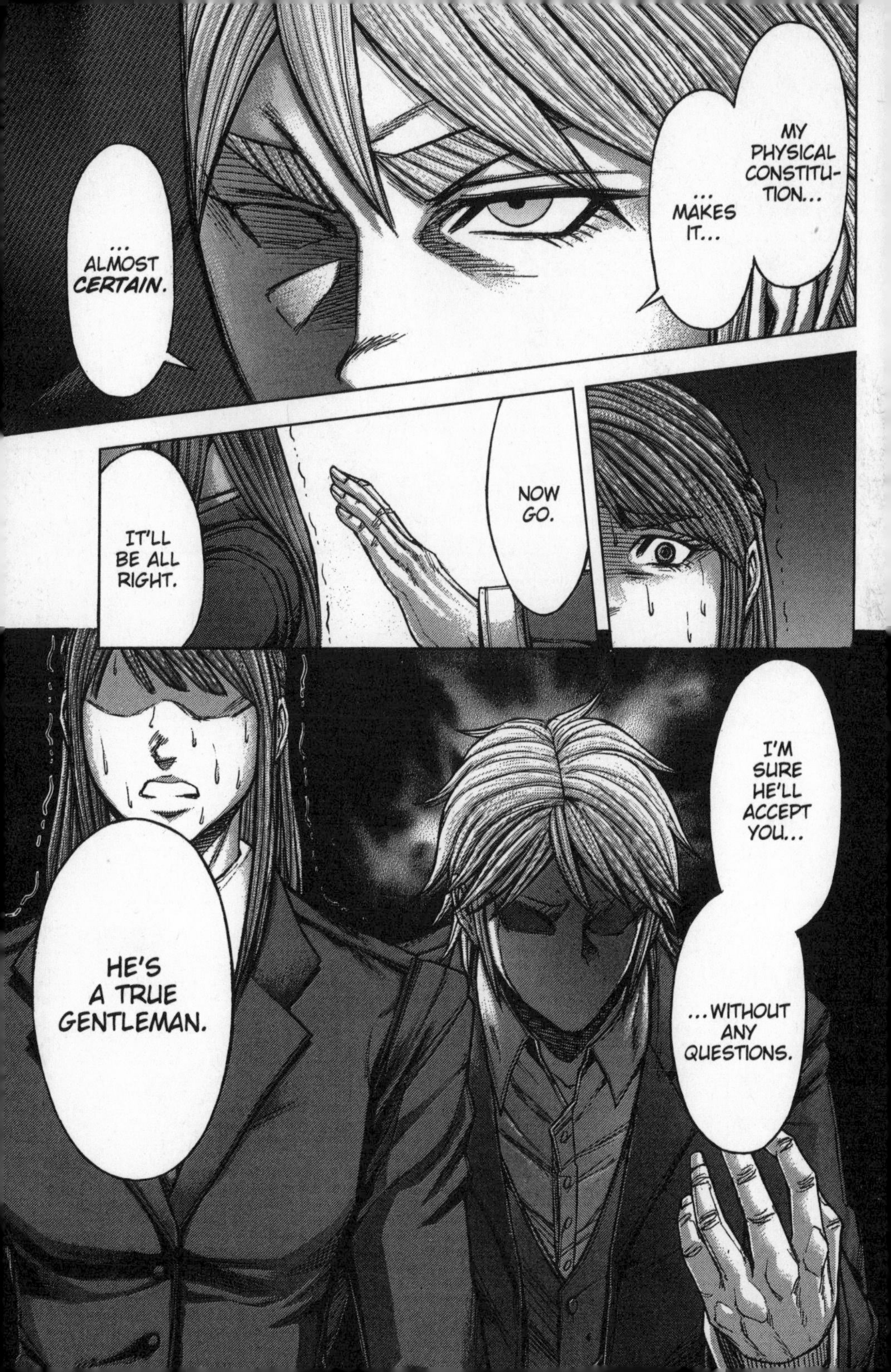
MY PHYSICAL CONSTITUTION... ...MAKES IT...
...ALMOST CERTAIN.
NOW GO.
IT'LL BE ALL RIGHT.
I'M SURE HE'LL ACCEPT YOU...
...WITHOUT ANY QUESTIONS.
HE'S A TRUE GENTLEMAN.

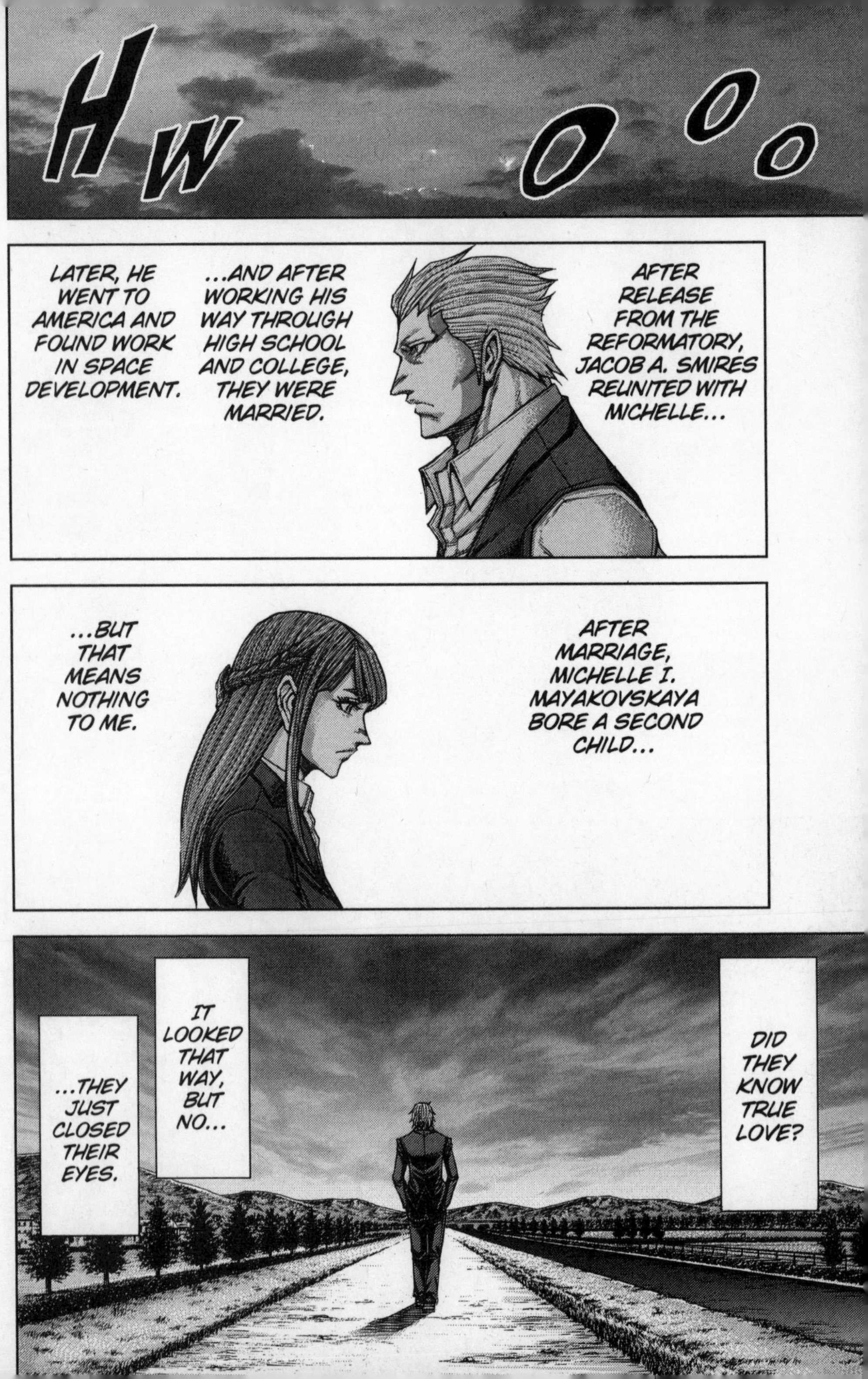
HWOOO
AFTER RELEASE FROM THE REFORMATORY, JACOB A. SMIRES REUNITED WITH MICHELLE...
...AND AFTER WORKING HIS WAY THROUGH HIGH SCHOOL AND COLLEGE, THEY WERE MARRIED.
LATER, HE WENT TO AMERICA AND FOUND WORK IN SPACE DEVELOPMENT.
AFTER MARRIAGE, MICHELLE I. MAYAKOVSKAYA BORE A SECOND CHILD...
...BUT THAT MEANS NOTHING TO ME.
DID THEY KNOW TRUE LOVE?
IT LOOKED THAT WAY, BUT NO...
...THEY JUST CLOSED THEIR EYES.

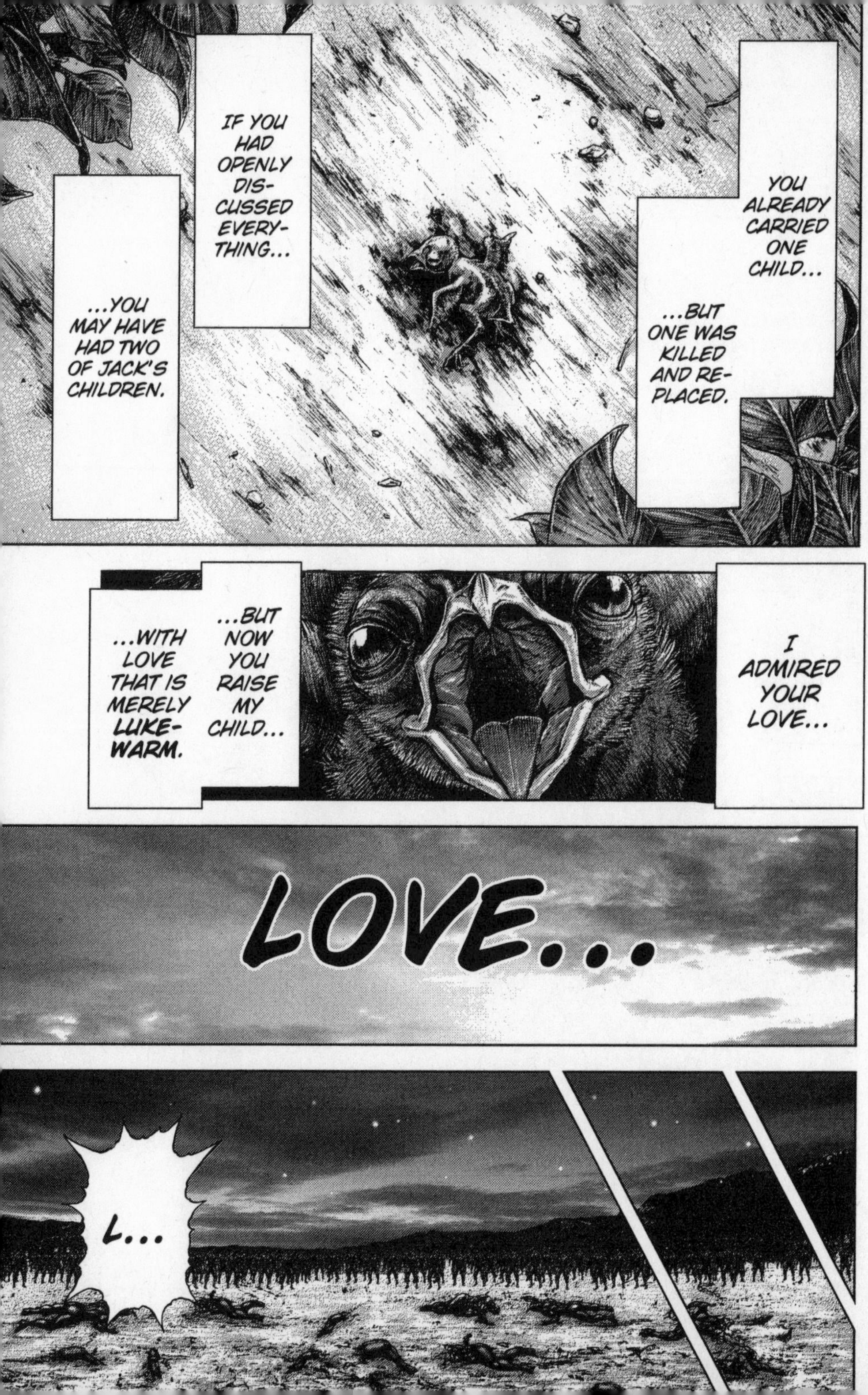
YOU ALREADY CARRIED ONE CHILD...
...BUT ONE WAS KILLED AND RE-PLACED.
IF YOU HAD OPENLY DIS-CUSSED EVERY-THING...
...YOU MAY HAVE HAD TWO OF JACK'S CHILDREN.
I ADMIRED YOUR LOVE...
...BUT NOW YOU RAISE MY CHILD...
...WITH LOVE THAT IS MERELY LUKE-WARM.
LOVE...
L...

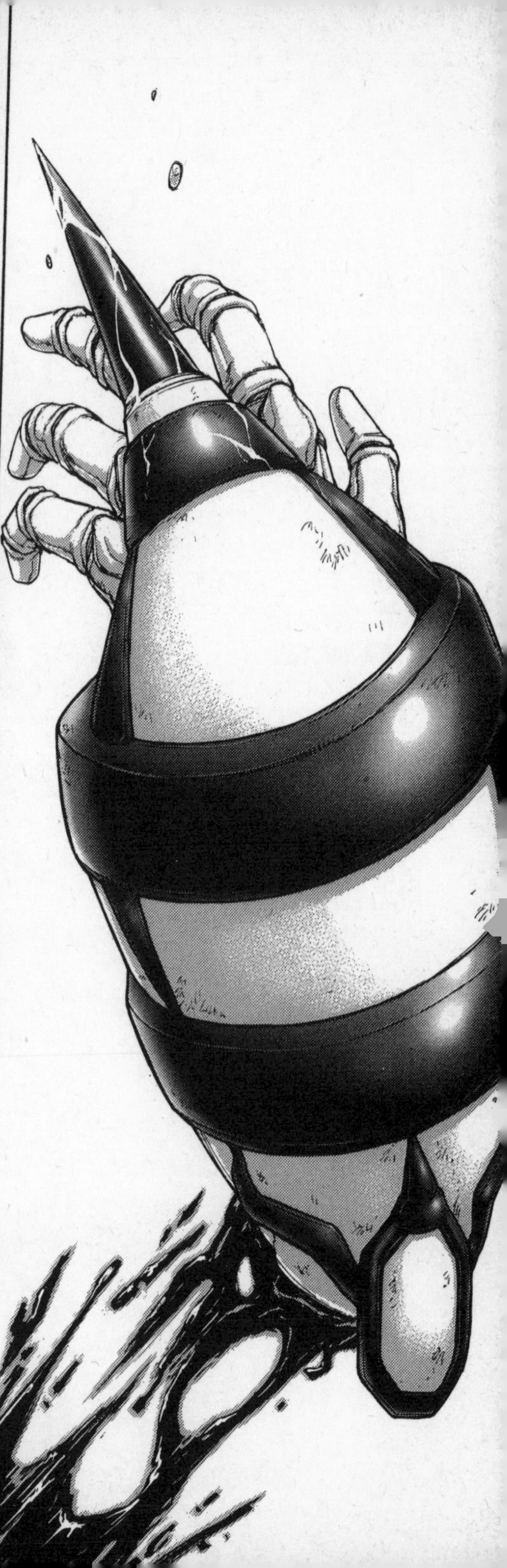

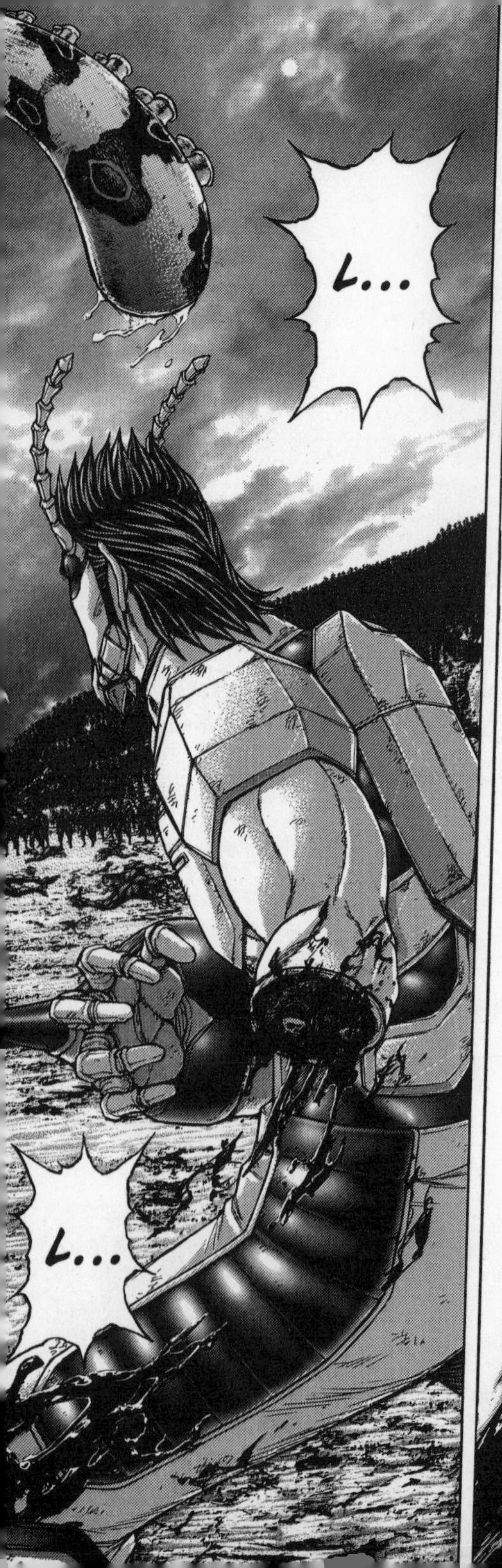
L...
L...

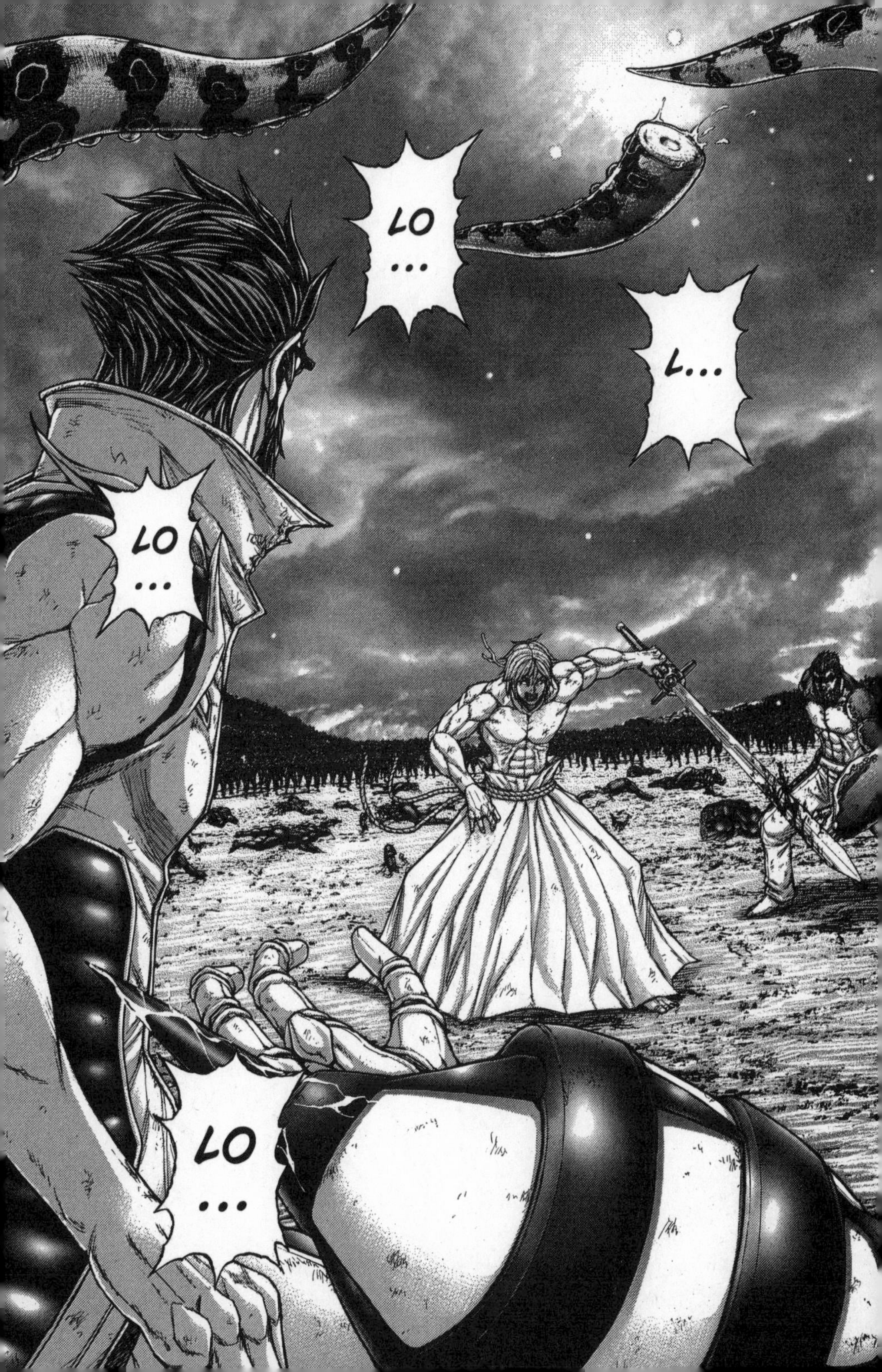
LO ...
L...
LO ...
LO ...

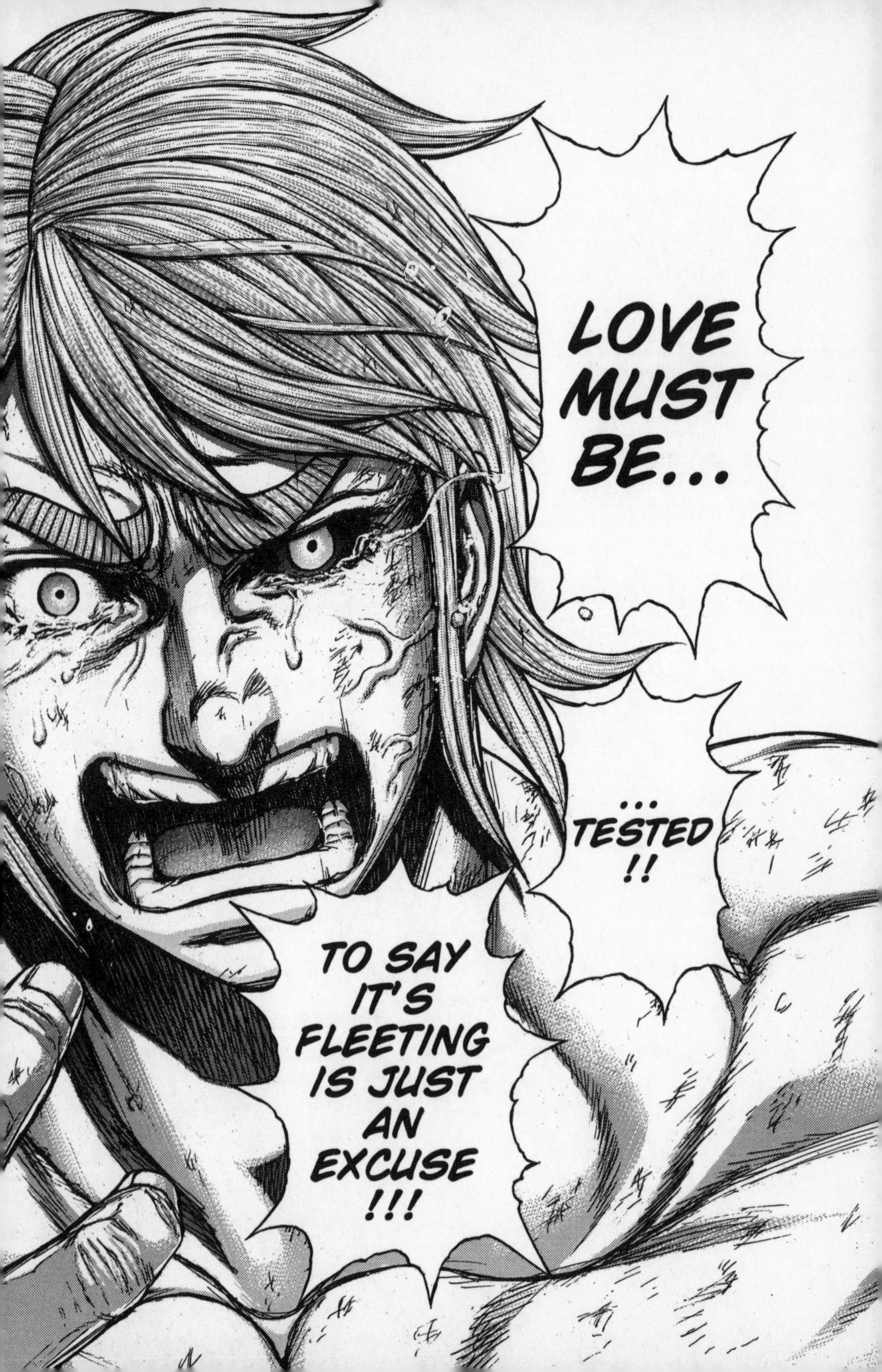
LOVE MUST BE...
... TESTED !!
TO SAY IT'S FLEETING IS JUST AN EXCUSE !!!

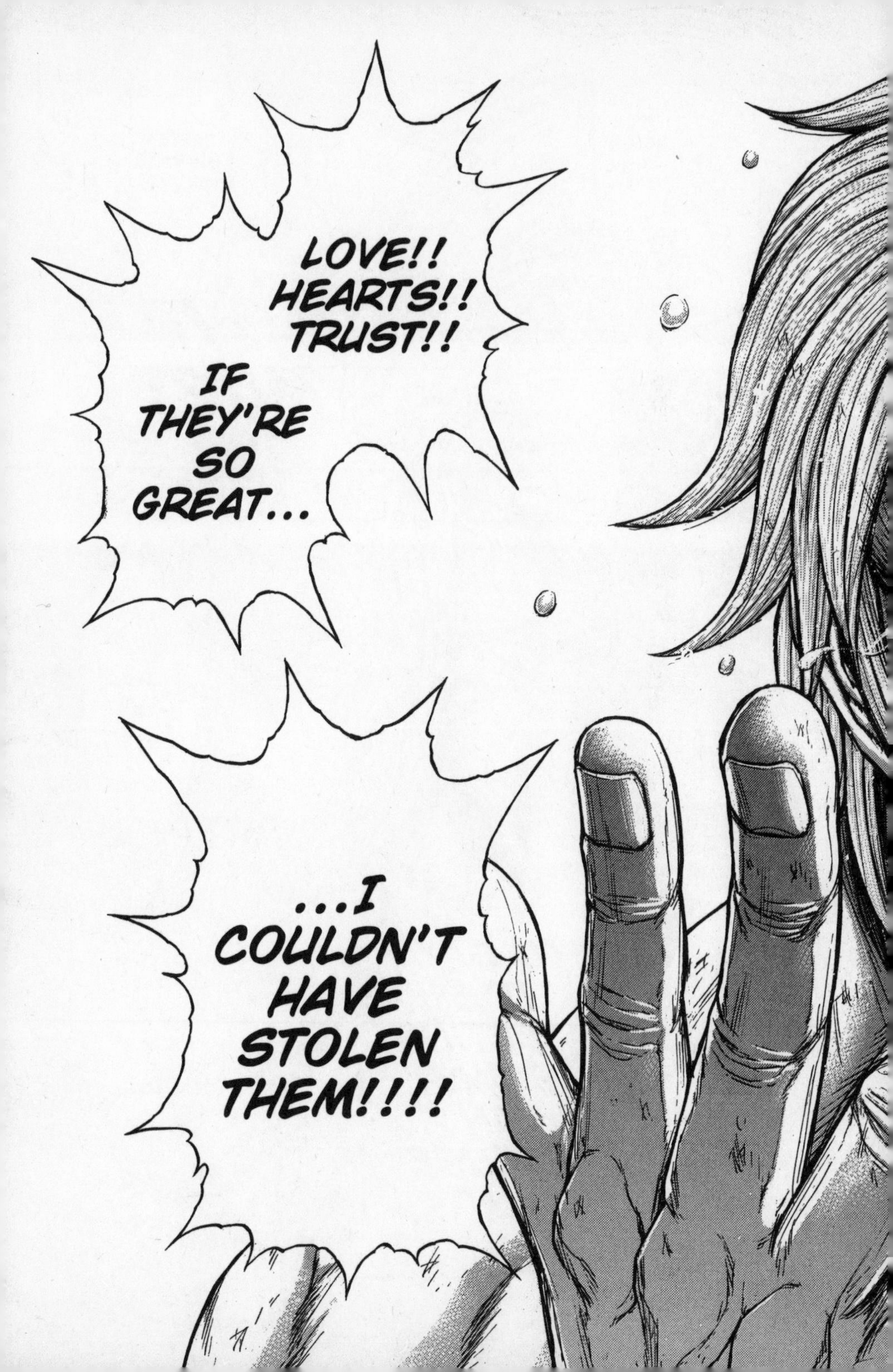
LOVE!! HEARTS!! TRUST!! IF THEY'RE SO GREAT...
...I COULDN'T HAVE STOLEN THEM!!!!

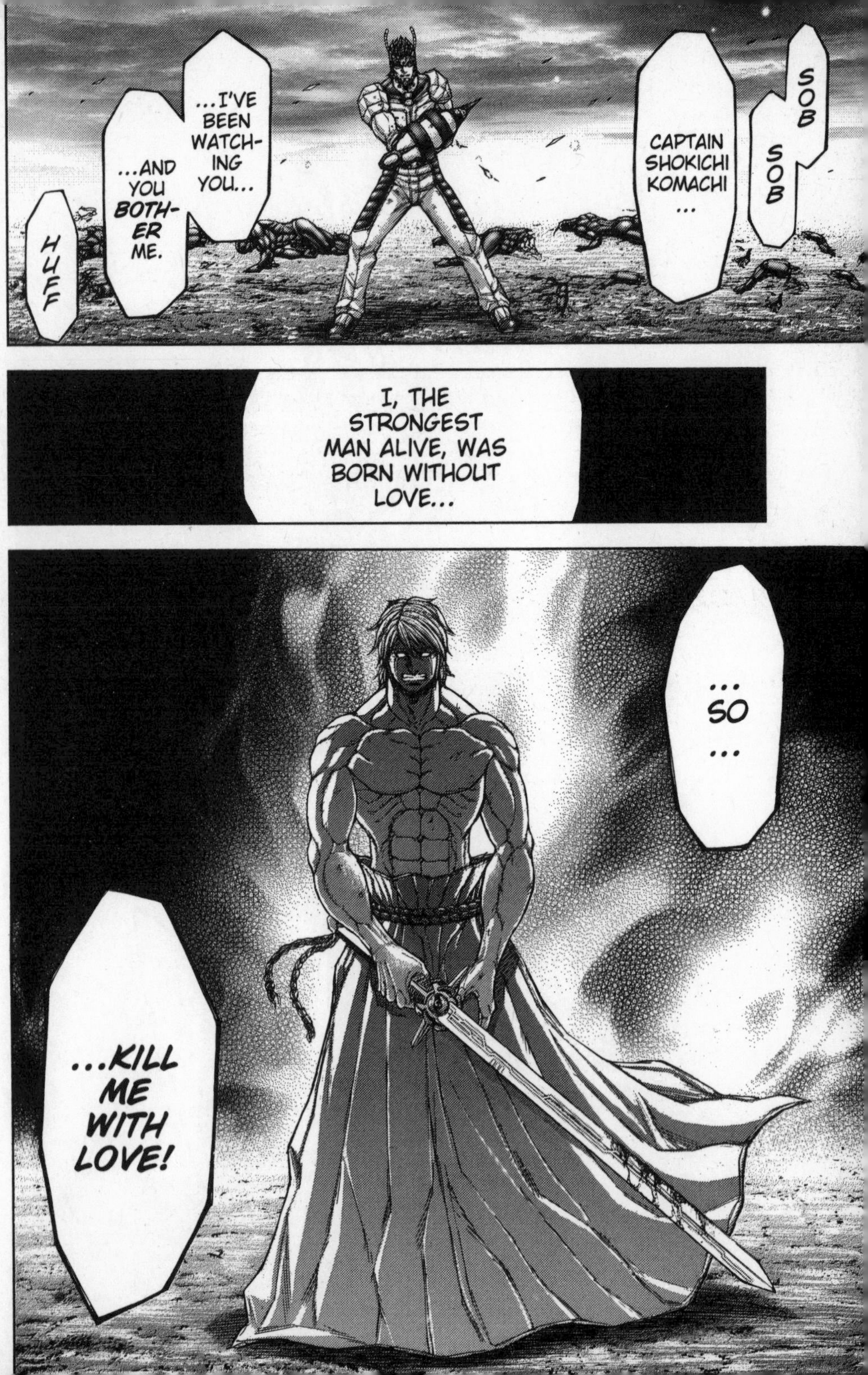
SOB SOB
CAPTAIN SHOKICHI KOMACHI...
...I'VE BEEN WATCHING YOU...
...AND YOU BOTHER ME.
HUFF
I, THE STRONGEST MAN ALIVE, WAS BORN WITHOUT LOVE...
...SO...
...KILL ME WITH LOVE!

CHAPTER 156: ELECTRO HEART

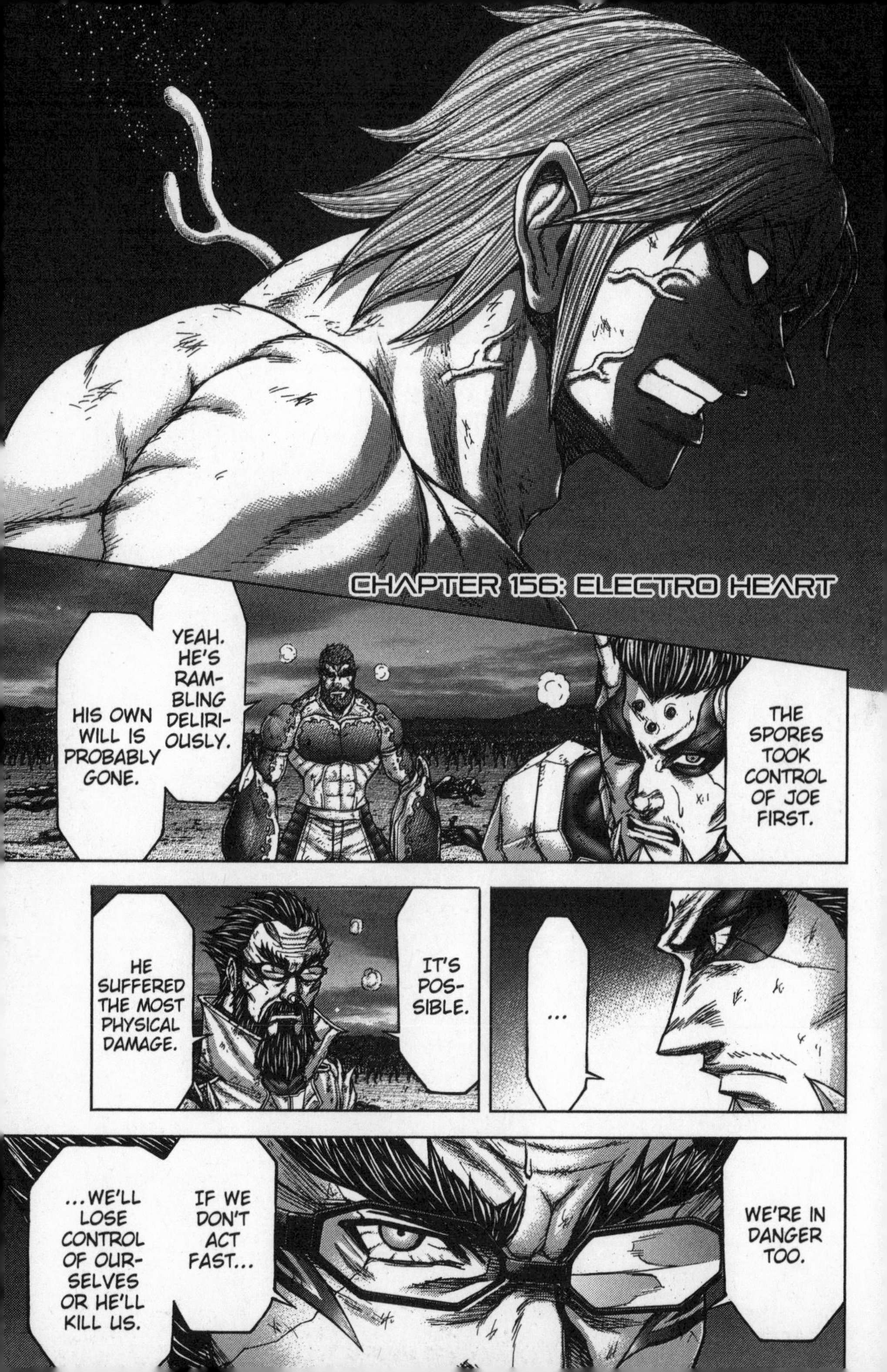
THE SPORES TOOK CONTROL OF JOE FIRST.
YEAH. HE'S RAMBLING DELIRIOUSLY.
HIS OWN WILL IS PROBABLY GONE.
...
IT'S POSSIBLE.
HE SUFFERED THE MOST PHYSICAL DAMAGE.
WE'RE IN DANGER TOO.
IF WE DON'T ACT FAST...
...WE'LL LOSE CONTROL OF OURSELVES OR HE'LL KILL US.

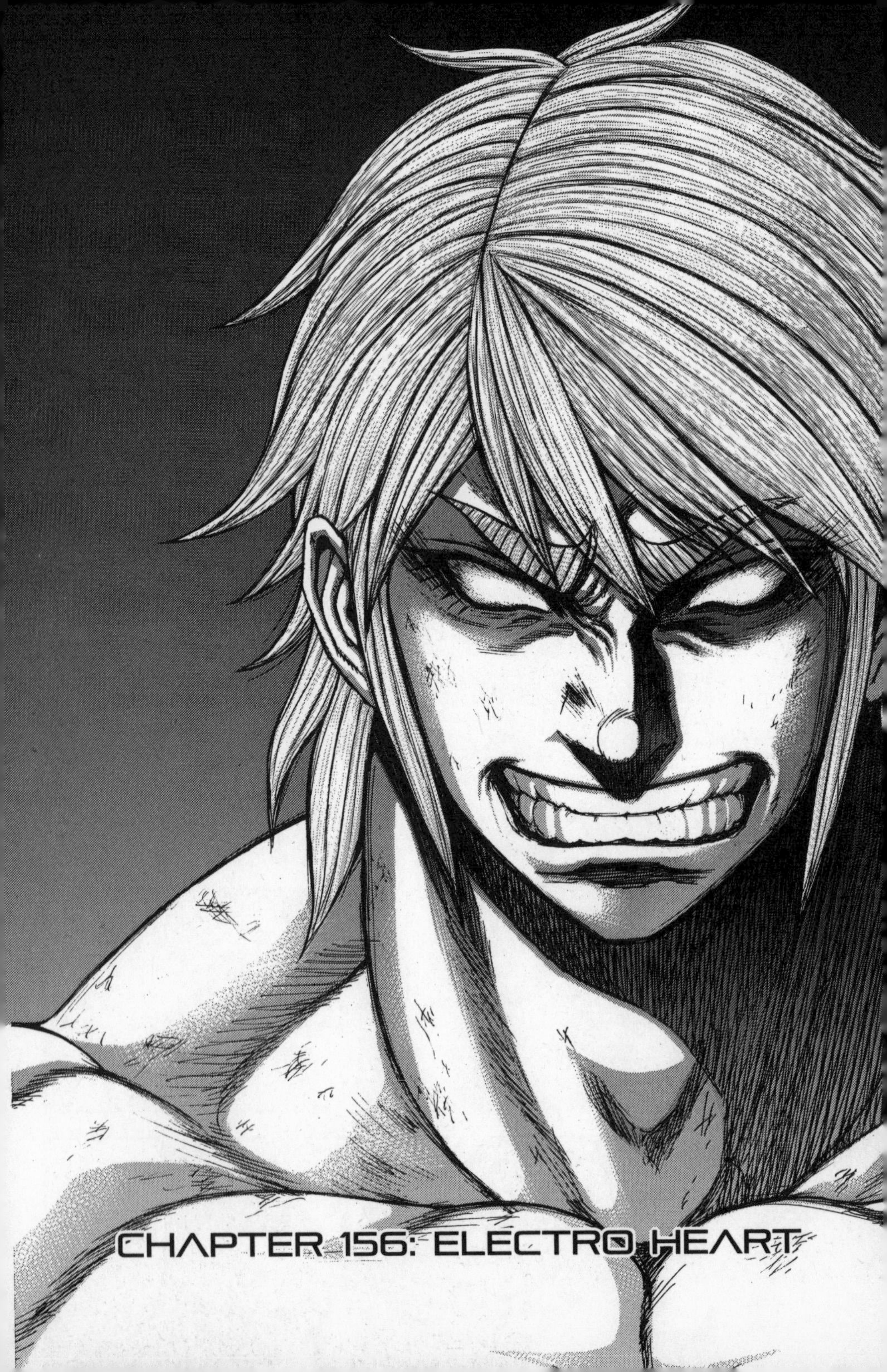
CHAPTER 156: ELECTRO HEART

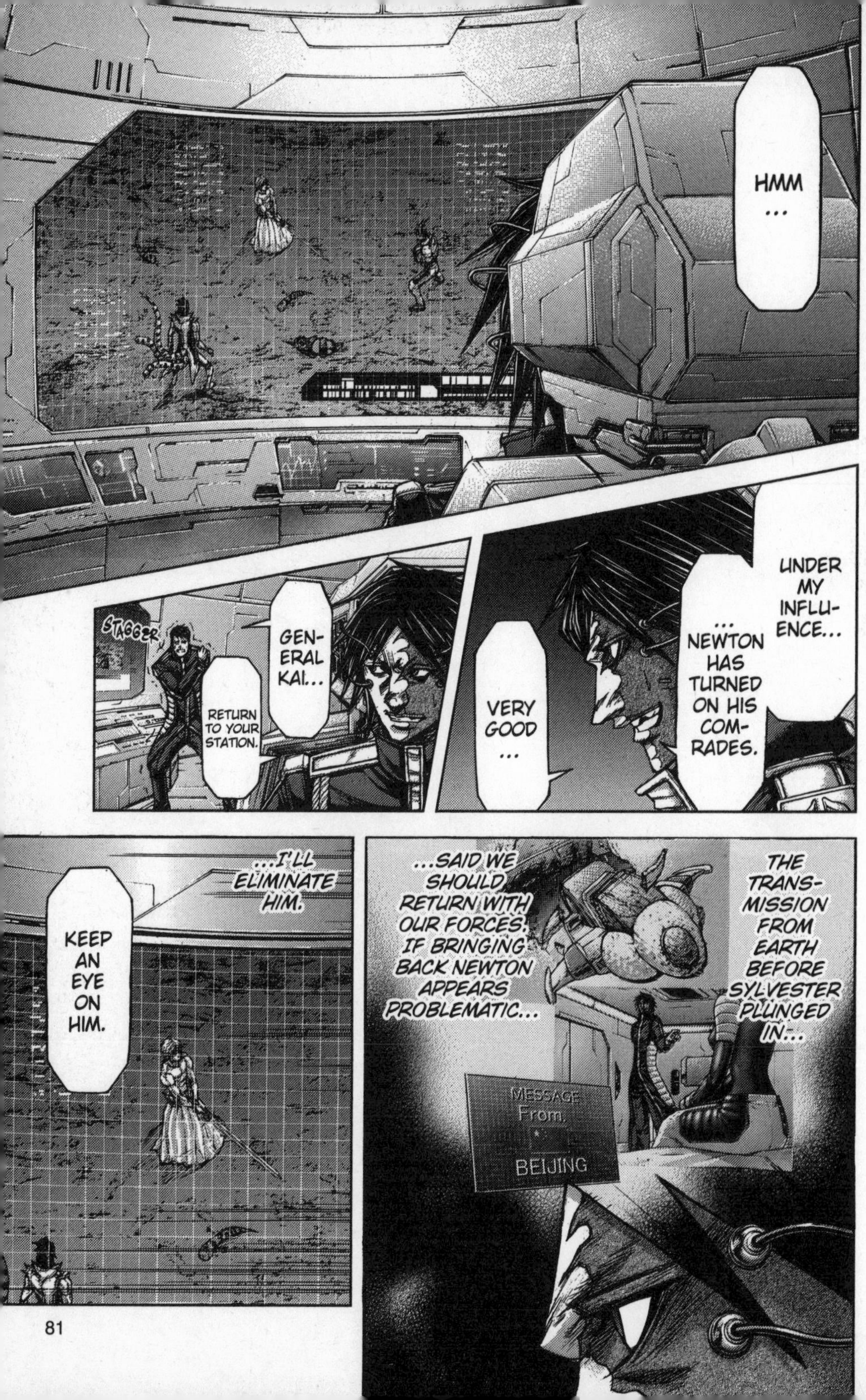
HMM...
UNDER MY INFLUENCE...
...NEWTON HAS TURNED ON HIS COMRADES.
VERY GOOD...
GENERAL KAI...
STAGGER
RETURN TO YOUR STATION.
THE TRANSMISSION FROM EARTH BEFORE SYLVESTER PLUNGED IN...
...SAID WE SHOULD RETURN WITH OUR FORCES. IF BRINGING BACK NEWTON APPEARS PROBLEMATIC...
MESSAGE From
BEIJING
...I'LL ELIMINATE HIM.
KEEP AN EYE ON HIM.

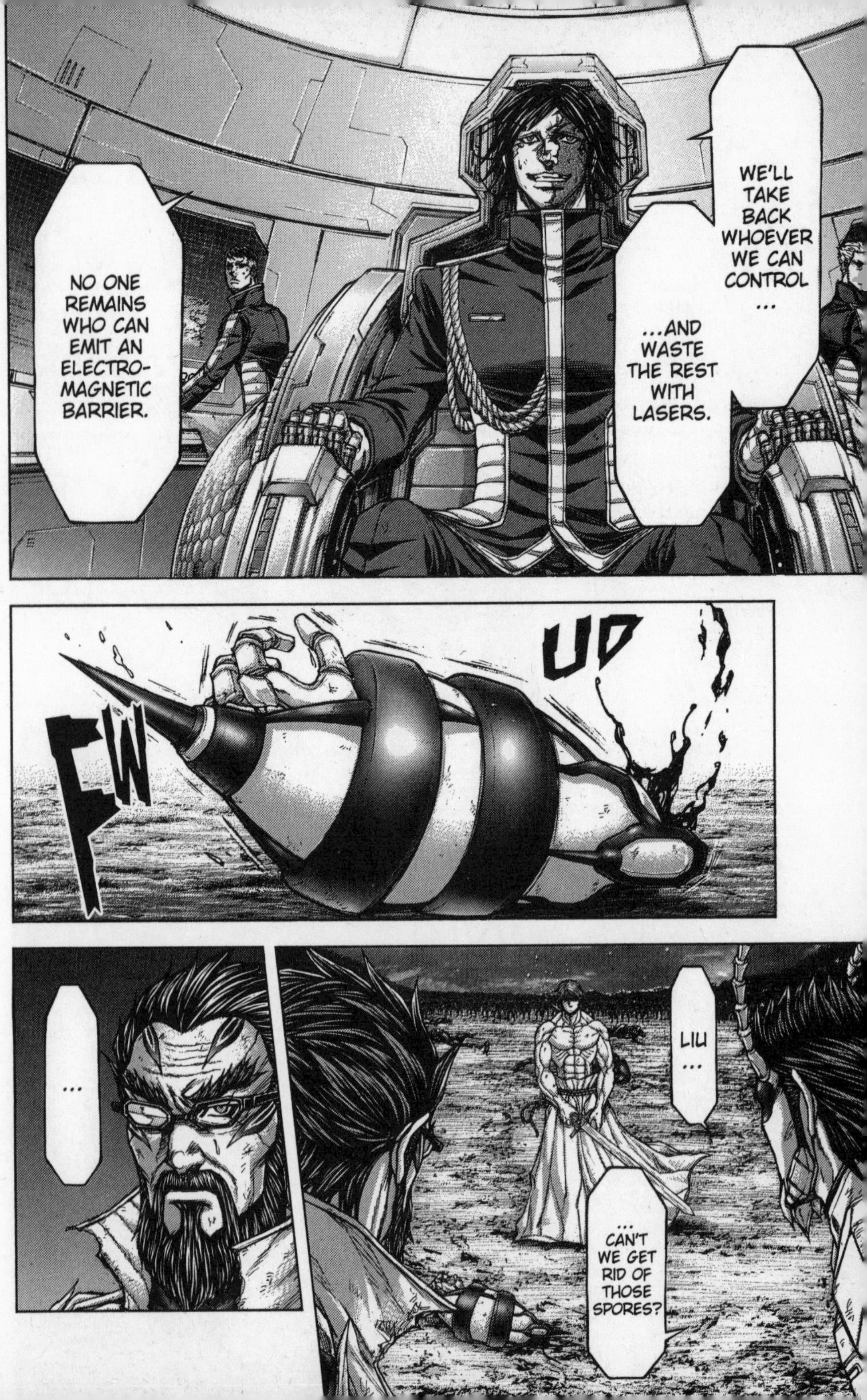
WE'LL TAKE BACK WHOEVER WE CAN CONTROL ...
...AND WASTE THE REST WITH LASERS.
NO ONE REMAINS WHO CAN EMIT AN ELECTRO-MAGNETIC BARRIER.
FW
UD
LIU ...
... CAN'T WE GET RID OF THOSE SPORES?
...

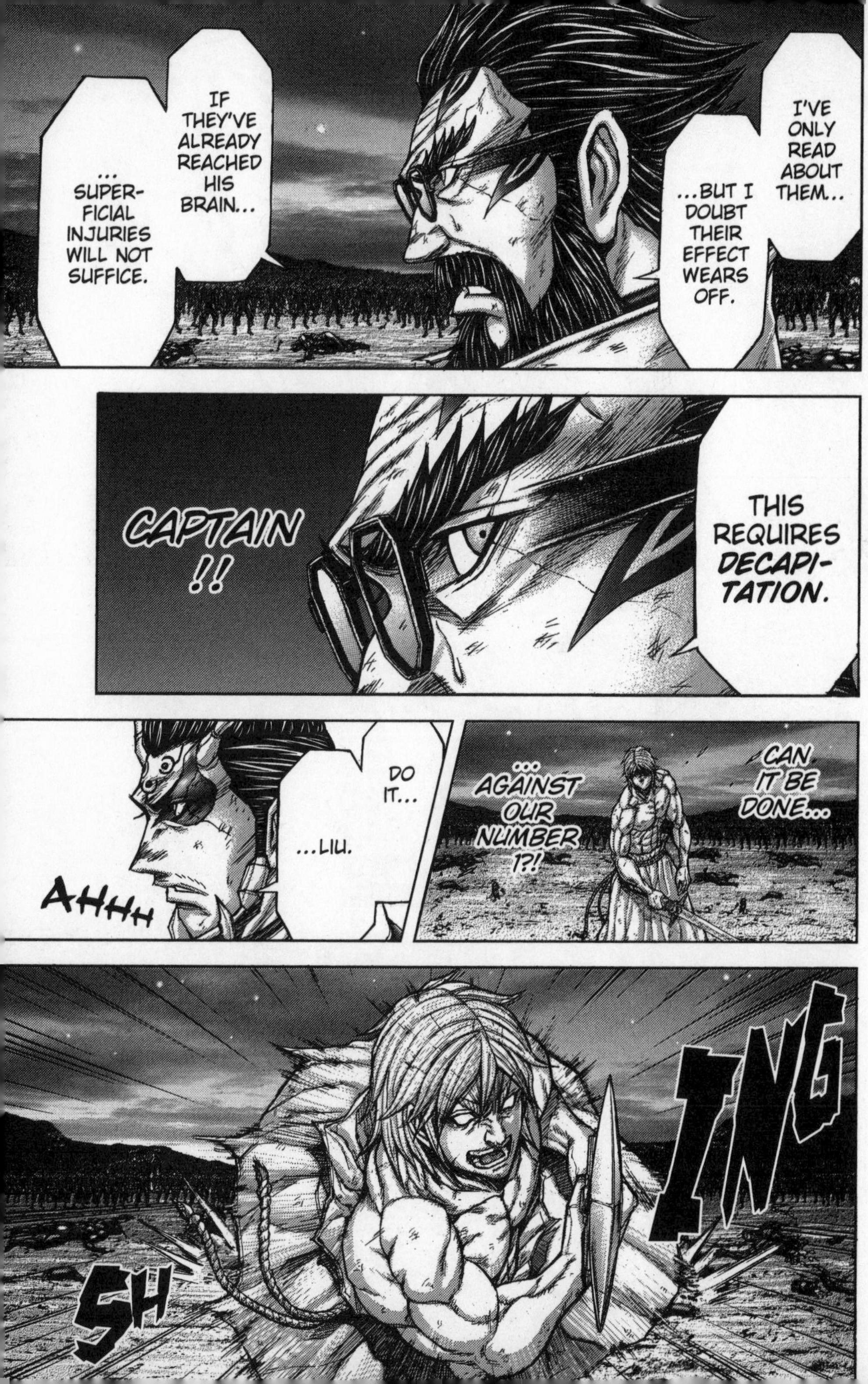
I'VE ONLY READ ABOUT THEM...
...BUT I DOUBT THEIR EFFECT WEARS OFF.
IF THEY'VE ALREADY REACHED HIS BRAIN...
...SUPER-FICIAL INJURIES WILL NOT SUFFICE.
THIS REQUIRES DECAPI-TATION.
CAPTAIN!!
CAN IT BE DONE...
...AGAINST OUR NUMBER 1?!
DO IT...
...LIU.
AHHH
TNG
SH

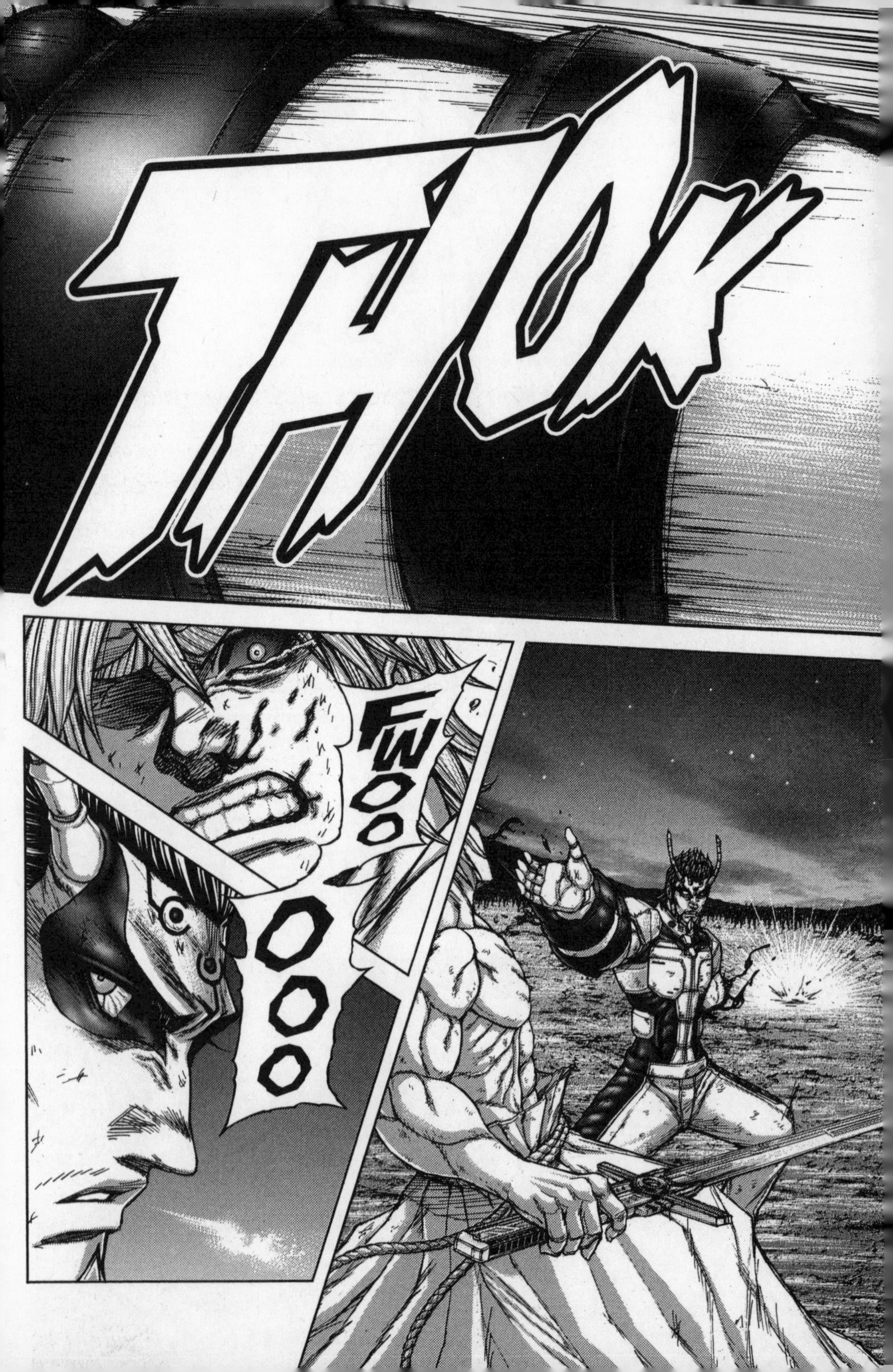
THOK
FWOOOOOO

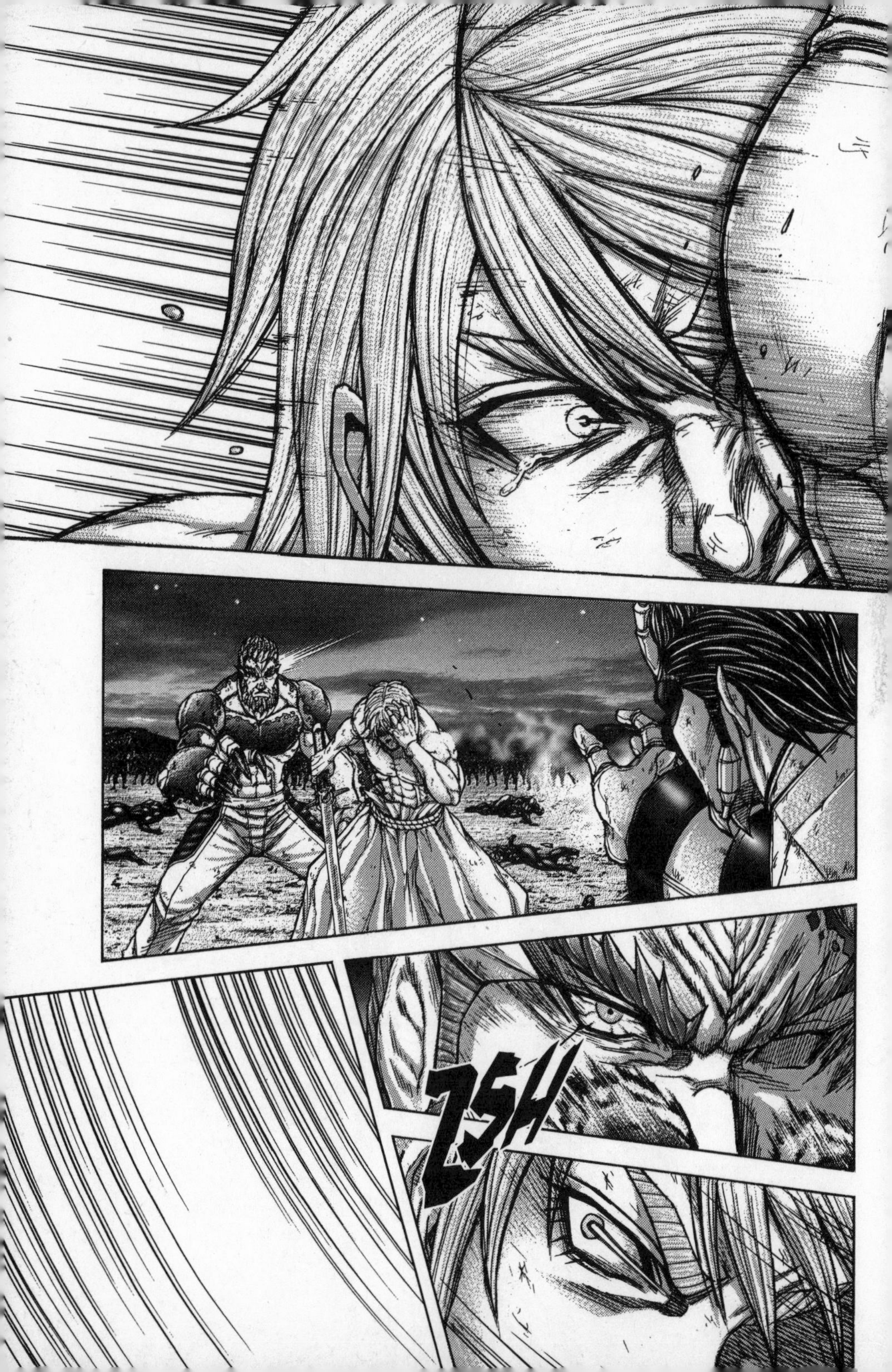
ZSH

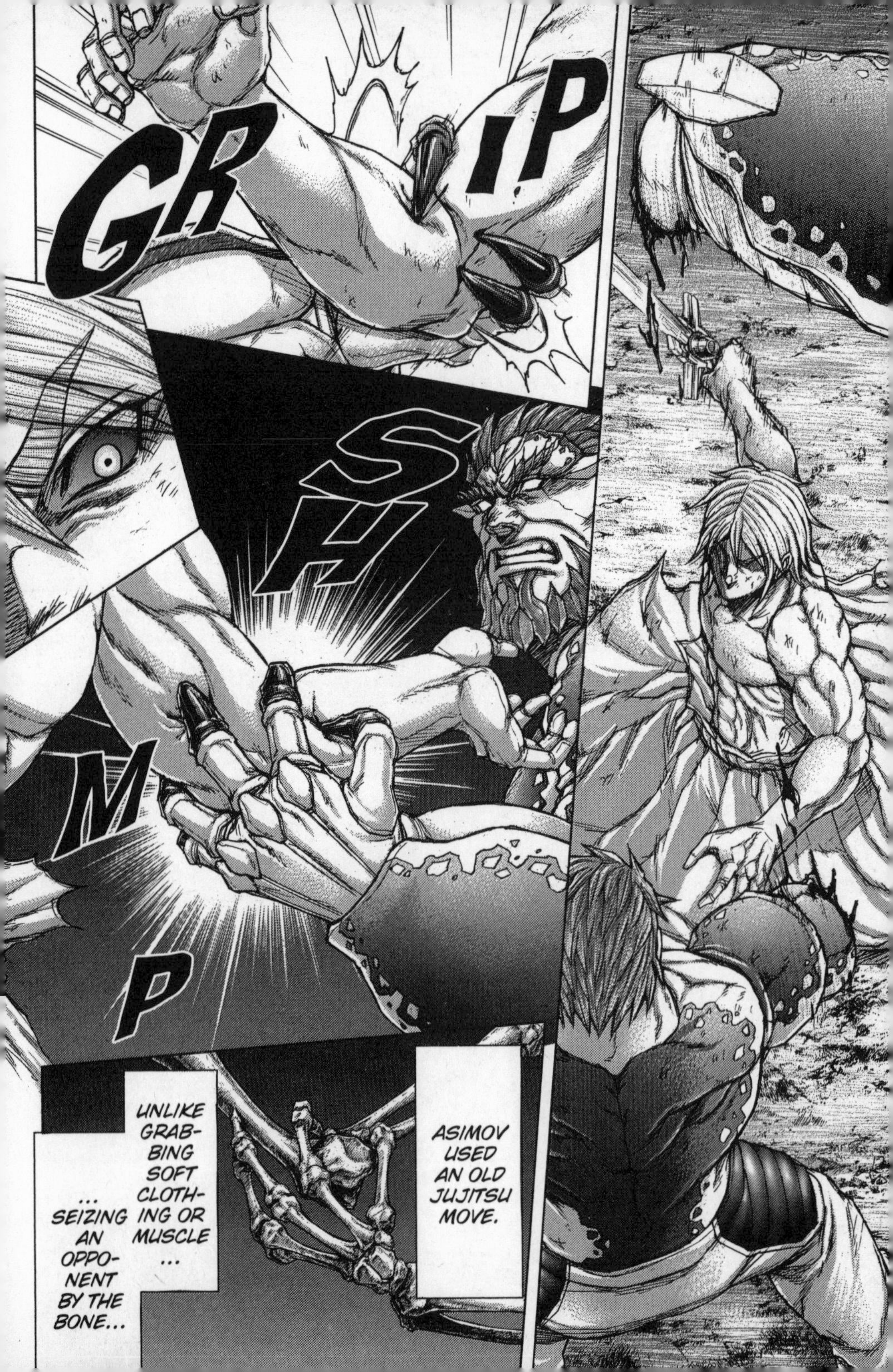
GRIP
SH
MP
ASIMOV USED AN OLD JUJITSU MOVE.
UNLIKE GRABBING SOFT CLOTHING OR MUSCLE...
...SEIZING AN OPPONENT BY THE BONE...

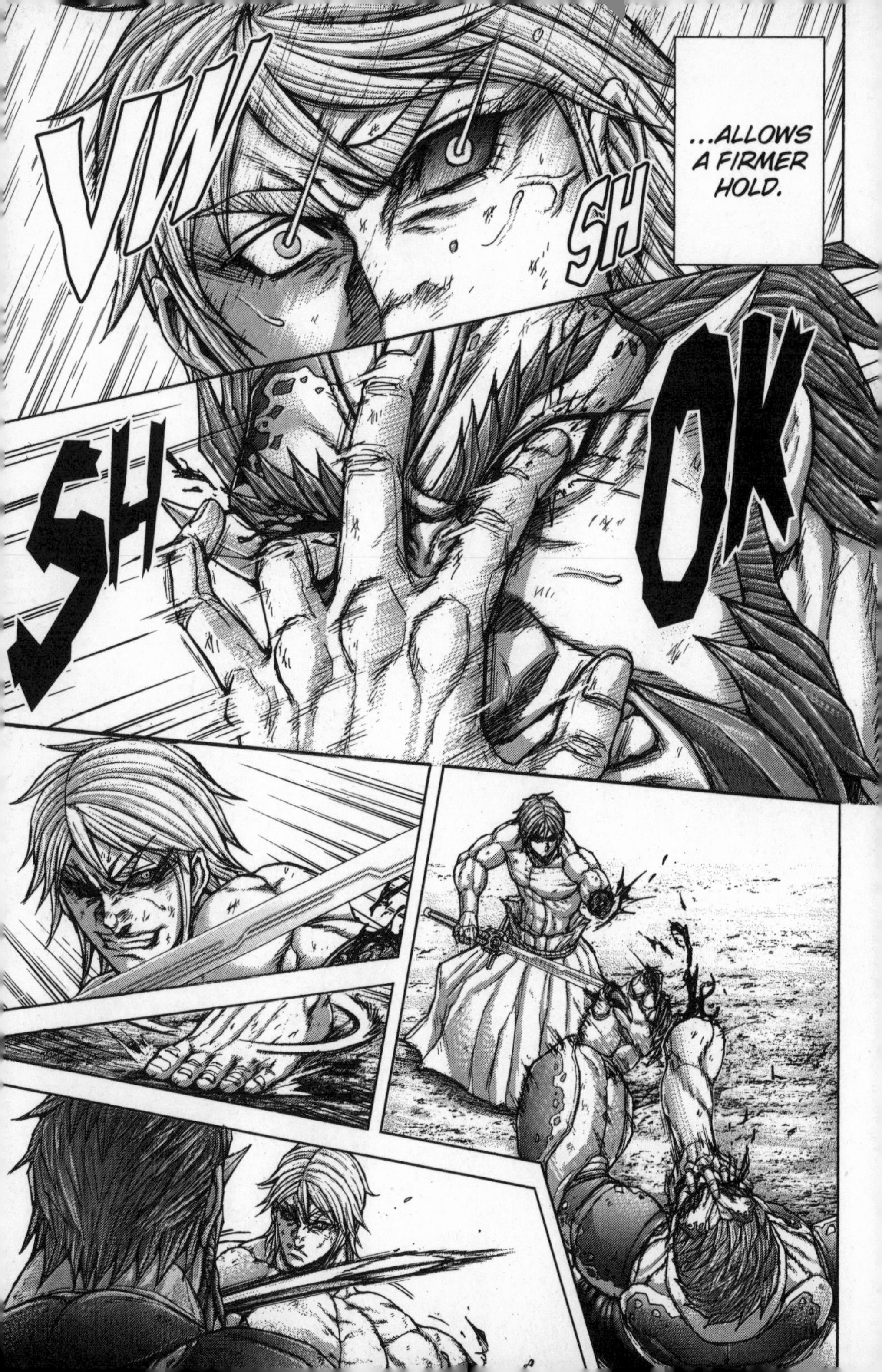
...ALLOWS A FIRMER HOLD.
VIN
SH
SH
OK

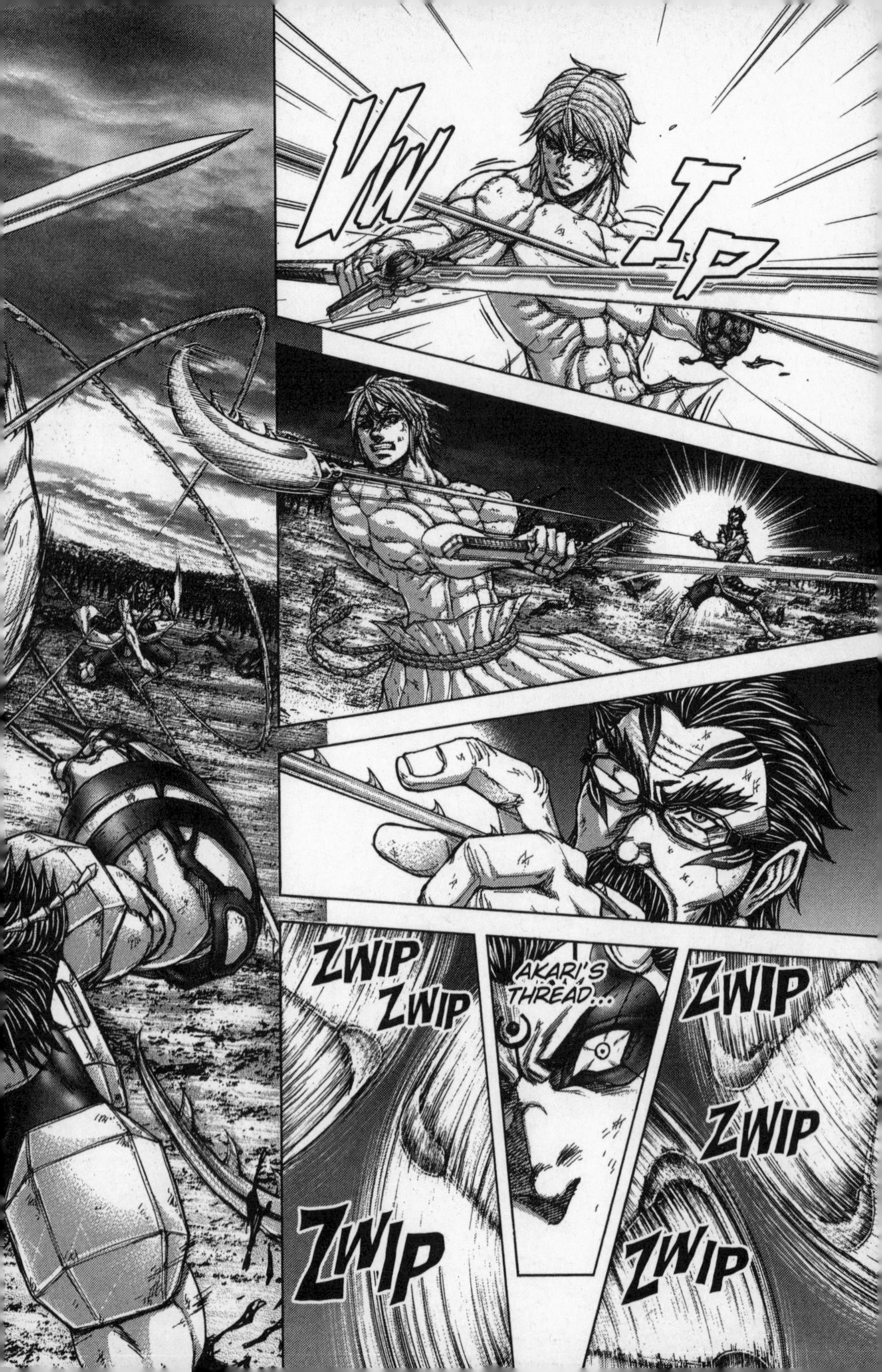
ZWIP
ZWIP
ZWIP
AKARI'S THREAD...
ZWIP
ZWIP
ZWIP

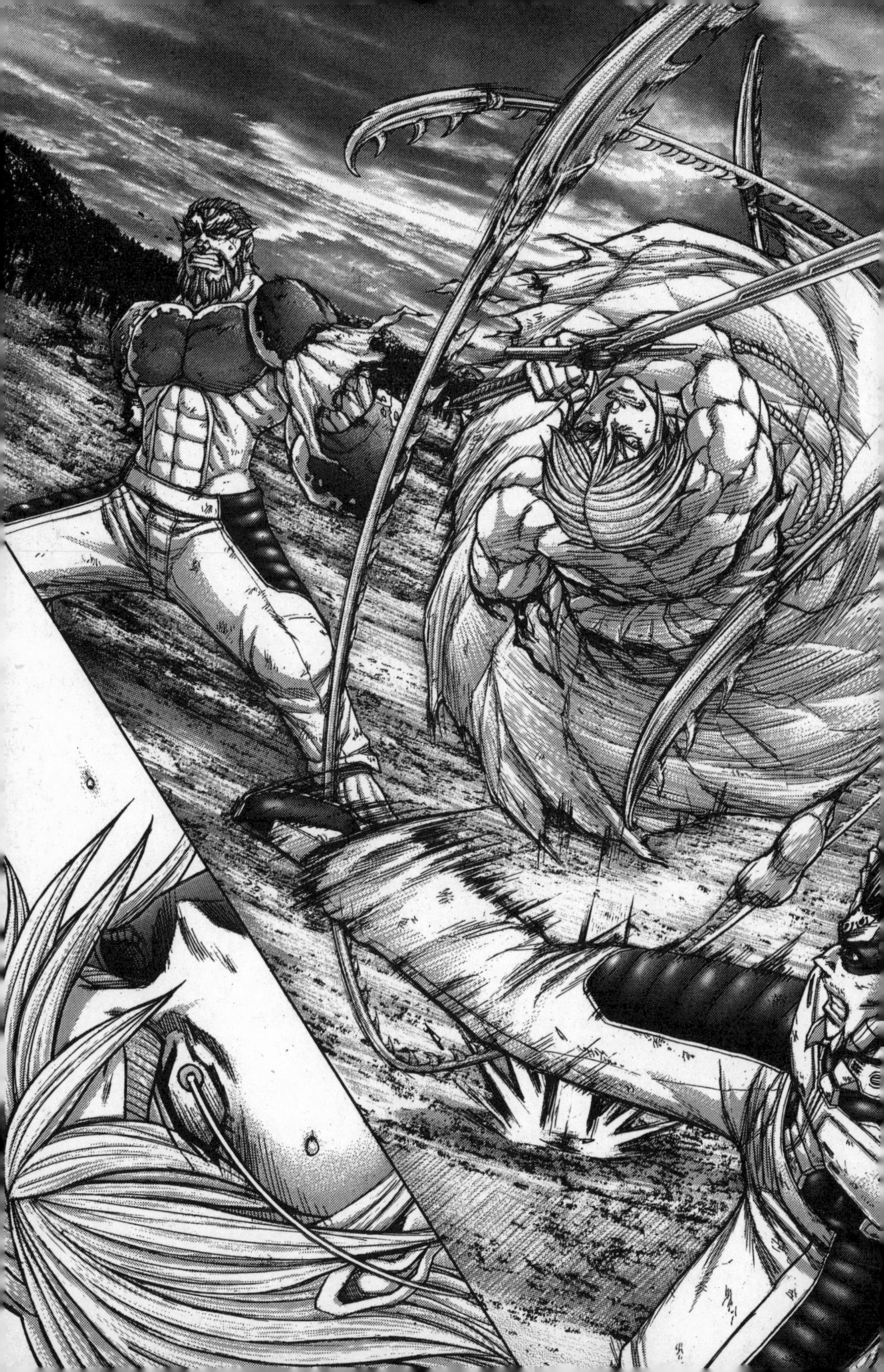

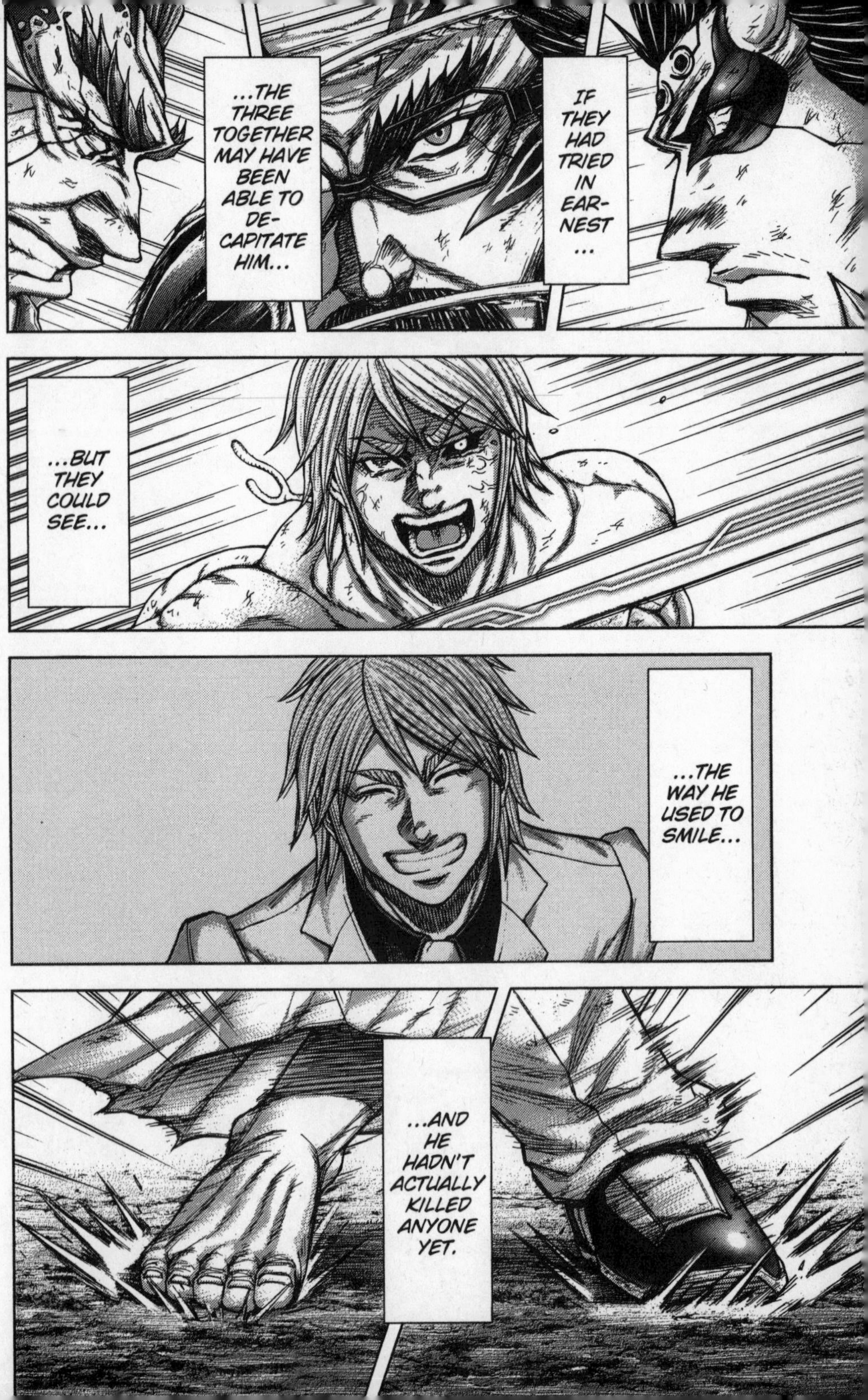
IF THEY HAD TRIED IN EAR-NEST...
...THE THREE TOGETHER MAY HAVE BEEN ABLE TO DE-CAPITATE HIM...
...BUT THEY COULD SEE...
...THE WAY HE USED TO SMILE...
...AND HE HADN'T ACTUALLY KILLED ANYONE YET.

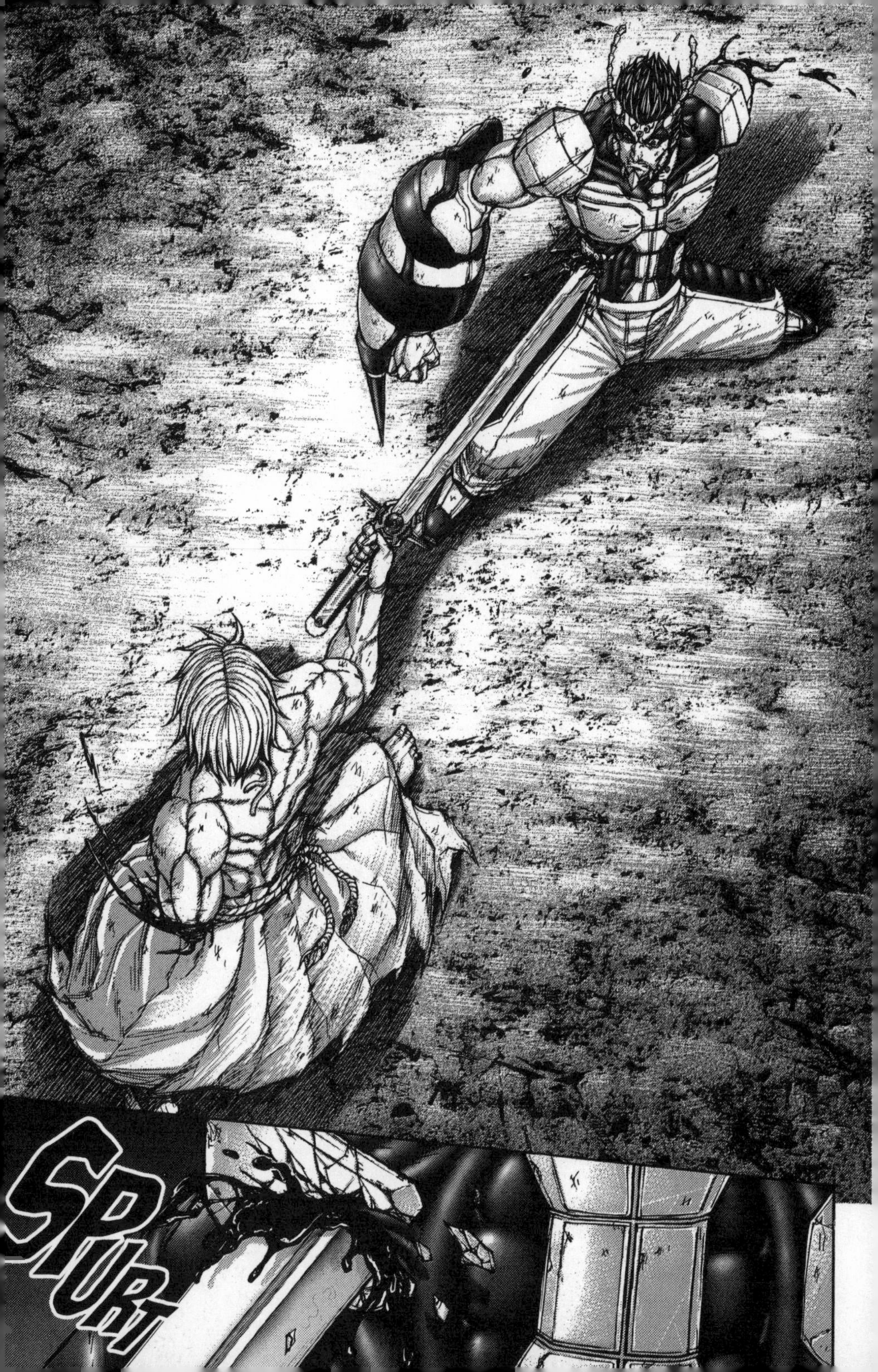
SPURT

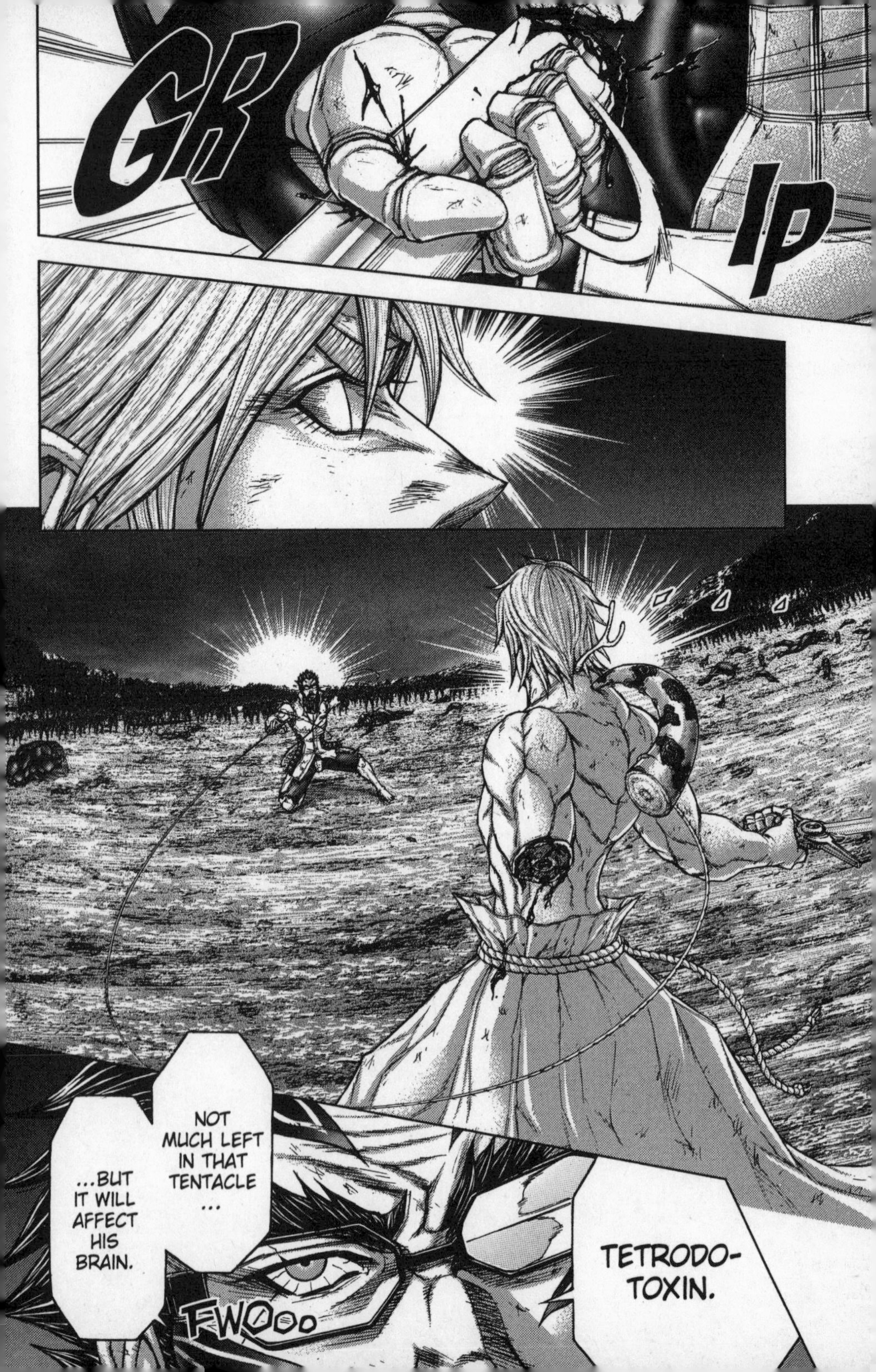
GRIP
NOT MUCH LEFT IN THAT TENTACLE ...
...BUT IT WILL AFFECT HIS BRAIN.
TETRODO-TOXIN.
FWOooo

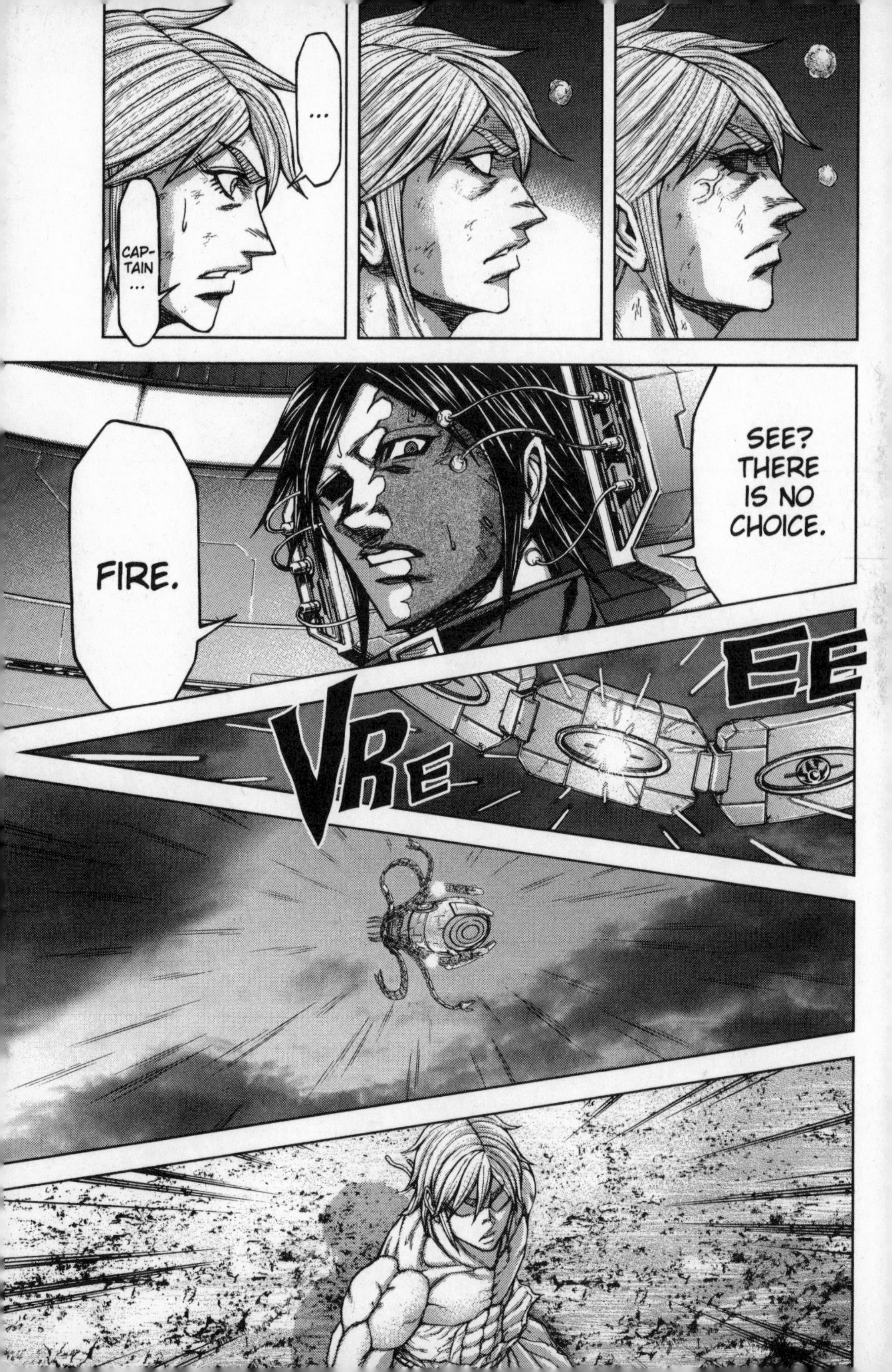
...
CAP-
TAIN
...
SEE? THERE IS NO CHOICE.
FIRE.
VREEE

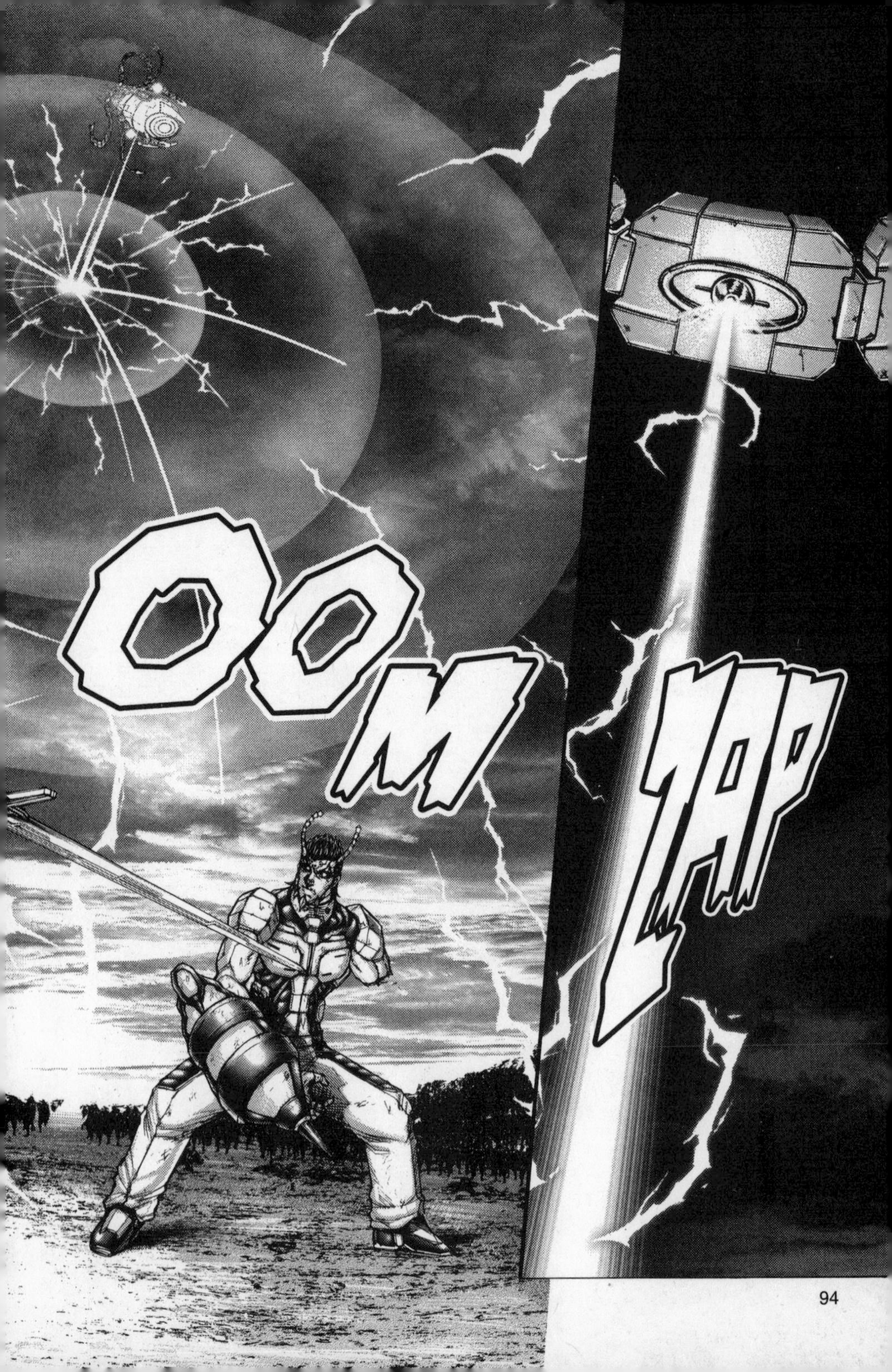
ZAP
OOM

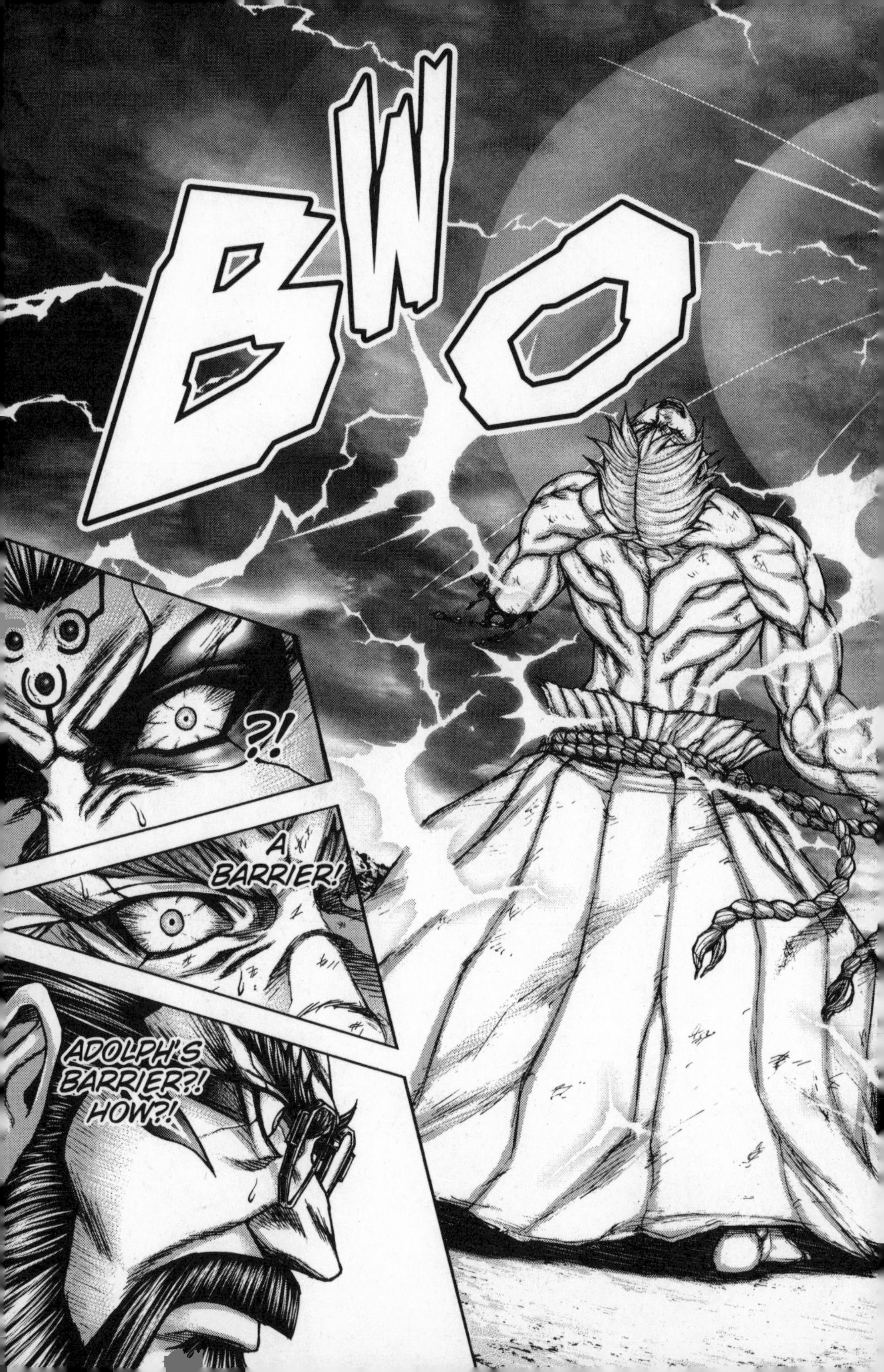
BWO
?!
A BARRIER!
ADOLPH'S BARRIER?! HOW?!

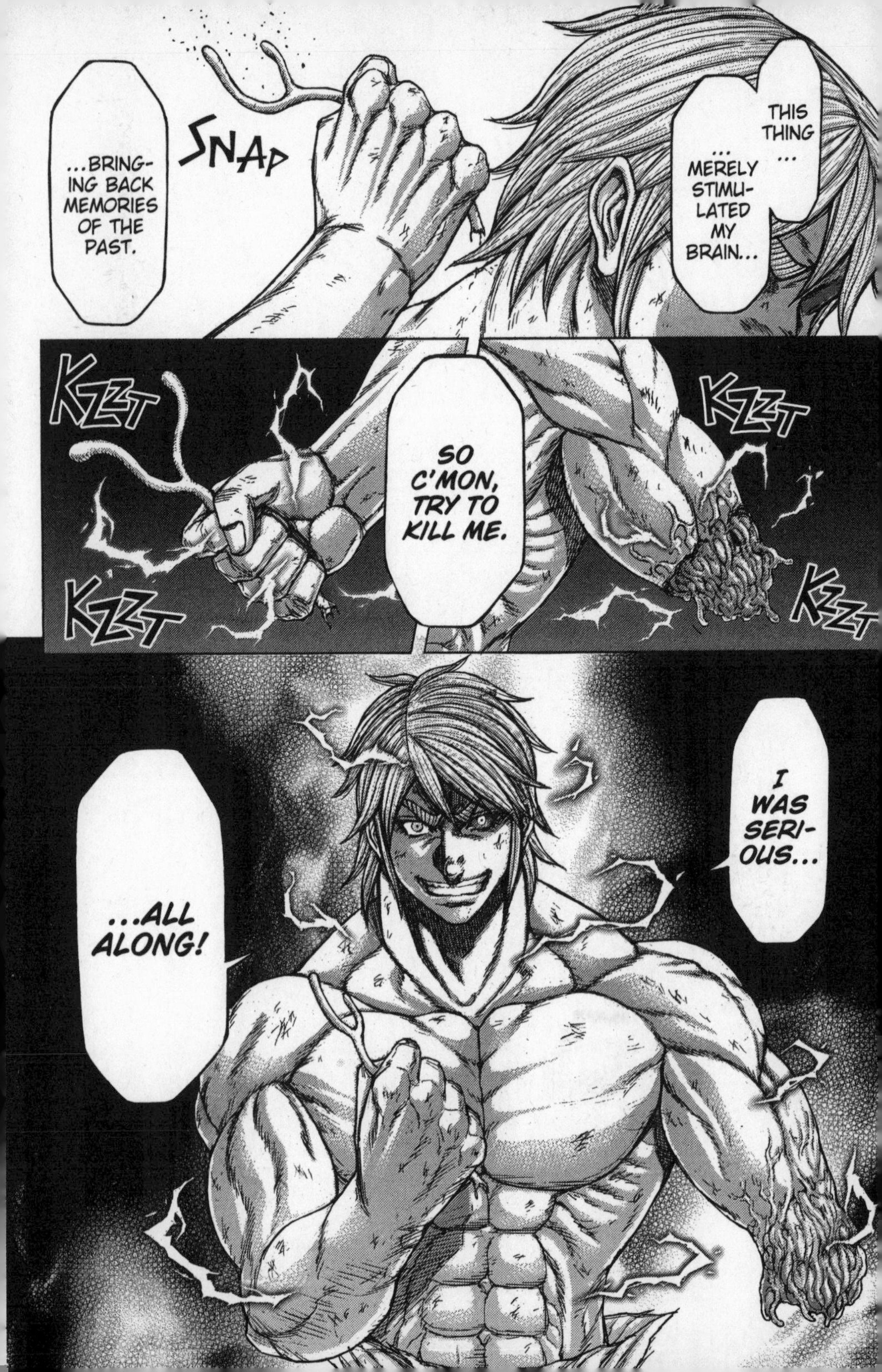

THIS THING ... ... MERELY STIMULATED MY BRAIN...
SNAP
...BRINGING BACK MEMORIES OF THE PAST.
KZZT
KZZT
SO C'MON, TRY TO KILL ME.
KZZT
KZZT
I WAS SERIOUS...
...ALL ALONG!

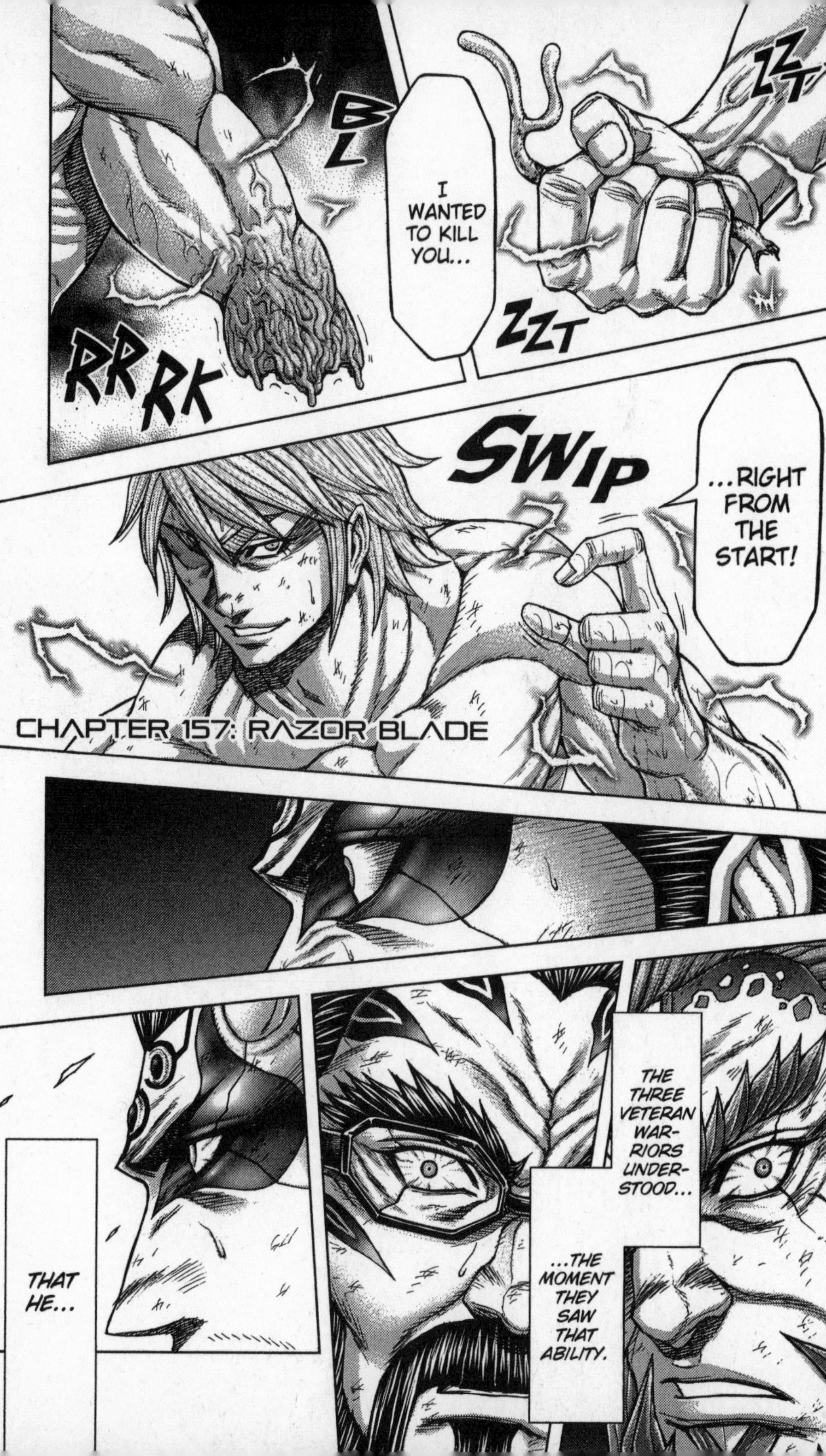
ZZT
I WANTED TO KILL YOU...
ZZT
BL
RRRK
SWIP
...RIGHT FROM THE START!
CHAPTER 157: RAZOR BLADE
THE THREE VETERAN WAR-RIORS UNDER-STOOD...
...THE MOMENT THEY SAW THAT ABILITY.
THAT HE...

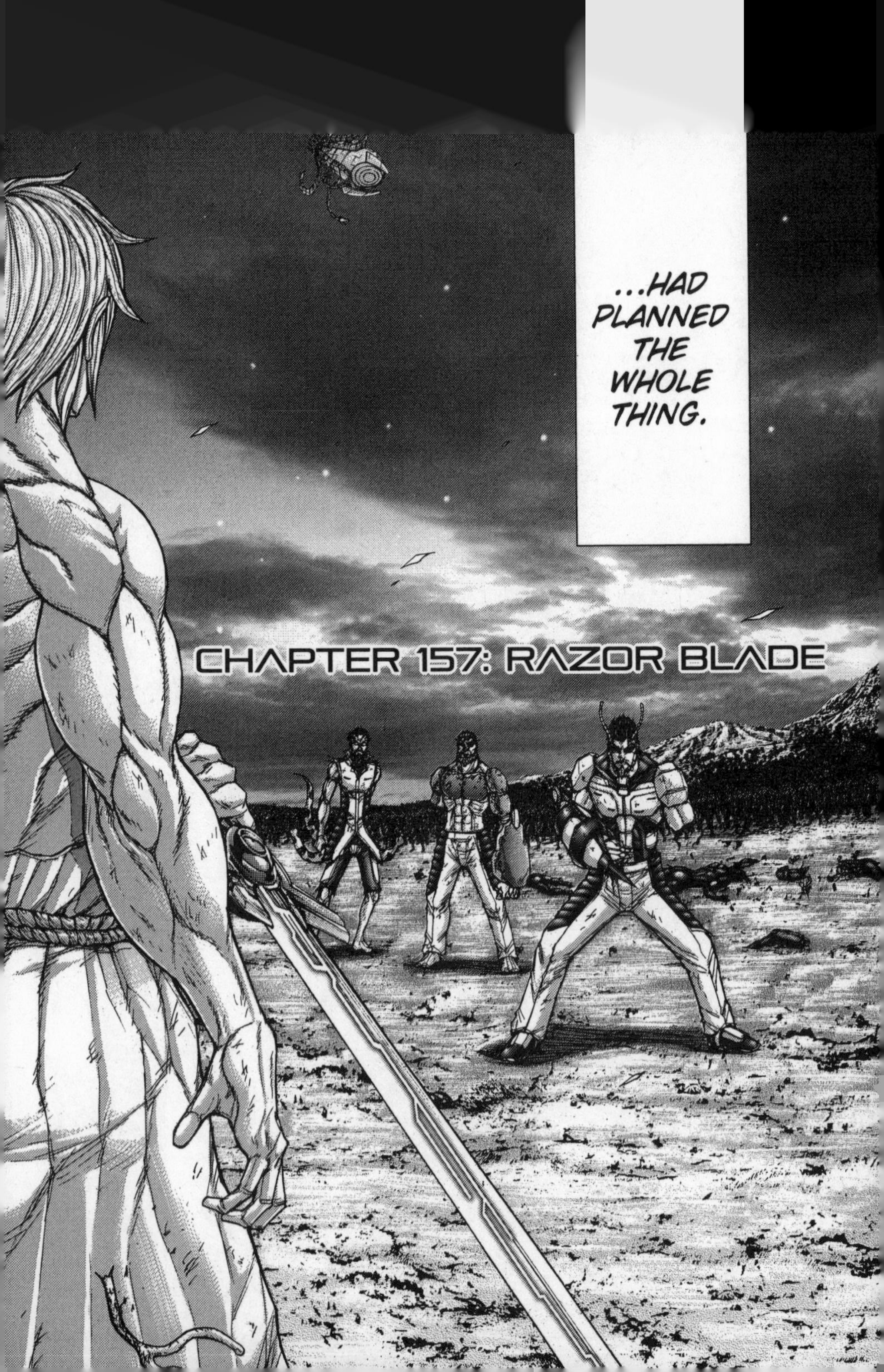
...HAD PLANNED THE WHOLE THING.
CHAPTER 157: RAZOR BLADE

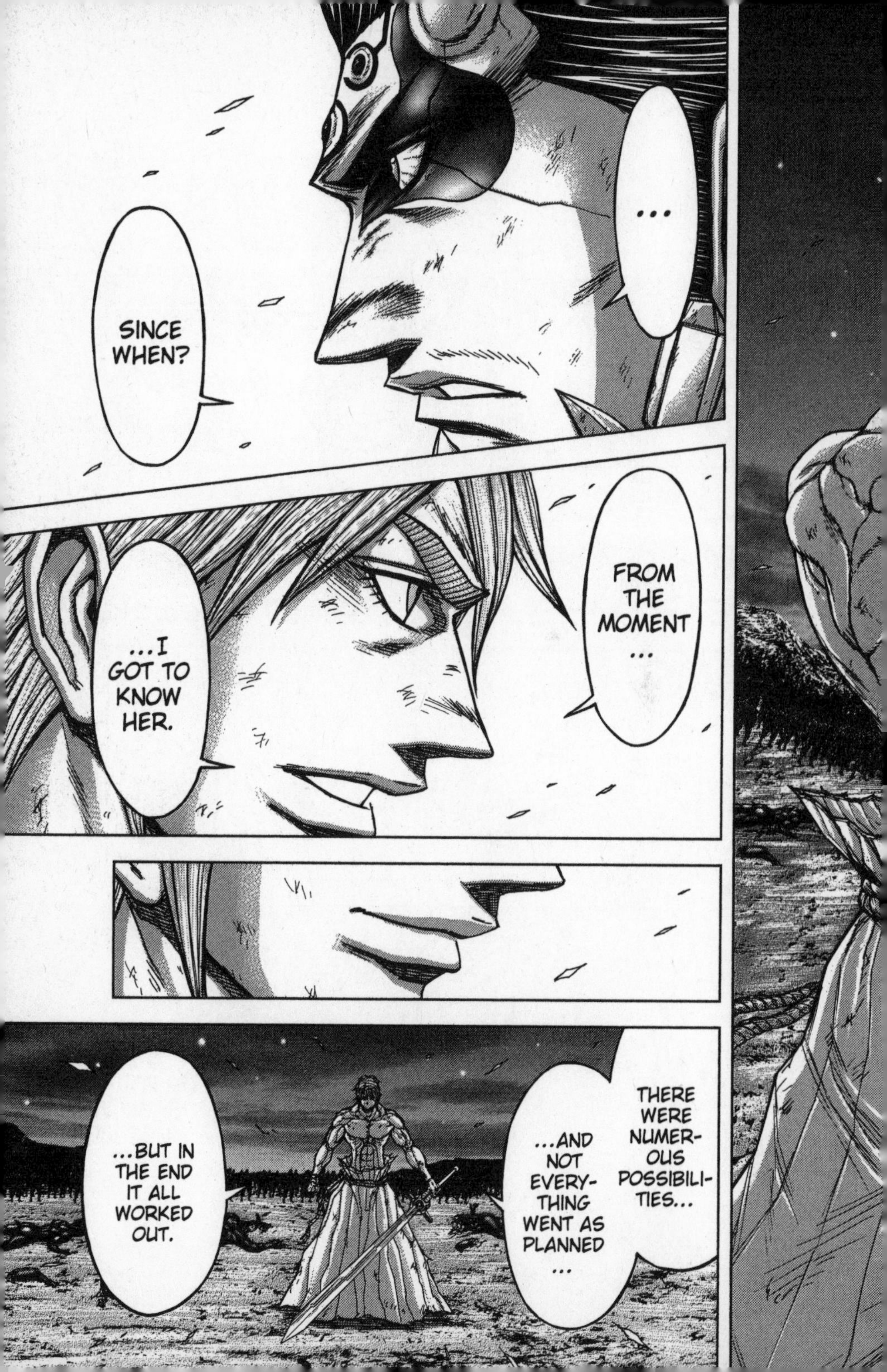
...
SINCE WHEN?
FROM THE MOMENT...
...I GOT TO KNOW HER.
THERE WERE NUMER-OUS POSSIBILI-TIES...
...AND NOT EVERY-THING WENT AS PLANNED...
...BUT IN THE END IT ALL WORKED OUT.

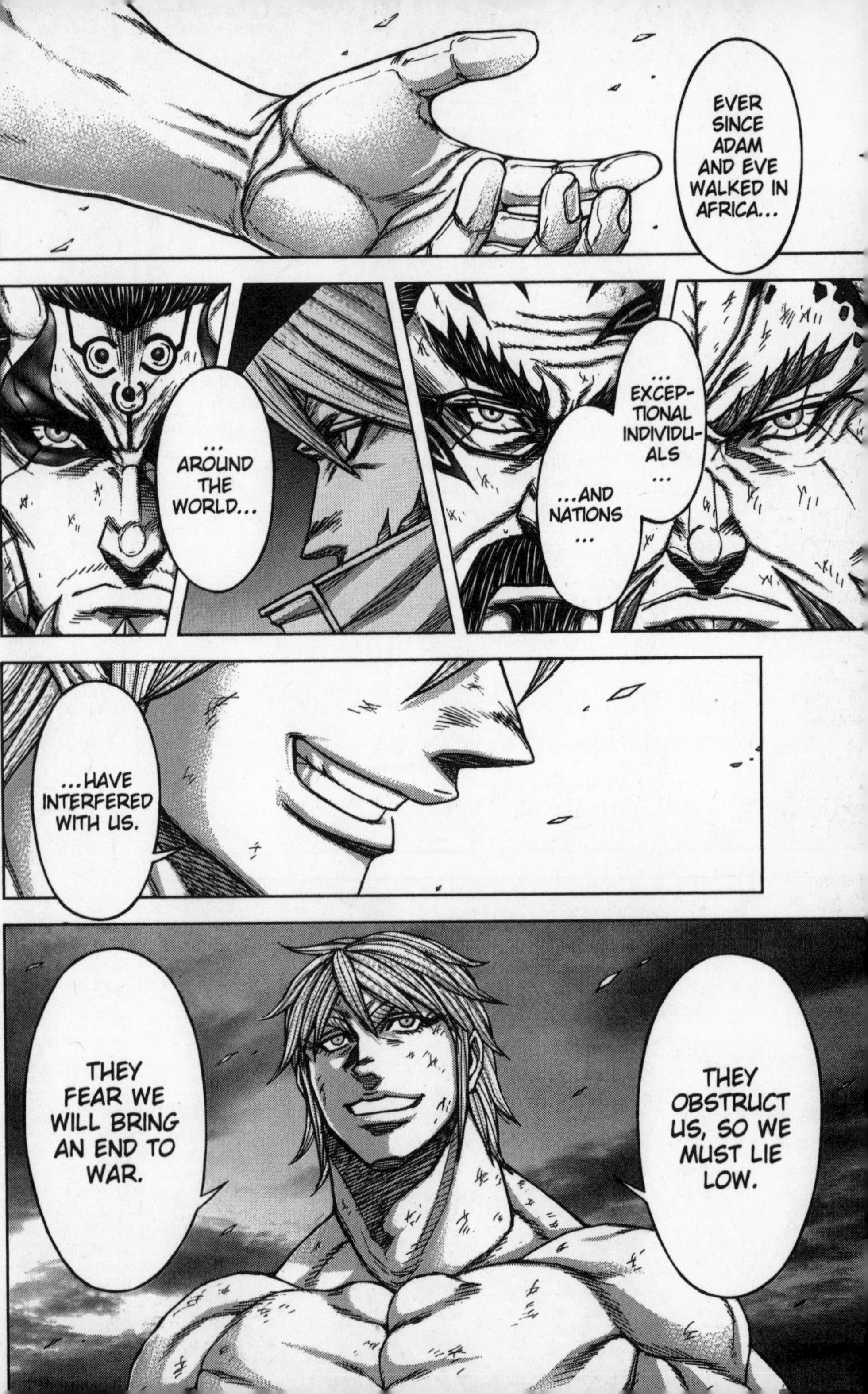
EVER SINCE ADAM AND EVE WALKED IN AFRICA...
...EXCEPTIONAL INDIVIDUALS...
...AND NATIONS...
...AROUND THE WORLD...
...HAVE INTERFERED WITH US.
THEY OBSTRUCT US, SO WE MUST LIE LOW.
THEY FEAR WE WILL BRING AN END TO WAR.

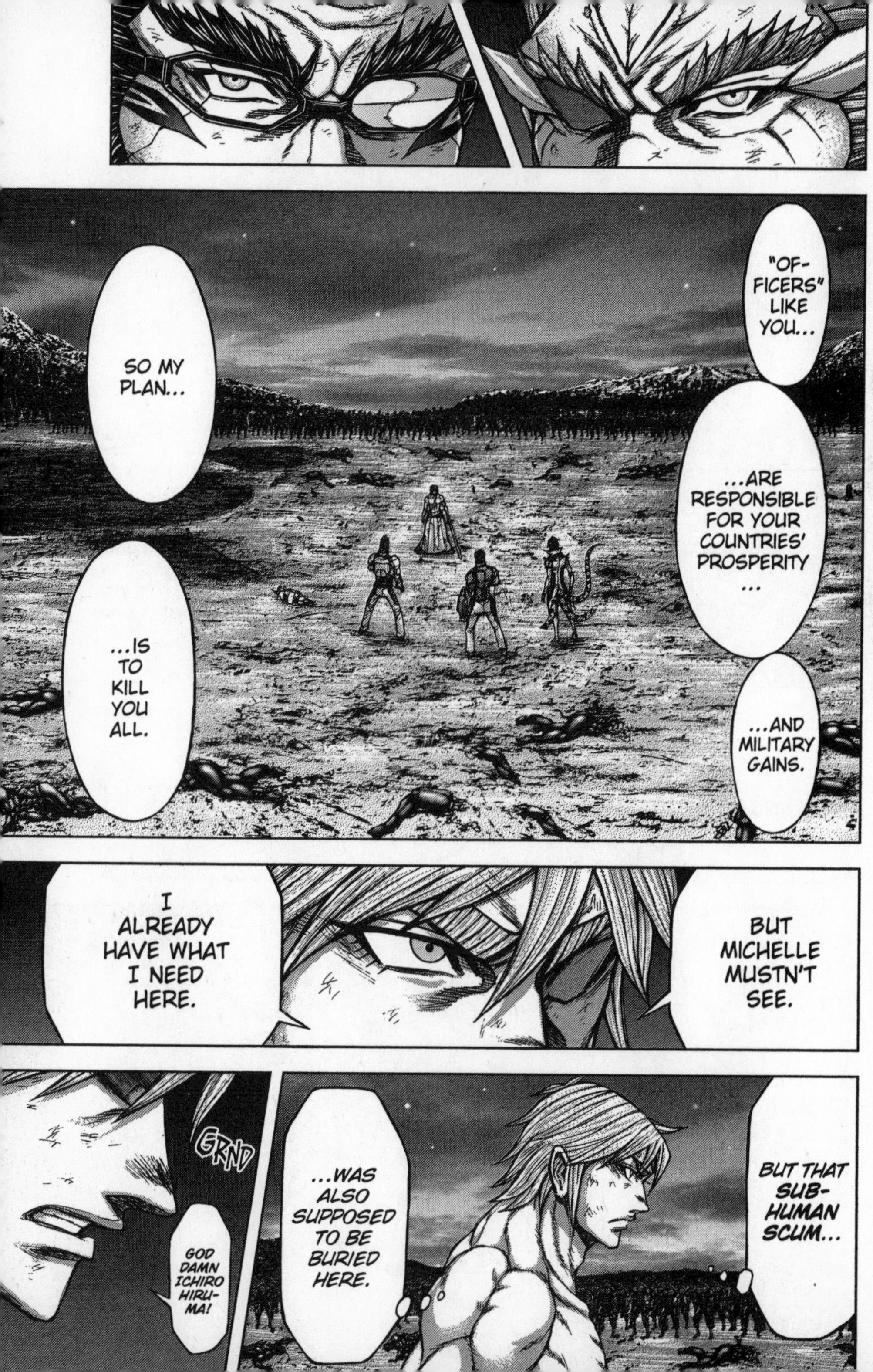
"OF-FICERS" LIKE YOU...
...ARE RESPONSIBLE FOR YOUR COUNTRIES' PROSPERITY...
...AND MILITARY GAINS.
SO MY PLAN...
...IS TO KILL YOU ALL.
BUT MICHELLE MUSTN'T SEE.
I ALREADY HAVE WHAT I NEED HERE.
BUT THAT SUB-HUMAN SCUM...
...WAS ALSO SUPPOSED TO BE BURIED HERE.
GRND
GOD DAMN ICHIRO HIRU-MA!

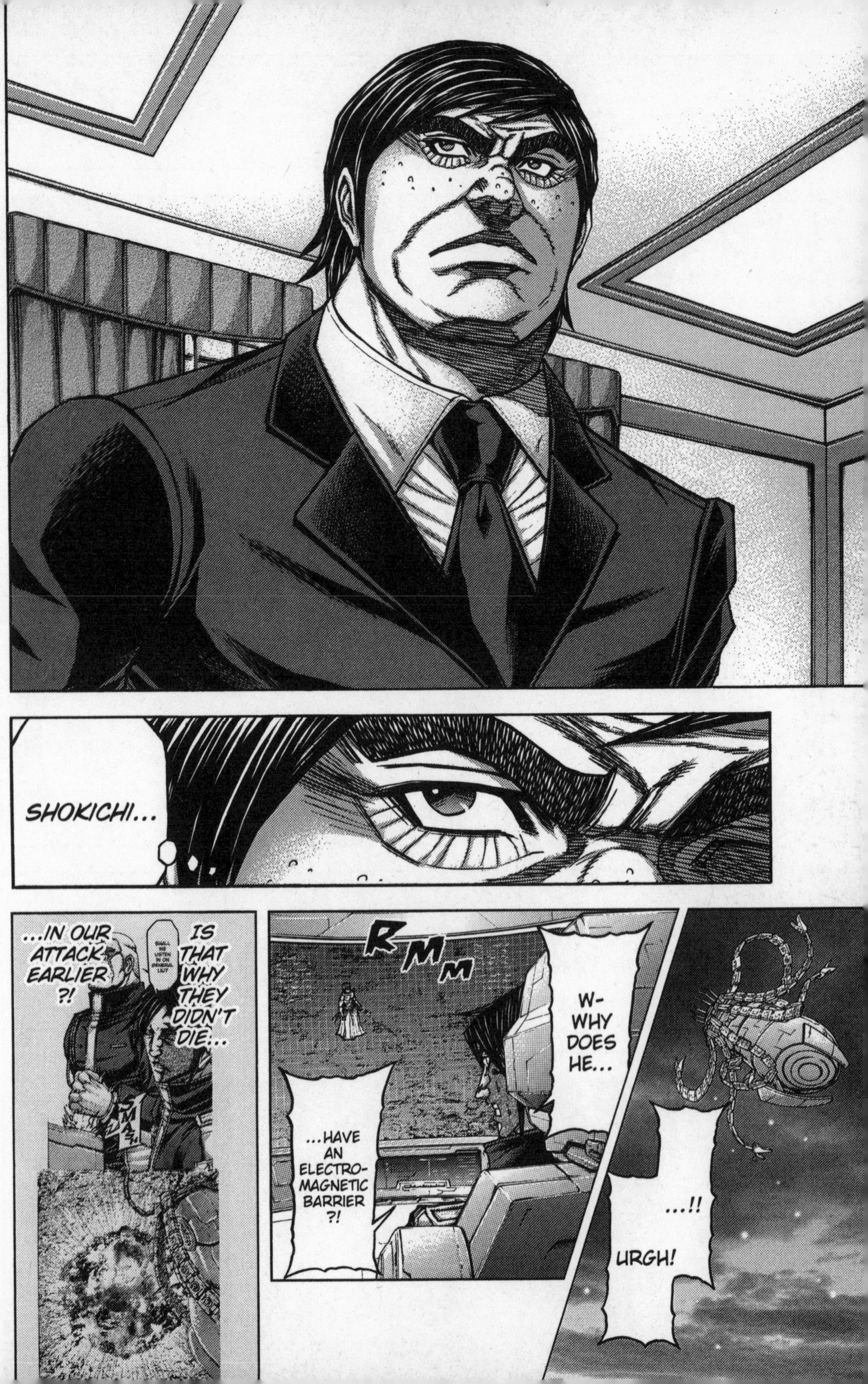
SHOKICHI...
...!!
URGH!
RMM
W-WHY DOES HE...
...HAVE AN ELECTROMAGNETIC BARRIER?!
SHALL WE LISTEN IN ON GENERAL LIU?
IS THAT WHY THEY DIDN'T DIE...
...IN OUR ATTACK EARLIER?!
SMASH

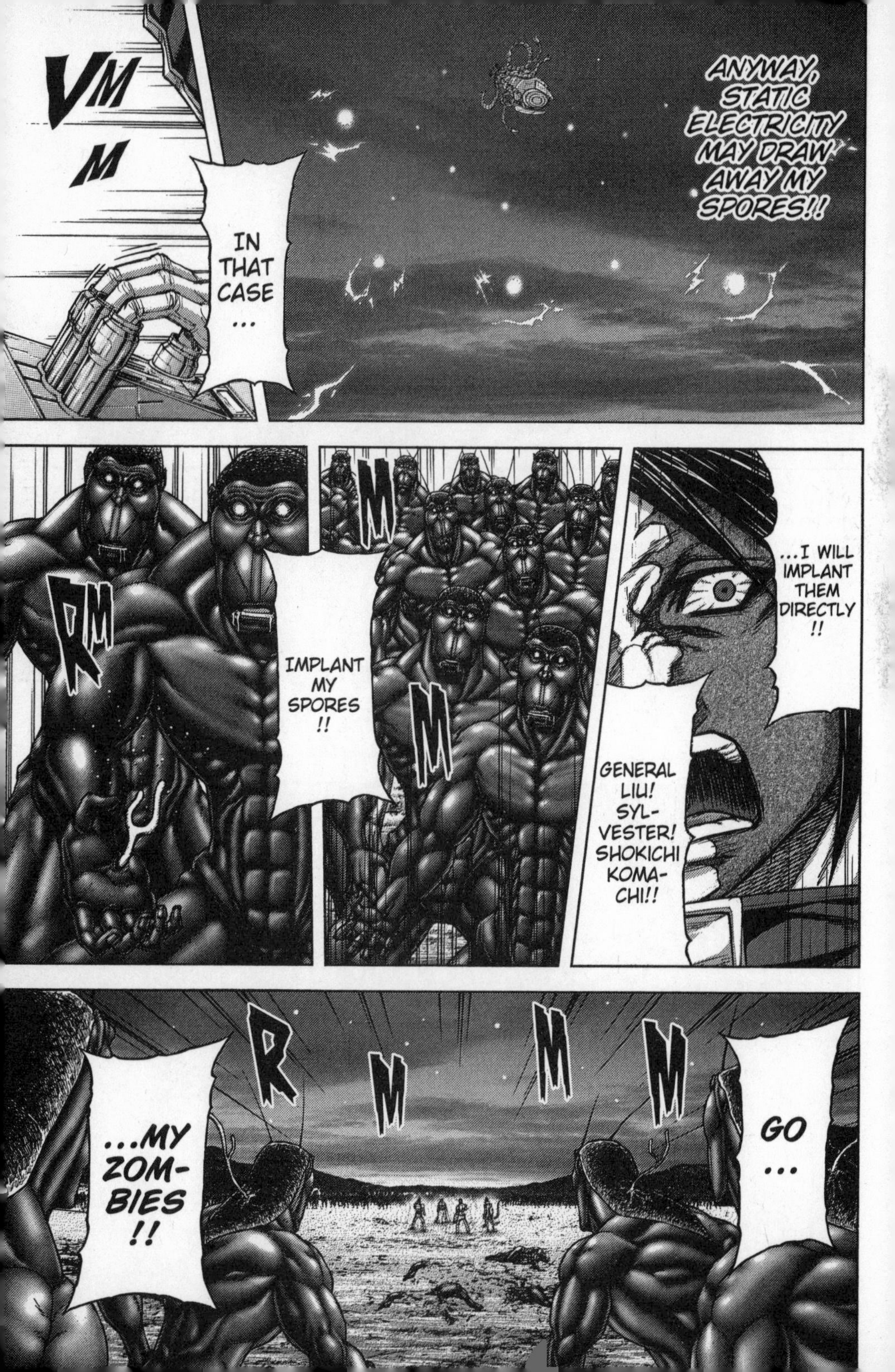

ANYWAY, STATIC ELECTRICITY MAY DRAW AWAY MY SPORES!!
IN THAT CASE...
VMM
...I WILL IMPLANT THEM DIRECTLY!!
GENERAL LIU! SYL-VESTER! SHOKICHI KOMA-CHI!!
IMPLANT MY SPORES!!
RMM
GO...
...MY ZOM-BIES!!
RMMM

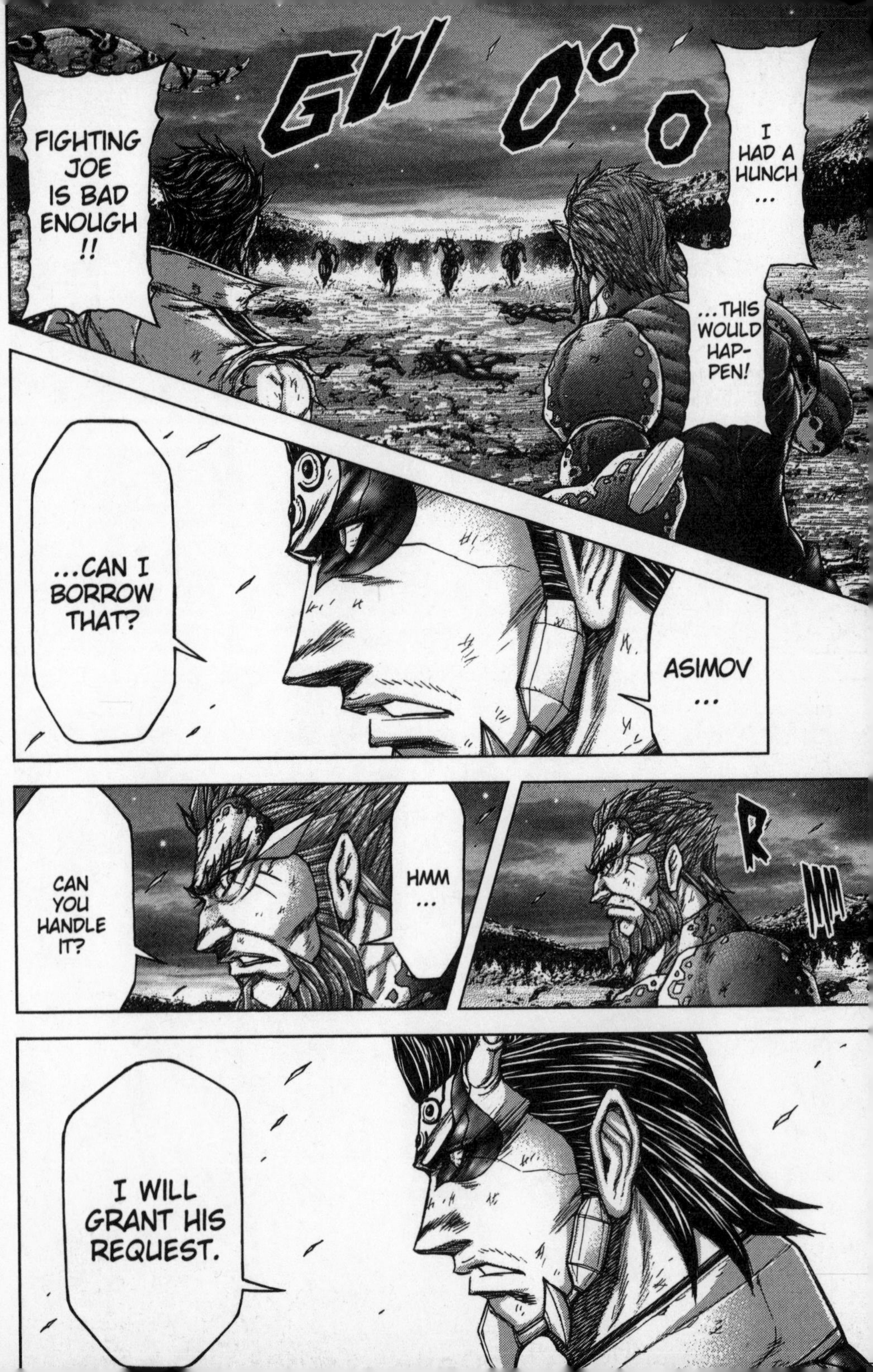
I HAD A HUNCH ...
...THIS WOULD HAP-PEN!
GW OOO
FIGHTING JOE IS BAD ENOUGH !!
ASIMOV ...
...CAN I BORROW THAT?
R MM
HMM ...
CAN YOU HANDLE IT?
I WILL GRANT HIS REQUEST.

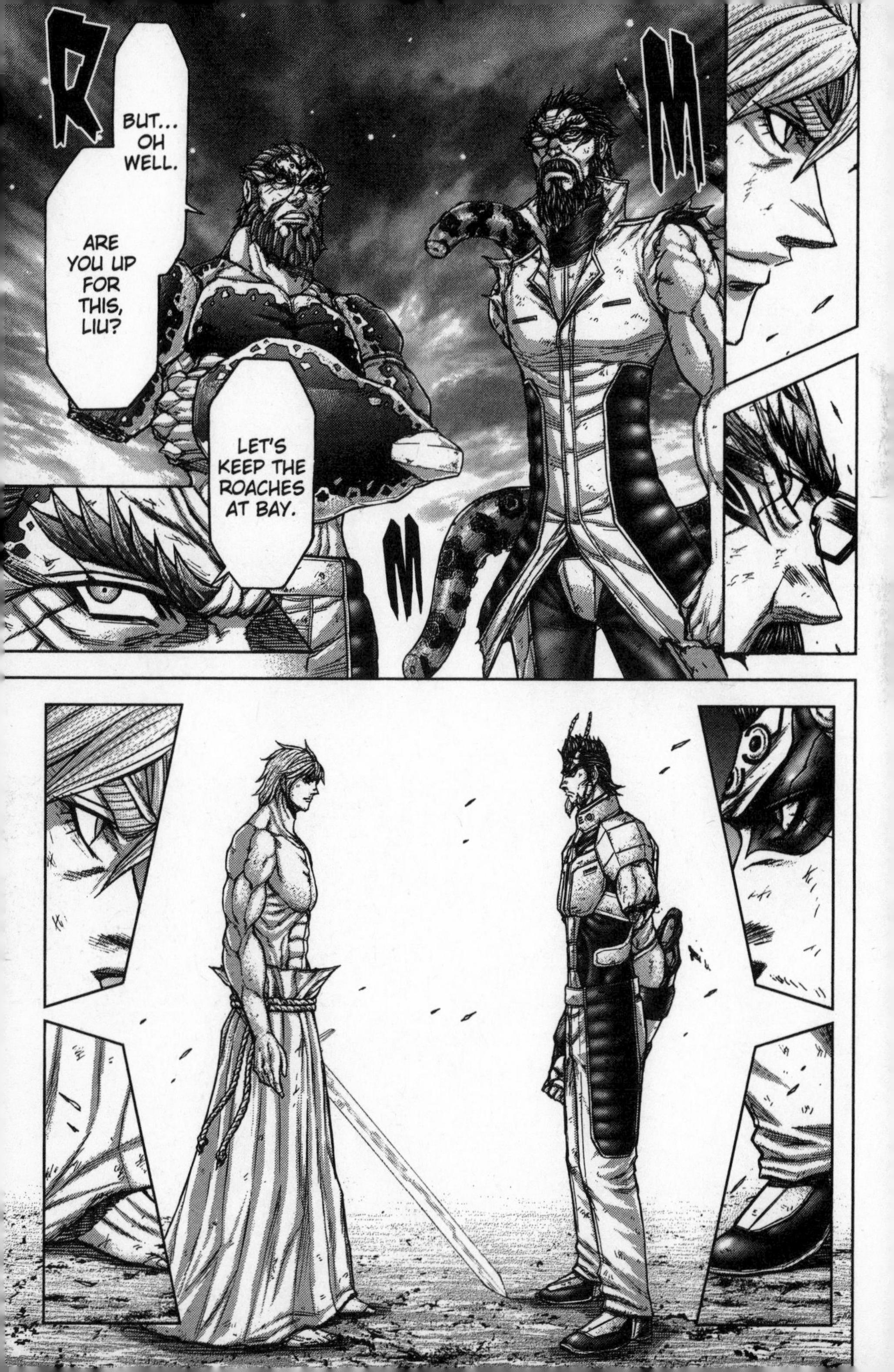
R
BUT... OH WELL.
ARE YOU UP FOR THIS, LIU?
M
LET'S KEEP THE ROACHES AT BAY.
M

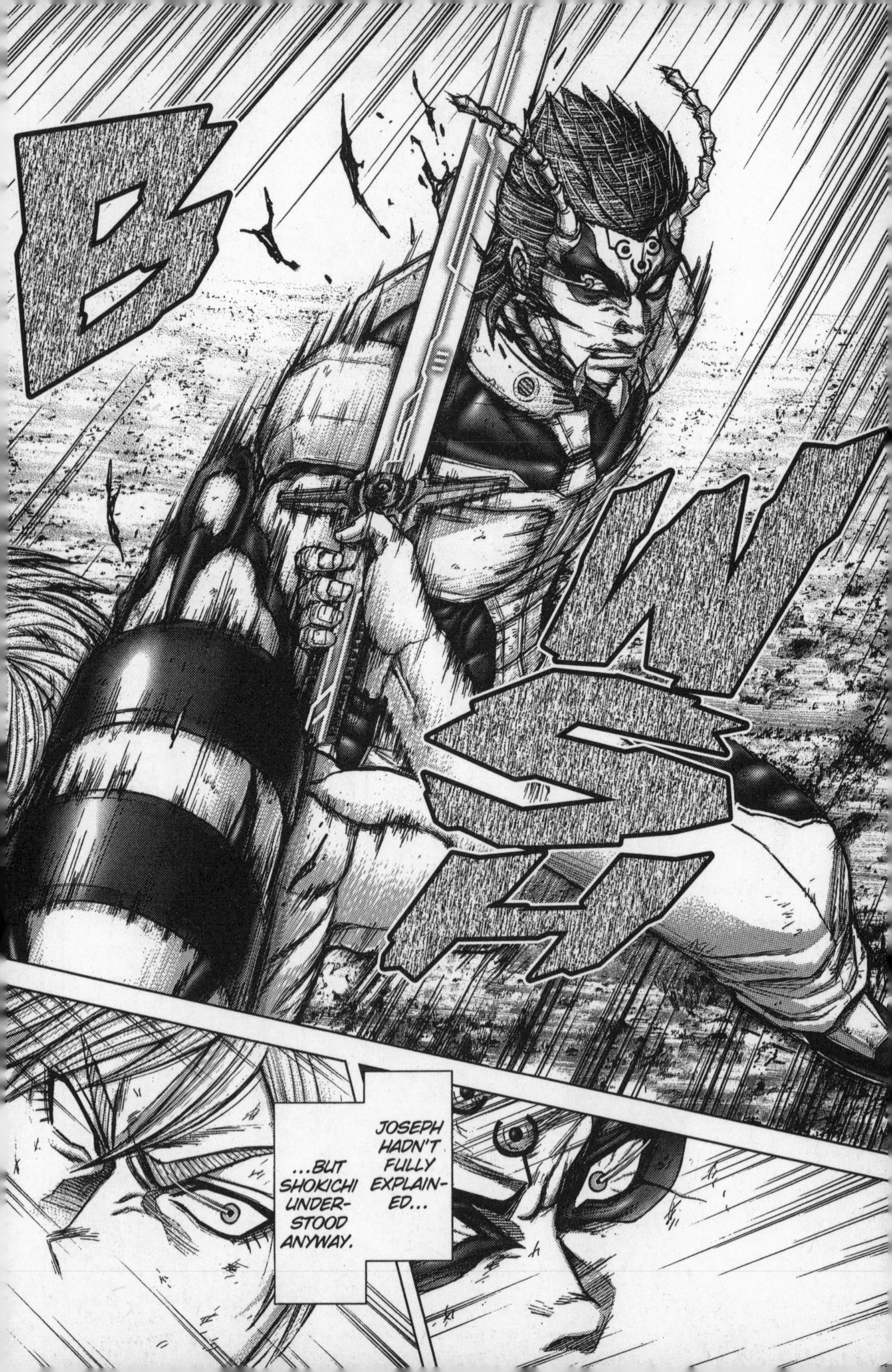
JOSEPH HADN'T FULLY EXPLAINED...
...BUT SHOKICHI UNDERSTOOD ANYWAY.

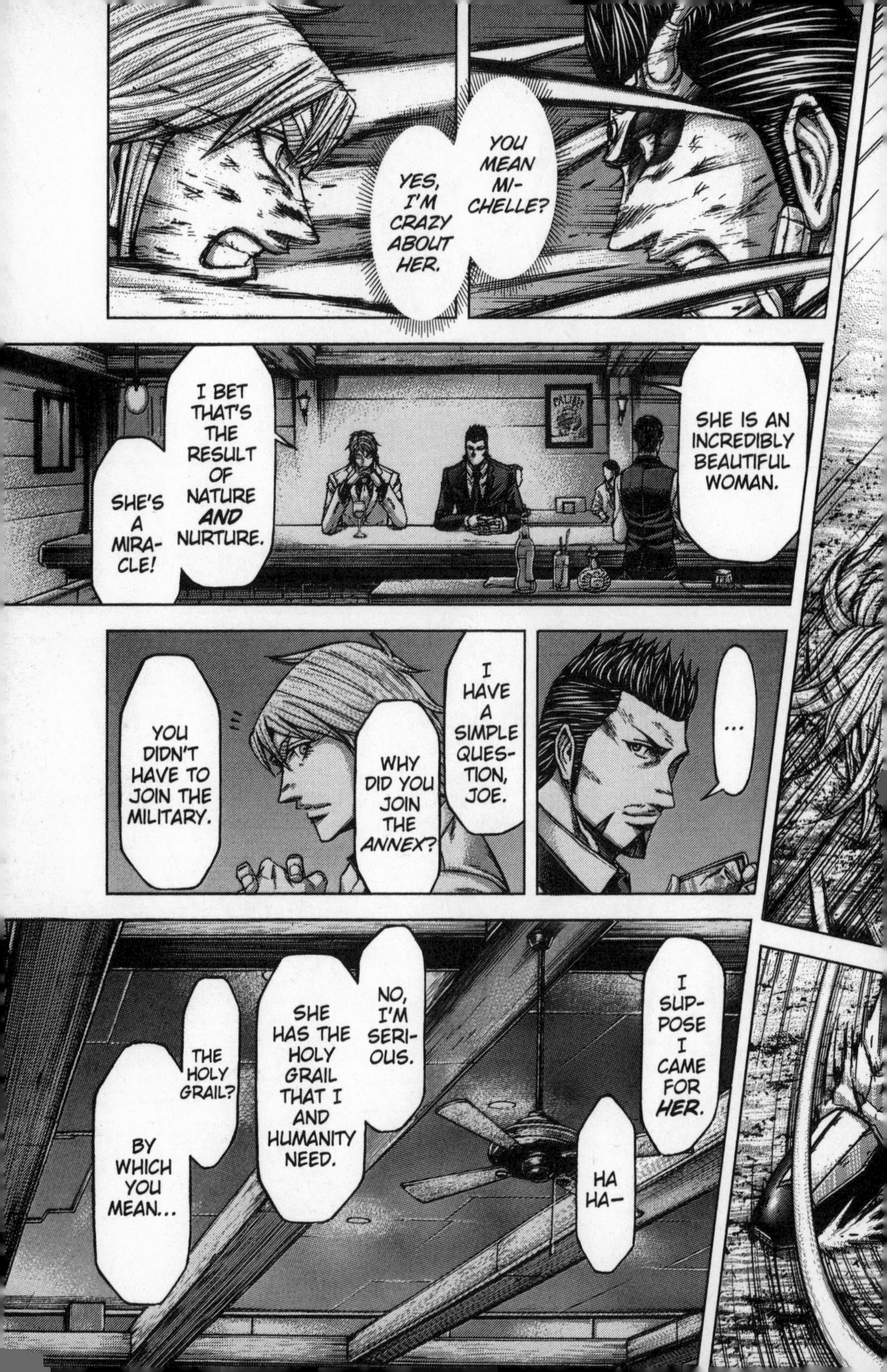
YOU MEAN MI-CHELLE?
YES, I'M CRAZY ABOUT HER.
SHE IS AN INCREDIBLY BEAUTIFUL WOMAN.
I BET THAT'S THE RESULT OF NATURE *AND* NURTURE.
SHE'S A MIRA-CLE!
...
I HAVE A SIMPLE QUES-TION, JOE.
WHY DID YOU JOIN THE *ANNEX*?
YOU DIDN'T HAVE TO JOIN THE MILITARY.
I SUP-POSE I CAME FOR *HER*.
HA HA-
NO, I'M SERI-OUS.
SHE HAS THE HOLY GRAIL THAT I AND HUMANITY NEED.
THE HOLY GRAIL?
BY WHICH YOU MEAN...

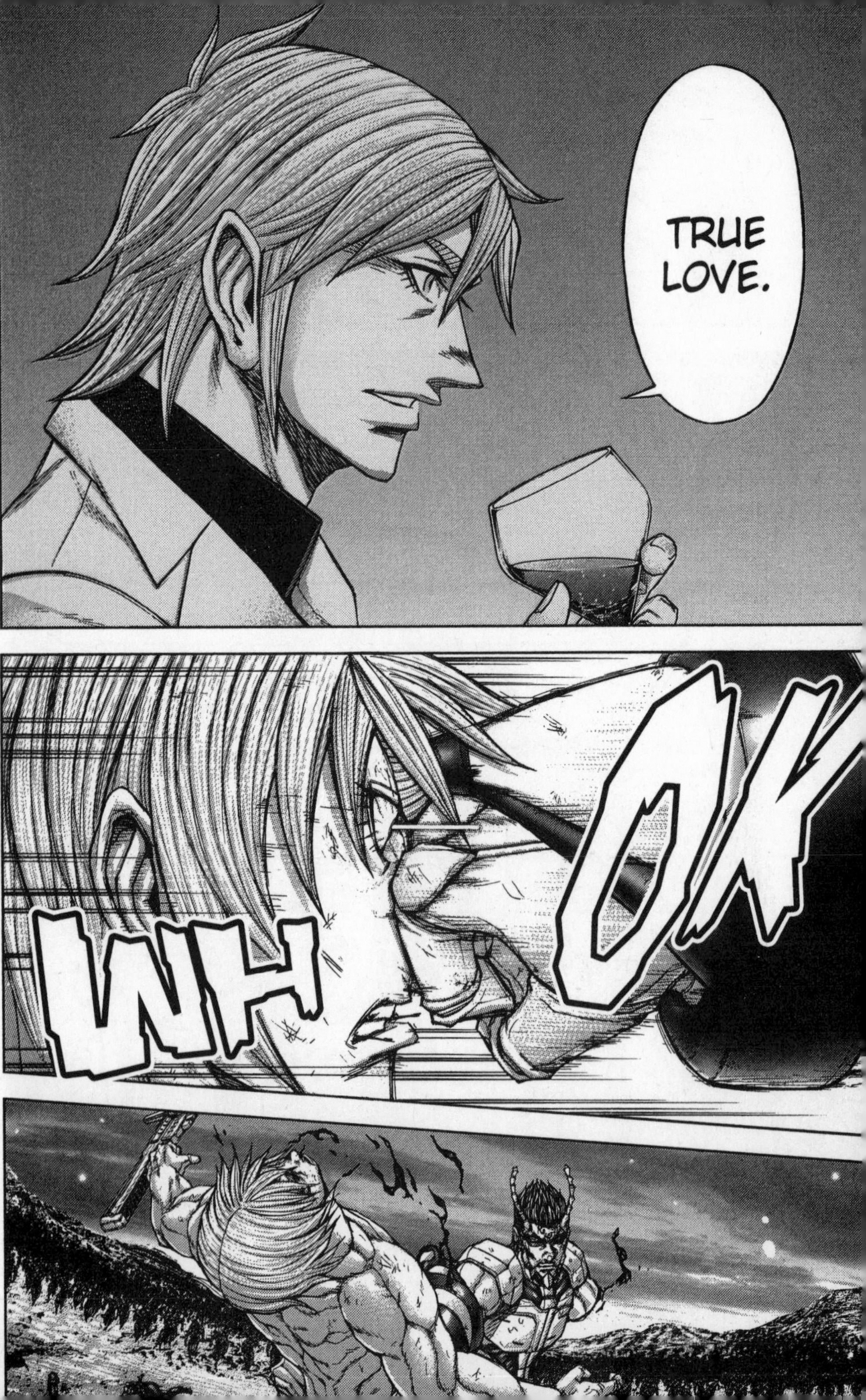
TRUE LOVE.
WH
OK

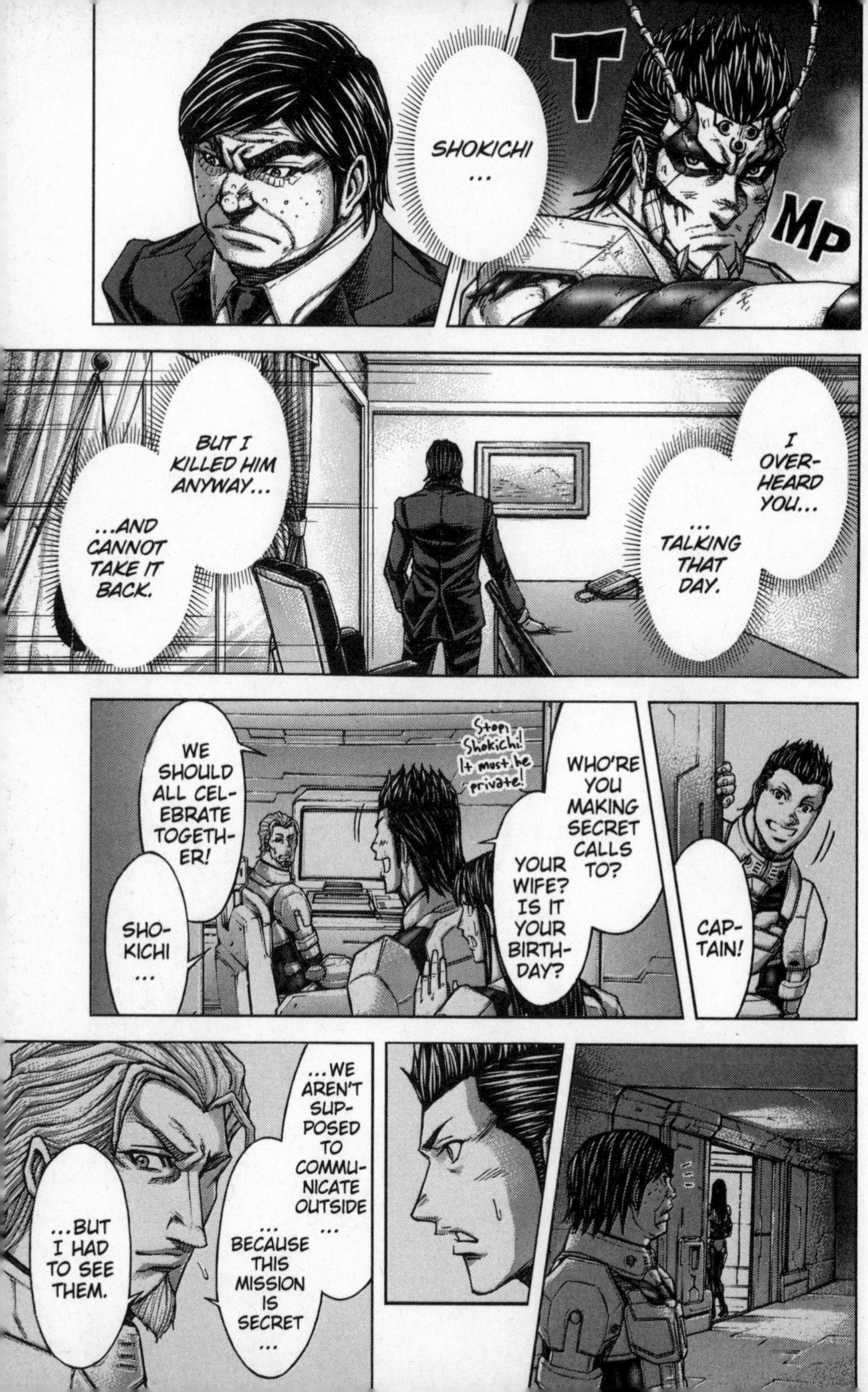

T
SHOKICHI ...
MP
I OVERHEARD YOU...
... TALKING THAT DAY.
BUT I KILLED HIM ANYWAY...
...AND CANNOT TAKE IT BACK.
CAPTAIN!
WHO'RE YOU MAKING SECRET CALLS TO?
YOUR WIFE? IS IT YOUR BIRTHDAY?
Stop! Shokichi! It must be private!
WE SHOULD ALL CELEBRATE TOGETHER!
SHOKICHI ...
...WE AREN'T SUPPOSED TO COMMUNICATE OUTSIDE ...
... BECAUSE THIS MISSION IS SECRET ...
...BUT I HAD TO SEE THEM.

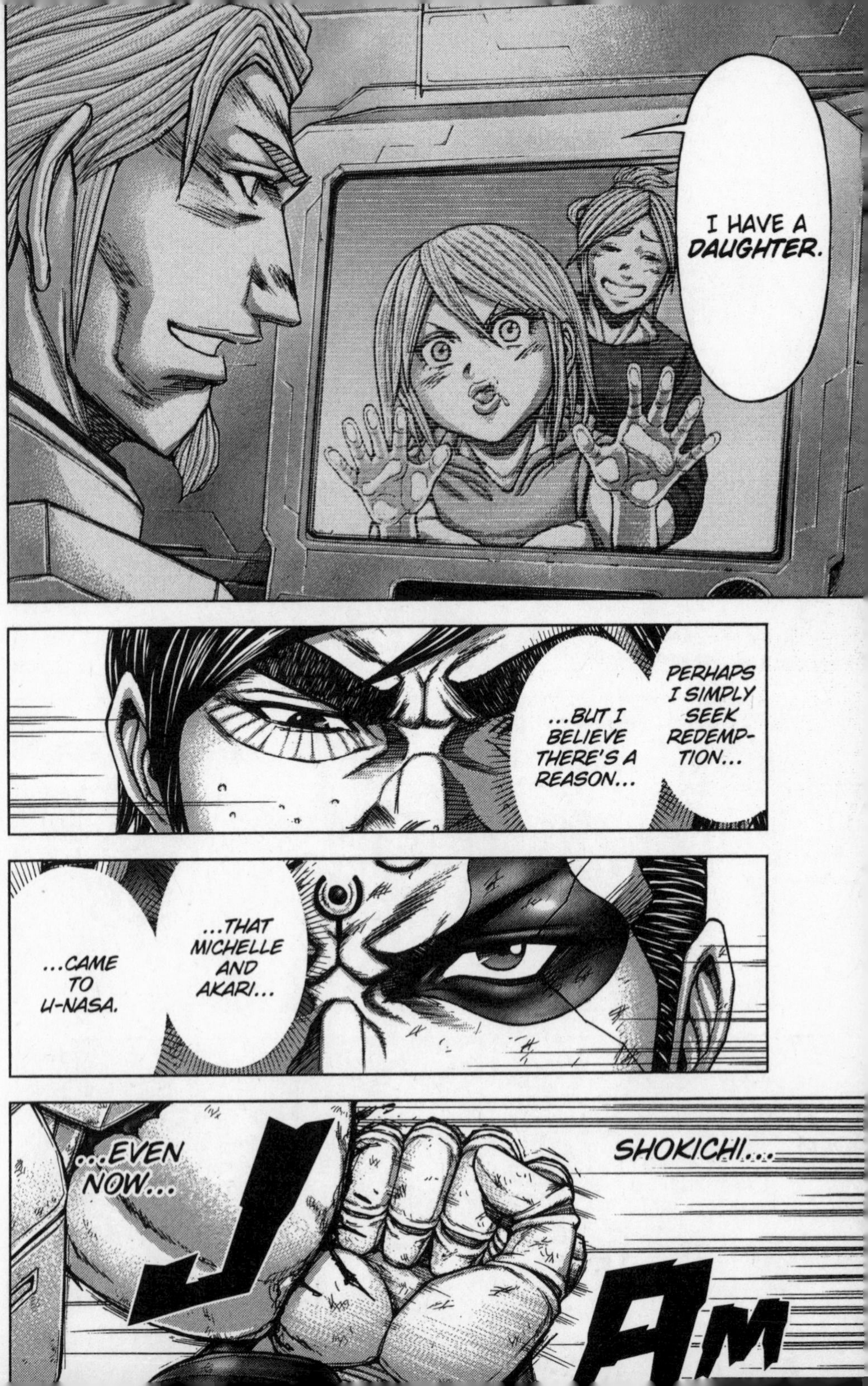
I HAVE A DAUGHTER.
PERHAPS I SIMPLY SEEK REDEMPTION...
...BUT I BELIEVE THERE'S A REASON...
...THAT MICHELLE AND AKARI...
...CAME TO U-NASA.
SHOKICHI...
...EVEN NOW...
JAM

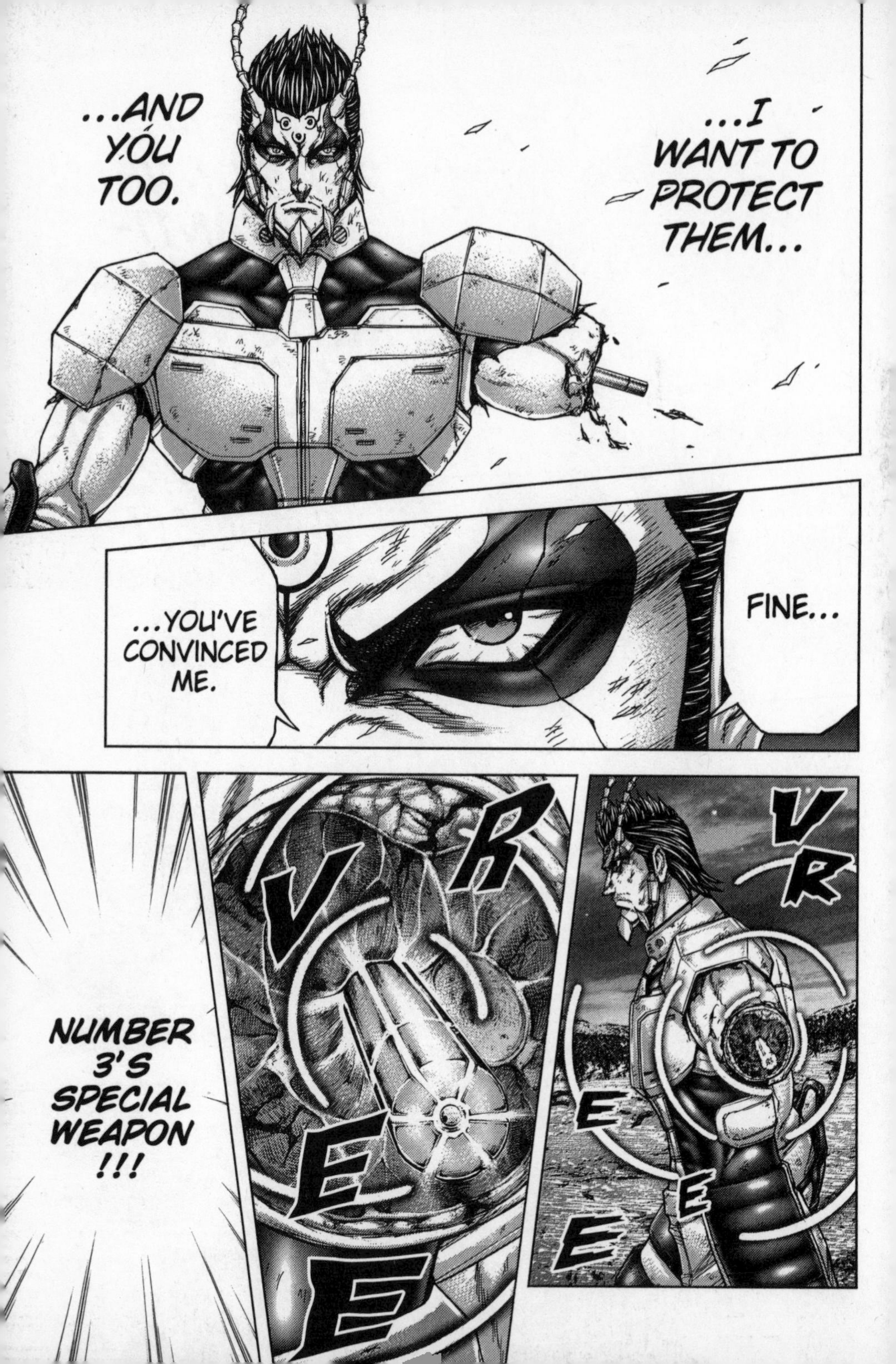
...I WANT TO PROTECT THEM...
...AND YOU TOO.
FINE...
...YOU'VE CONVINCED ME.
VREEE
VREE
NUMBER 3'S SPECIAL WEAPON!!!

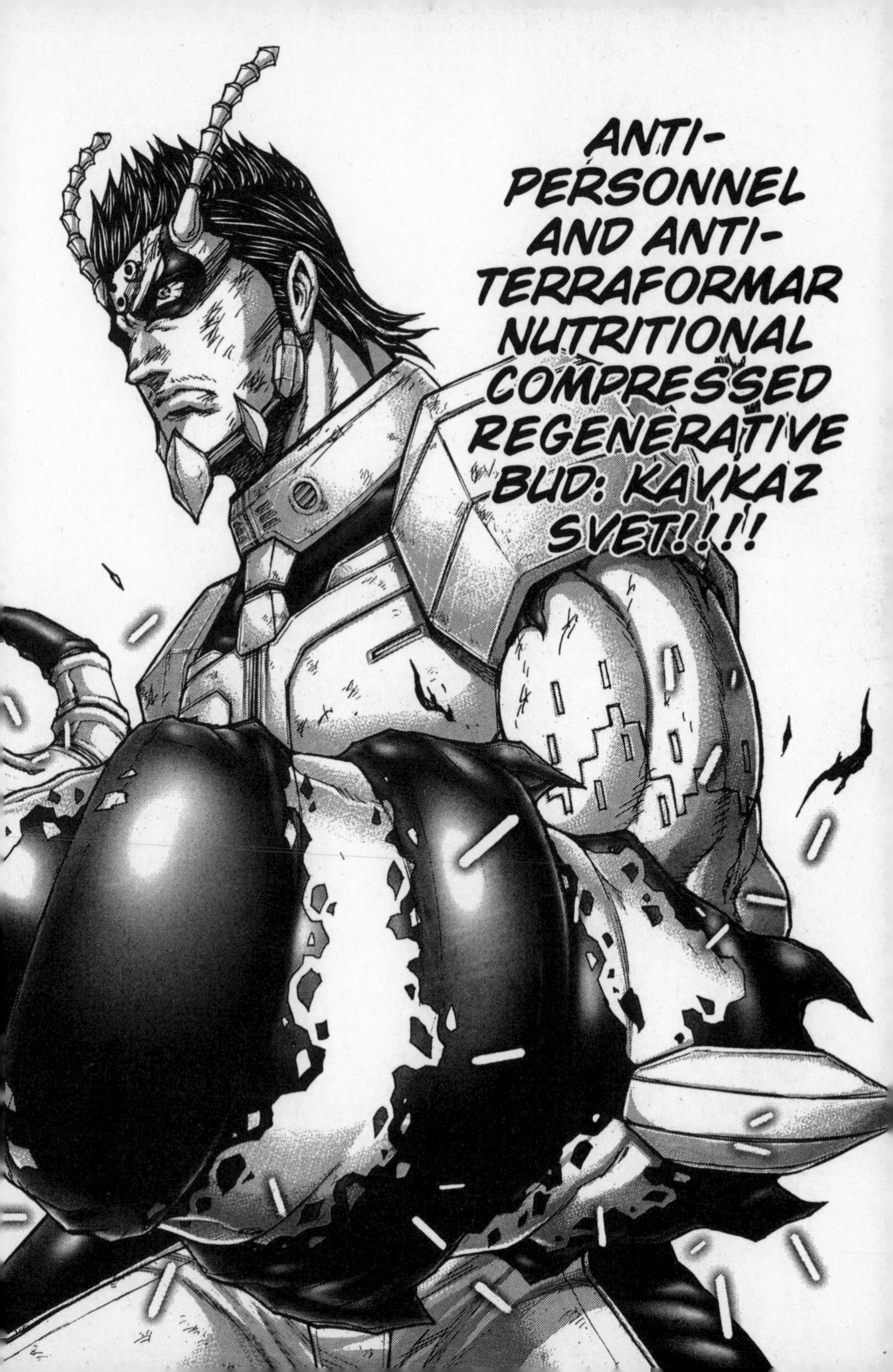
ANTI-PERSONNEL AND ANTI-TERRAFORMAR NUTRITIONAL COMPRESSED REGENERATIVE BUD: KAVKAZ SVET!!!!

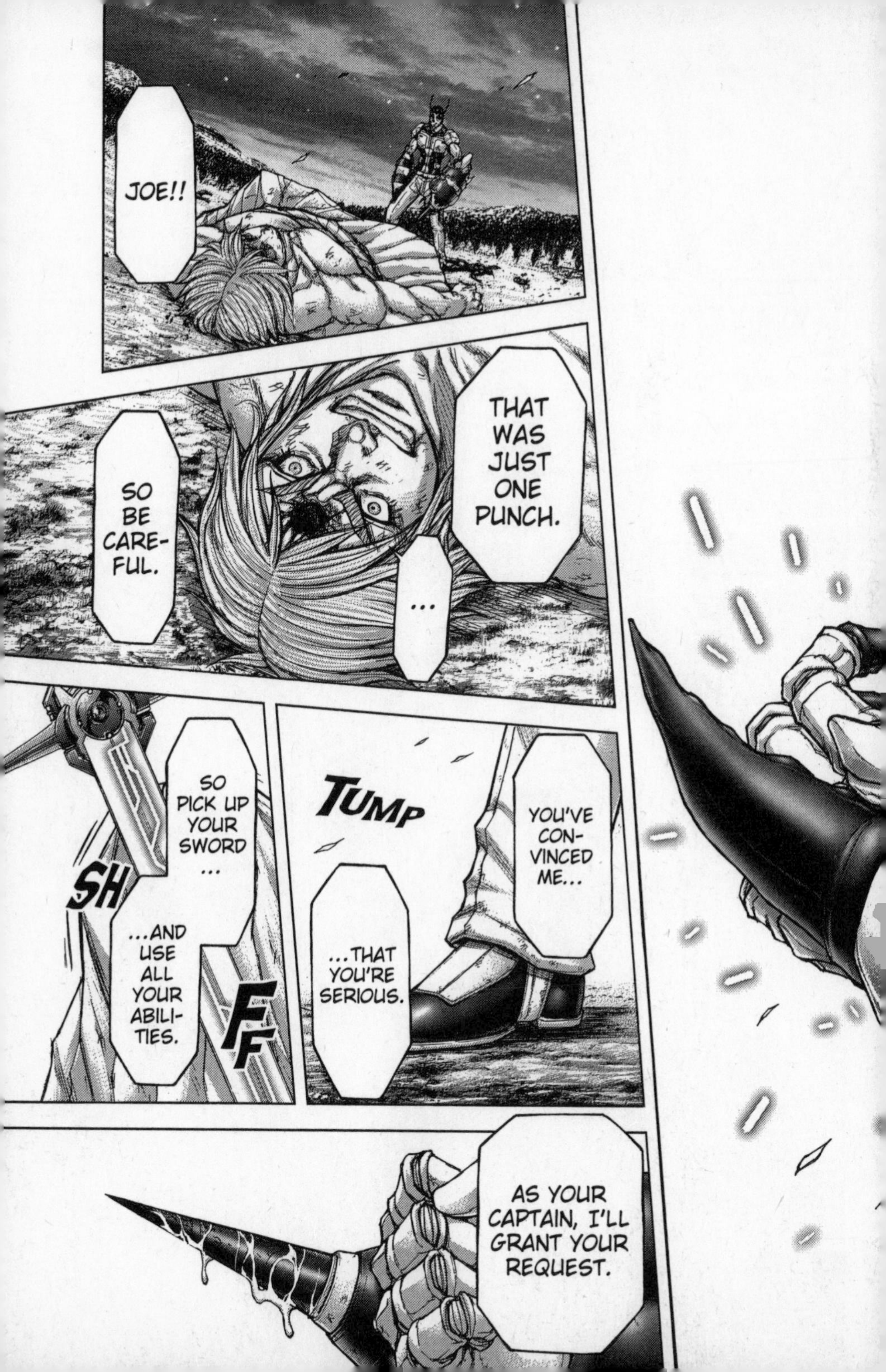
JOE!!
THAT WAS JUST ONE PUNCH.
...
SO BE CARE-FUL.
YOU'VE CON-VINCED ME...
TUMP
...THAT YOU'RE SERIOUS.
SO PICK UP YOUR SWORD...
SH
FF
...AND USE ALL YOUR ABILI-TIES.
AS YOUR CAPTAIN, I'LL GRANT YOUR REQUEST.

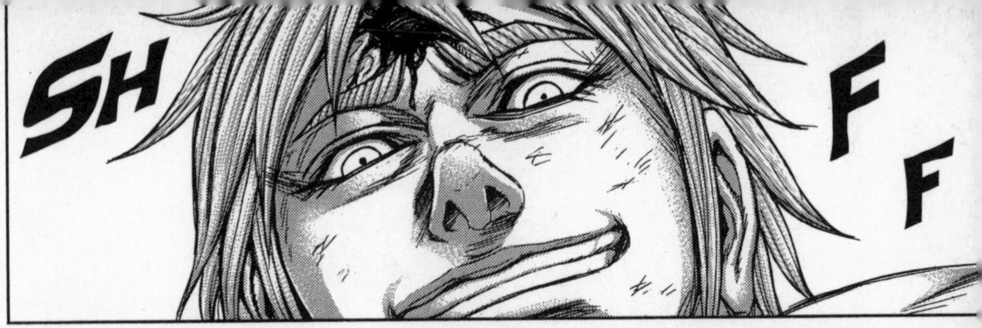
SH
F
F
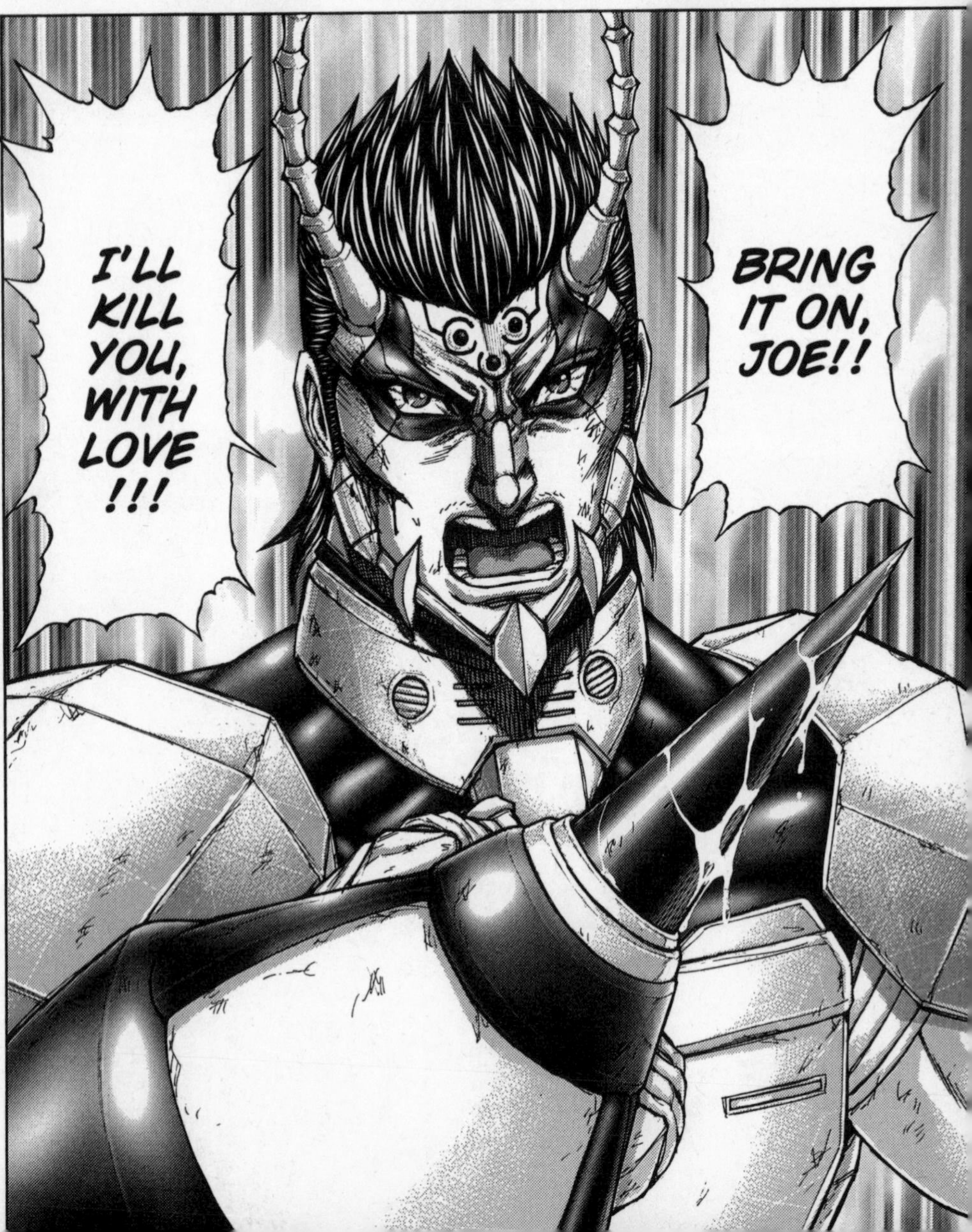
BRING IT ON, JOE!!
I'LL KILL YOU, WITH LOVE!!!

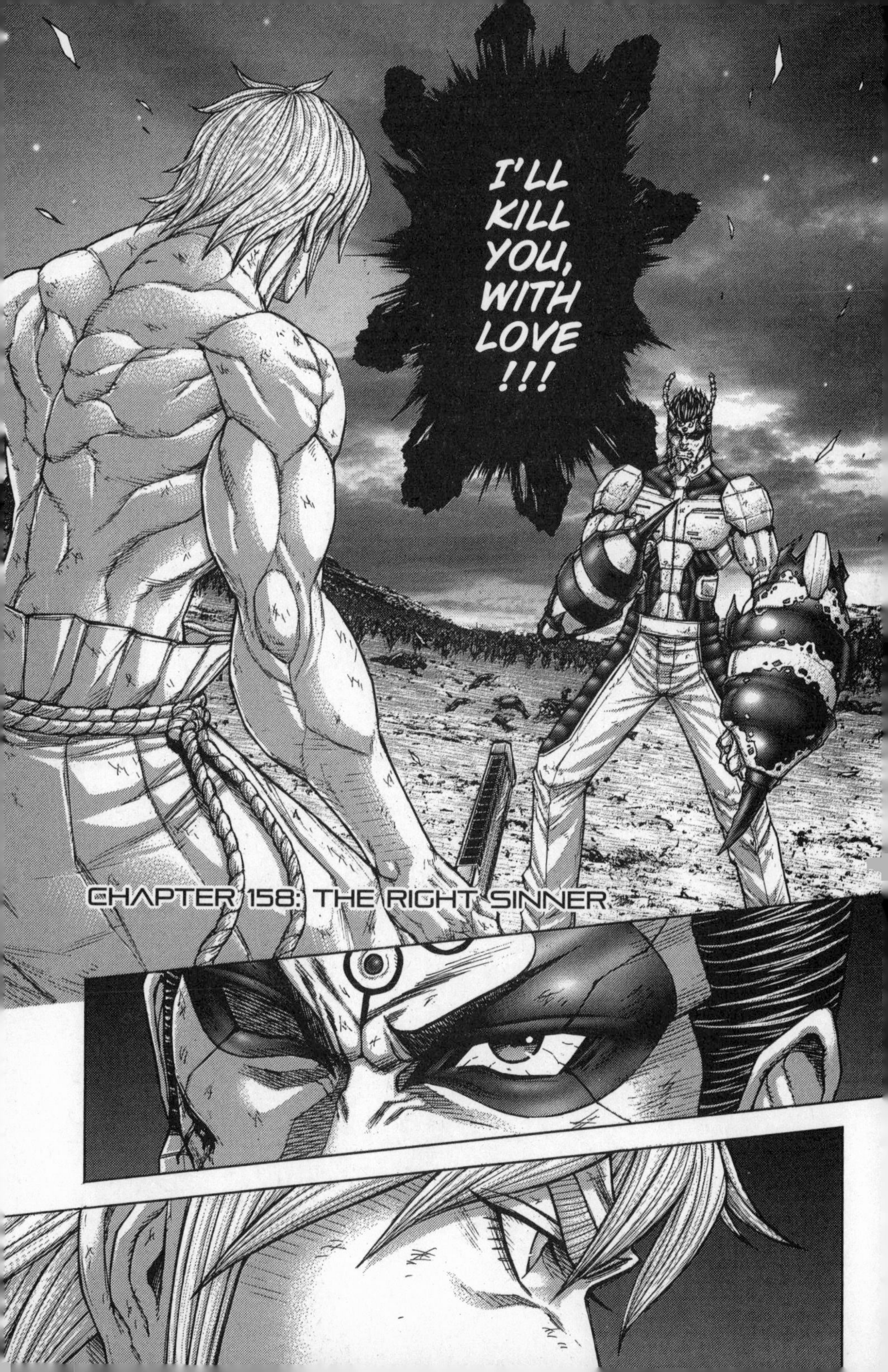
I'LL KILL YOU, WITH LOVE !!!
CHAPTER 158: THE RIGHT SINNER

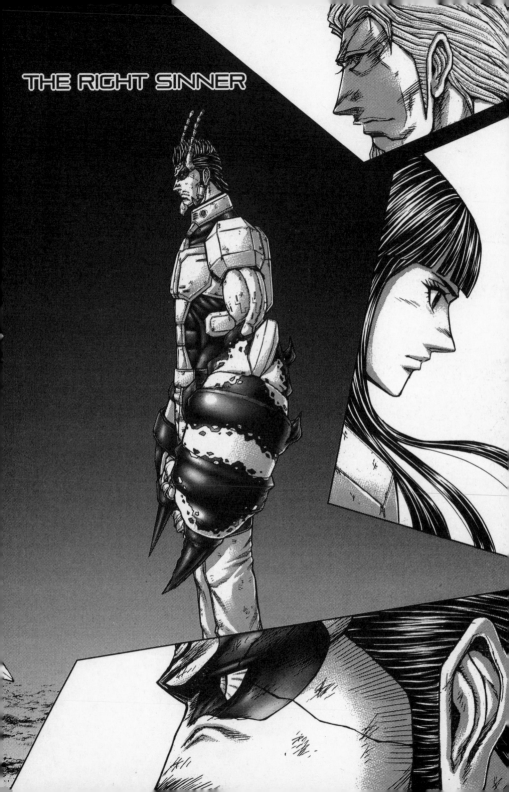

THE RIGHT SINNER

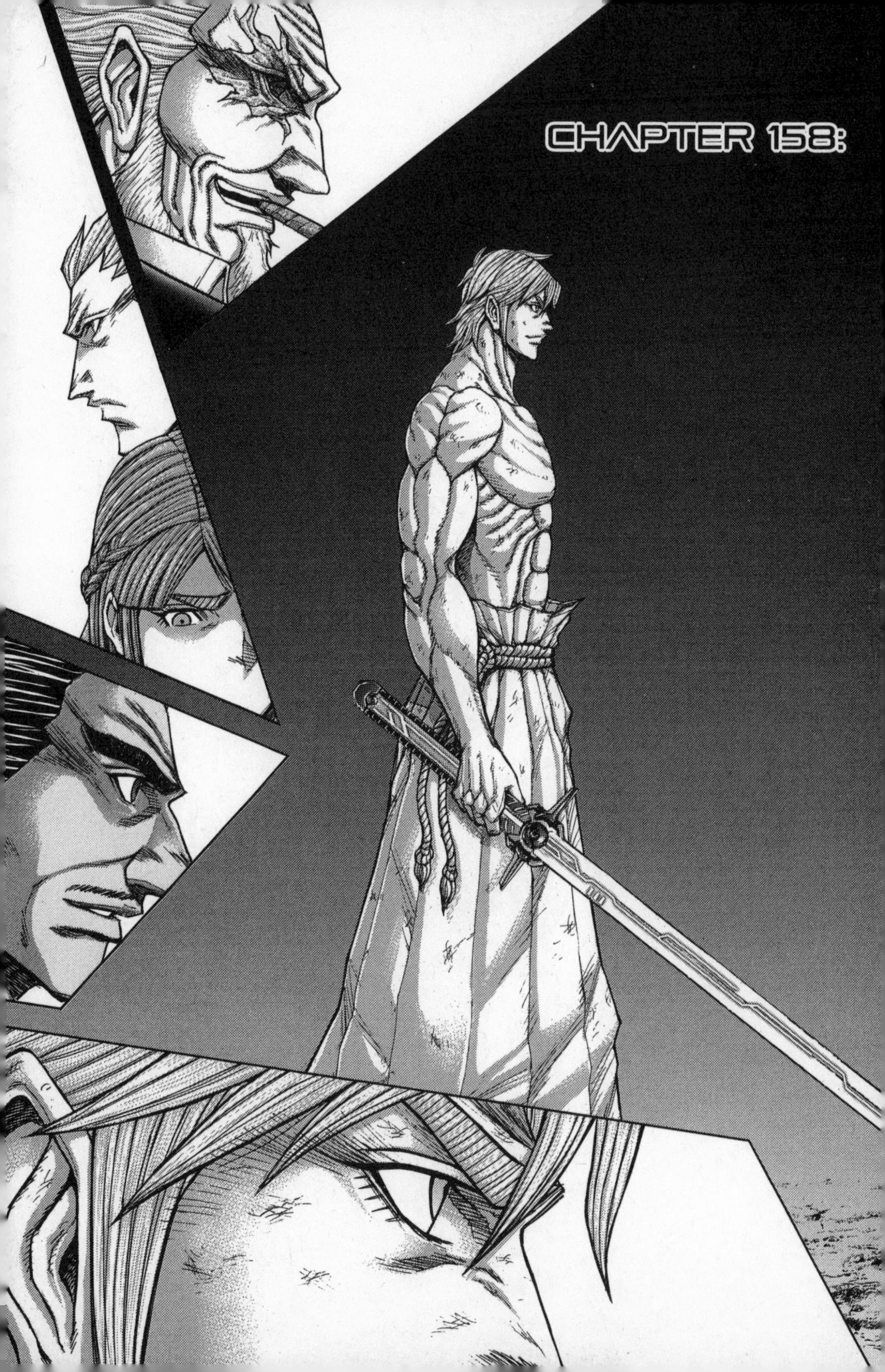
CHAPTER 158:

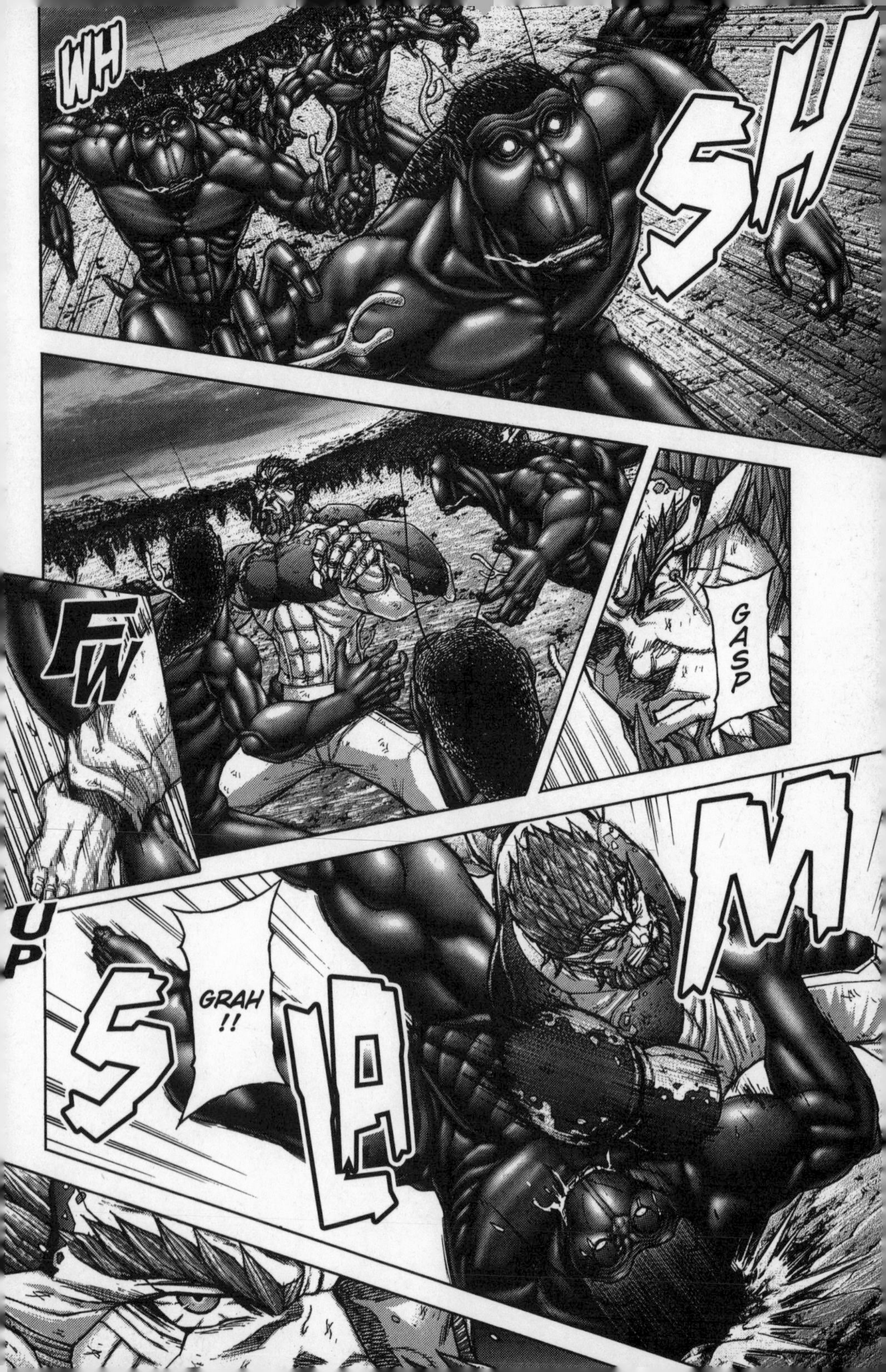
WH
SH
GASP
FW
UP
M
GRAH !!
S
LA

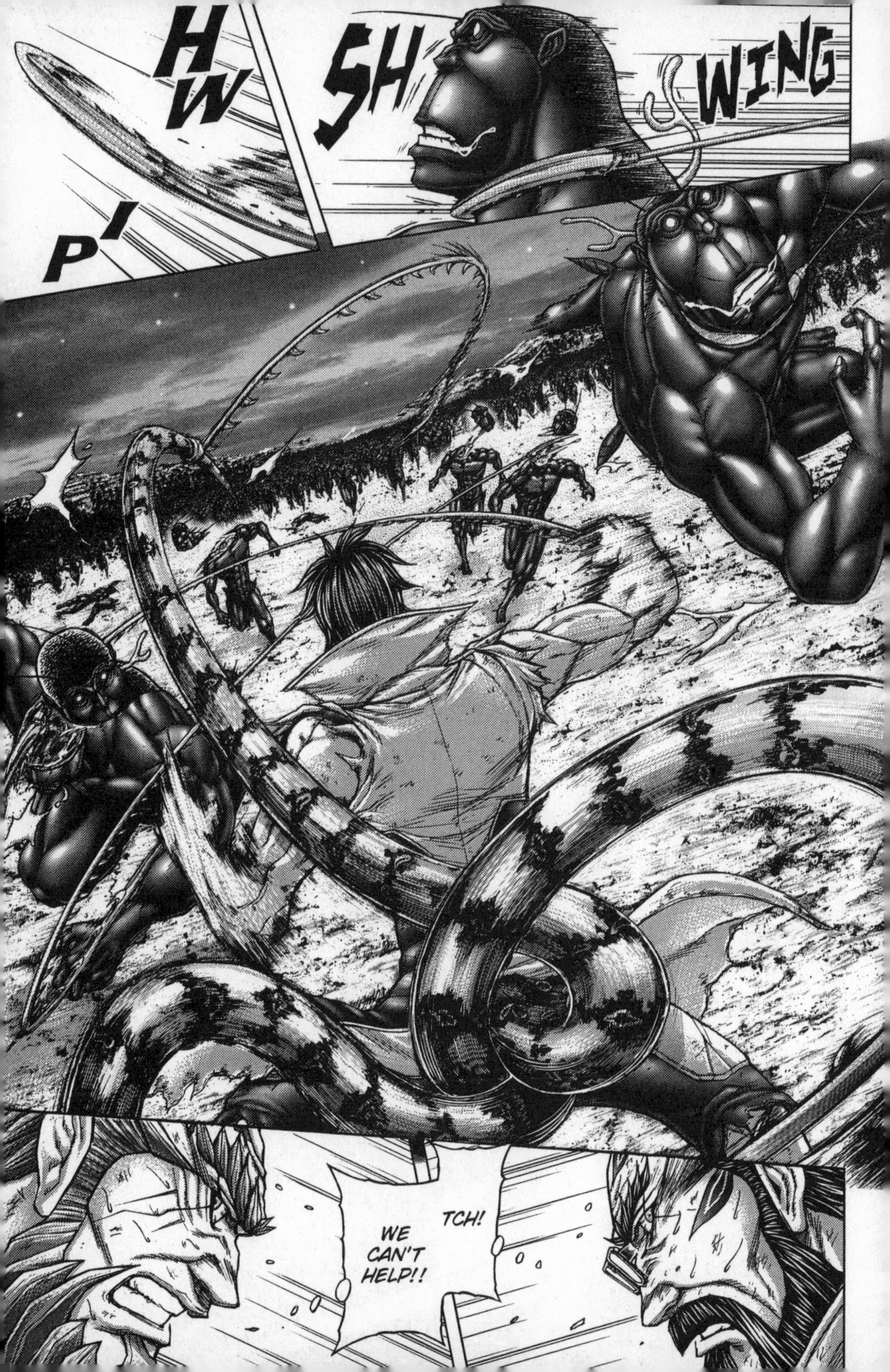
SHWING
HWIP
TCH!
WE CAN'T HELP!!

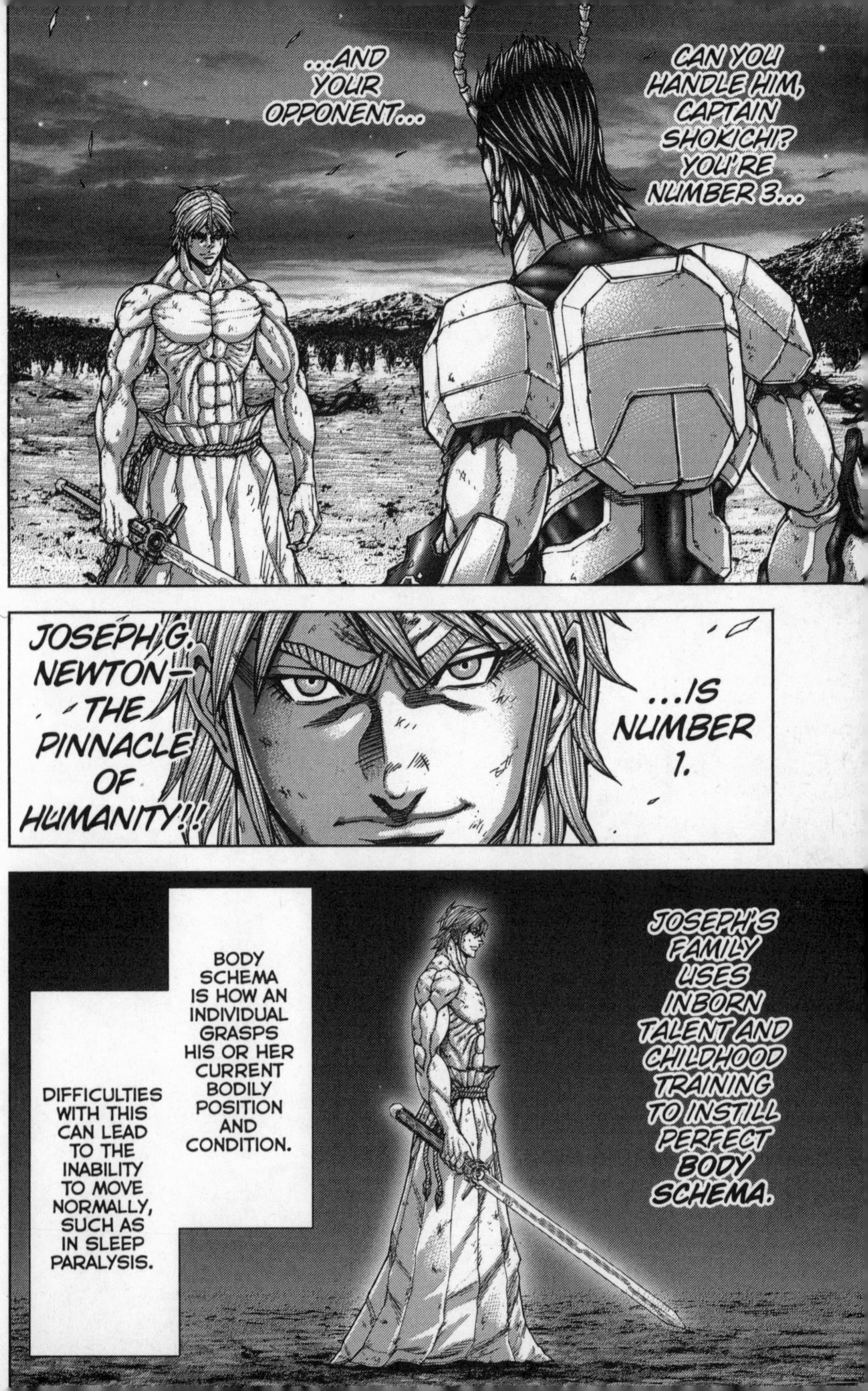
CAN YOU HANDLE HIM, CAPTAIN SHOKICHI? YOU'RE NUMBER 3...
...AND YOUR OPPONENT...
JOSEPH G. NEWTON—THE PINNACLE OF HUMANITY!!
...IS NUMBER 1.
JOSEPH'S FAMILY USES INBORN TALENT AND CHILDHOOD TRAINING TO INSTILL PERFECT BODY SCHEMA.
BODY SCHEMA IS HOW AN INDIVIDUAL GRASPS HIS OR HER CURRENT BODILY POSITION AND CONDITION.
DIFFICULTIES WITH THIS CAN LEAD TO THE INABILITY TO MOVE NORMALLY, SUCH AS IN SLEEP PARALYSIS.

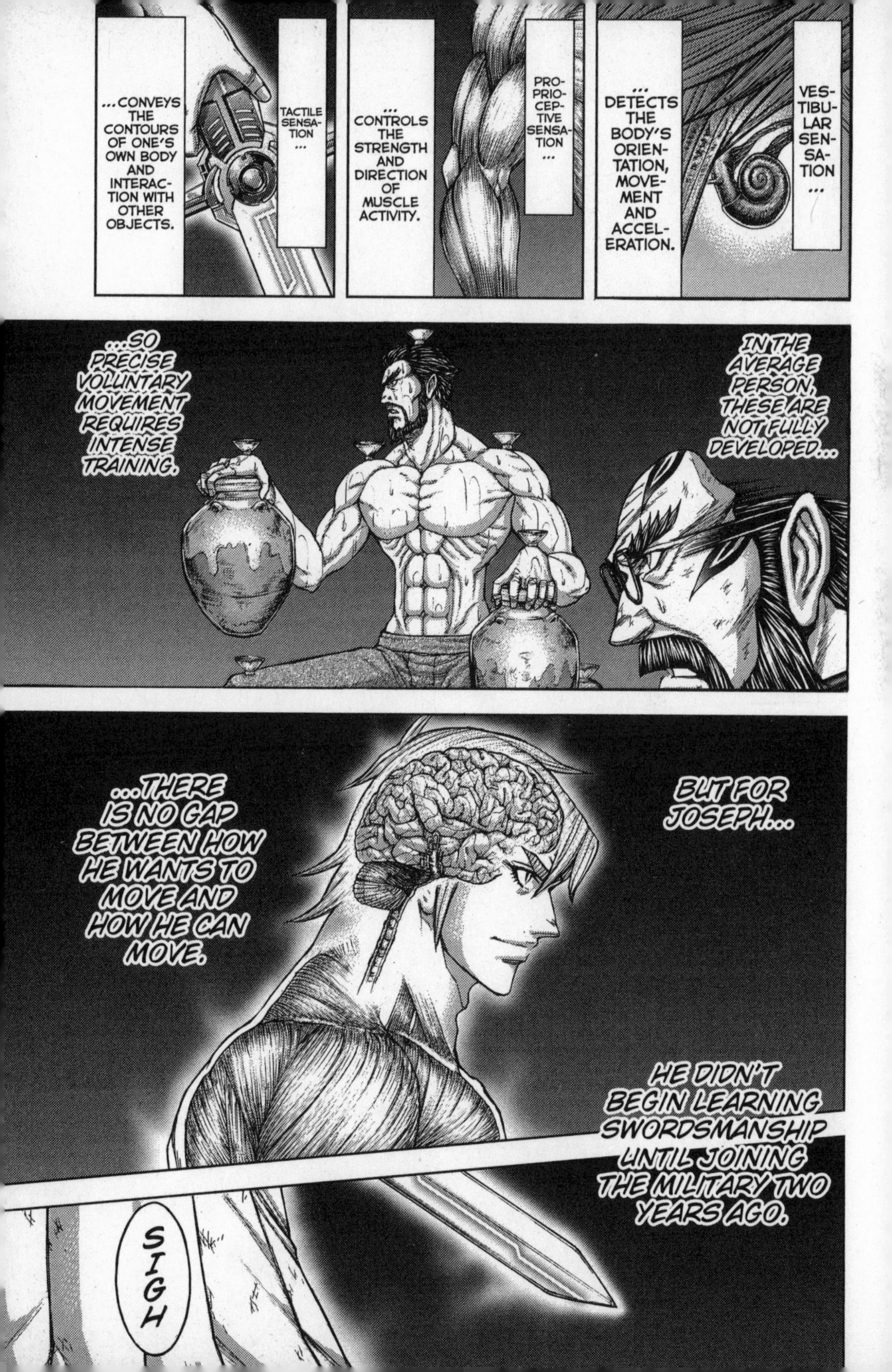
VESTIBULAR SENSATION...
...DETECTS THE BODY'S ORIENTATION, MOVEMENT AND ACCELERATION.
PROPRIOCEPTIVE SENSATION...
...CONTROLS THE STRENGTH AND DIRECTION OF MUSCLE ACTIVITY.
TACTILE SENSATION...
...CONVEYS THE CONTOURS OF ONE'S OWN BODY AND INTERACTION WITH OTHER OBJECTS.
IN THE AVERAGE PERSON, THESE ARE NOT FULLY DEVELOPED...
...SO PRECISE VOLUNTARY MOVEMENT REQUIRES INTENSE TRAINING.
BUT FOR JOSEPH...
...THERE IS NO GAP BETWEEN HOW HE WANTS TO MOVE AND HOW HE CAN MOVE.
HE DIDN'T BEGIN LEARNING SWORDSMANSHIP UNTIL JOINING THE MILITARY TWO YEARS AGO.
SIGH

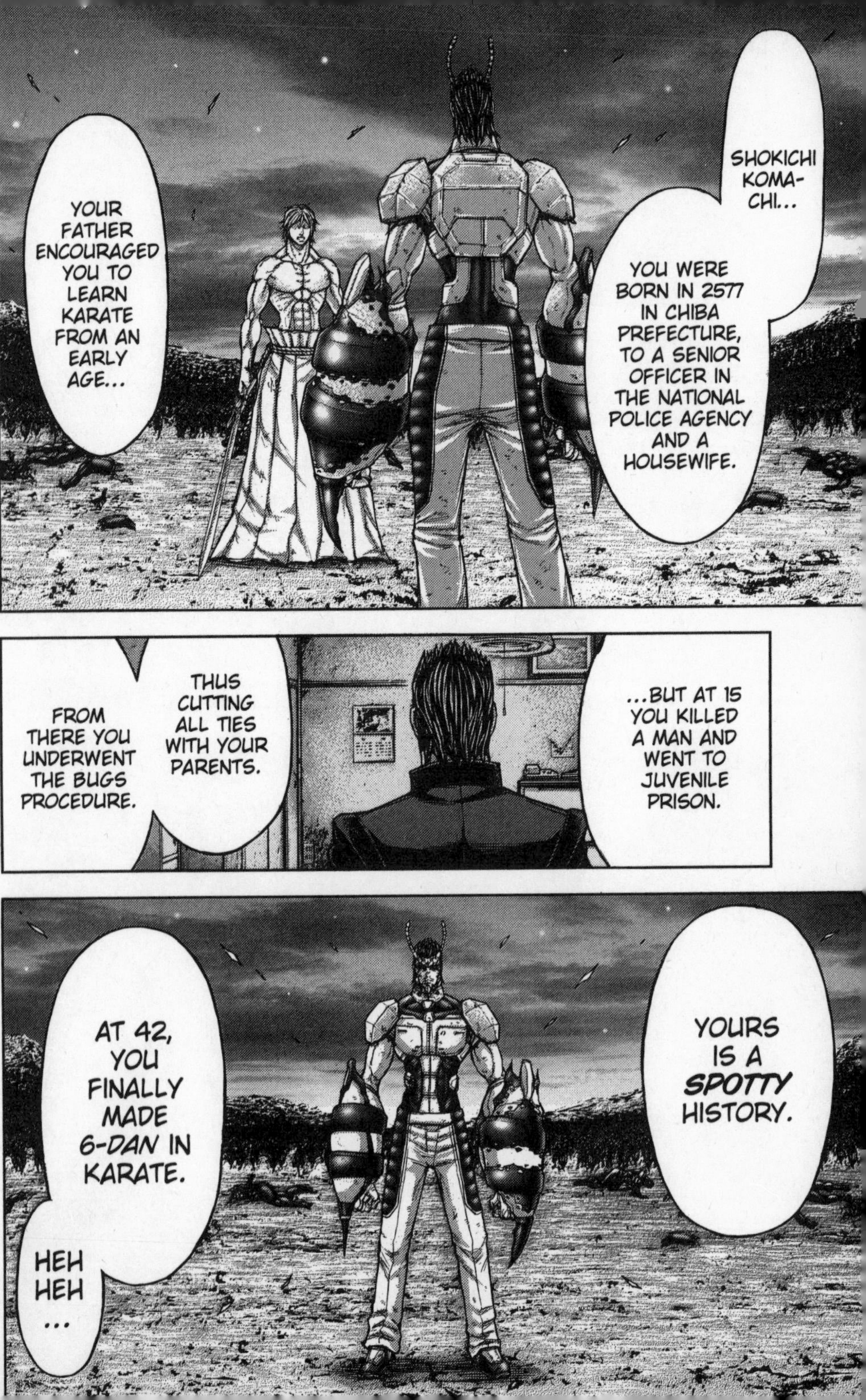
SHOKICHI KOMACHI... YOU WERE BORN IN 2577 IN CHIBA PREFECTURE, TO A SENIOR OFFICER IN THE NATIONAL POLICE AGENCY AND A HOUSEWIFE.
YOUR FATHER ENCOURAGED YOU TO LEARN KARATE FROM AN EARLY AGE...
...BUT AT 15 YOU KILLED A MAN AND WENT TO JUVENILE PRISON.
FROM THERE YOU UNDERWENT THE BUGS PROCEDURE.
THUS CUTTING ALL TIES WITH YOUR PARENTS.
YOURS IS A *SPOTTY* HISTORY.
AT 42, YOU FINALLY MADE 6-*DAN* IN KARATE.
HEH HEH ...

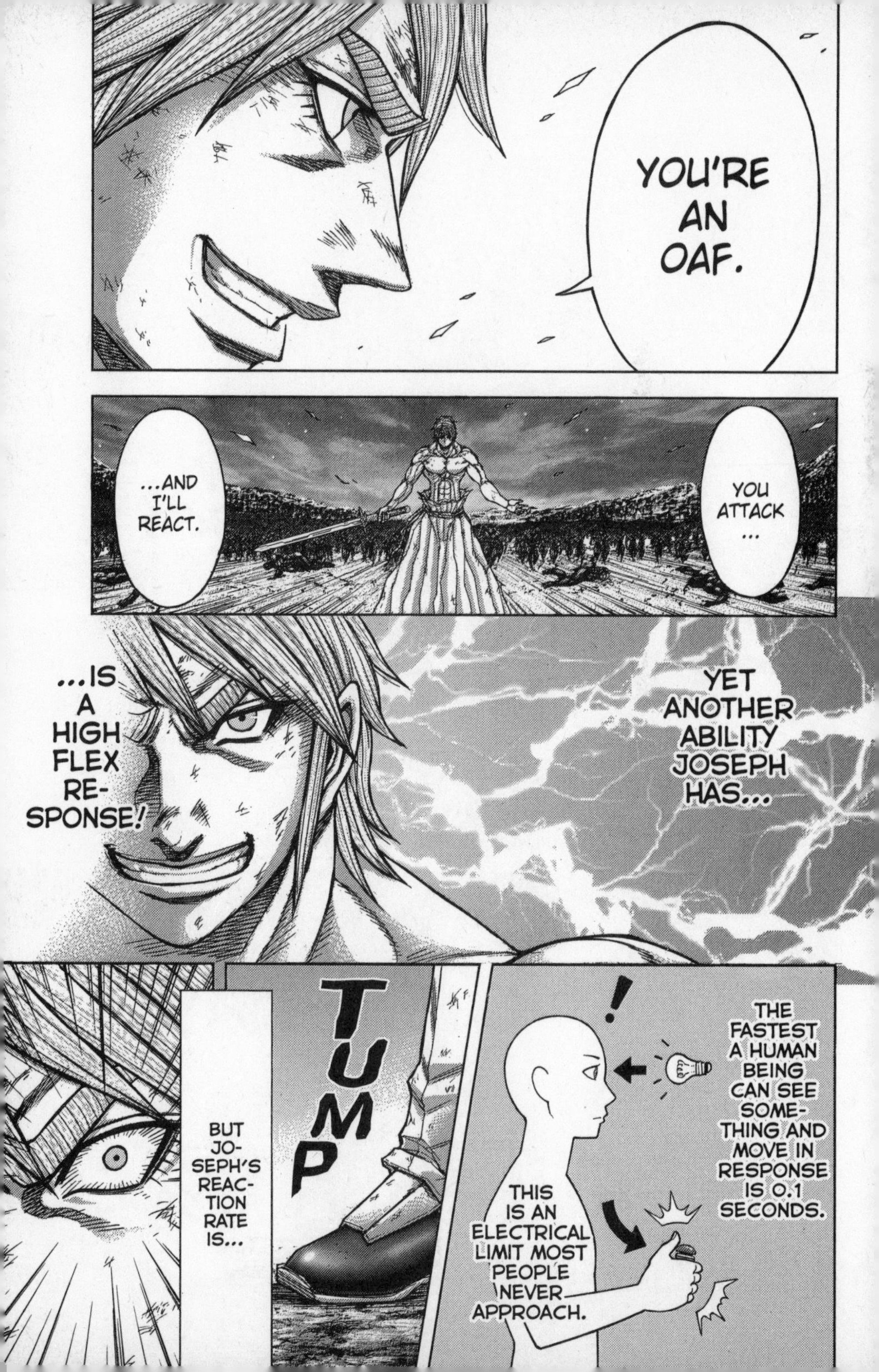
YOU'RE AN OAF.
YOU ATTACK ...
...AND I'LL REACT.
YET ANOTHER ABILITY JOSEPH HAS...
...IS A HIGH FLEX RE-SPONSE!
!
THE FASTEST A HUMAN BEING CAN SEE SOME-THING AND MOVE IN RESPONSE IS 0.1 SECONDS.
THIS IS AN ELECTRICAL LIMIT MOST PEOPLE NEVER APPROACH.
TUMP
BUT JO-SEPH'S REAC-TION RATE IS...

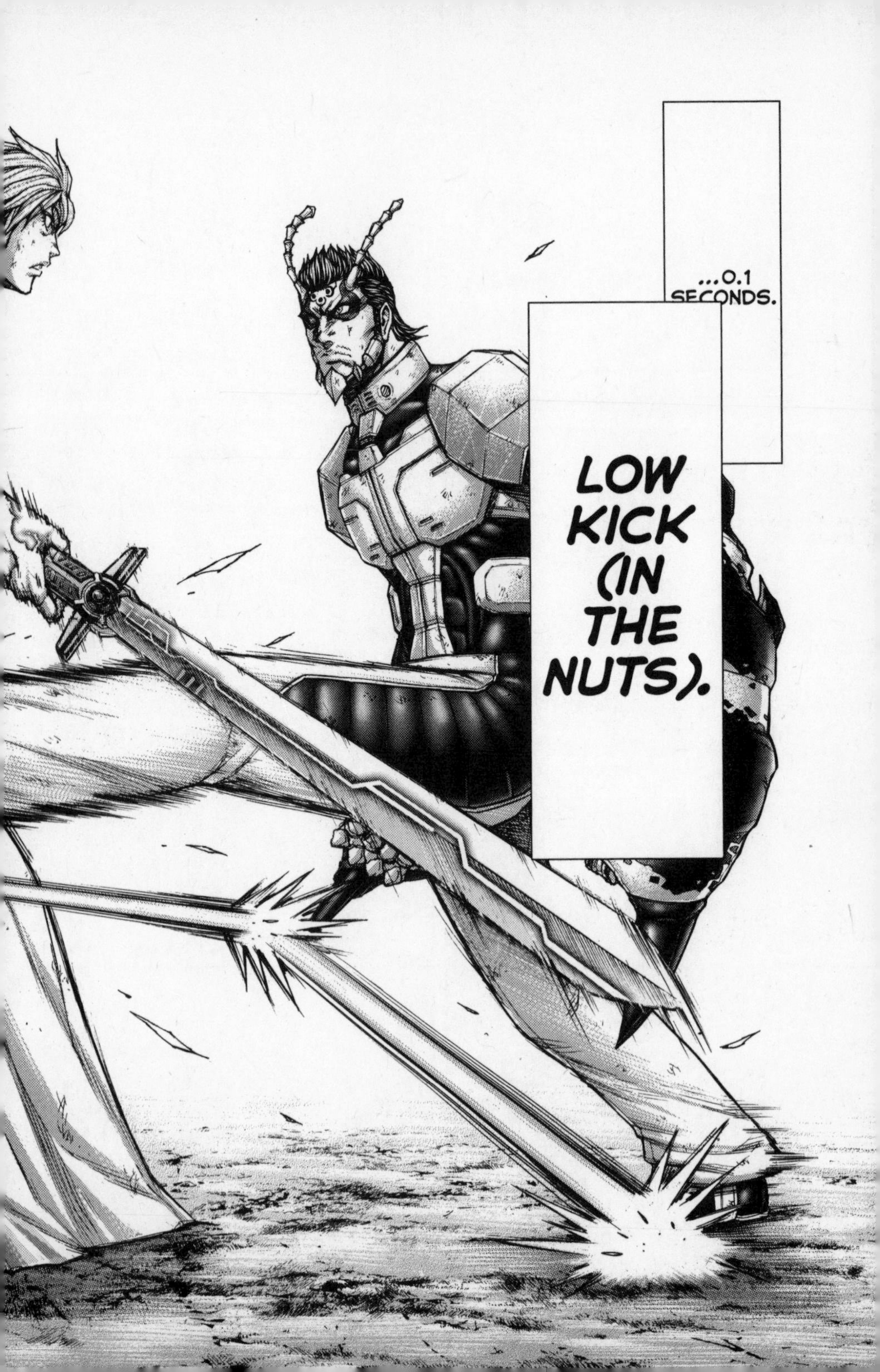
...0.1 SECONDS.
LOW KICK (IN THE NUTS).

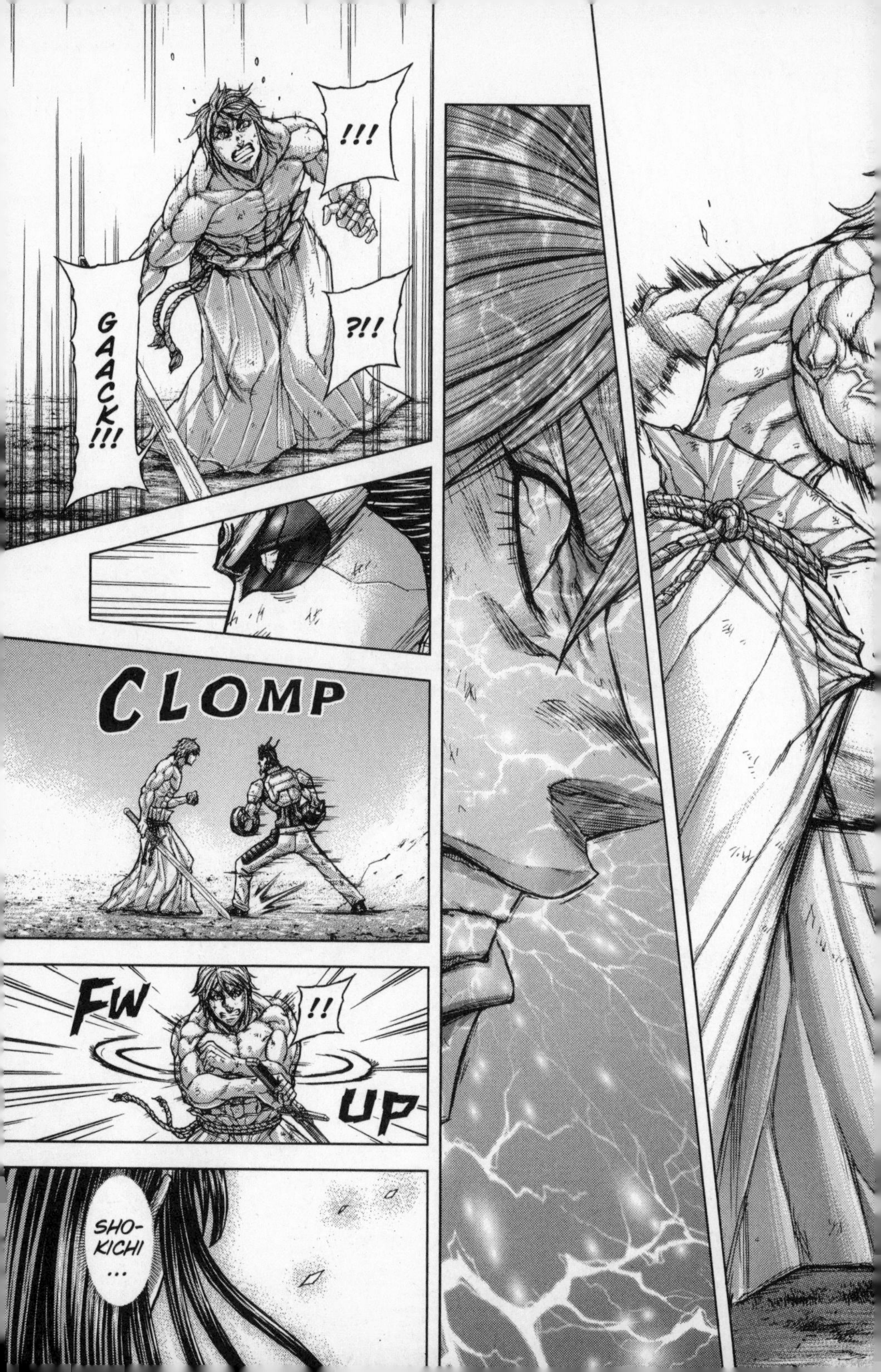
!!!
?!!
GAACK!!!
CLOMP
FW UP
!!
SHO-KICHI ...

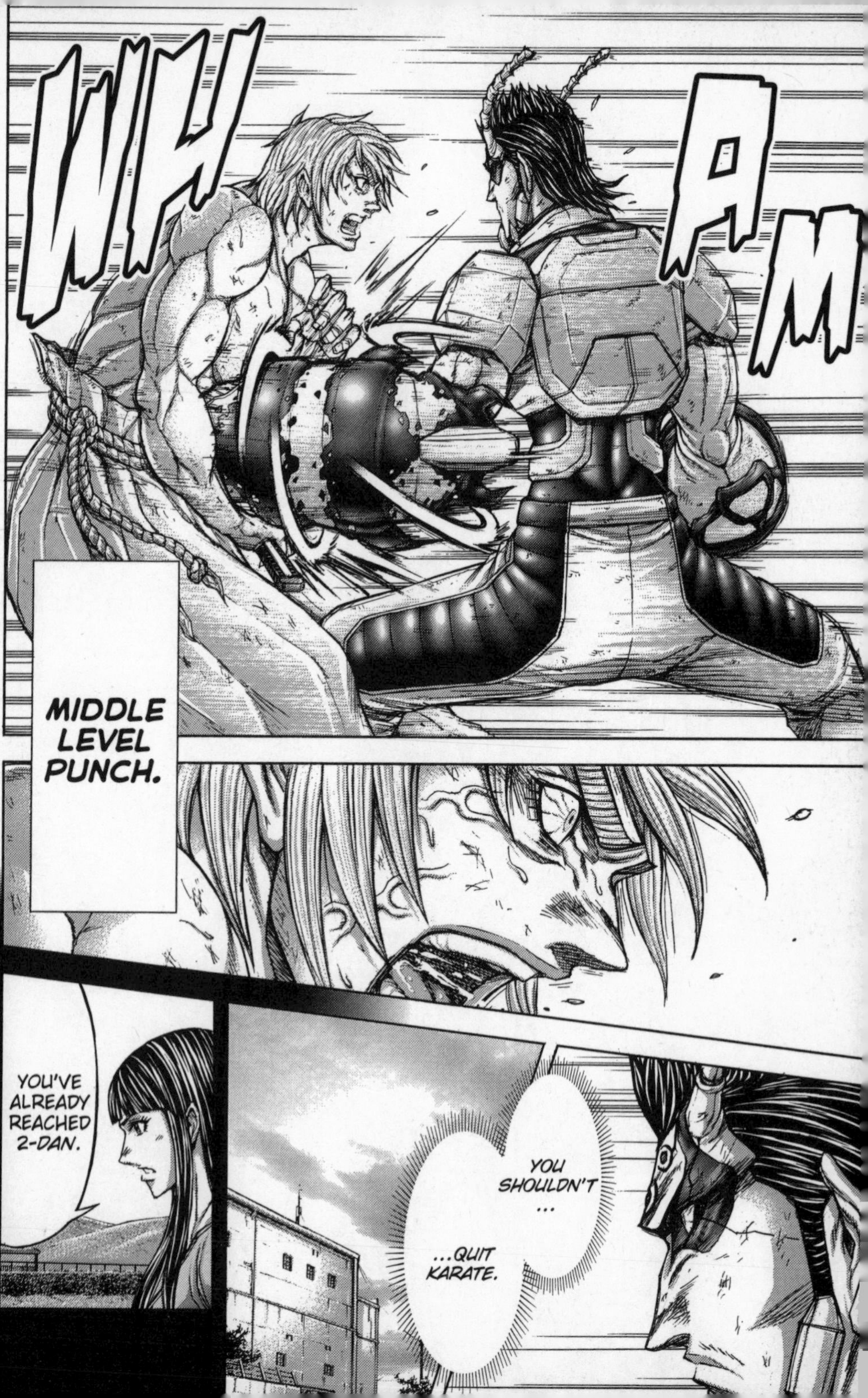
WHAM
MIDDLE LEVEL PUNCH.
YOU SHOULDN'T...
...QUIT KARATE.
YOU'VE ALREADY REACHED 2-DAN.

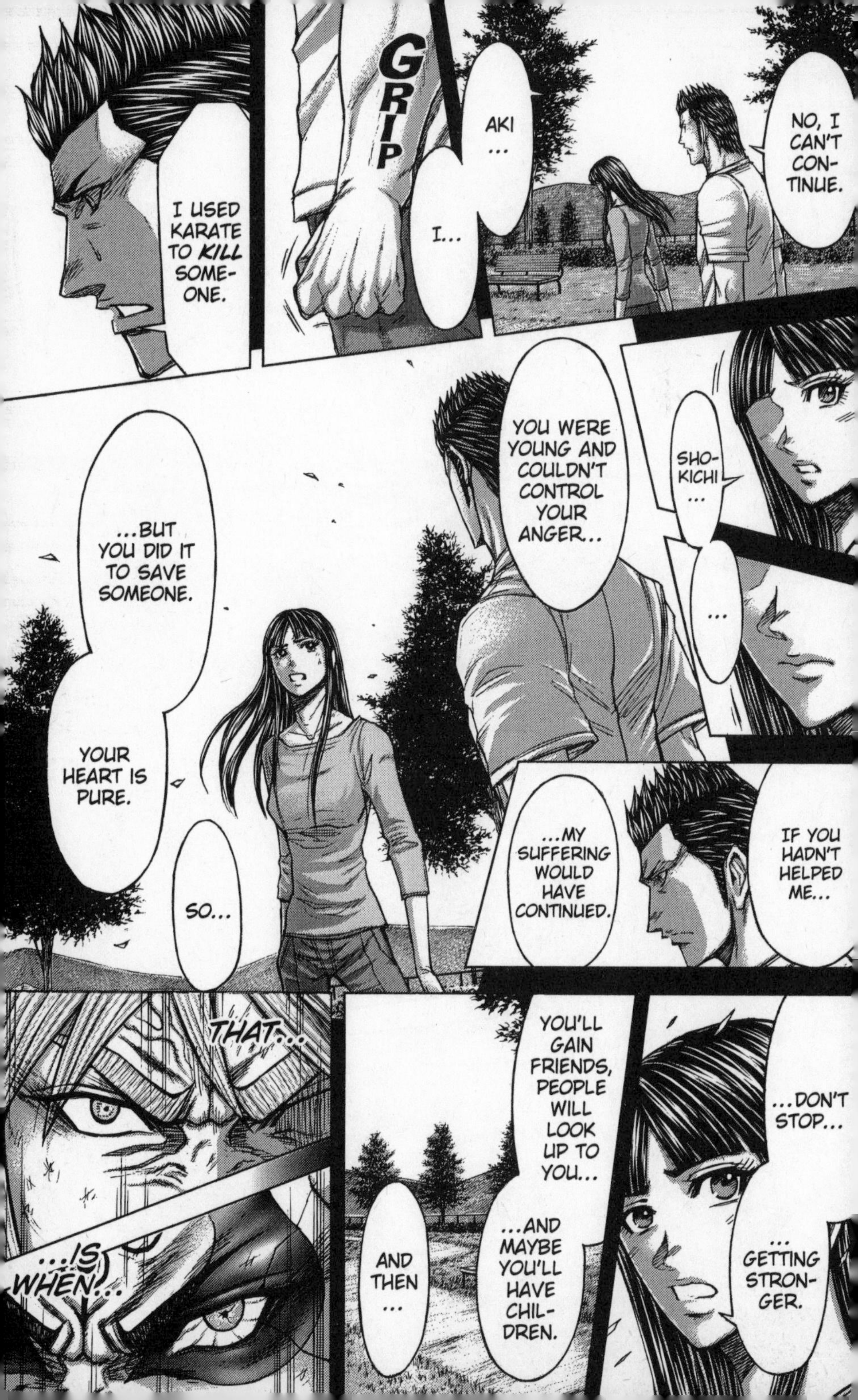

NO, I CAN'T CONTINUE.
AKI...
I...
GRIP
I USED KARATE TO KILL SOMEONE.
SHO-KICHI...
...
YOU WERE YOUNG AND COULDN'T CONTROL YOUR ANGER...
...BUT YOU DID IT TO SAVE SOMEONE.
YOUR HEART IS PURE.
IF YOU HADN'T HELPED ME...
...MY SUFFERING WOULD HAVE CONTINUED.
SO...
...DON'T STOP...
...GETTING STRONGER.
YOU'LL GAIN FRIENDS, PEOPLE WILL LOOK UP TO YOU...
...AND MAYBE YOU'LL HAVE CHILDREN.
AND THEN...
THAT...
...IS WHEN...

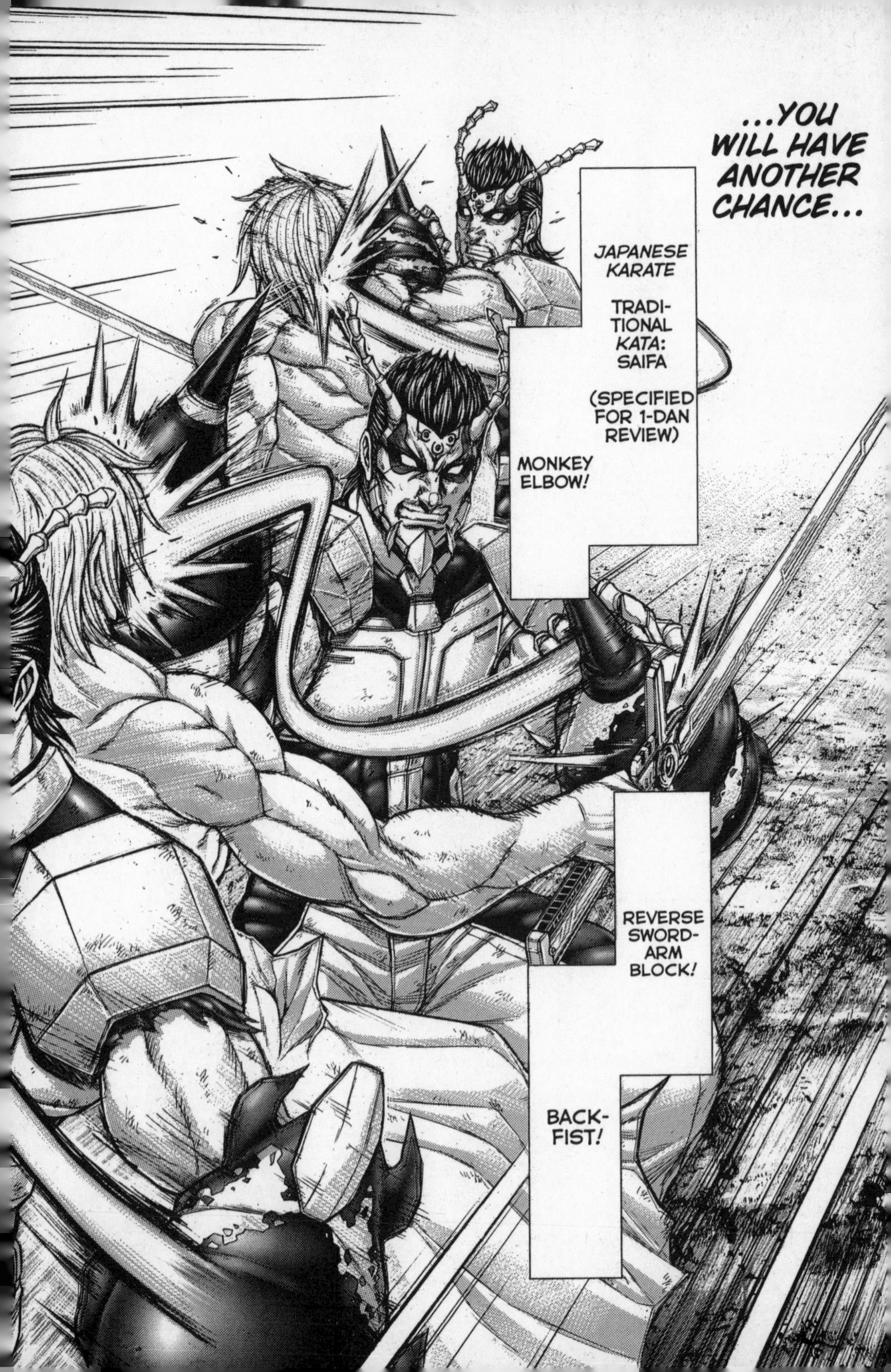
...YOU WILL HAVE ANOTHER CHANCE...
JAPANESE KARATE
TRADI-TIONAL KATA: SAIFA
(SPECIFIED FOR 1-DAN REVIEW)
MONKEY ELBOW!
REVERSE SWORD-ARM BLOCK!
BACK-FIST!

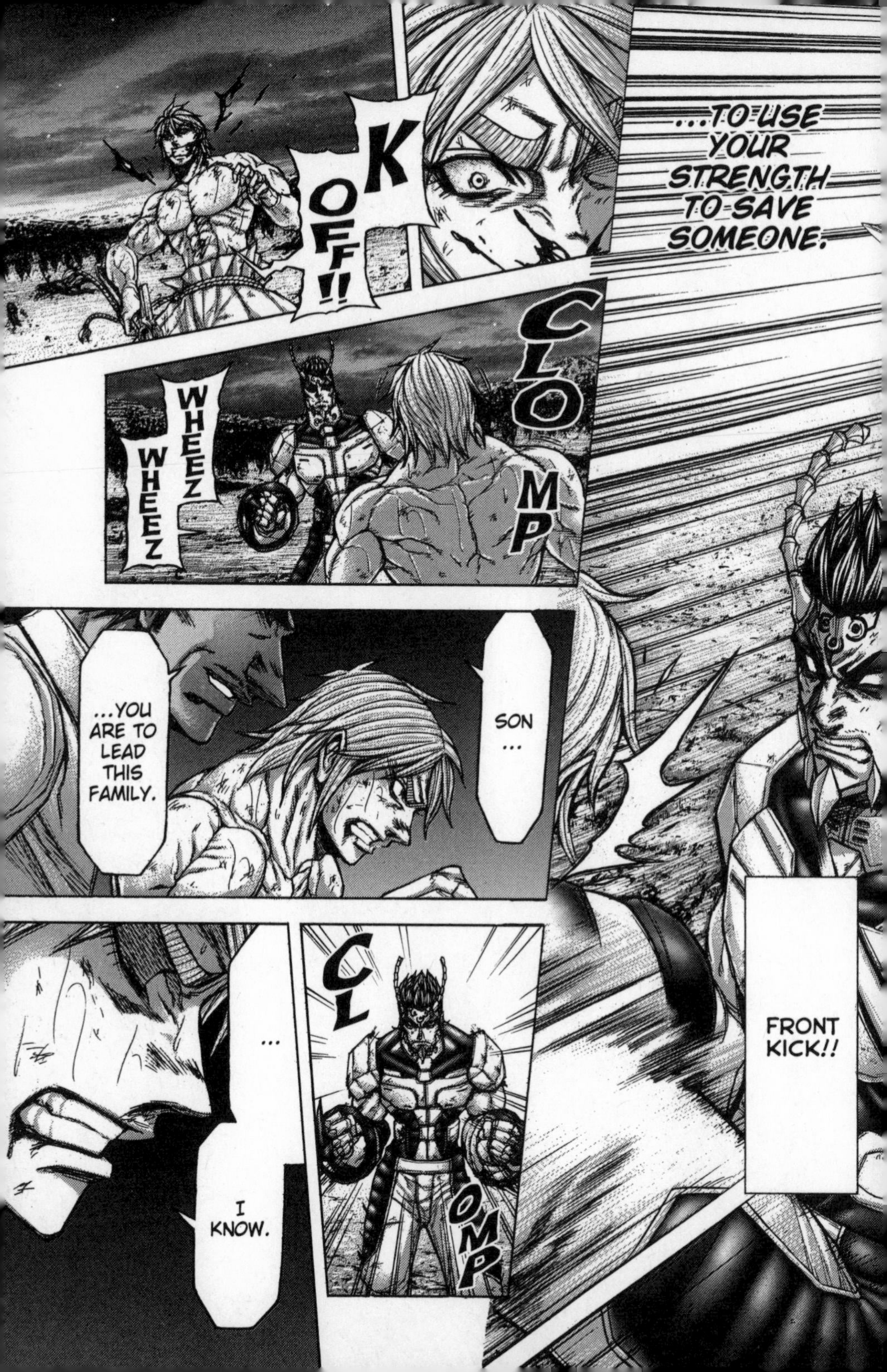
...TO USE YOUR STRENGTH TO SAVE SOMEONE.
KOFF!!
CLOMP
WHEEZ WHEEZ WHEEZ
SON...
...YOU ARE TO LEAD THIS FAMILY.
CLOMP
...
I KNOW.
FRONT KICK!!

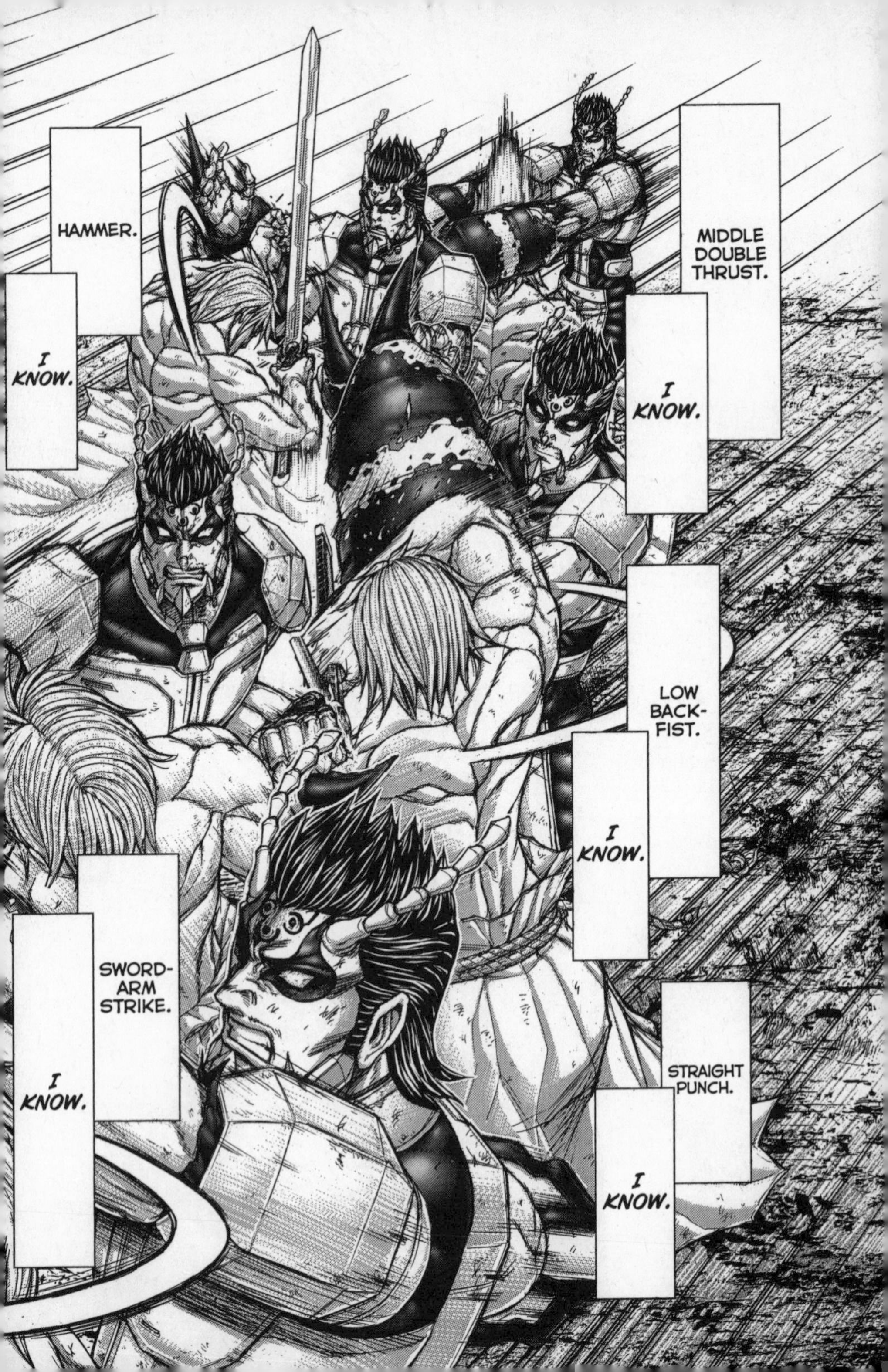
MIDDLE DOUBLE THRUST.
I KNOW.
HAMMER.
I KNOW.
LOW BACK-FIST.
I KNOW.
STRAIGHT PUNCH.
I KNOW.
SWORD-ARM STRIKE.
I KNOW.

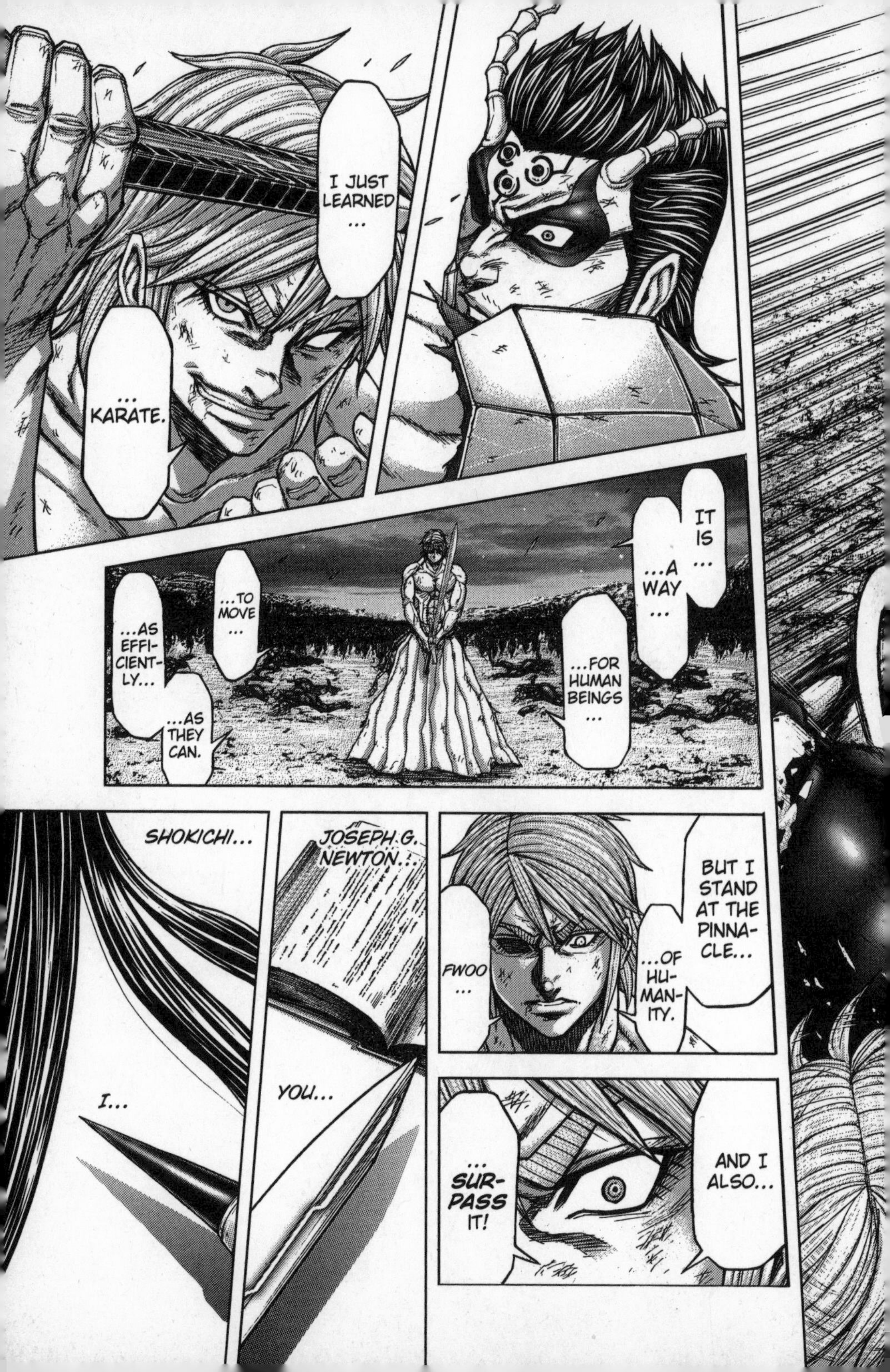
I JUST LEARNED ...
... KARATE.
IT IS ...
...A WAY ...
...FOR HUMAN BEINGS ...
...TO MOVE ...
...AS EFFICIENTLY...
...AS THEY CAN.
BUT I STAND AT THE PINNACLE...
...OF HUMANITY.
FWOO ...
AND I ALSO...
... SURPASS IT!
JOSEPH G. NEWTON...
YOU...
SHOKICHI...
I...

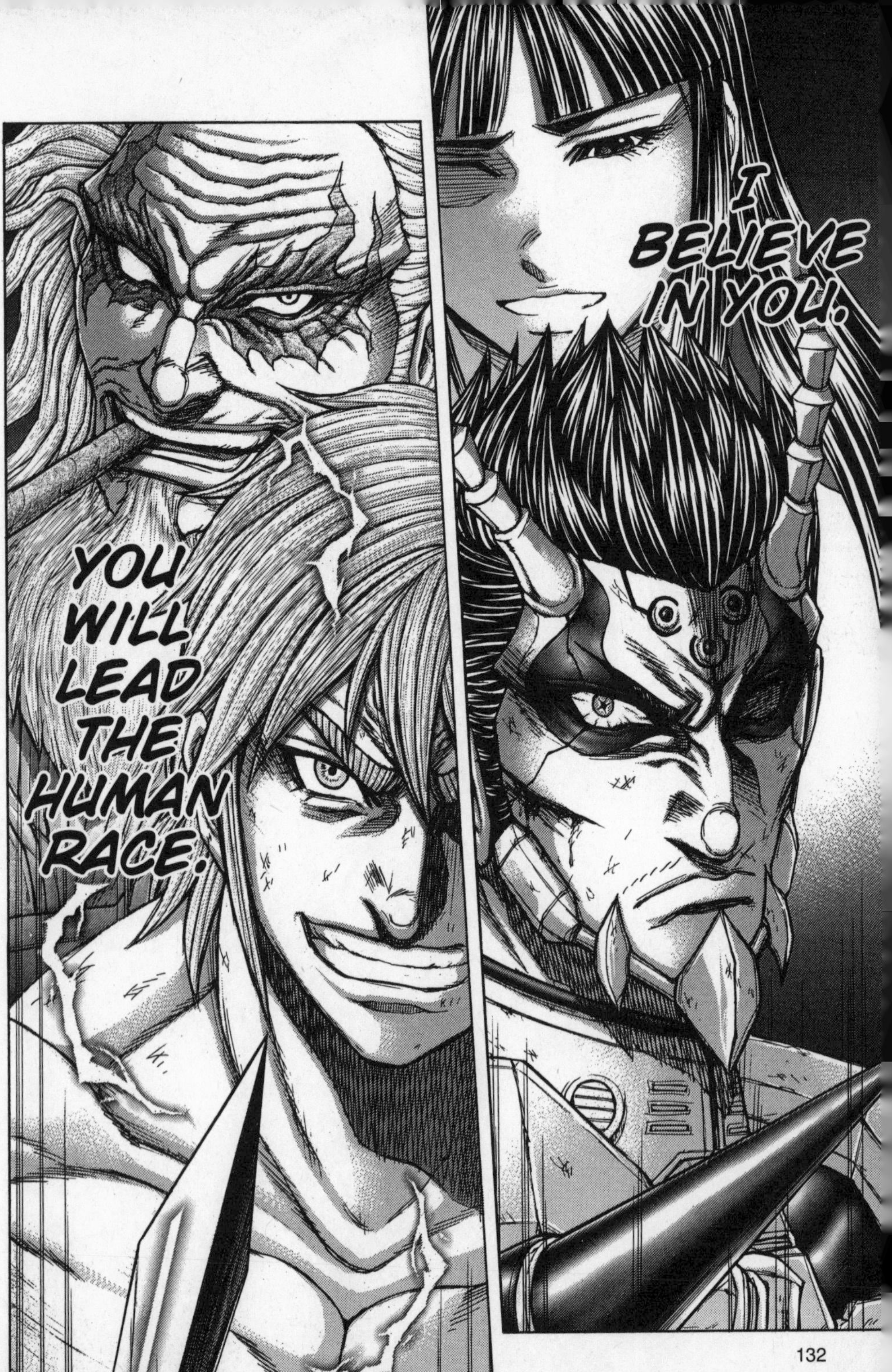
I BELIEVE IN YOU.
YOU WILL LEAD THE HUMAN RACE.

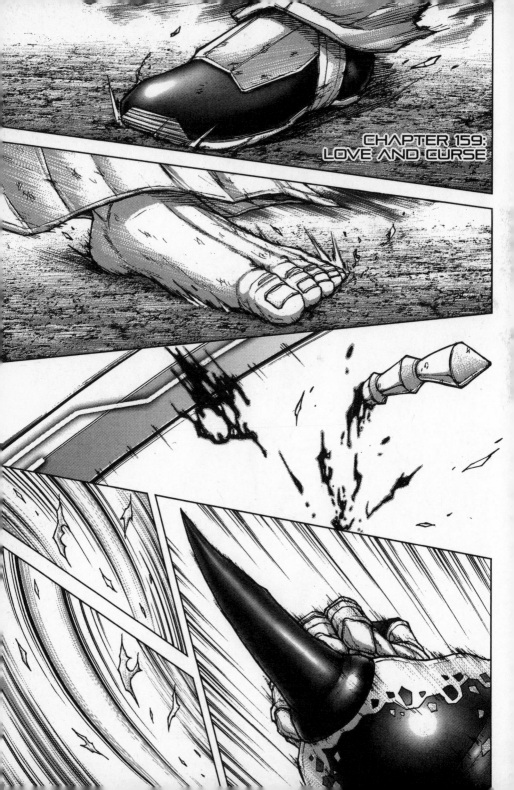

CHAPTER 159:
LOVE AND CURSE

CHAPTER 159: LOVE AND CURSE

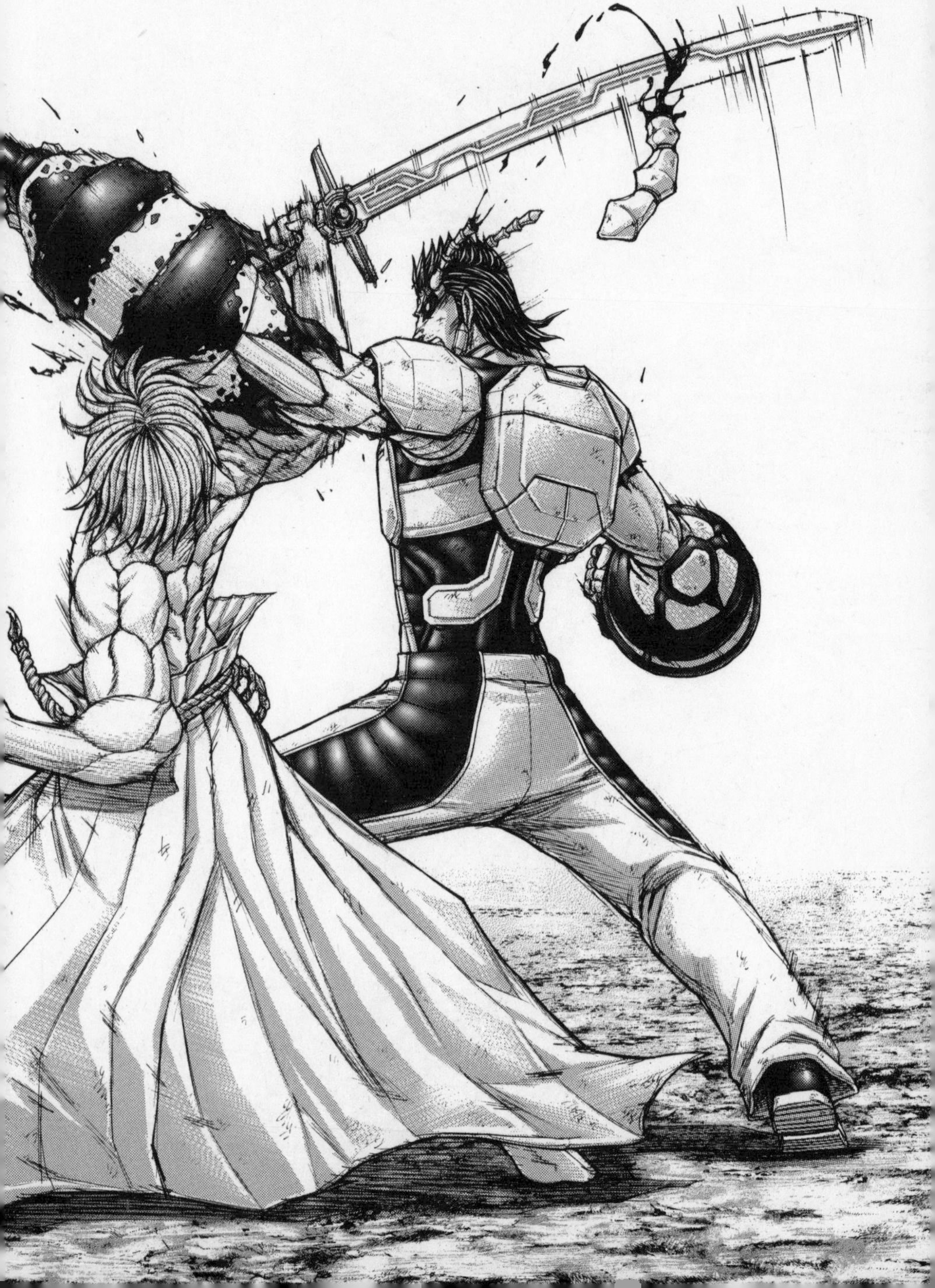

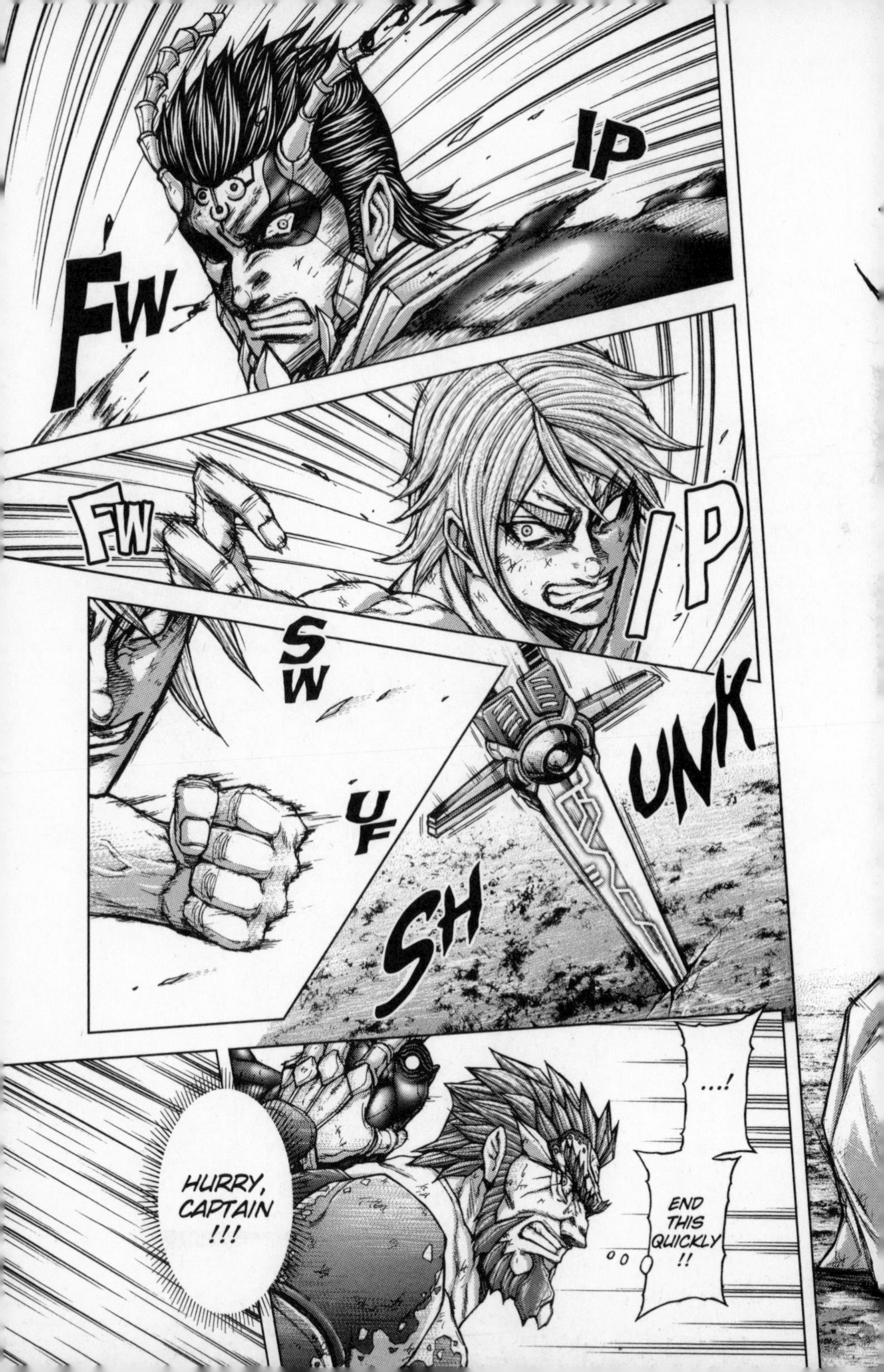
IP
FW
IP
FW
UNK
SW
SH
UF
...!
END THIS QUICKLY !!
HURRY, CAPTAIN !!!

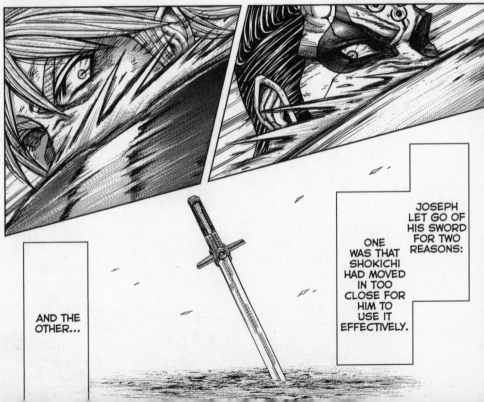

JOSEPH LET GO OF HIS SWORD FOR TWO REASONS:

ONE WAS THAT SHOKICHI HAD MOVED IN TOO CLOSE FOR HIM TO USE IT EFFECTIVELY.

AND THE OTHER...

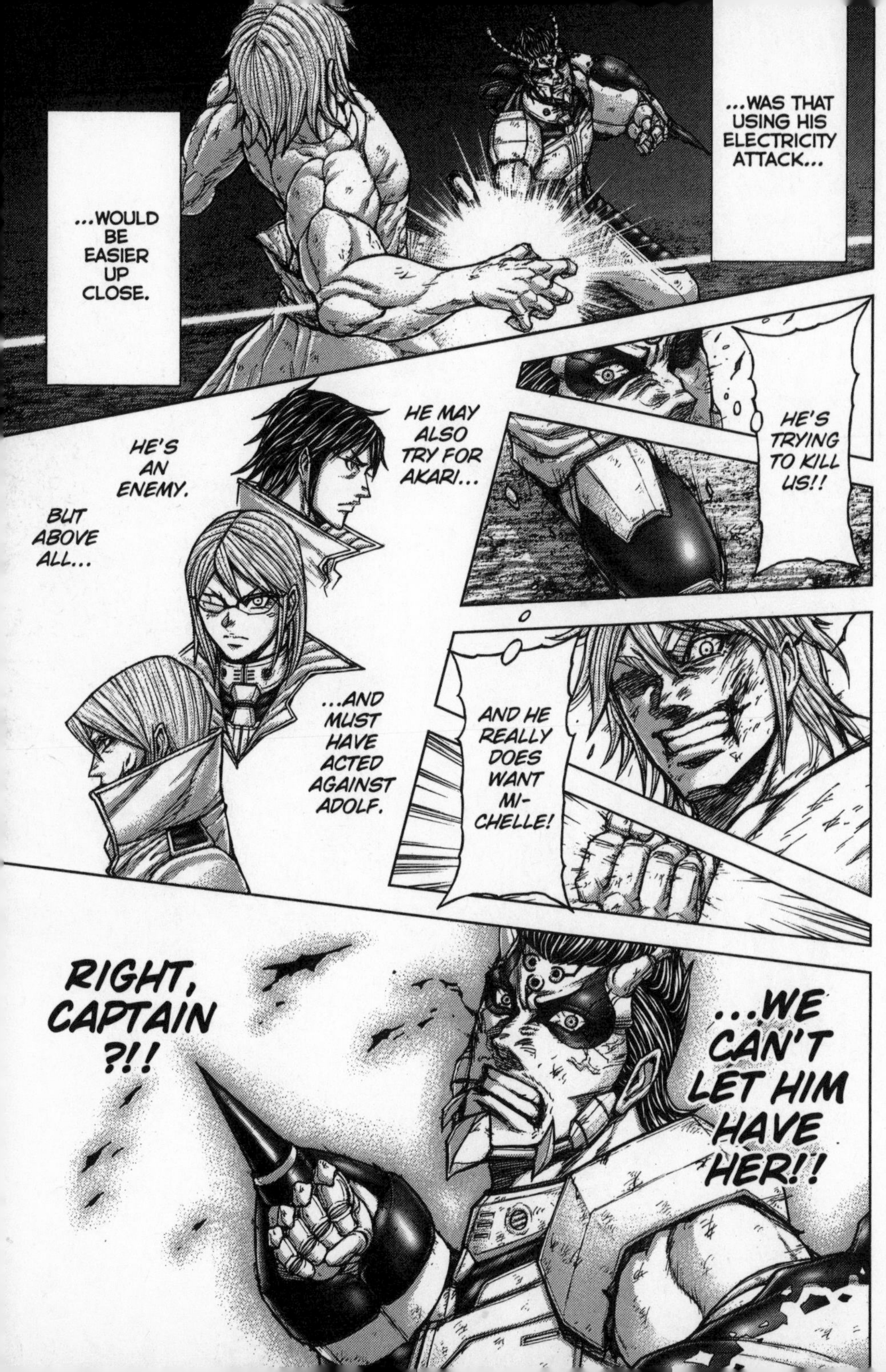
...WAS THAT USING HIS ELECTRICITY ATTACK...
...WOULD BE EASIER UP CLOSE.
HE'S TRYING TO KILL US!!
AND HE REALLY DOES WANT MI-CHELLE!
HE MAY ALSO TRY FOR AKARI...
HE'S AN ENEMY.
BUT ABOVE ALL...
...AND MUST HAVE ACTED AGAINST ADOLF.
...WE CAN'T LET HIM HAVE HER!!
RIGHT, CAPTAIN?!!

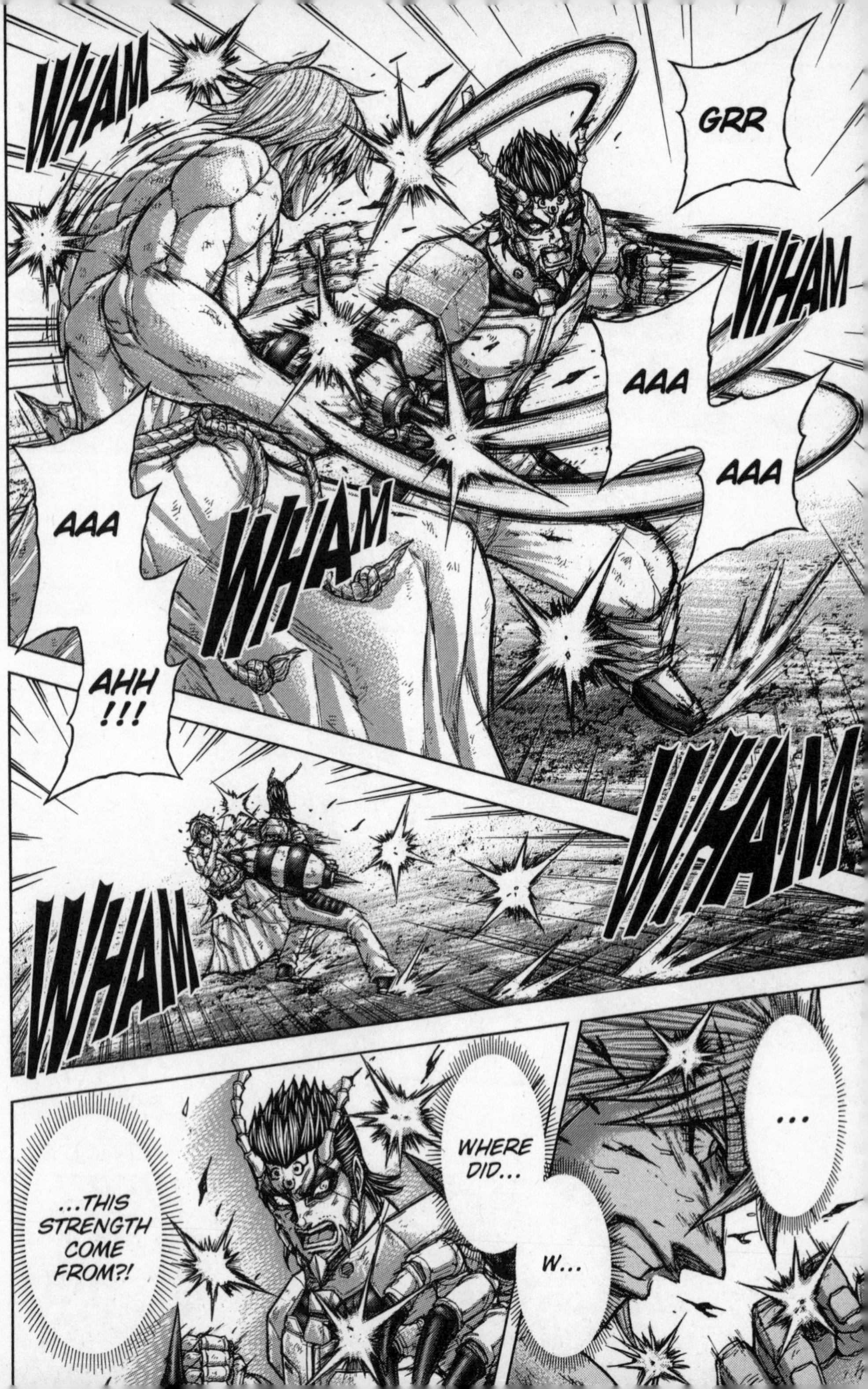
GRR
WHAM
AAA
AAA
WHAM
AAA
WHAM
AHH!!!
WHAM
WHAM
...
WHERE DID...
W...
...THIS STRENGTH COME FROM?!

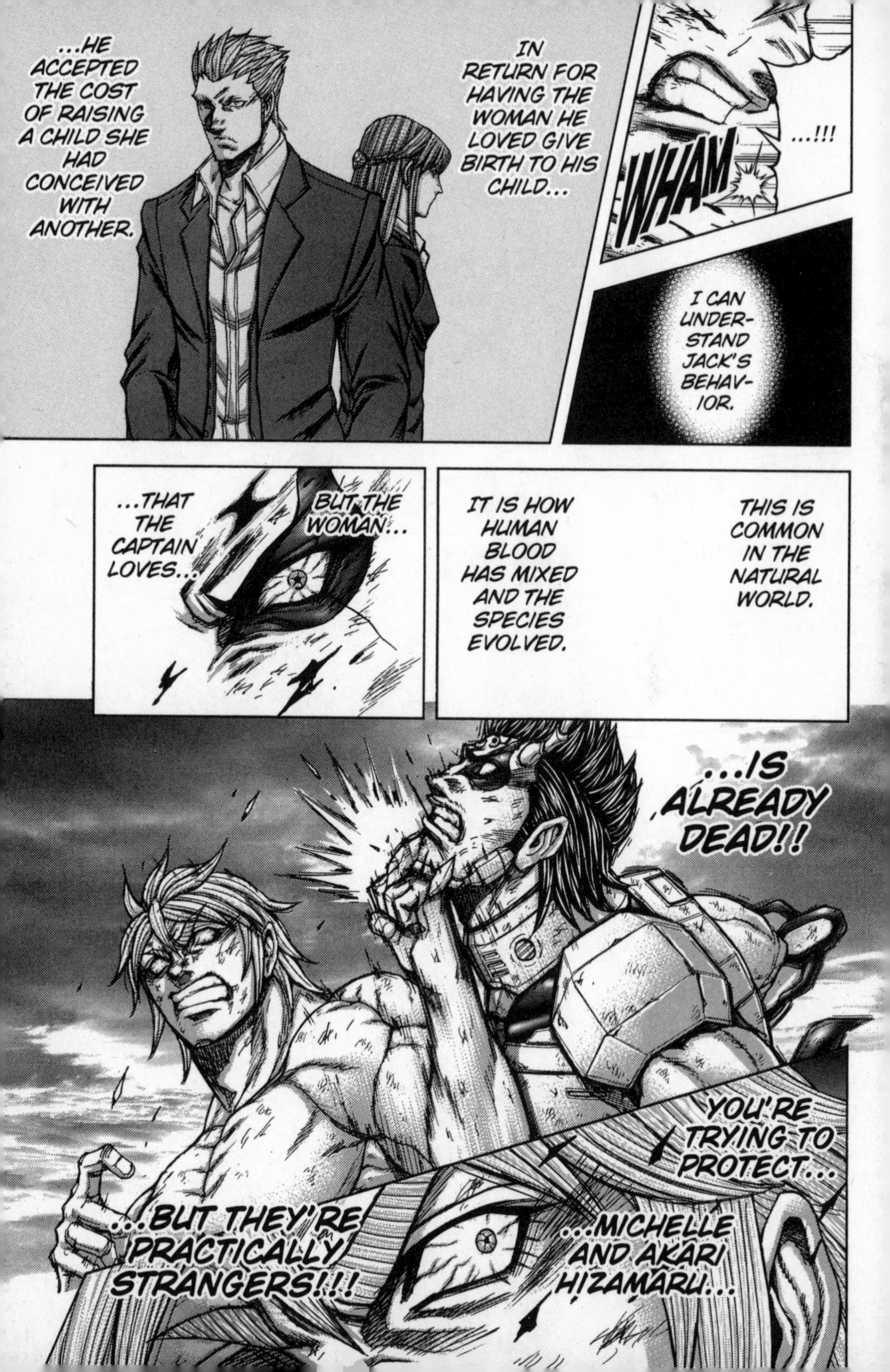

...!!!
WHAM
I CAN UNDER-STAND JACK'S BEHAV-IOR.
IN RETURN FOR HAVING THE WOMAN HE LOVED GIVE BIRTH TO HIS CHILD...
...HE ACCEPTED THE COST OF RAISING A CHILD SHE HAD CONCEIVED WITH ANOTHER.
THIS IS COMMON IN THE NATURAL WORLD.
IT IS HOW HUMAN BLOOD HAS MIXED AND THE SPECIES EVOLVED.
BUT THE WOMAN...
...THAT THE CAPTAIN LOVES...
...IS ALREADY DEAD!!
YOU'RE TRYING TO PROTECT...
...MICHELLE AND AKARI HIZAMARU...
...BUT THEY'RE PRACTICALLY STRANGERS!!!

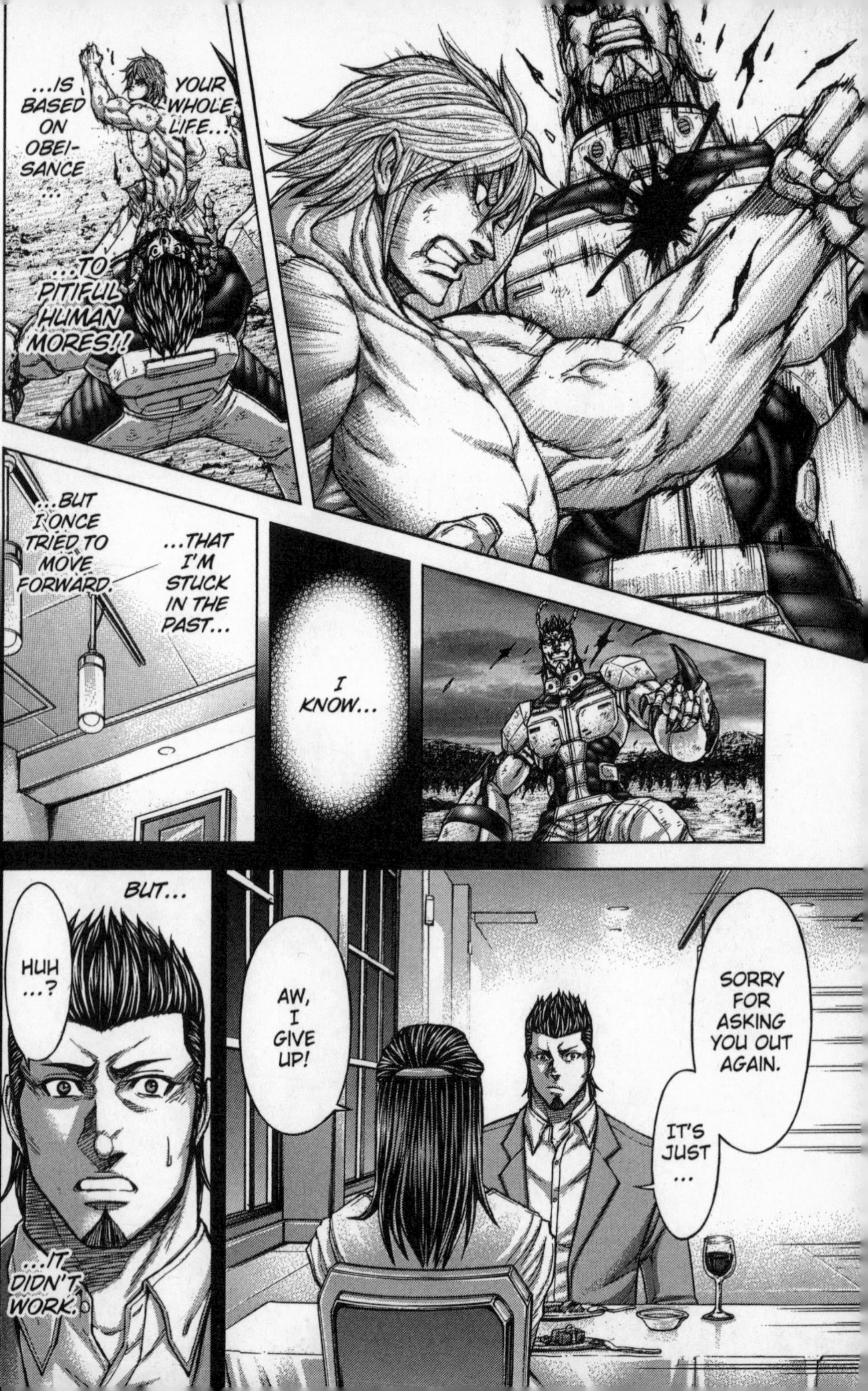
YOUR WHOLE LIFE...
...IS BASED ON OBEISANCE...
...TO PITIFUL HUMAN MORES!!
I KNOW...
...THAT I'M STUCK IN THE PAST...
...BUT I ONCE TRIED TO MOVE FORWARD.
SORRY FOR ASKING YOU OUT AGAIN.
IT'S JUST...
AW, I GIVE UP!
BUT...
HUH...?
...IT DIDN'T WORK.

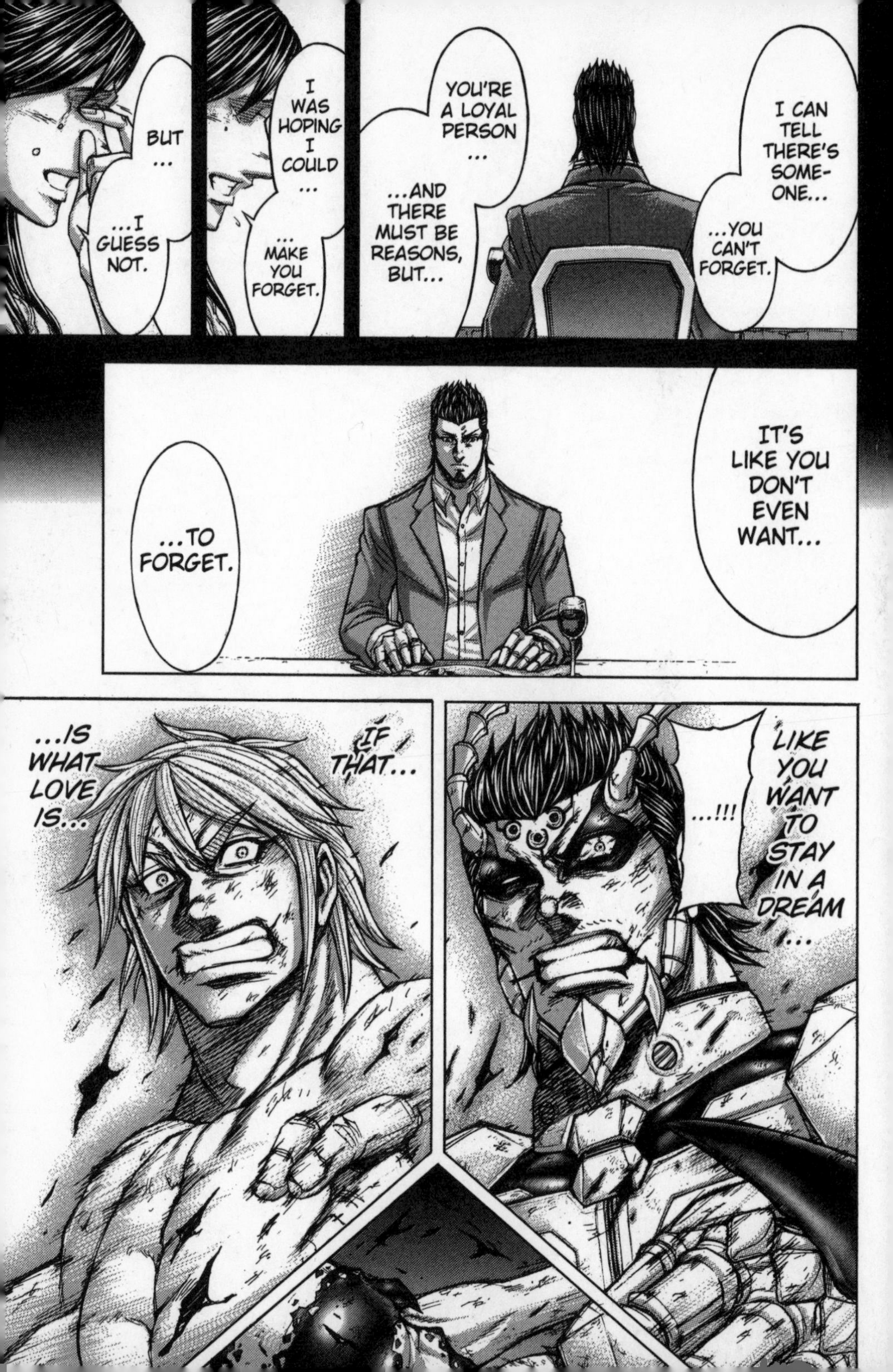
I CAN TELL THERE'S SOME-ONE... ...YOU CAN'T FORGET.
YOU'RE A LOYAL PERSON ...
...AND THERE MUST BE REASONS, BUT...
I WAS HOPING I COULD ...
... MAKE YOU FORGET.
BUT ...
...I GUESS NOT.
IT'S LIKE YOU DON'T EVEN WANT...
...TO FORGET.
LIKE YOU WANT TO STAY IN A DREAM ...
...!!!
IF THAT...
...IS WHAT LOVE IS...

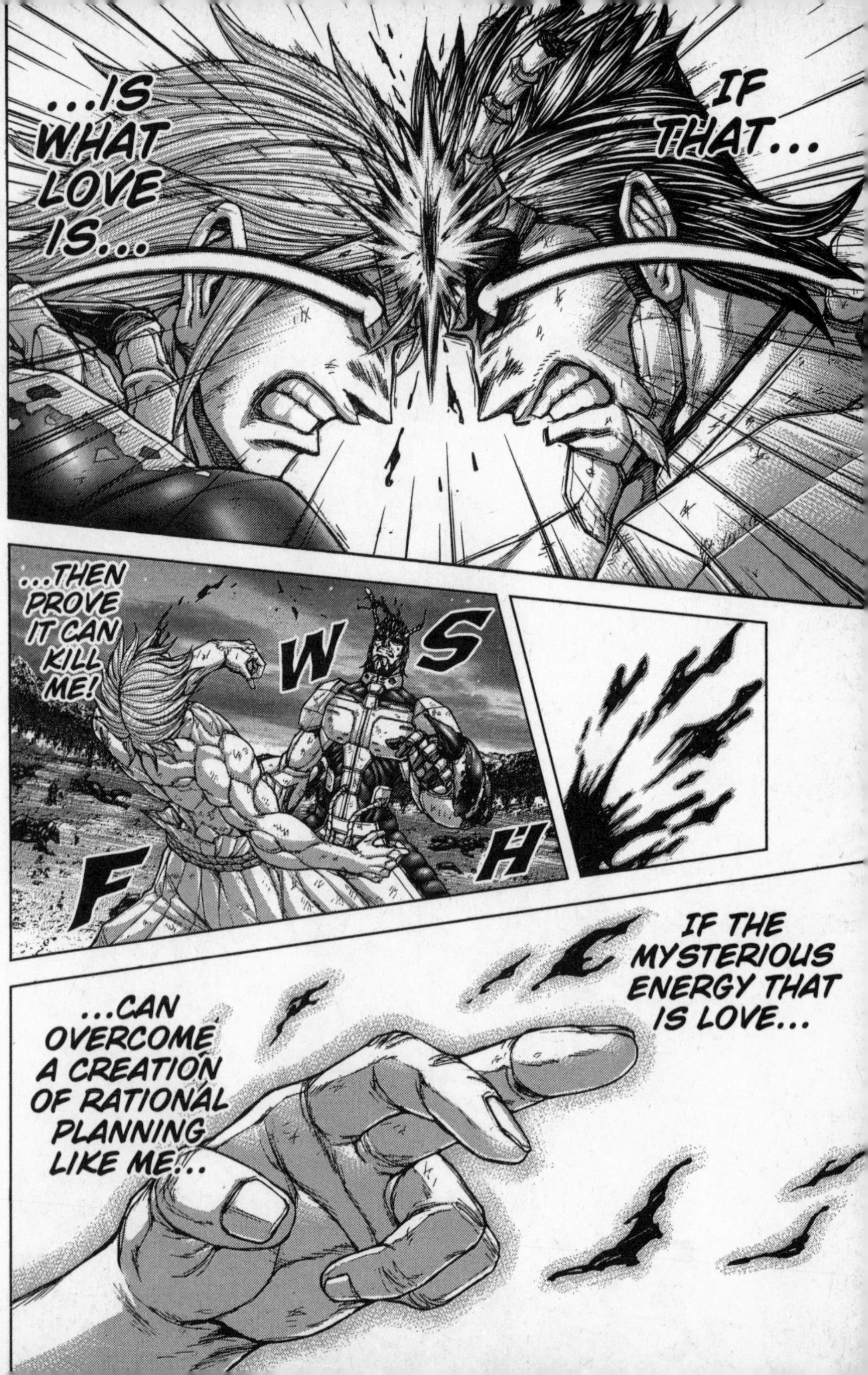
IF THAT...
...IS WHAT LOVE IS...
...THEN PROVE IT CAN KILL ME!
FWSH
IF THE MYSTERIOUS ENERGY THAT IS LOVE...
...CAN OVERCOME A CREATION OF RATIONAL PLANNING LIKE ME...

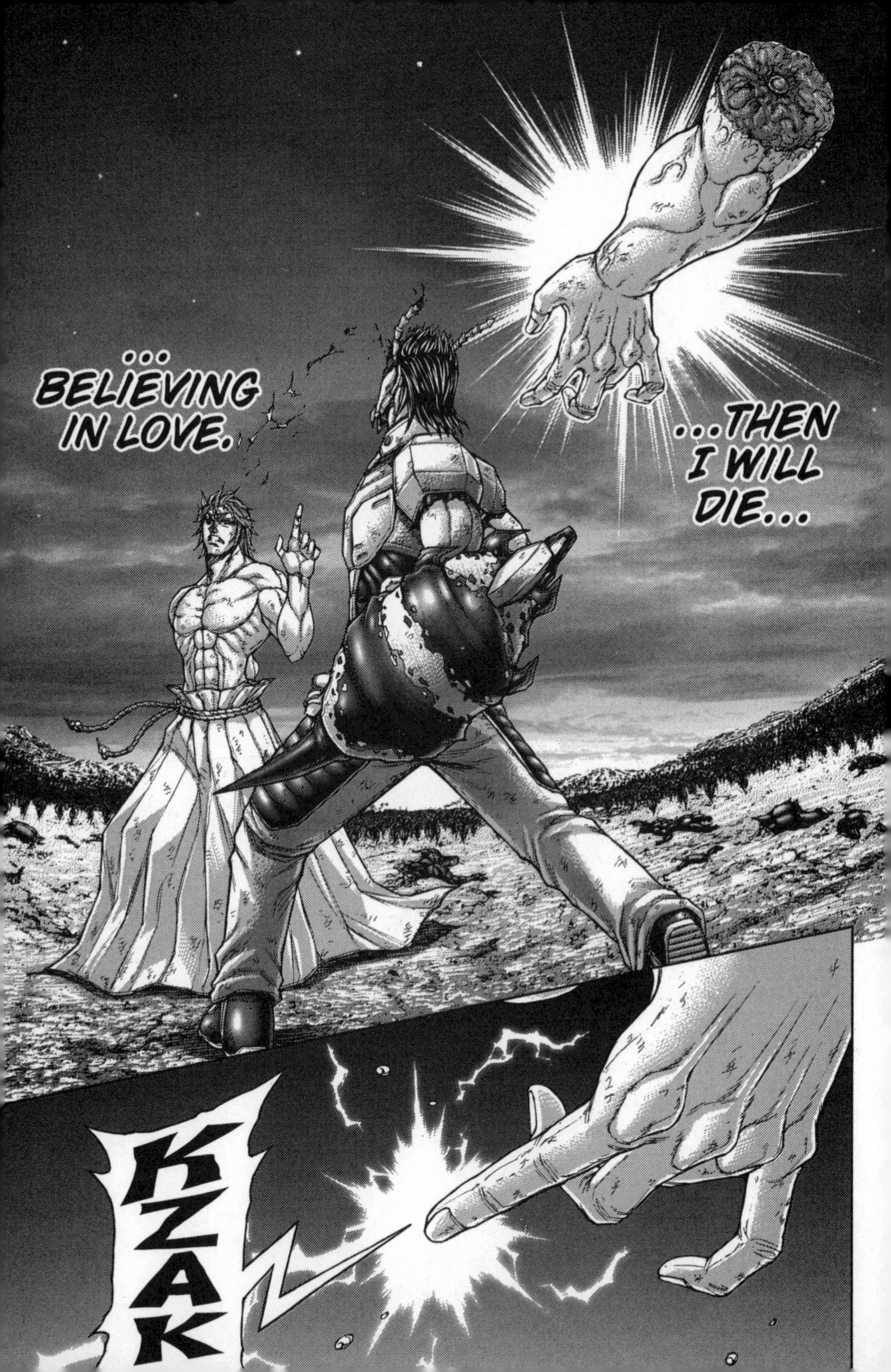
...THEN I WILL DIE...
...BELIEVING IN LOVE.
KZAK

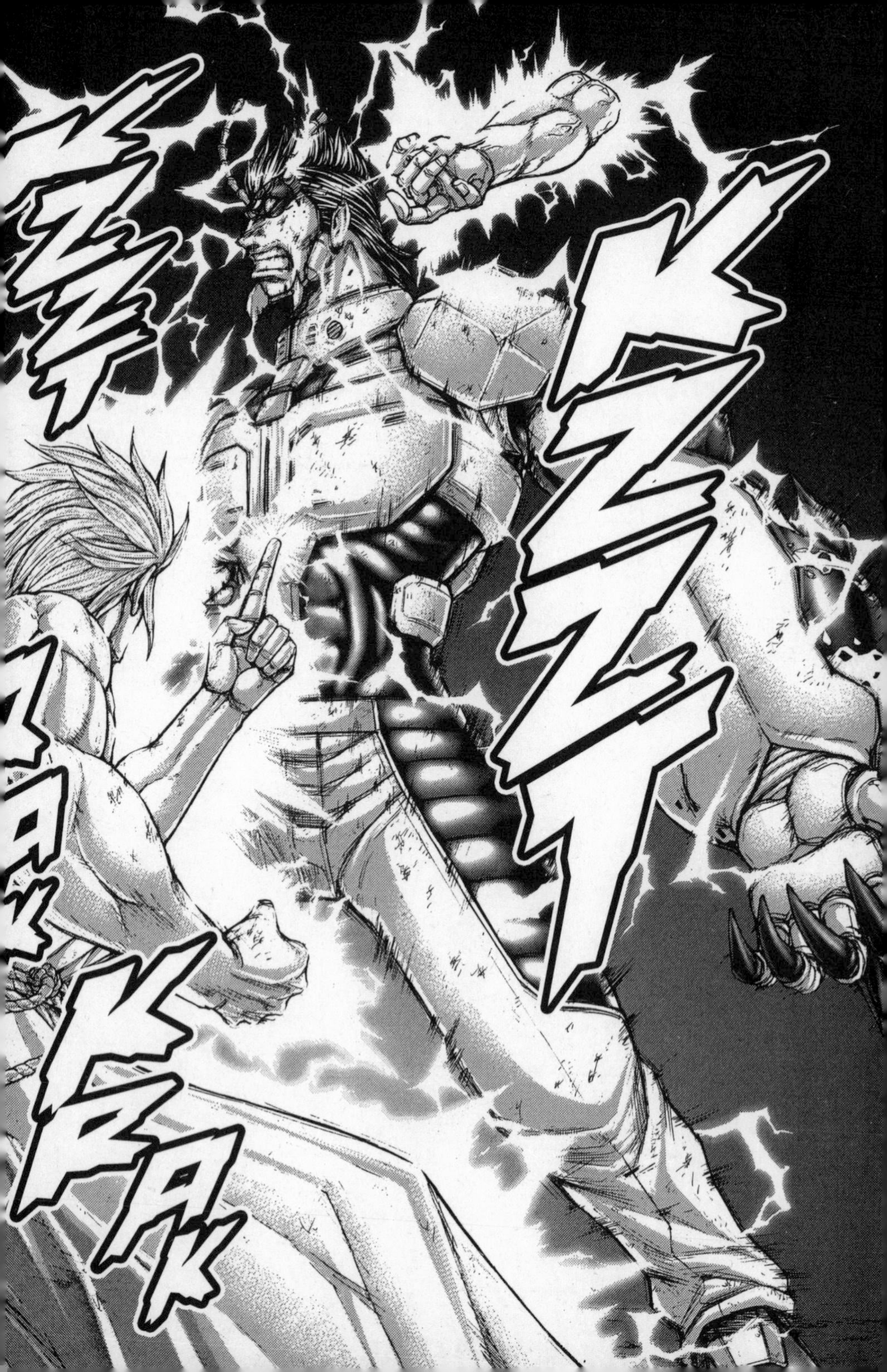
KZZZT

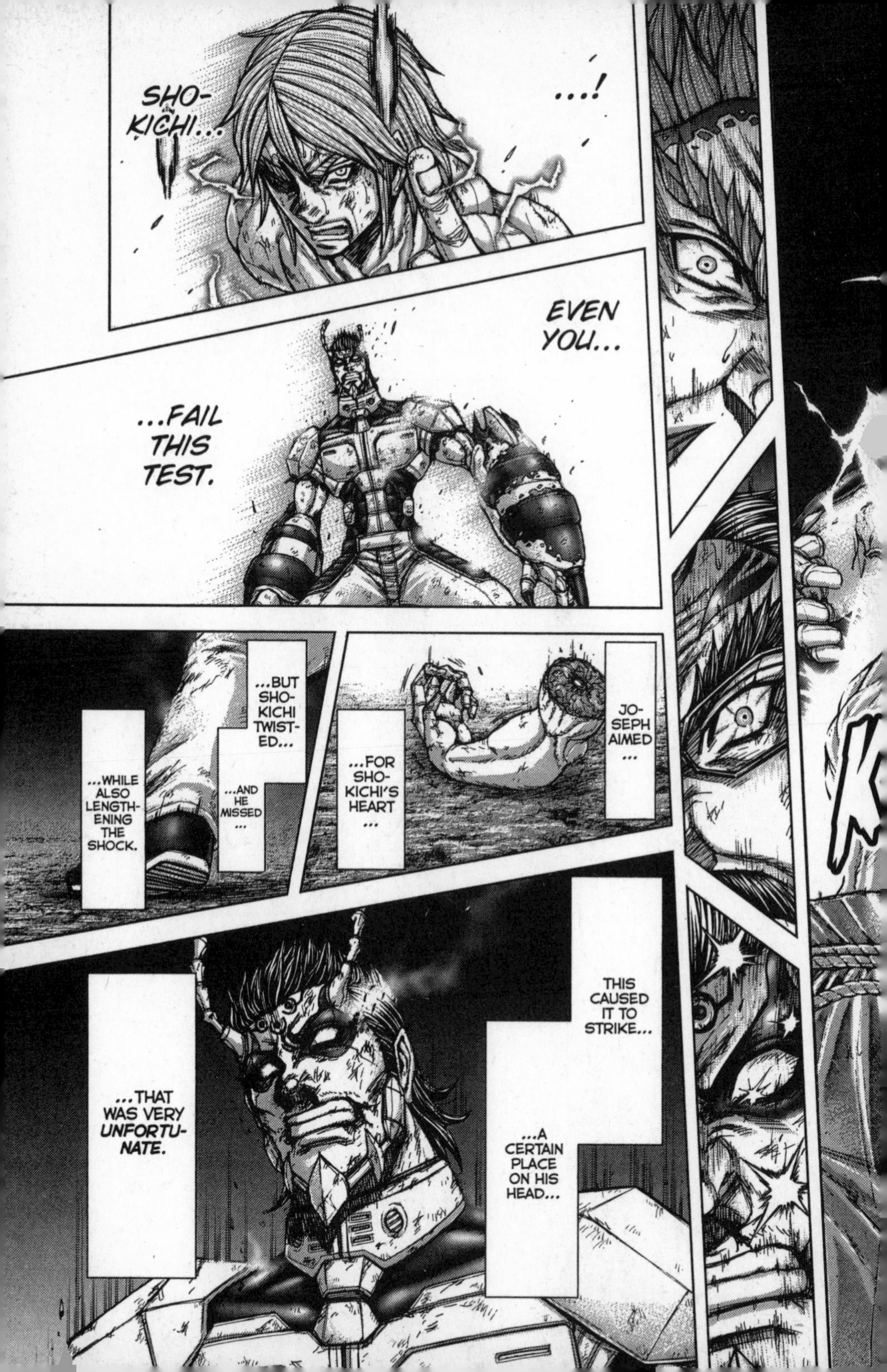
...!
SHO-KICHI...
EVEN YOU...
...FAIL THIS TEST.
JOSEPH AIMED...
...FOR SHOKICHI'S HEART...
...BUT SHOKICHI TWISTED...
...AND HE MISSED...
...WHILE ALSO LENGTHENING THE SHOCK.
THIS CAUSED IT TO STRIKE...
...A CERTAIN PLACE ON HIS HEAD...
...THAT WAS VERY *UNFORTUNATE.*

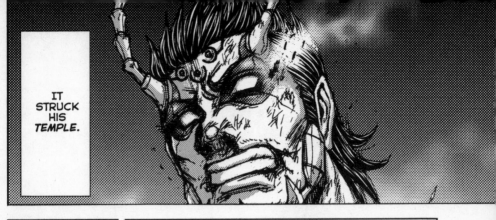

IT STRUCK HIS *TEMPLE.*
"TEMPLE" IS DERIVED FROM THE LATIN TEMPULA ...
...WHICH INDICATES A PLACE OF WORSHIP.
IN AN EXPERIMENT IN CANADA IN 1997...
...ELECTRICAL STIMULATION BEHIND THE TEMPLES ...
...CAUSED SUBJECTS TO SEE CHRIST, THE VIRGIN MARY AND THEIR DECEASED GRANDPARENTS.
THEY PERFORMED THE SAME TESTS ON NON-BELIEVERS.
AND THEY SAW ...
...SOMETHING LIKE ALIENS DESCENDING FROM HEAVEN.
SURPRISINGLY ...
...THE HUMAN BRAIN ...
... SENSES MUCH ...
... SUCH AS GODS ...
...AND GODDESSES...
...THAT IS BEYOND THE ORDINARY ORGANS OF PERCEPTION.

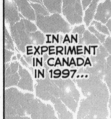

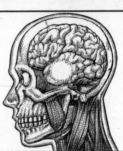

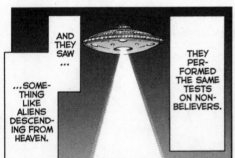

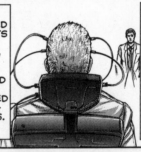

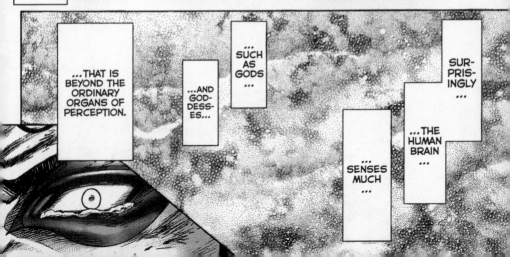

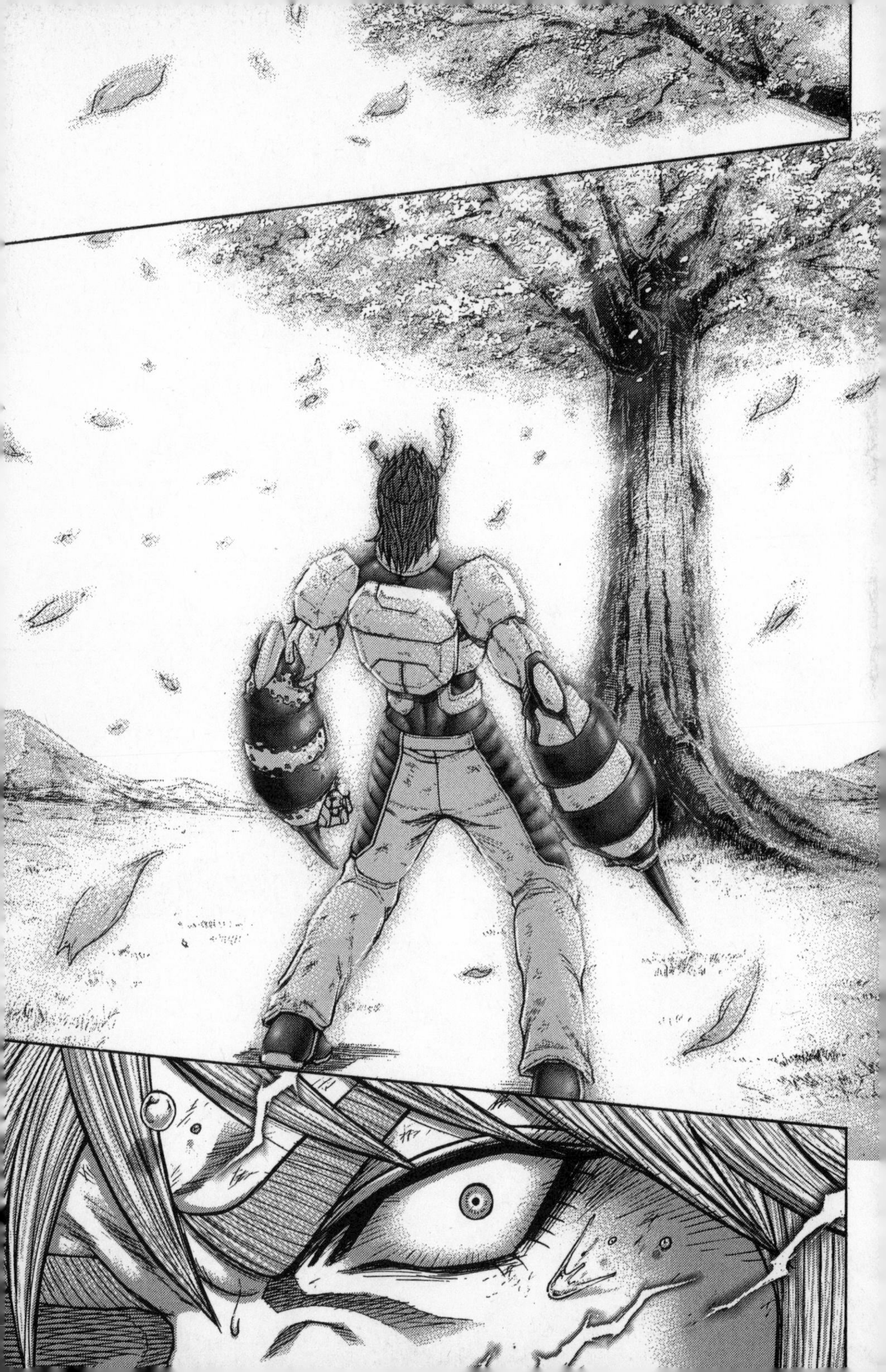

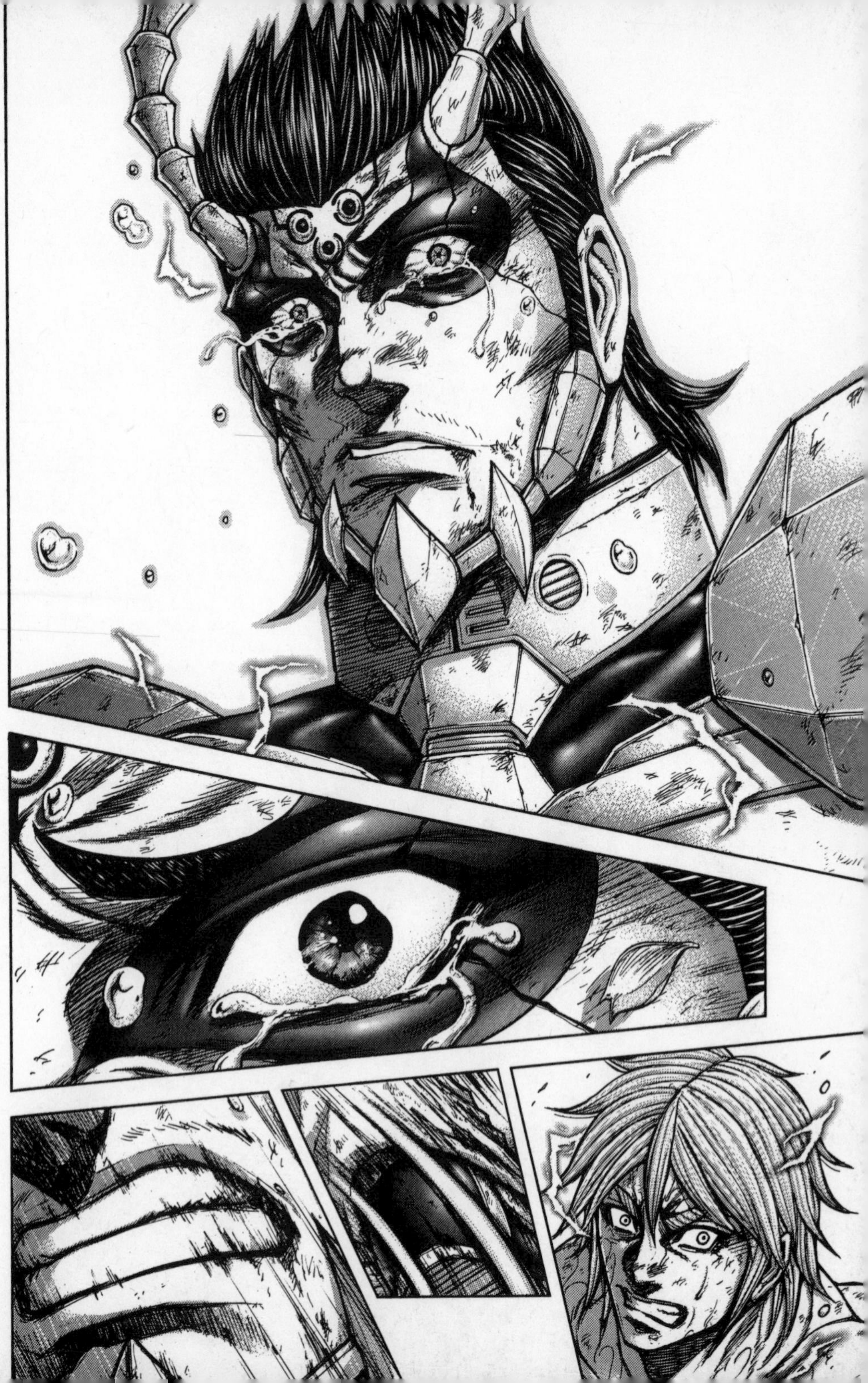

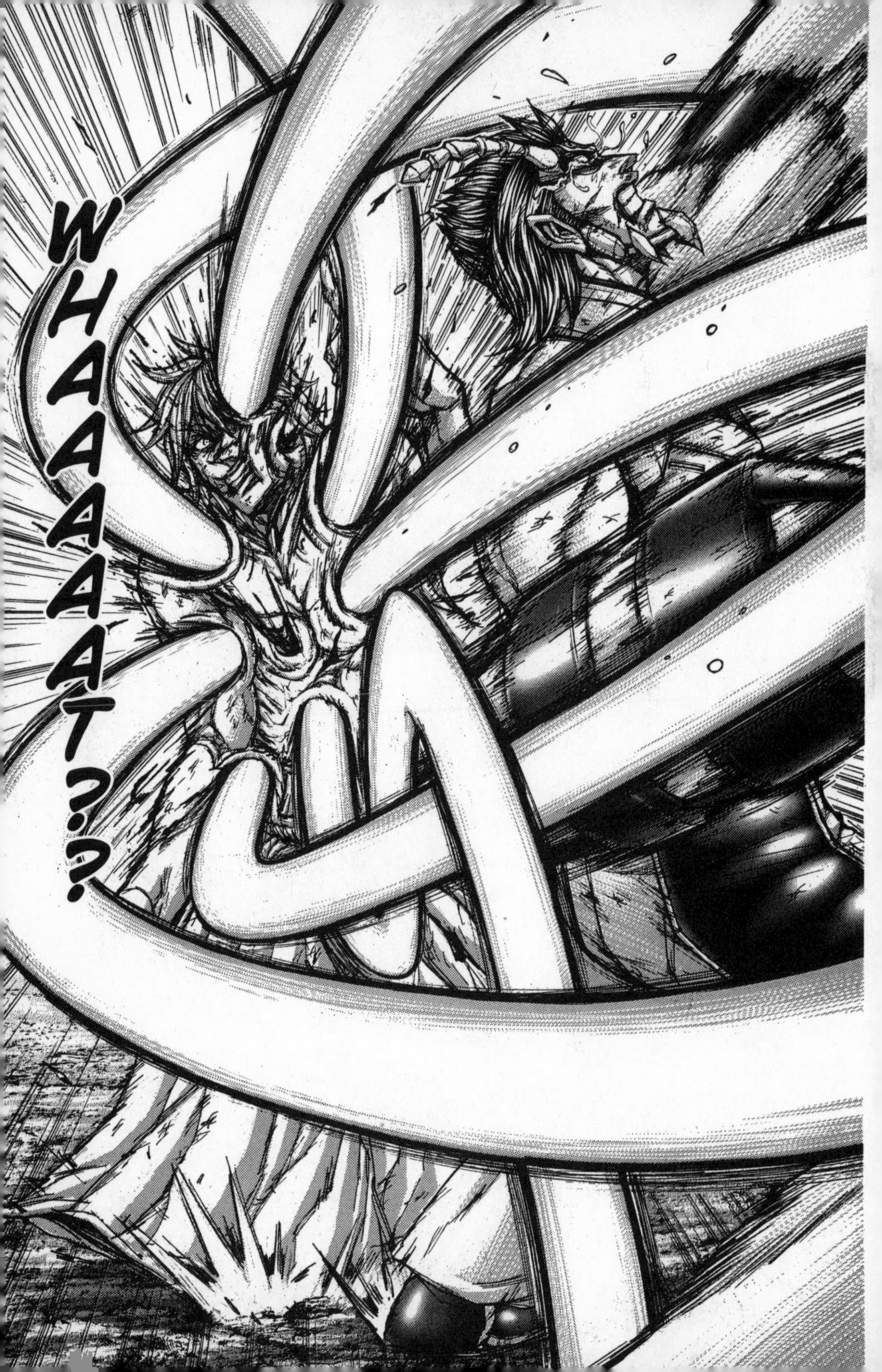
WHAAAAAT?!?!

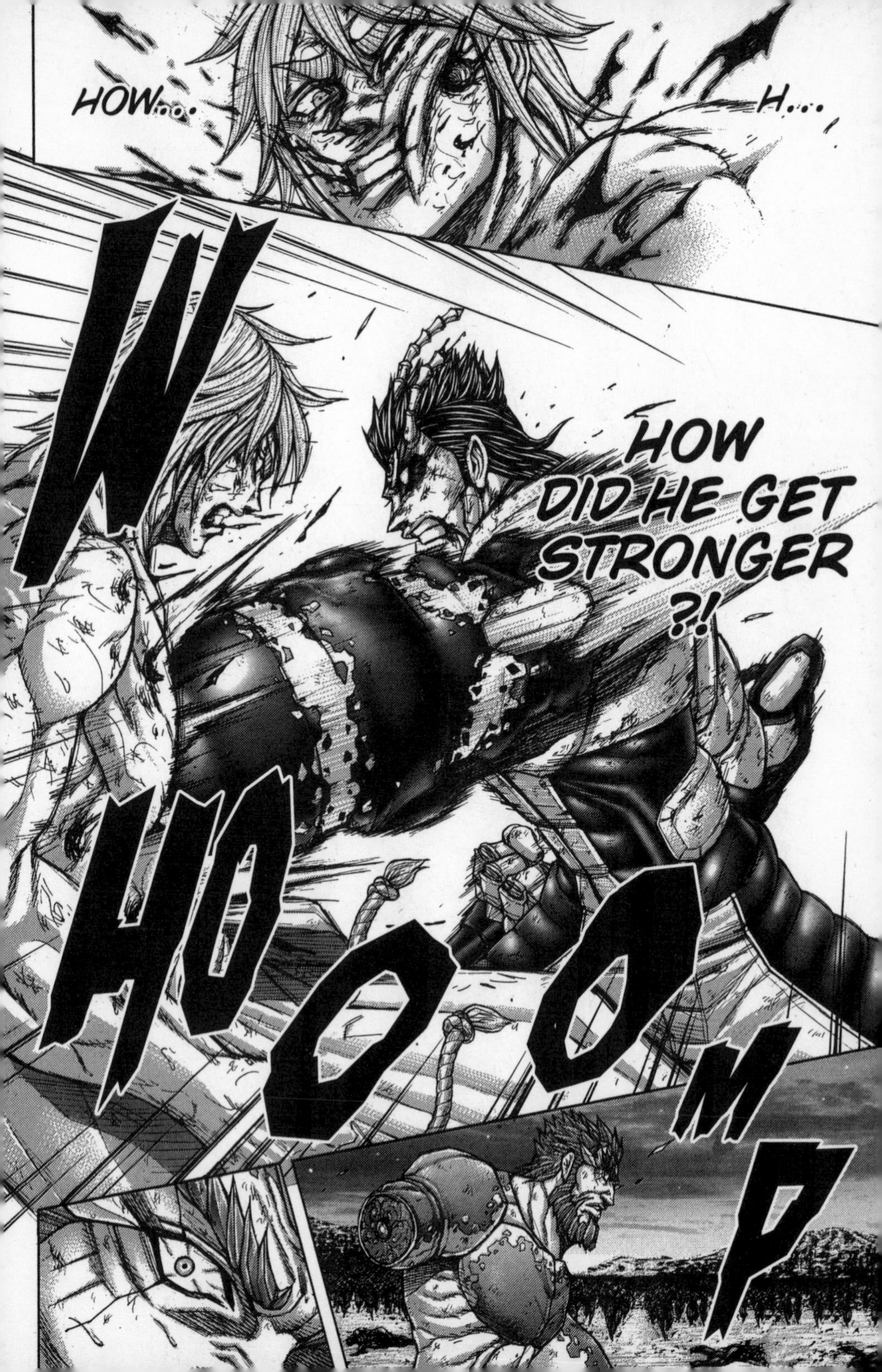
H...!
HOW...
HOW DID HE GET STRONGER ?!
WHOOOMP

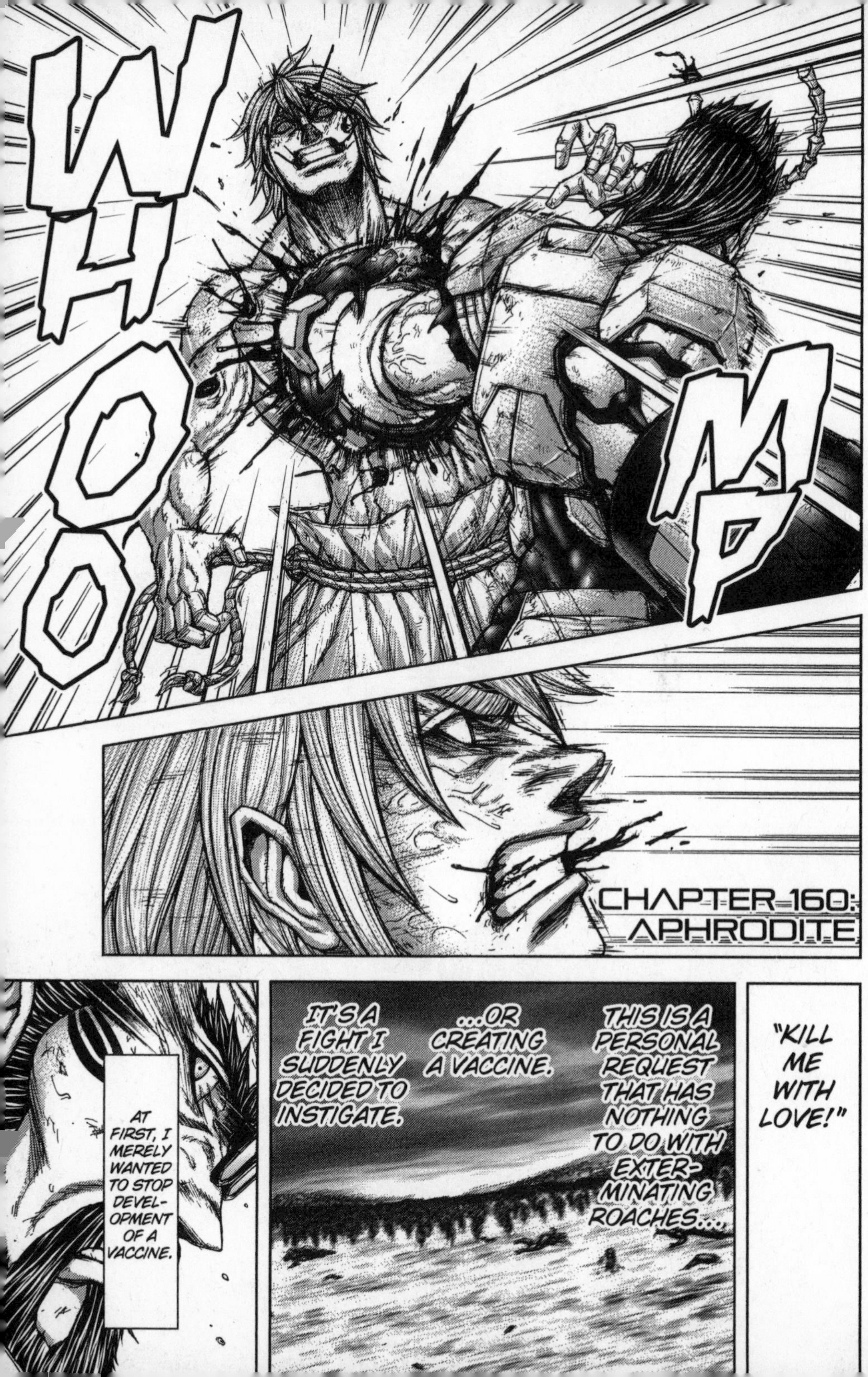
WHOOMP
CHAPTER 160: APHRODITE
"KILL ME WITH LOVE!"
THIS IS A PERSONAL REQUEST THAT HAS NOTHING TO DO WITH EXTERMINATING ROACHES...
...OR CREATING A VACCINE.
IT'S A FIGHT I SUDDENLY DECIDED TO INSTIGATE.
AT FIRST, I MERELY WANTED TO STOP DEVELOPMENT OF A VACCINE.

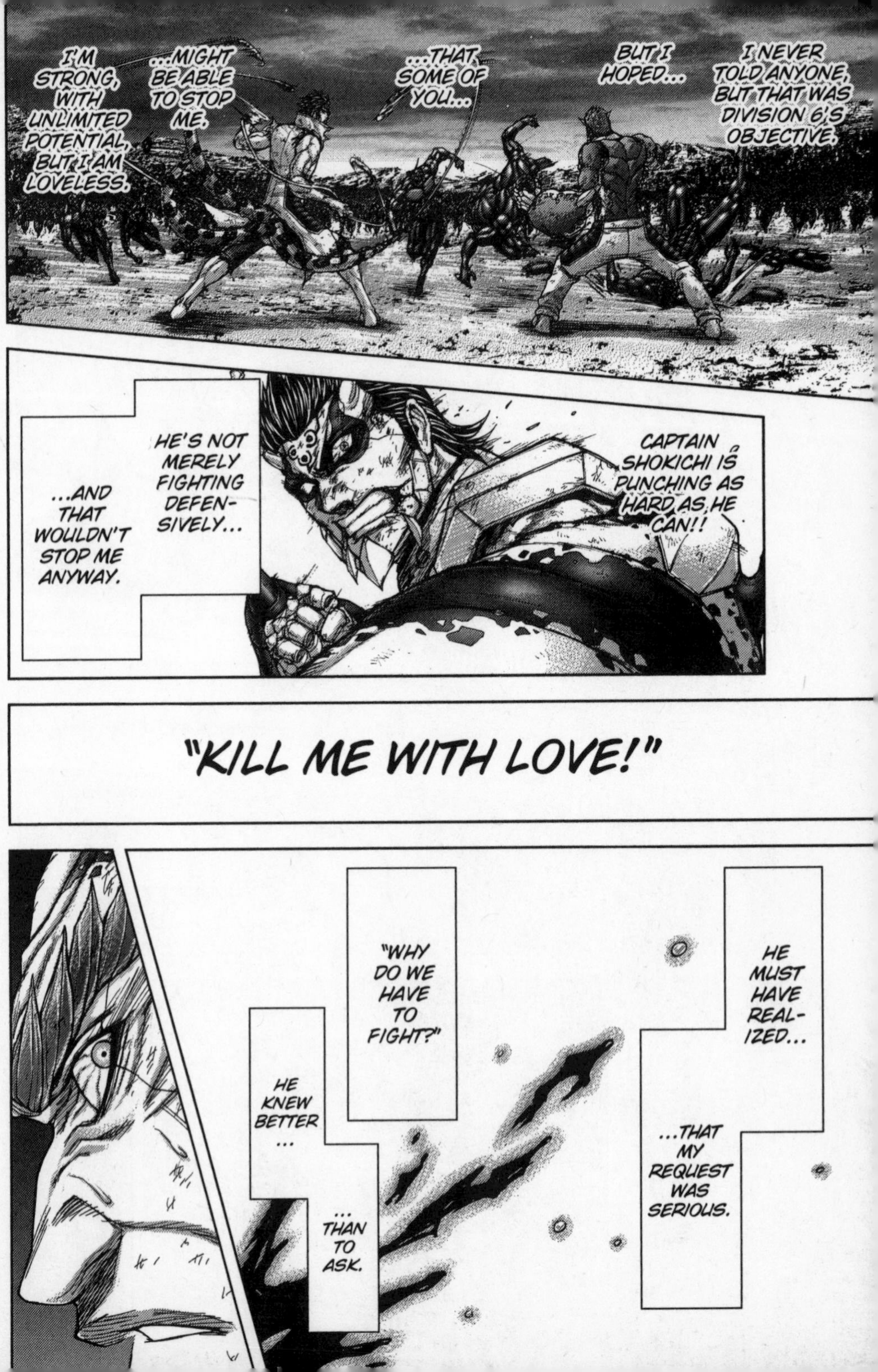
I NEVER TOLD ANYONE, BUT THAT WAS DIVISION 6'S OBJECTIVE.
BUT I HOPED...
...THAT SOME OF YOU...
...MIGHT BE ABLE TO STOP ME.
I'M STRONG, WITH UNLIMITED POTENTIAL, BUT I AM LOVELESS.
CAPTAIN SHOKICHI IS PUNCHING AS HARD AS HE CAN!!
HE'S NOT MERELY FIGHTING DEFEN-SIVELY...
...AND THAT WOULDN'T STOP ME ANYWAY.
"KILL ME WITH LOVE!"
HE MUST HAVE REAL-IZED...
...THAT MY REQUEST WAS SERIOUS.
"WHY DO WE HAVE TO FIGHT?"
HE KNEW BETTER...
...THAN TO ASK.

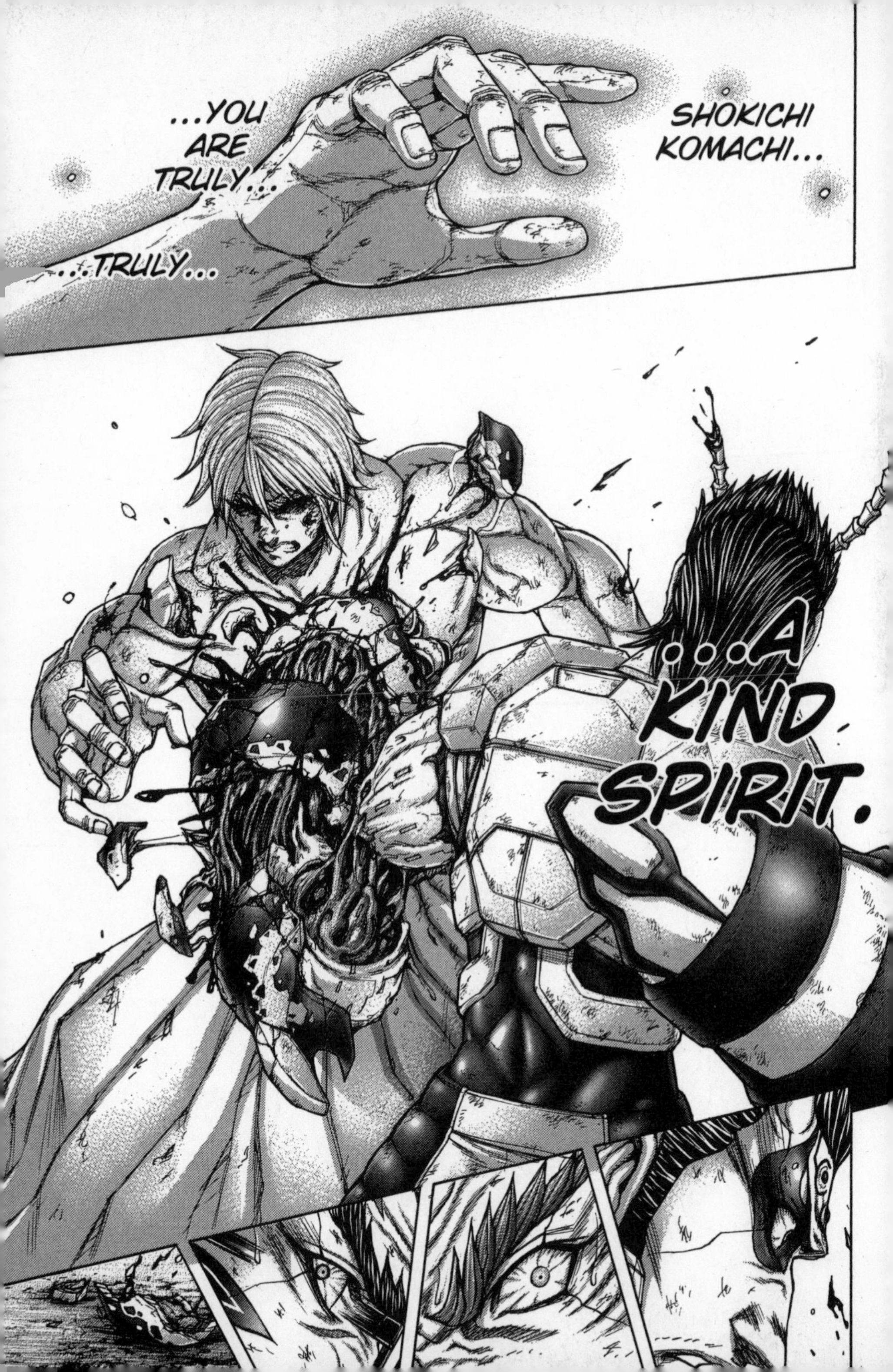
SHOKICHI KOMACHI...
...YOU ARE TRULY...
...TRULY...
...A KIND SPIRIT.

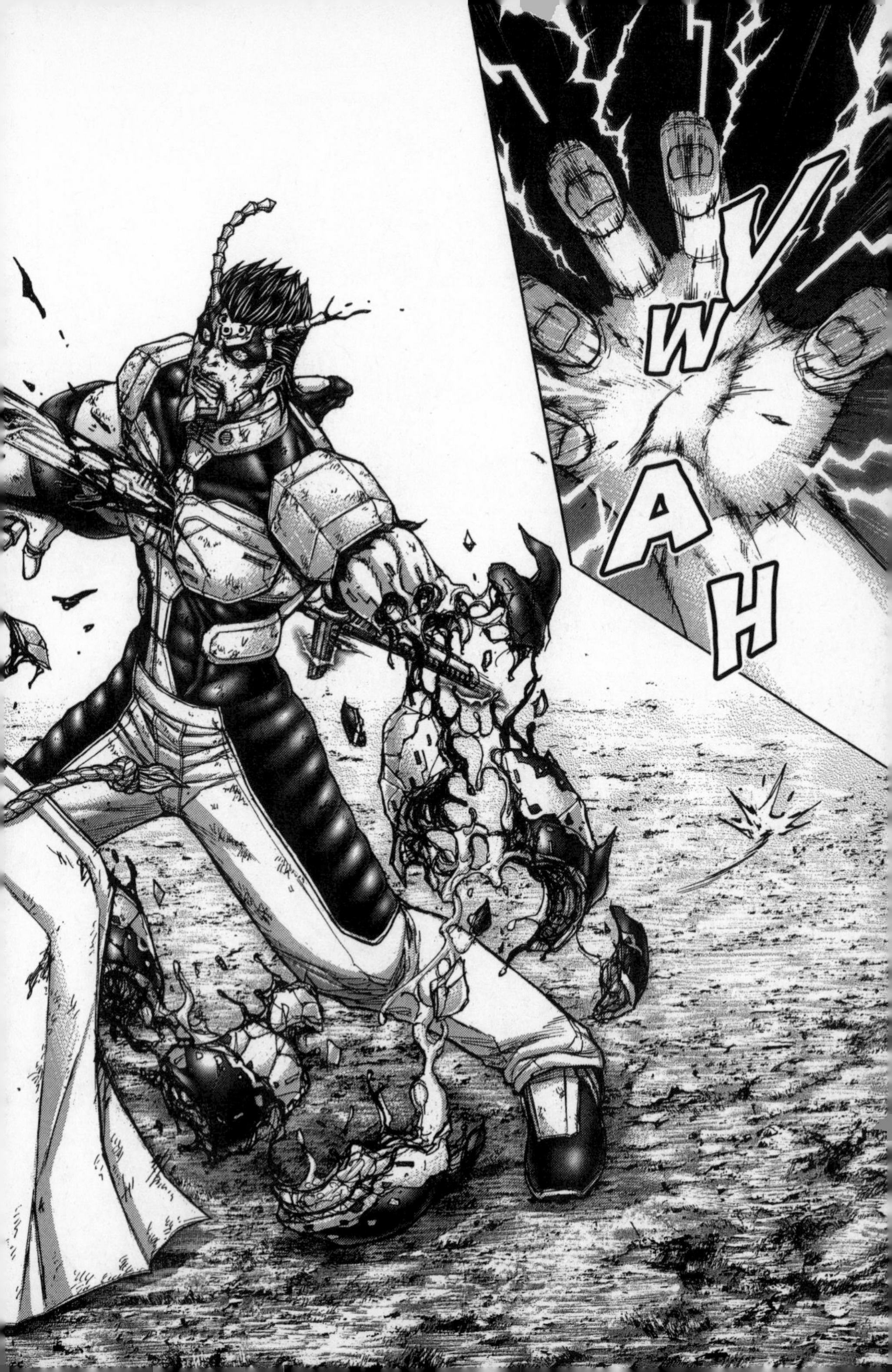
VWAH

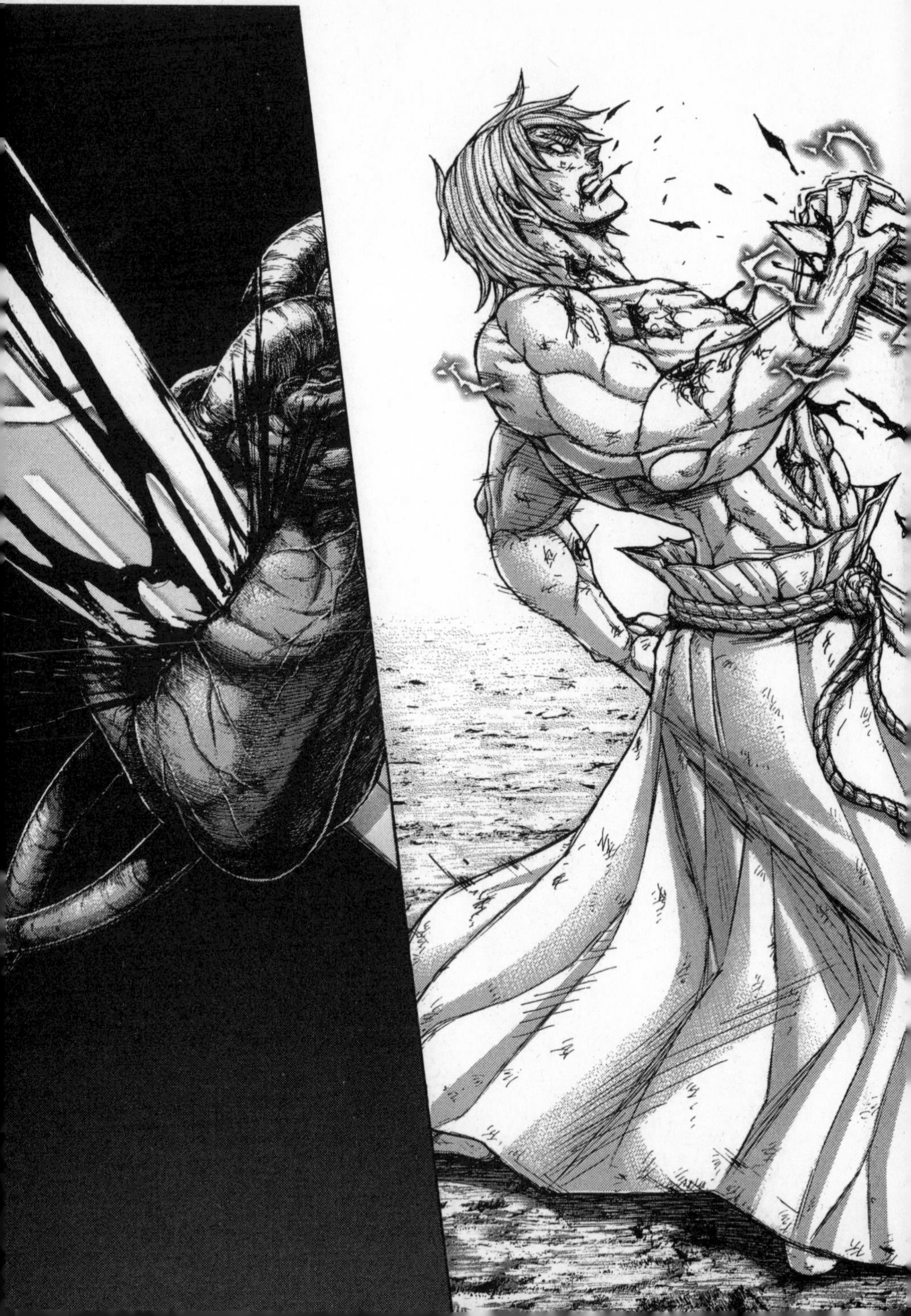

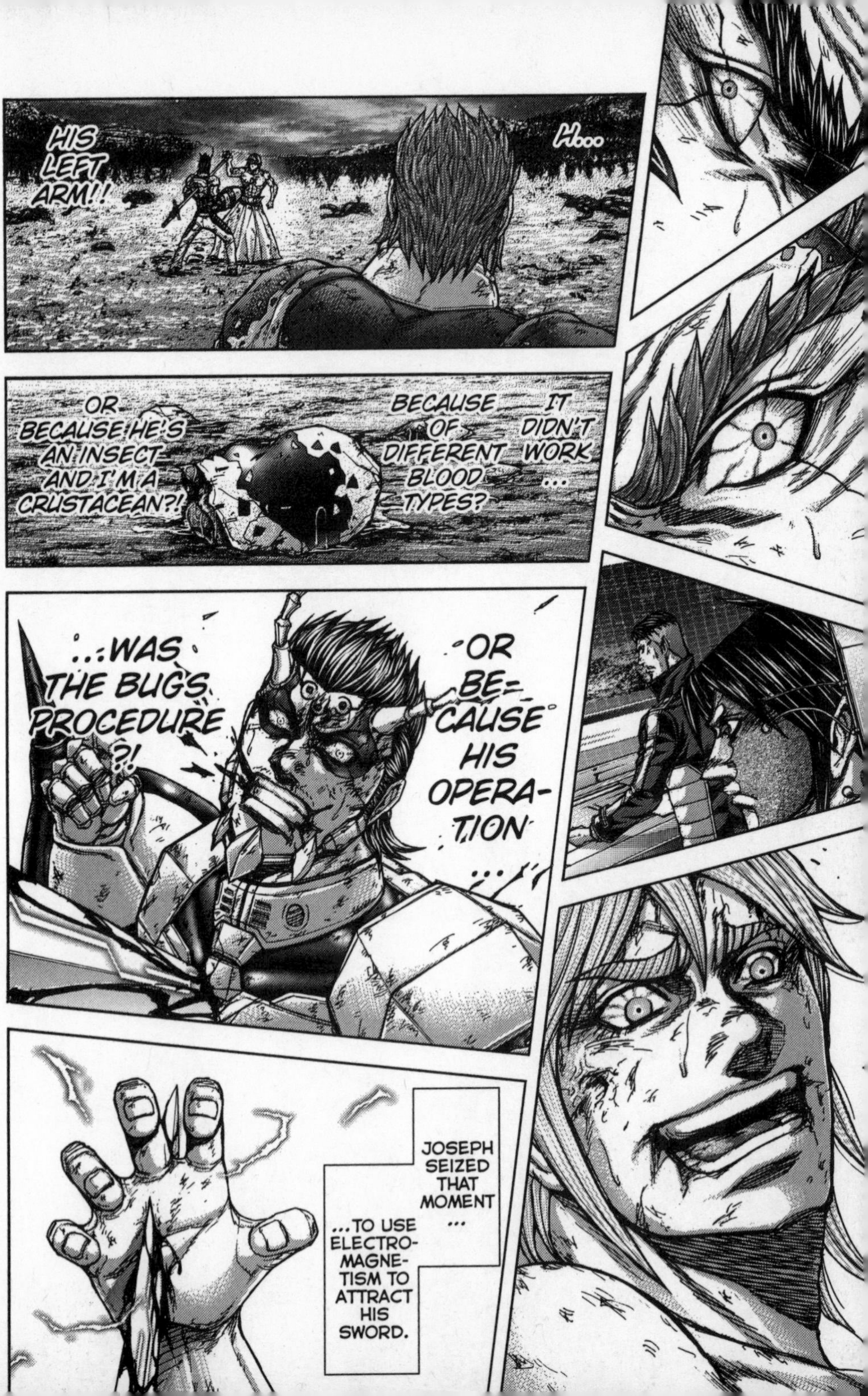
H...
HIS LEFT ARM!!
IT DIDN'T WORK...
BECAUSE OF DIFFERENT BLOOD TYPES?
OR BECAUSE HE'S AN INSECT AND I'M A CRUSTACEAN?!
OR BECAUSE HIS OPERATION...
...WAS THE BUGS PROCEDURE?!
JOSEPH SEIZED THAT MOMENT...
...TO USE ELECTRO-MAGNETISM TO ATTRACT HIS SWORD.

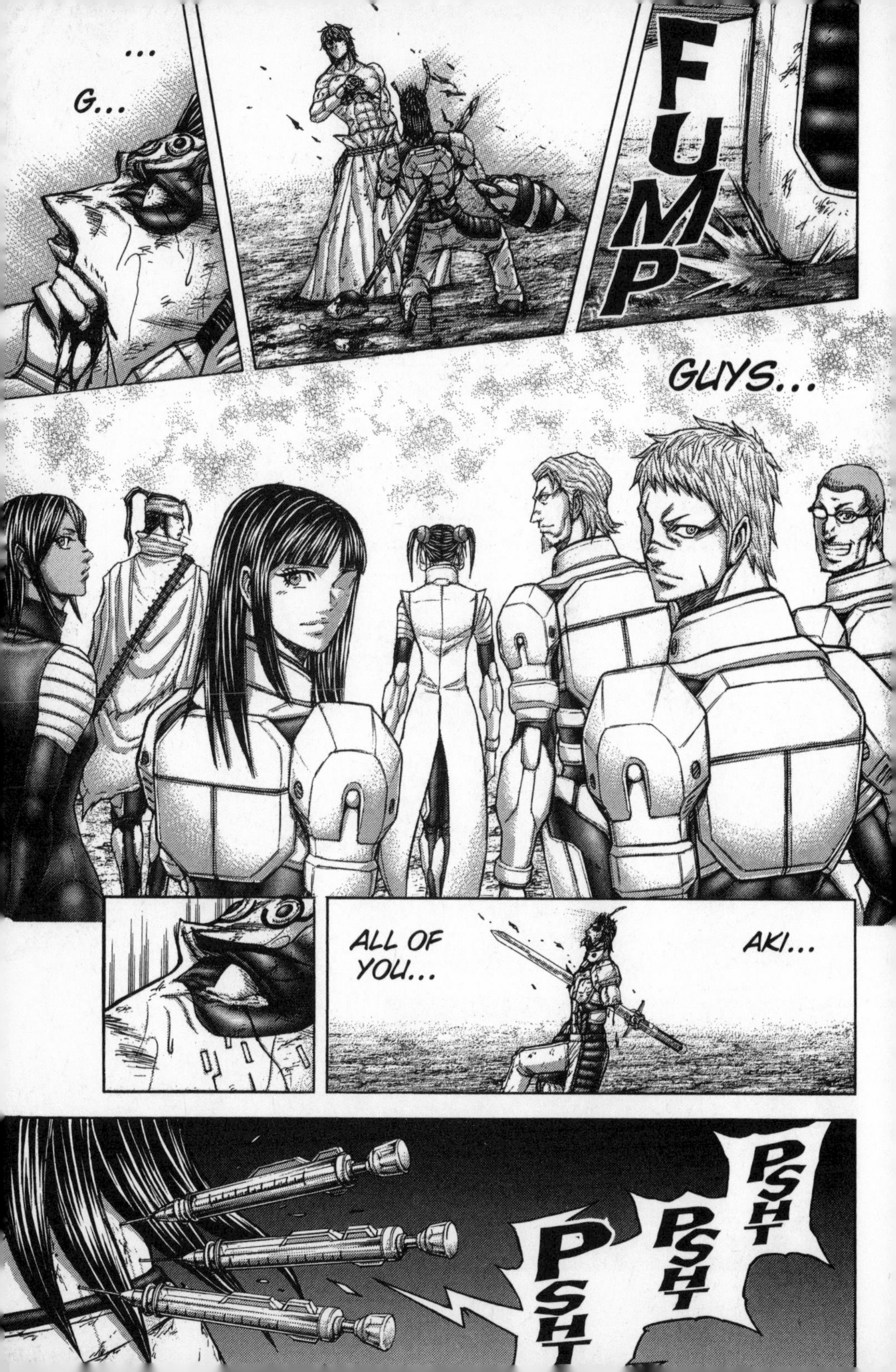
FUMP
...
G...
GUYS...
AKI...
ALL OF YOU...
PSHT
PSHT
PSHT

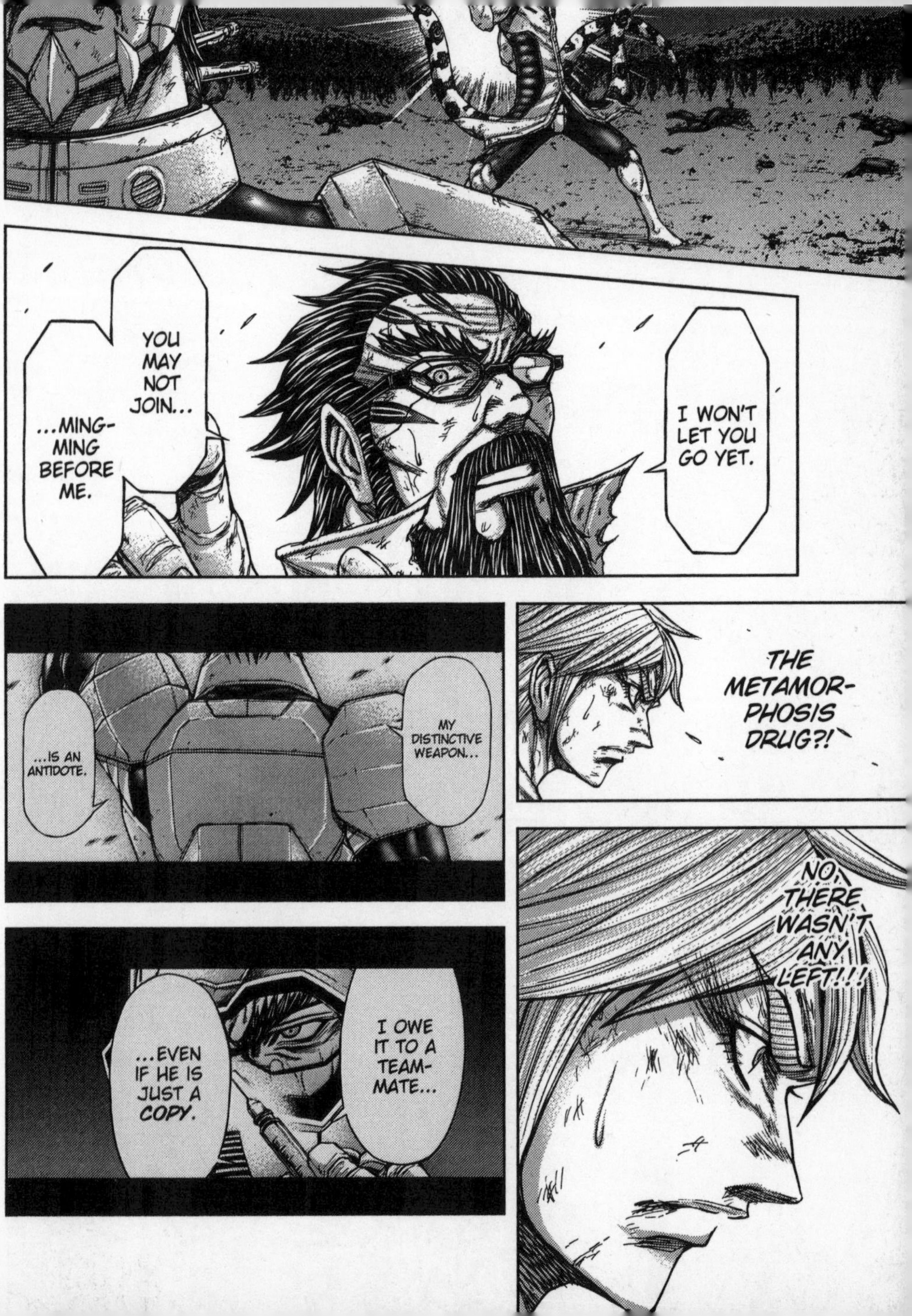
I WON'T LET YOU GO YET.
YOU MAY NOT JOIN...
...MING-MING BEFORE ME.
THE METAMORPHOSIS DRUG?!
MY DISTINCTIVE WEAPON...
...IS AN ANTIDOTE.
NO, THERE WASN'T ANY LEFT!!!
I OWE IT TO A TEAMMATE...
...EVEN IF HE IS JUST A COPY.

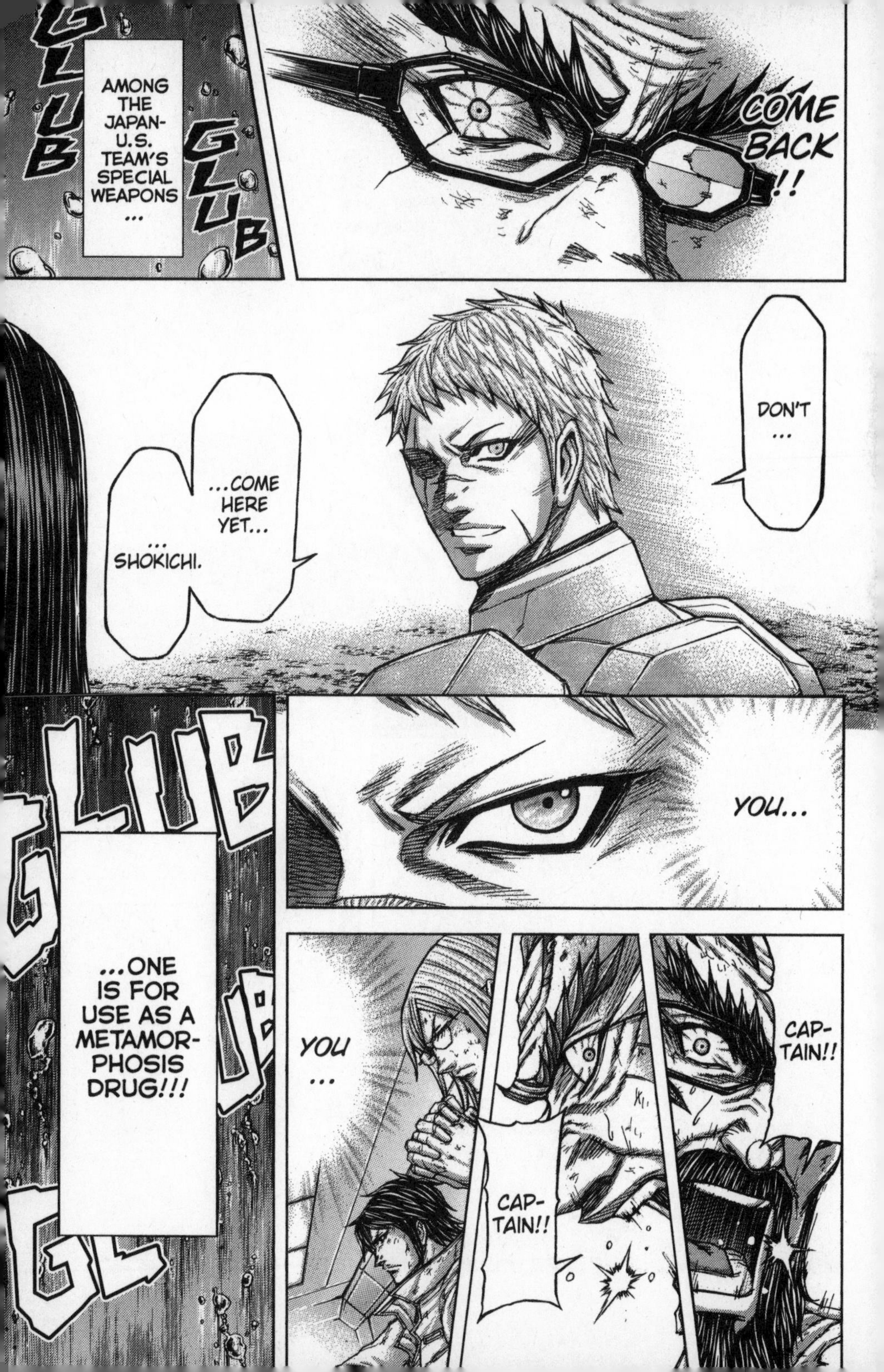
COME BACK!!
GLUB
GLUB
AMONG THE JAPAN-U.S. TEAM'S SPECIAL WEAPONS...
DON'T...
...COME HERE YET... ...SHOKICHI.
YOU...
CAP-TAIN!!
CAP-TAIN!!
YOU...
GLUB
GLUB
GLUB
...ONE IS FOR USE AS A METAMORPHOSIS DRUG!!!

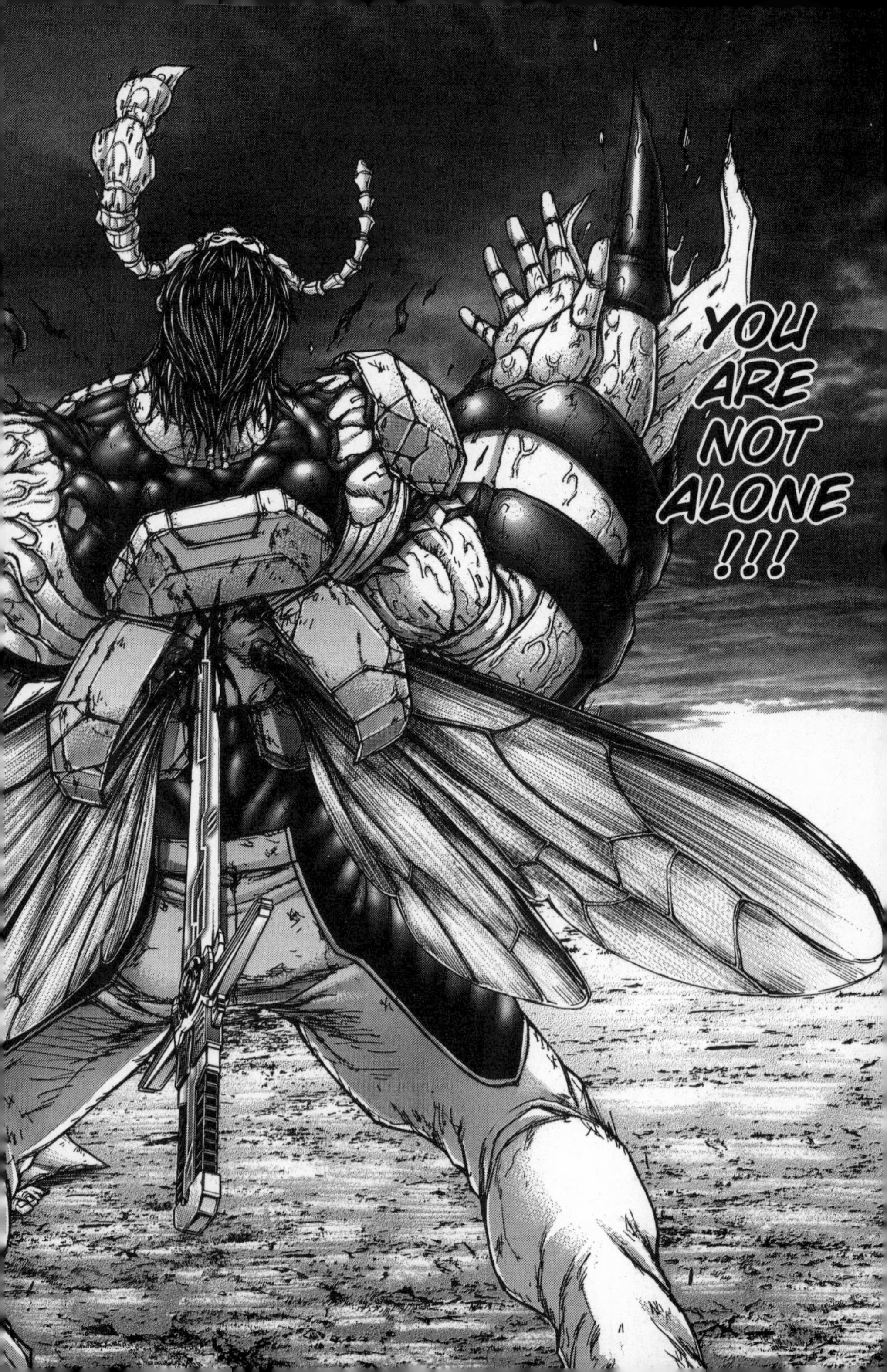
YOU ARE NOT ALONE !!!

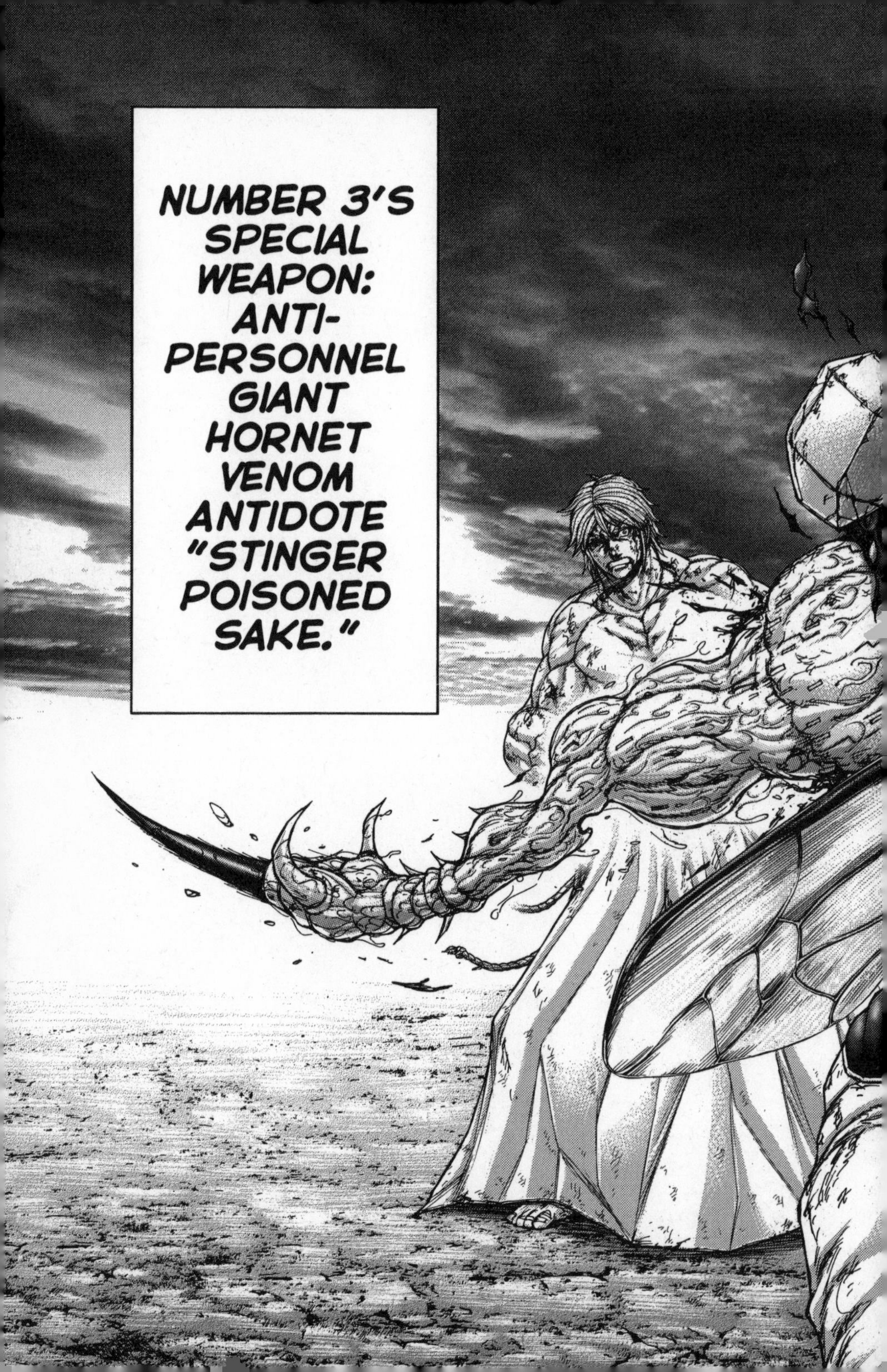
NUMBER 3'S SPECIAL WEAPON: ANTI-PERSONNEL GIANT HORNET VENOM ANTIDOTE "STINGER POISONED SAKE."

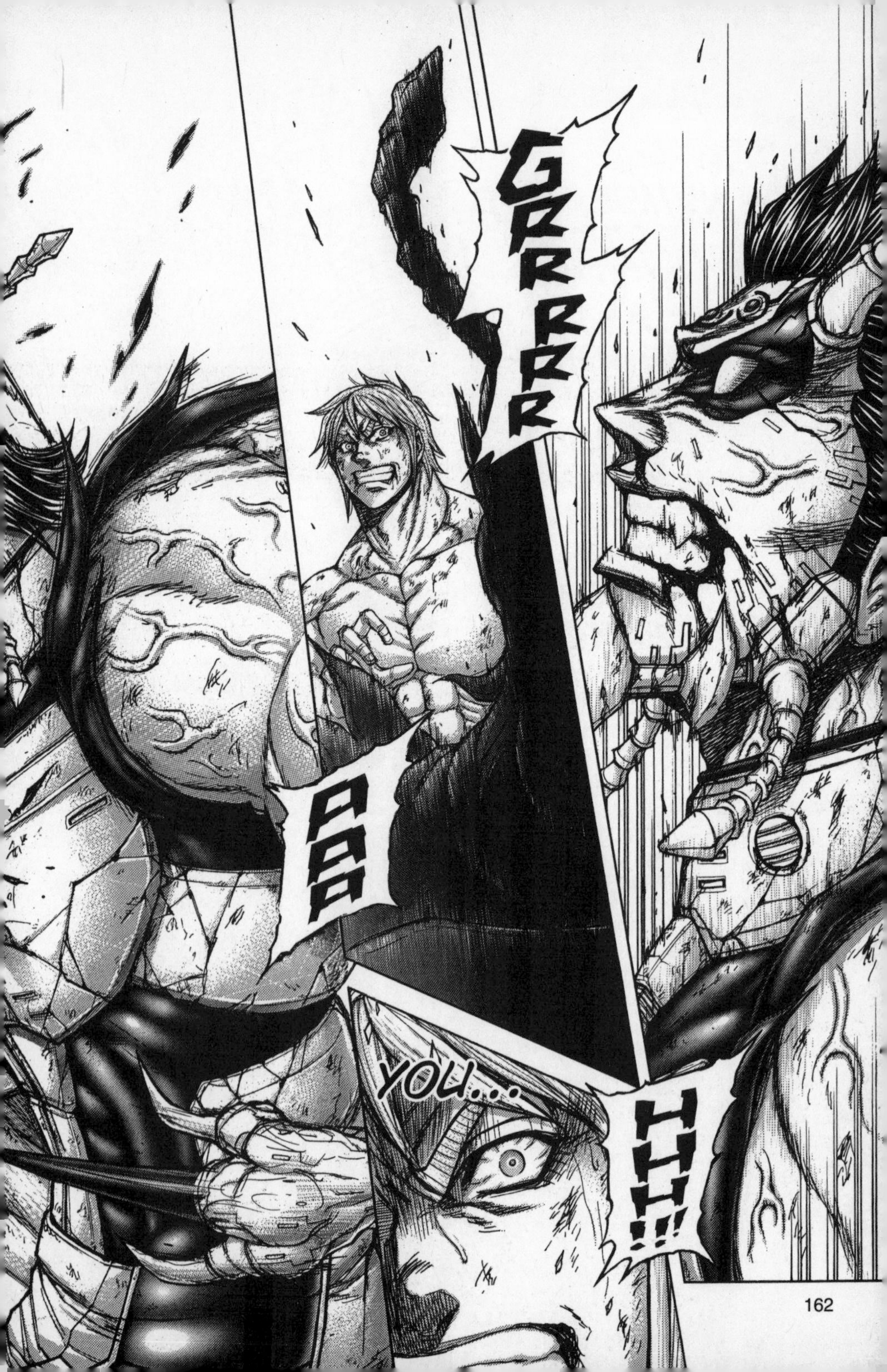
GRRRRR
AAA
HHH!!!
YOU...

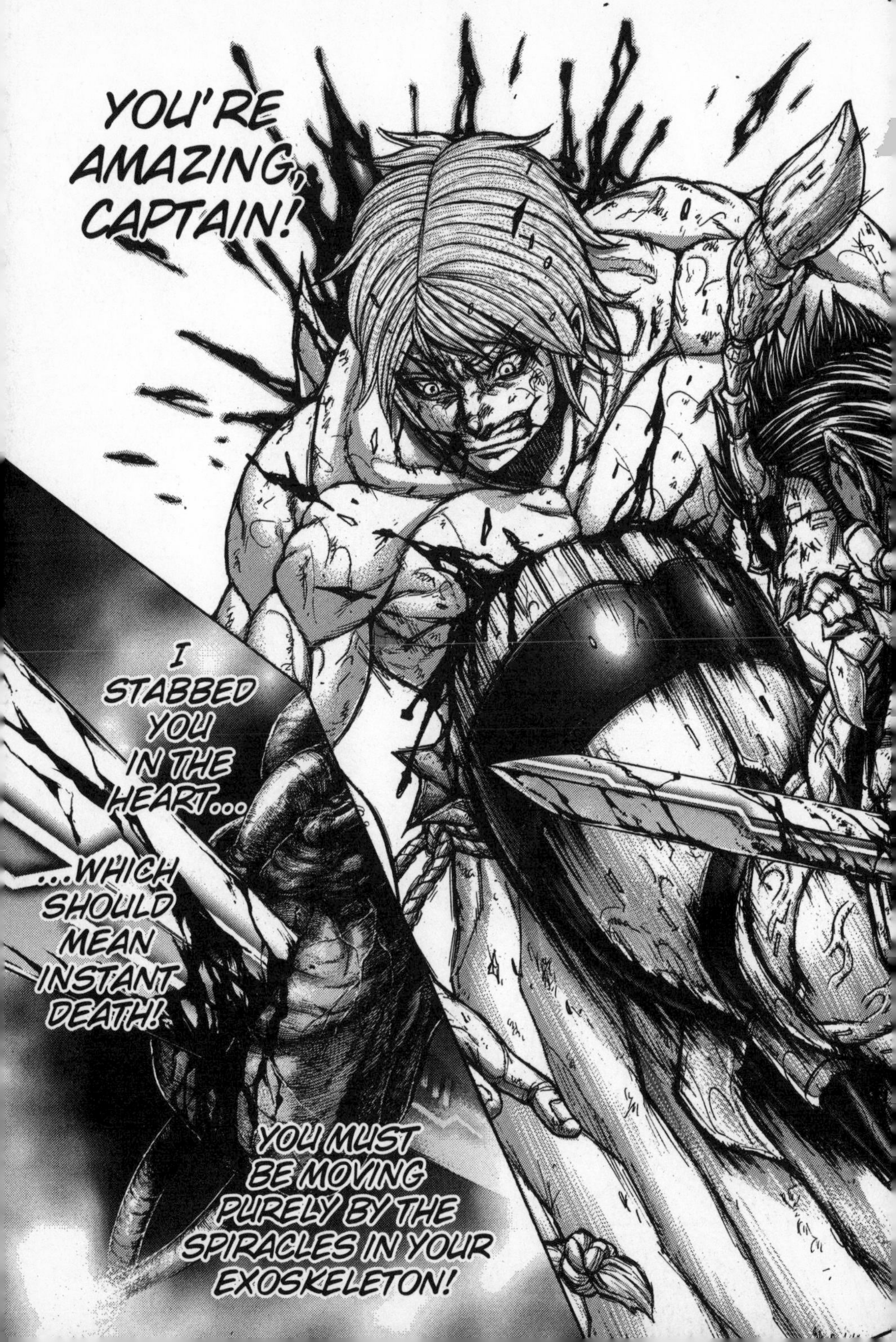
YOU'RE AMAZING, CAPTAIN!
I STABBED YOU IN THE HEART...
...WHICH SHOULD MEAN INSTANT DEATH!
YOU MUST BE MOVING PURELY BY THE SPIRACLES IN YOUR EXOSKELETON!

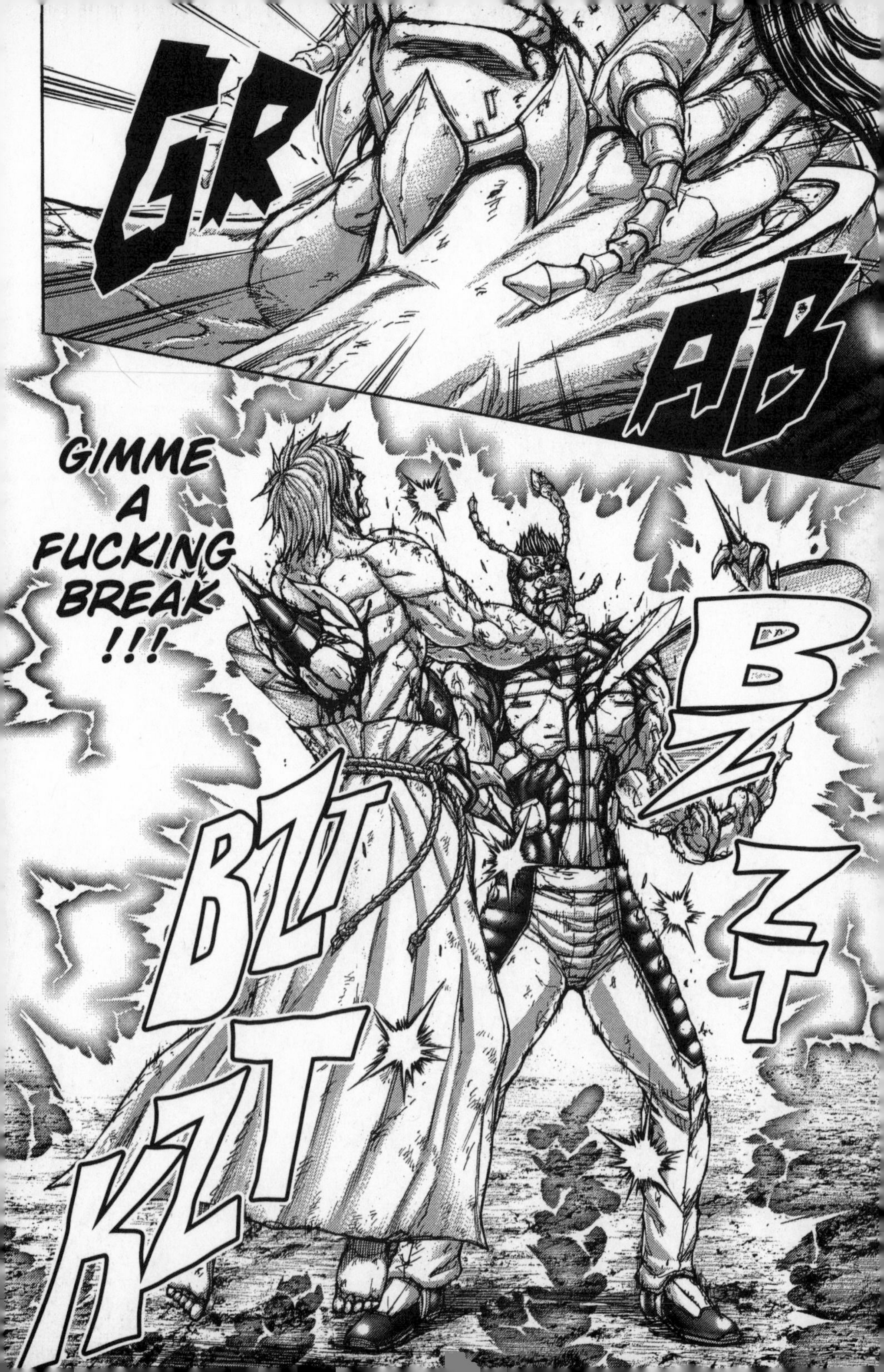
GR
AB
GIMME A FUCKING BREAK!!!
BZZT
BZZT
KZZT

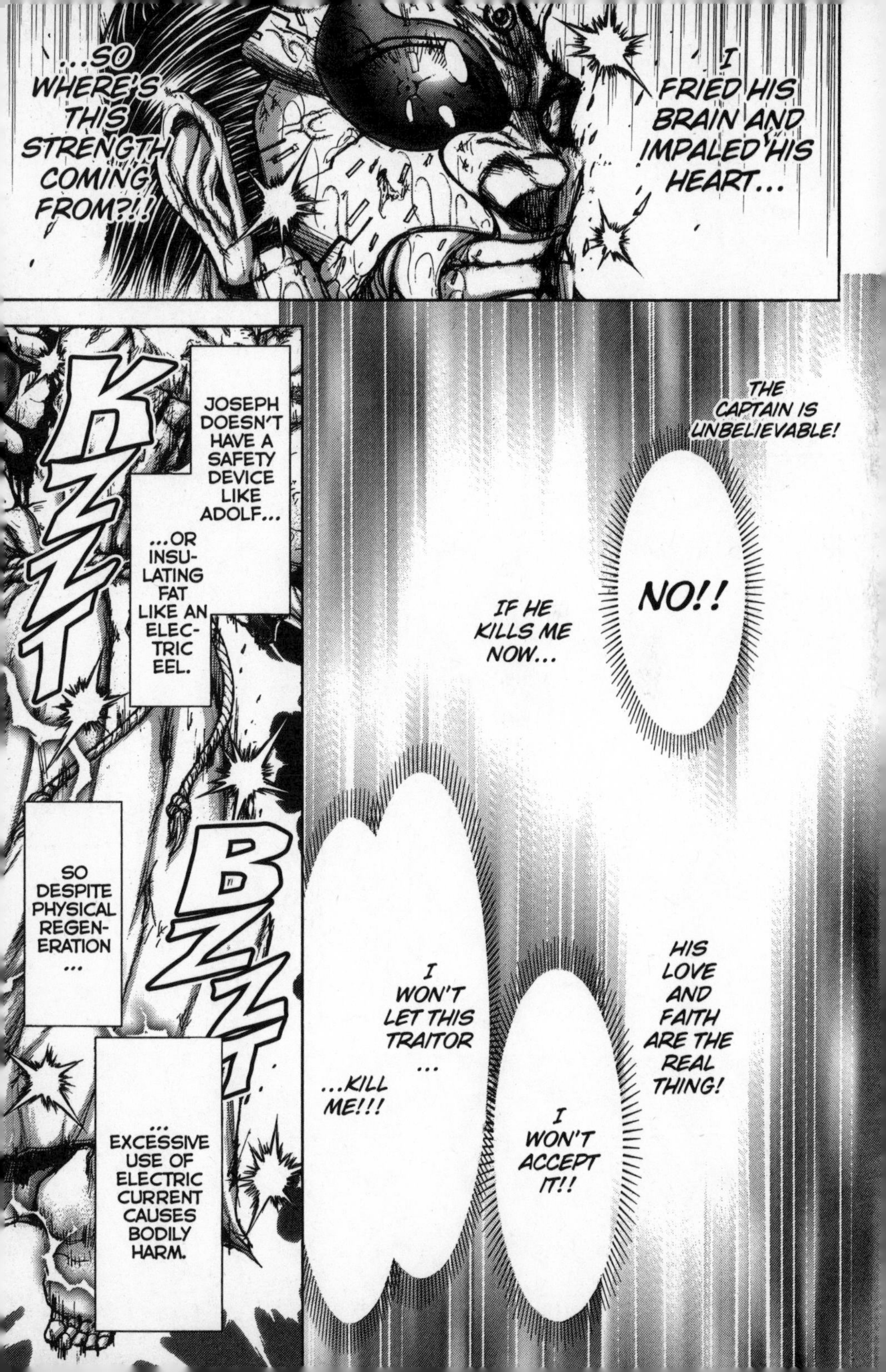
I FRIED HIS BRAIN AND IMPALED HIS HEART...
...SO WHERE'S THIS STRENGTH COMING FROM?!!
THE CAPTAIN IS UNBELIEVABLE!
NO!!
IF HE KILLS ME NOW...
HIS LOVE AND FAITH ARE THE REAL THING!
I WON'T ACCEPT IT!!
I WON'T LET THIS TRAITOR...
...KILL ME!!!
JOSEPH DOESN'T HAVE A SAFETY DEVICE LIKE ADOLF...
...OR INSU-LATING FAT LIKE AN ELEC-TRIC EEL.
KZZZT
SO DESPITE PHYSICAL REGEN-ERATION...
BZZZT
...EXCESSIVE USE OF ELECTRIC CURRENT CAUSES BODILY HARM.

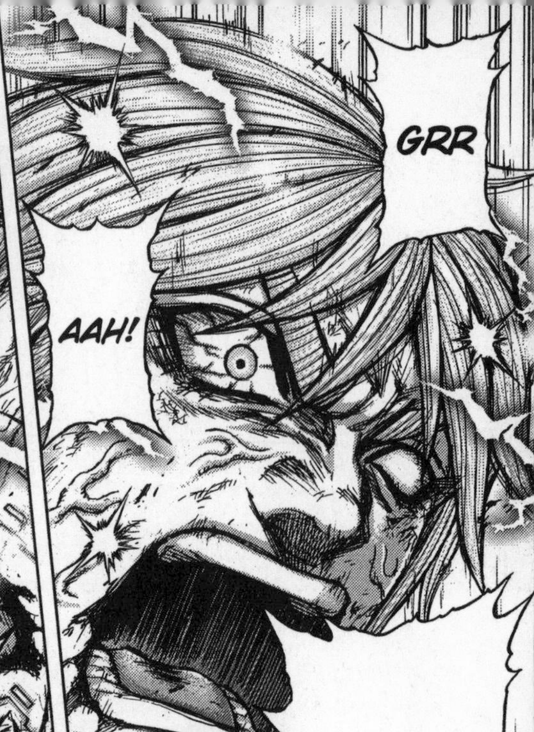
GRR
AAH!
I AM THE PINNACLE OF HUMANITY!!!!
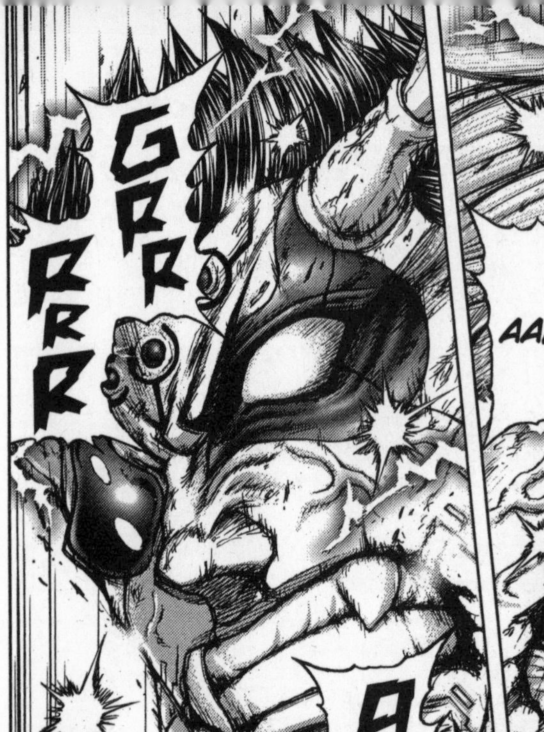
GRR
RRR
AAAAAH!!!!
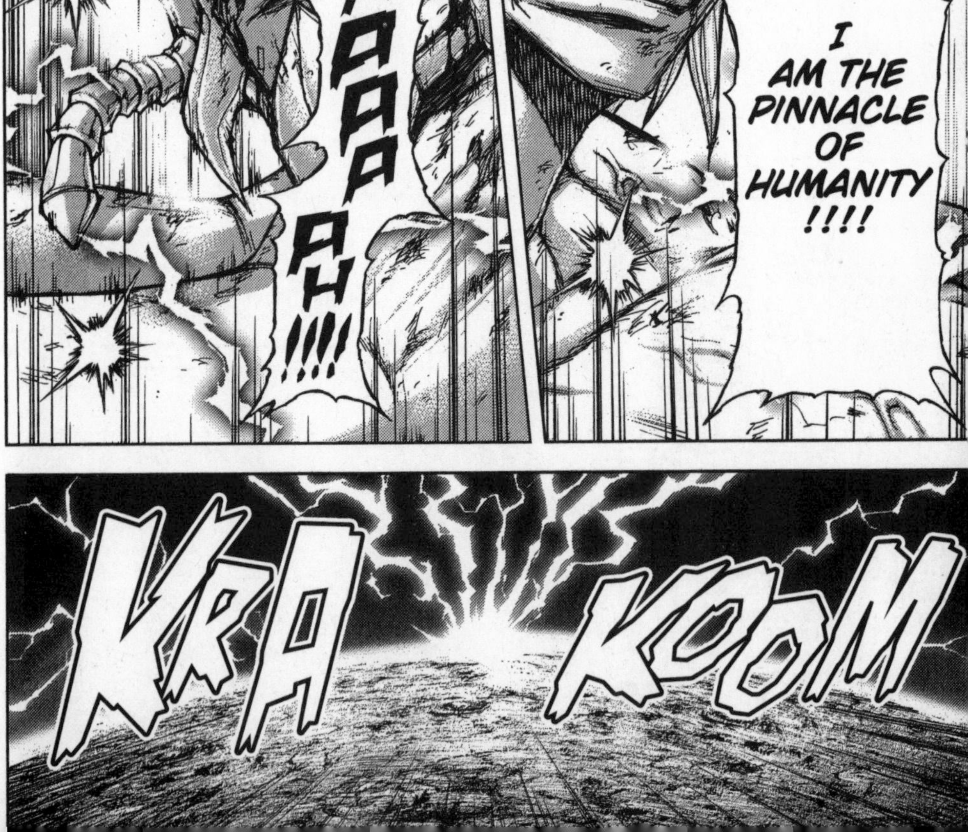
KRA
KOOM

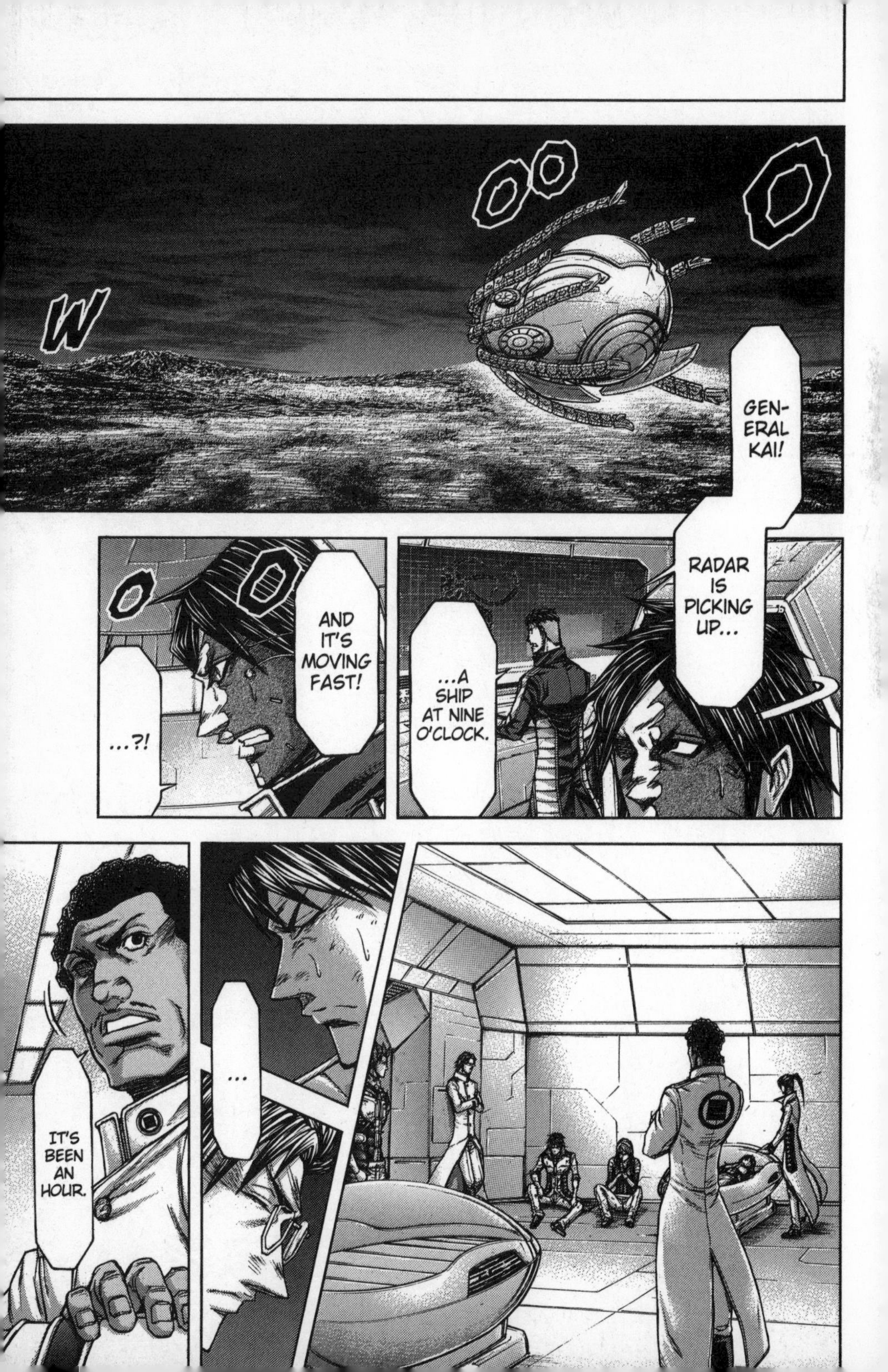
GEN-ERAL KAI!
RADAR IS PICKING UP...
...A SHIP AT NINE O'CLOCK.
AND IT'S MOVING FAST!
...?!
...
IT'S BEEN AN HOUR.

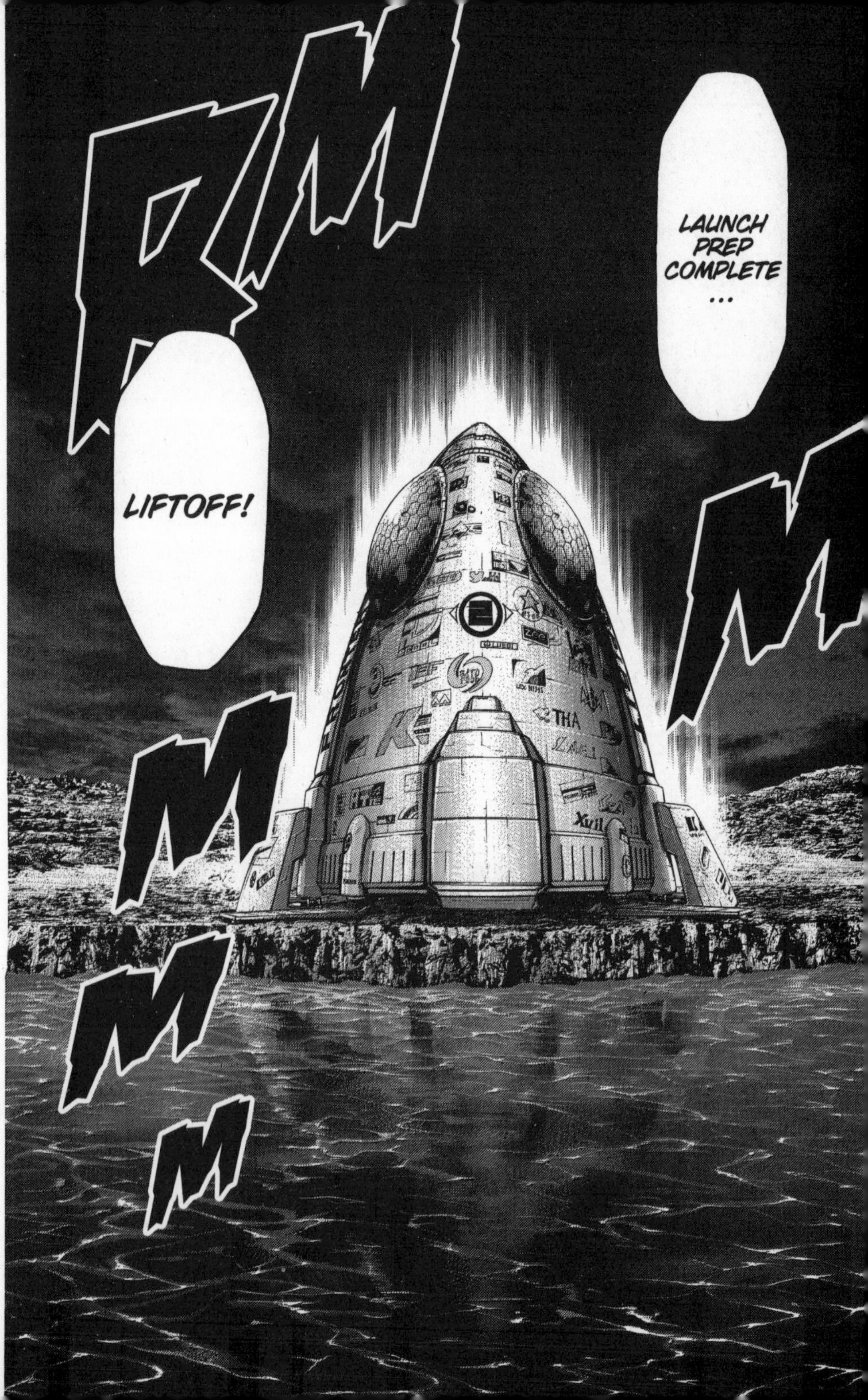
LAUNCH PREP COMPLETE ...
LIFTOFF!

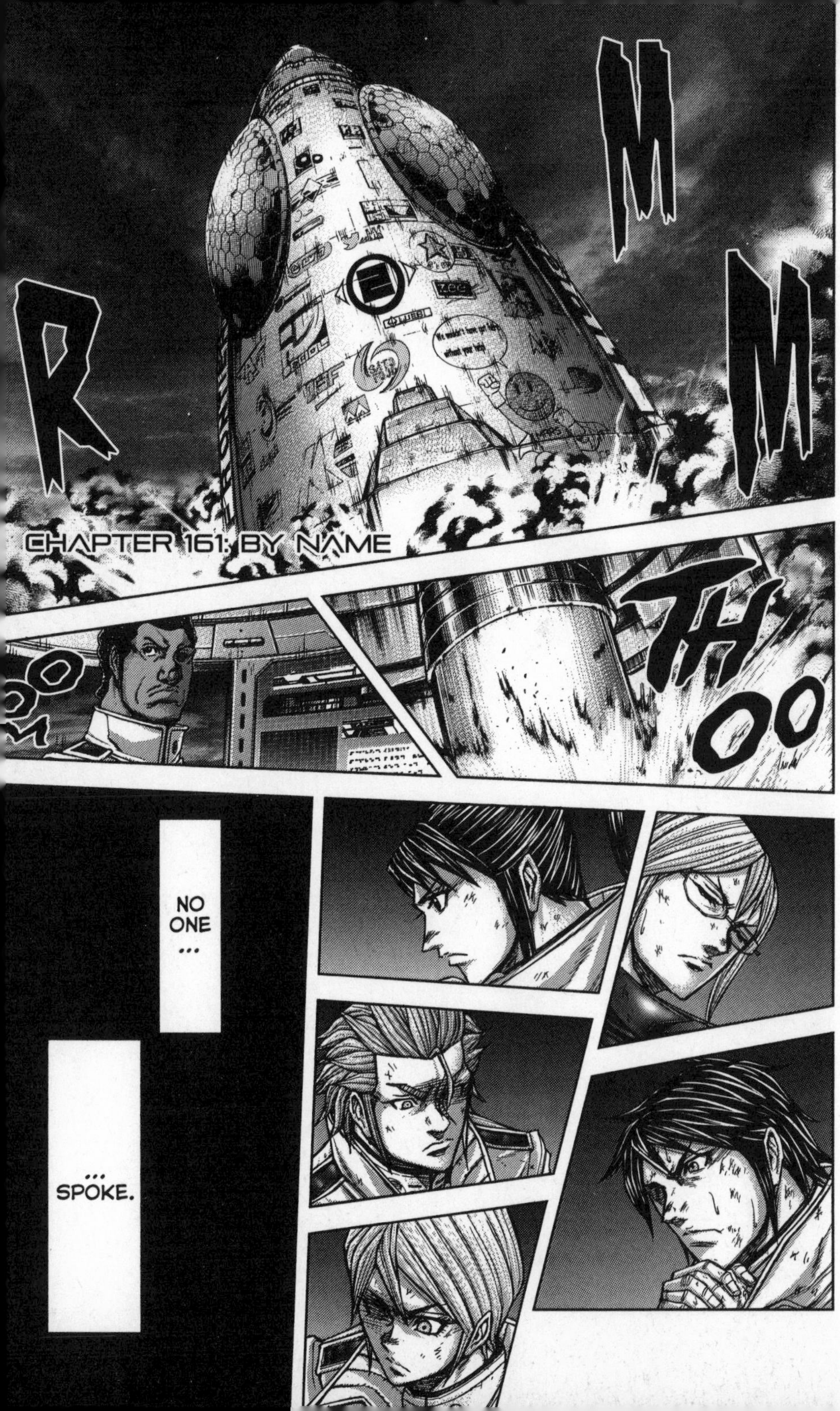
RMMM
CHAPTER 161: BY NAME
THOO
OOM
NO ONE ...
... SPOKE.

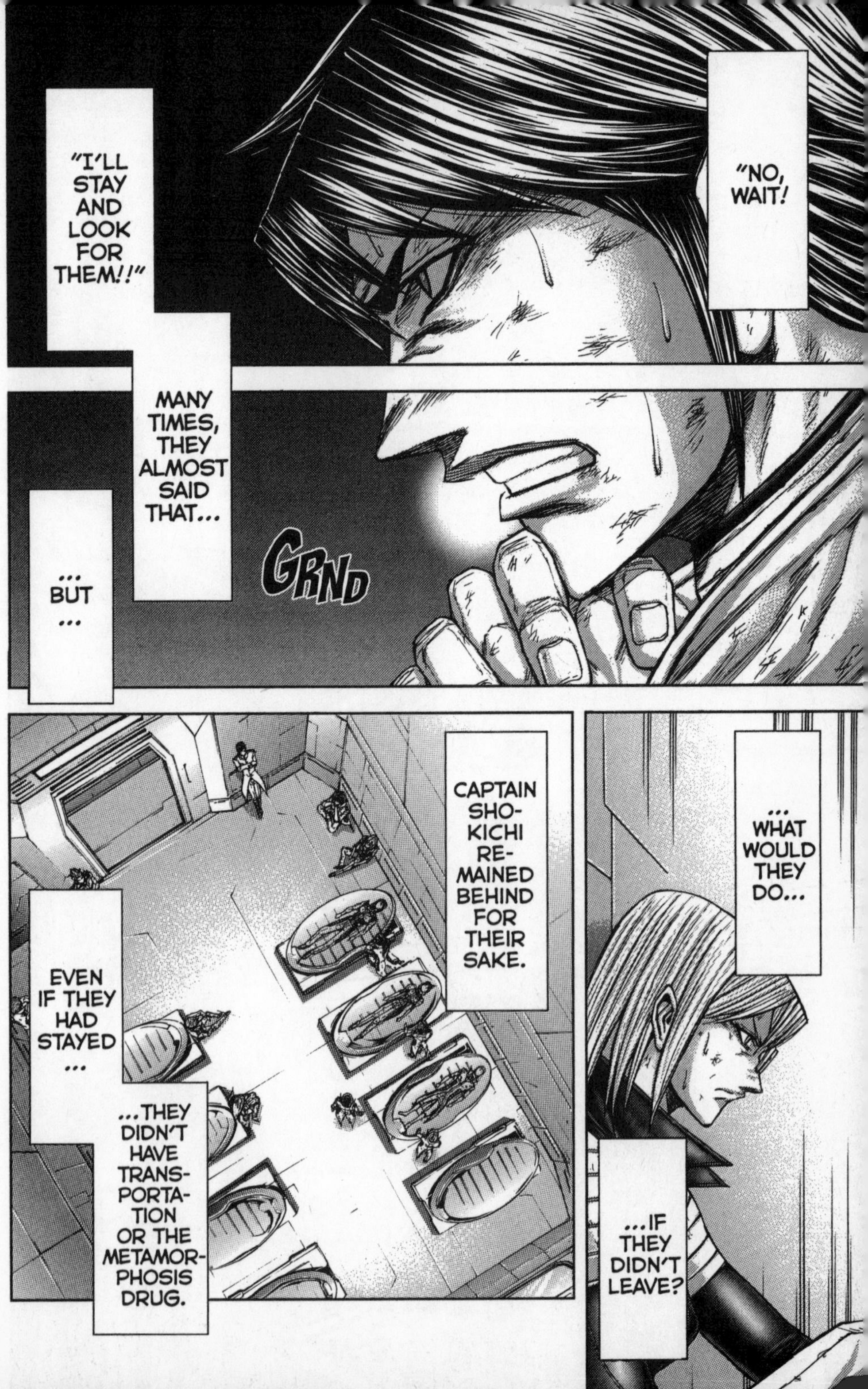
"NO, WAIT!
"I'LL STAY AND LOOK FOR THEM!!"
MANY TIMES, THEY ALMOST SAID THAT...
...BUT...
GRND
...WHAT WOULD THEY DO...
...IF THEY DIDN'T LEAVE?
CAPTAIN SHOKICHI REMAINED BEHIND FOR THEIR SAKE.
EVEN IF THEY HAD STAYED...
...THEY DIDN'T HAVE TRANSPORTATION OR THE METAMORPHOSIS DRUG.

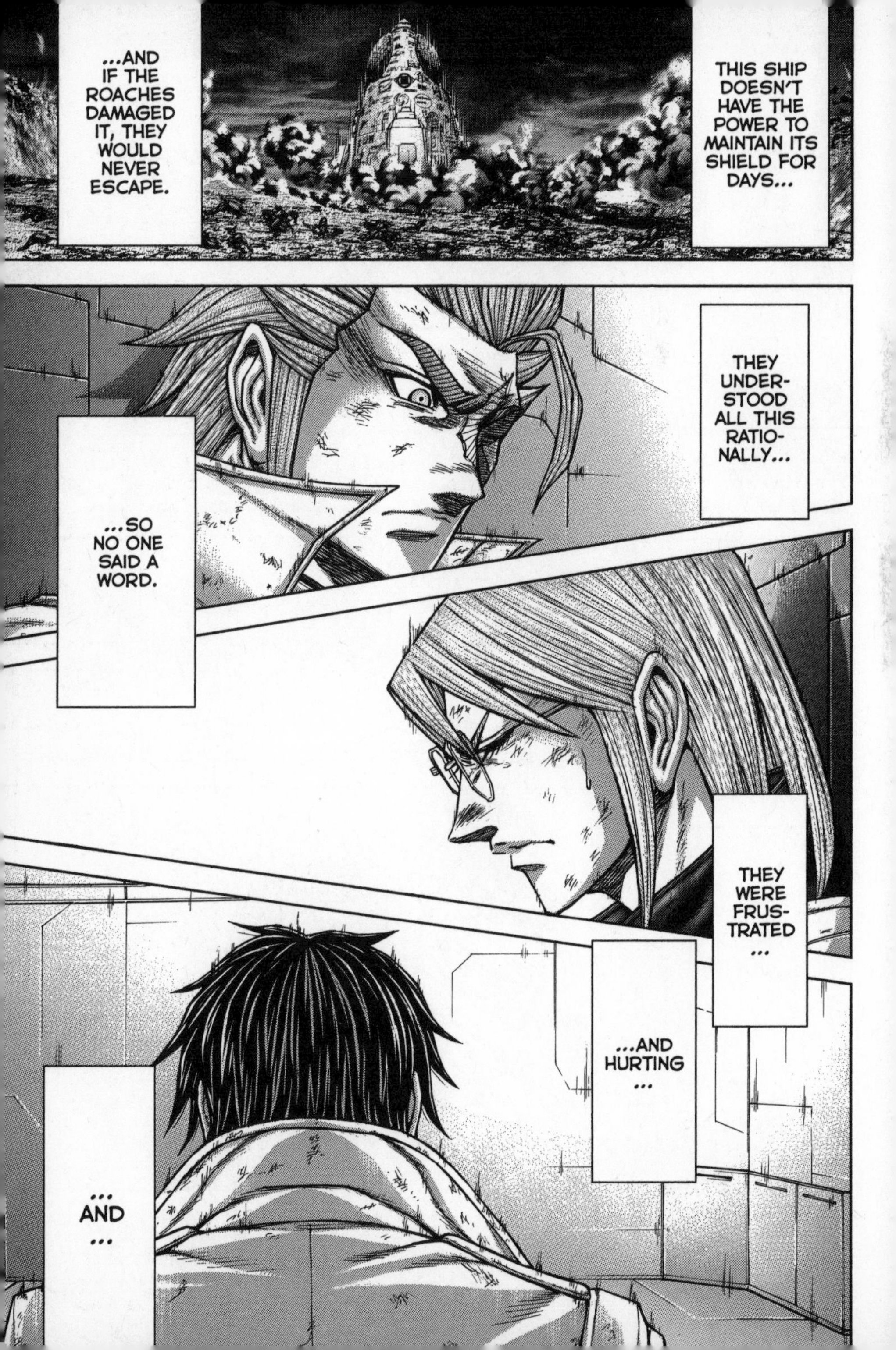
THIS SHIP DOESN'T HAVE THE POWER TO MAINTAIN ITS SHIELD FOR DAYS...
...AND IF THE ROACHES DAMAGED IT, THEY WOULD NEVER ESCAPE.
THEY UNDERSTOOD ALL THIS RATIONALLY...
...SO NO ONE SAID A WORD.
THEY WERE FRUSTRATED...
...AND HURTING...
...AND...

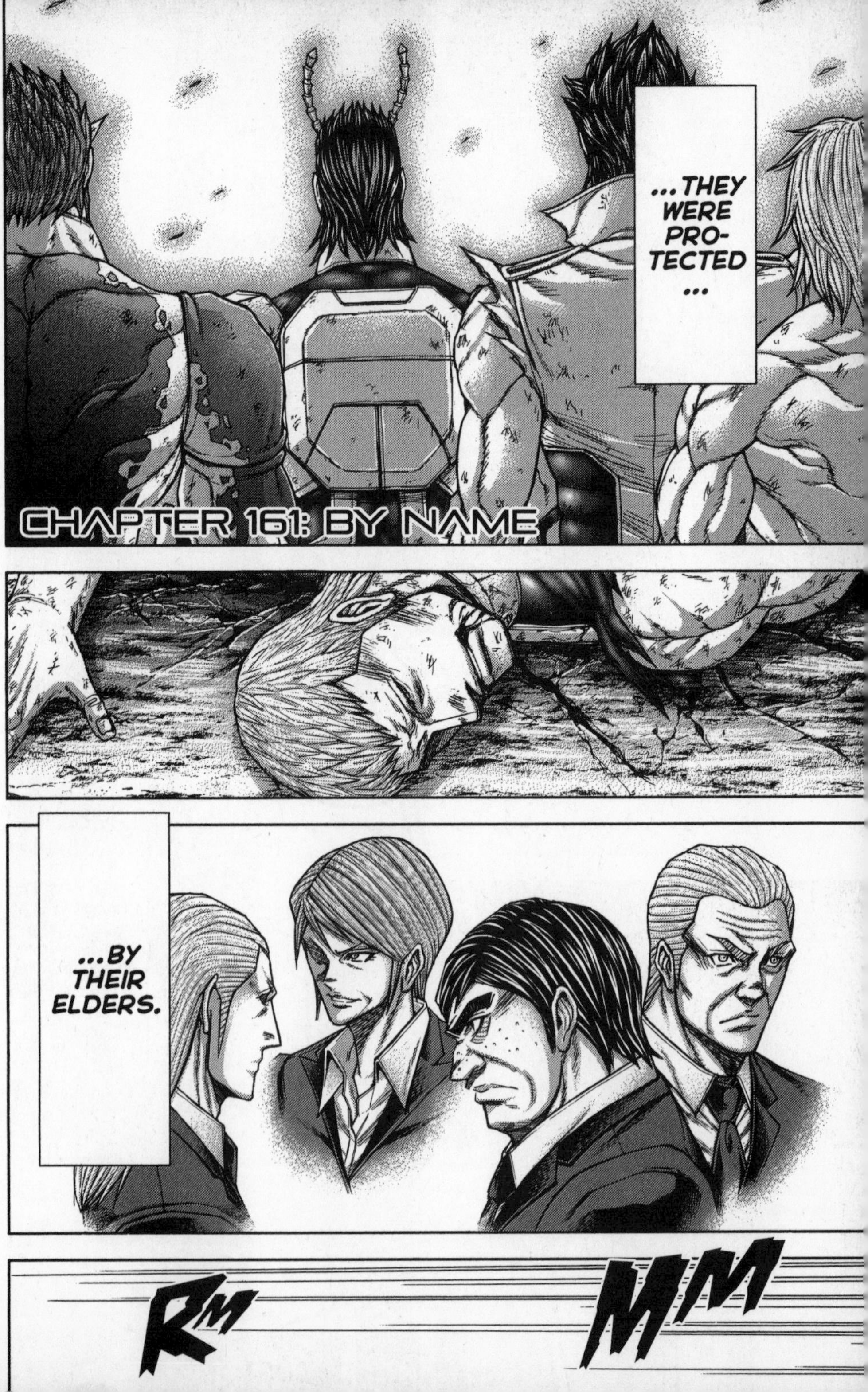
...THEY WERE PRO-TECTED...
CHAPTER 161: BY NAME
...BY THEIR ELDERS.
RM
MM

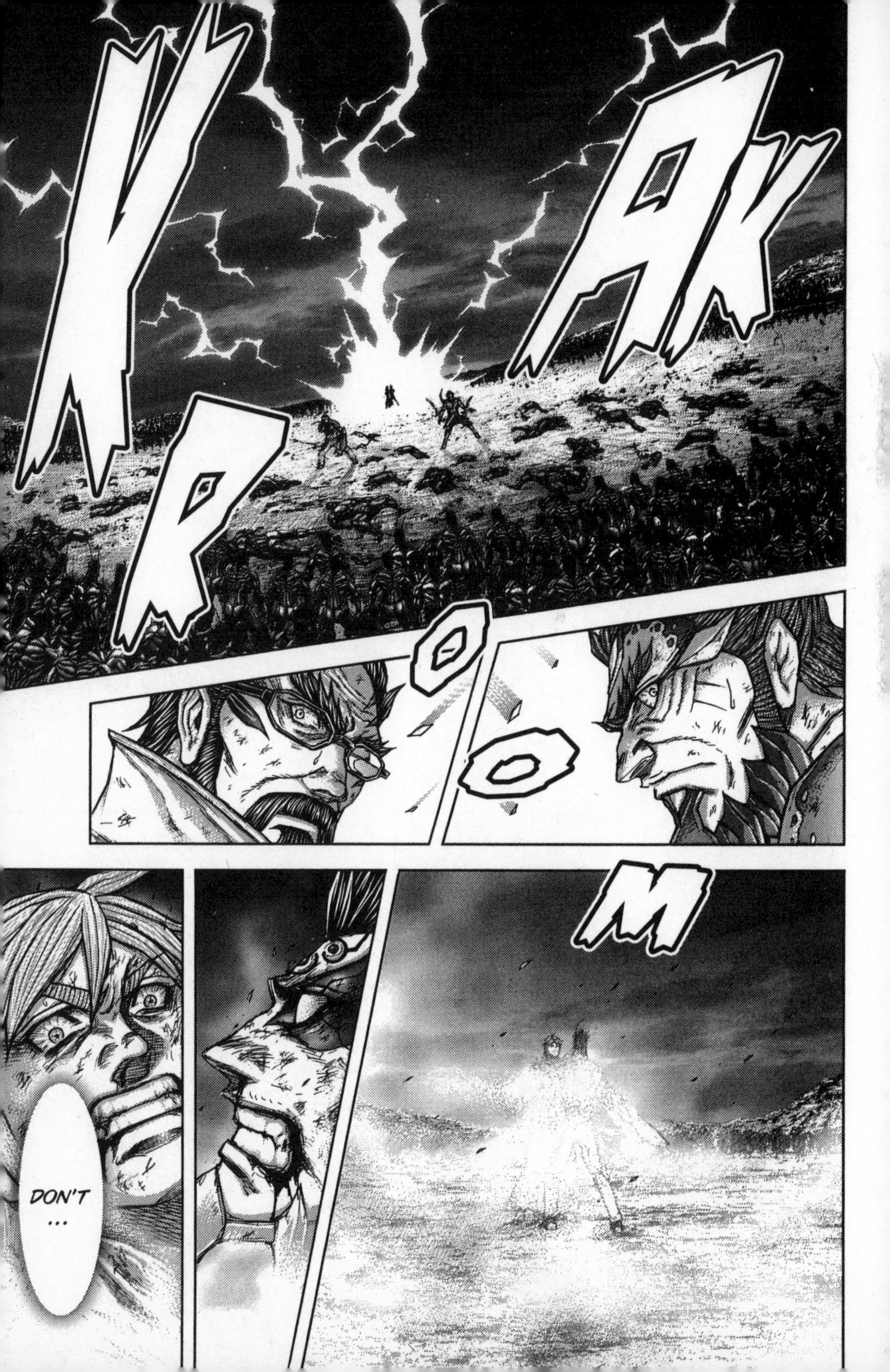

KRAK
OOM
DON'T ...

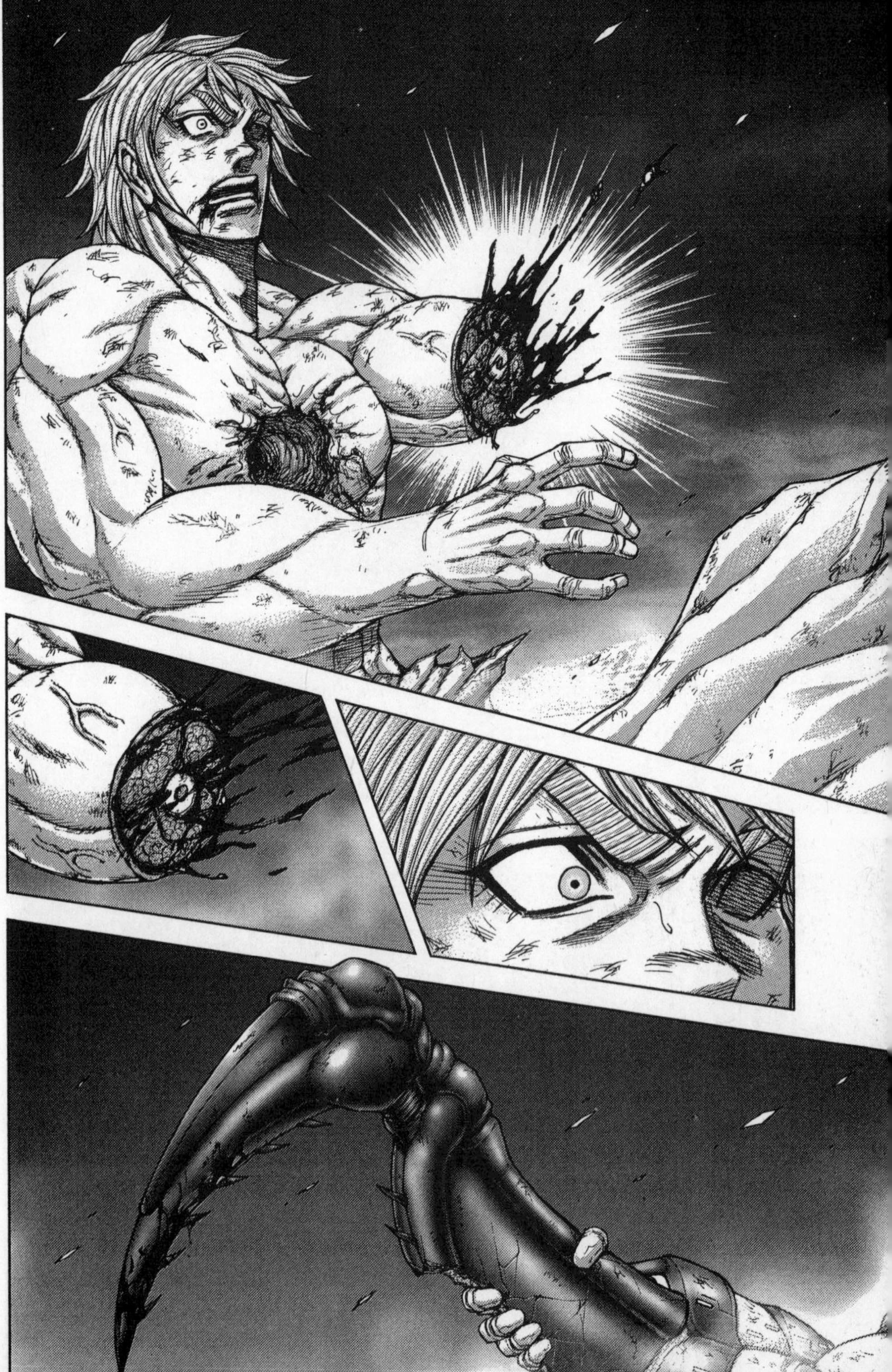

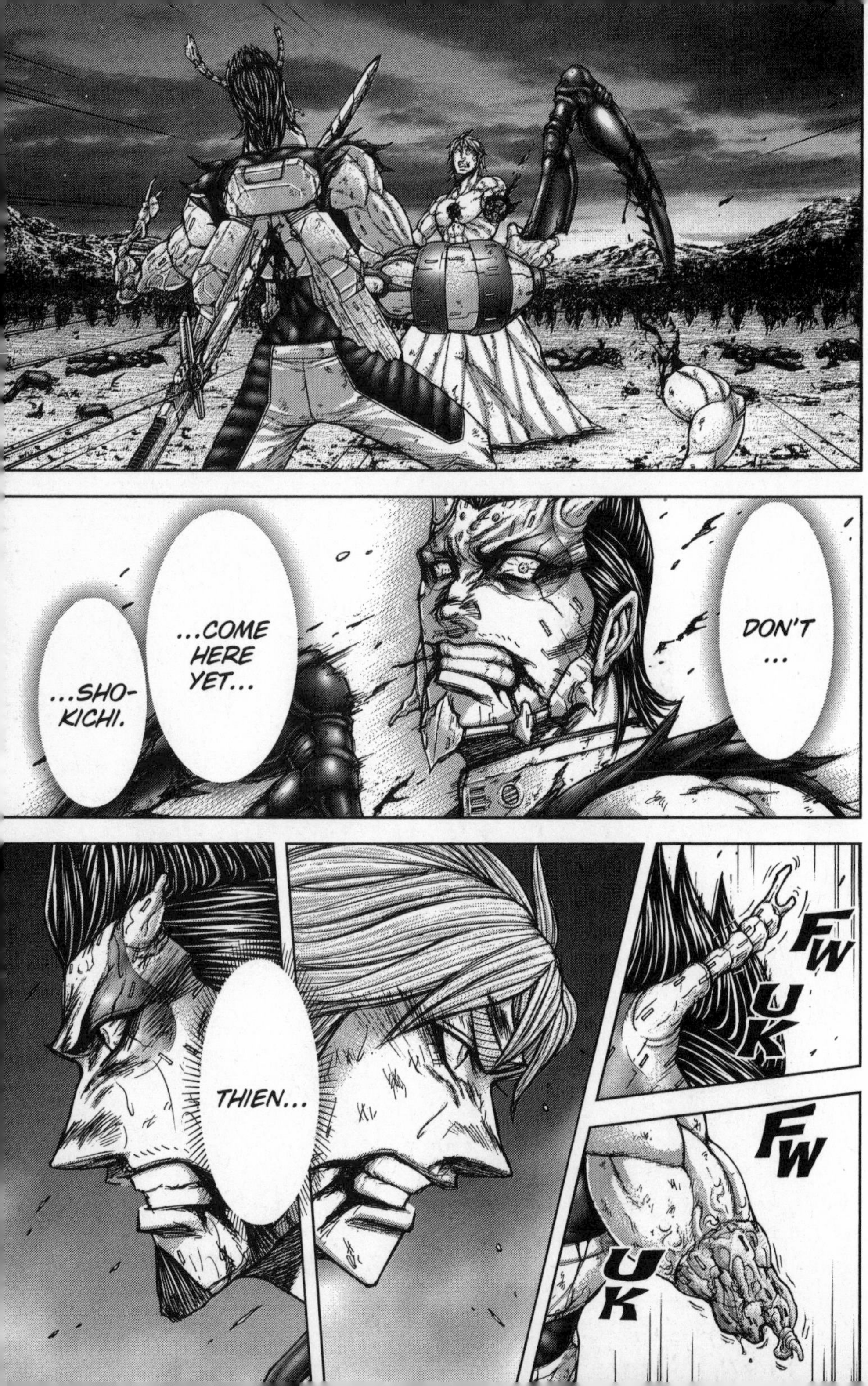
DON'T ...
...COME HERE YET...
...SHO-KICHI.
FWUK
FWUK
THIEN...

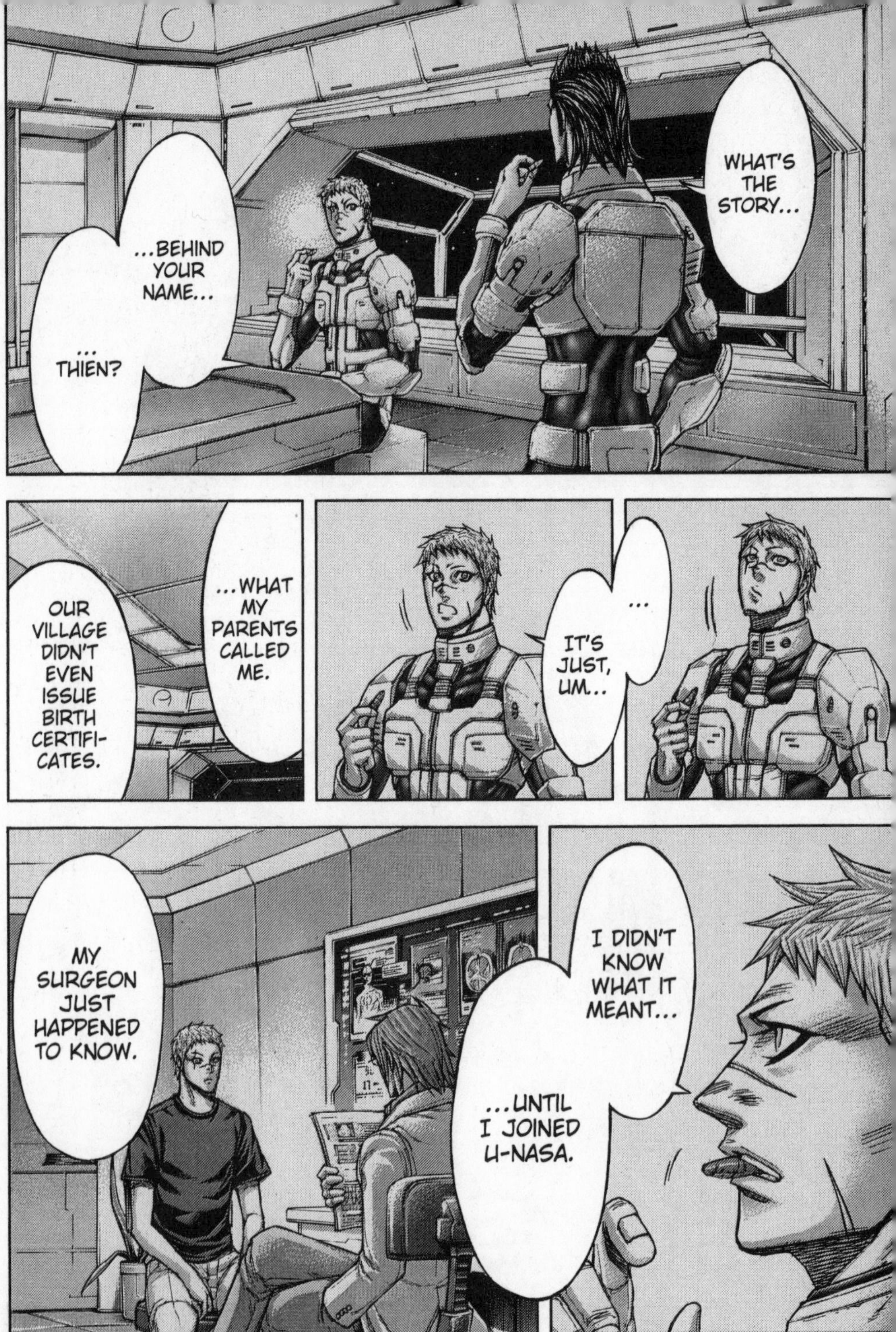
WHAT'S THE STORY...
...BEHIND YOUR NAME...
... THIEN?
...
IT'S JUST, UM...
...WHAT MY PARENTS CALLED ME.
OUR VILLAGE DIDN'T EVEN ISSUE BIRTH CERTIFICATES.
I DIDN'T KNOW WHAT IT MEANT...
...UNTIL I JOINED U-NASA.
MY SURGEON JUST HAPPENED TO KNOW.

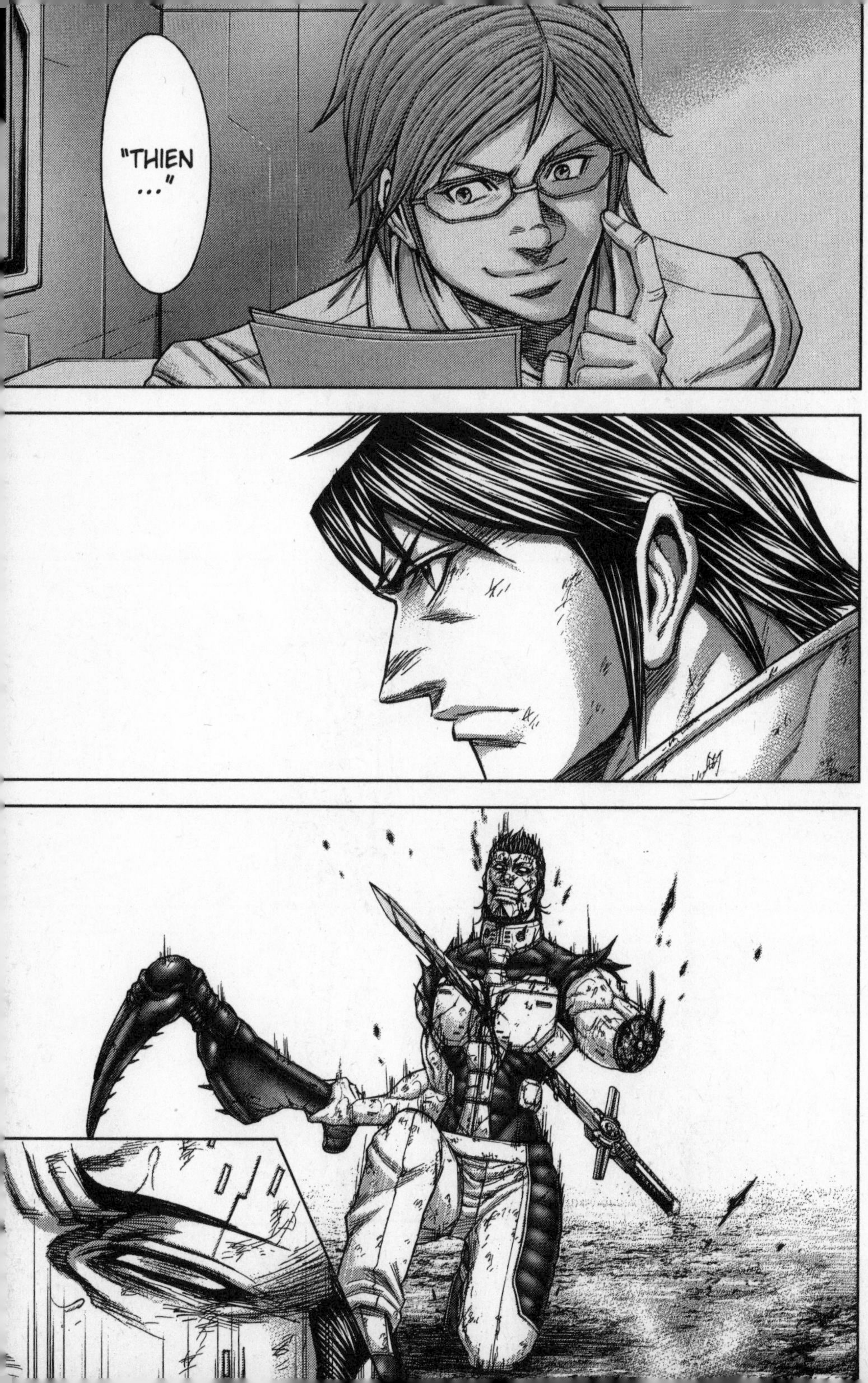
"THIEN ..."

...MEANS A BEACON OF LIGHT.

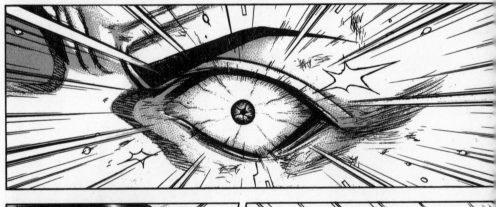

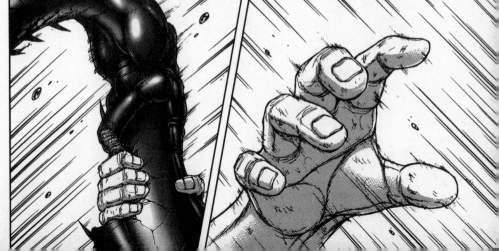

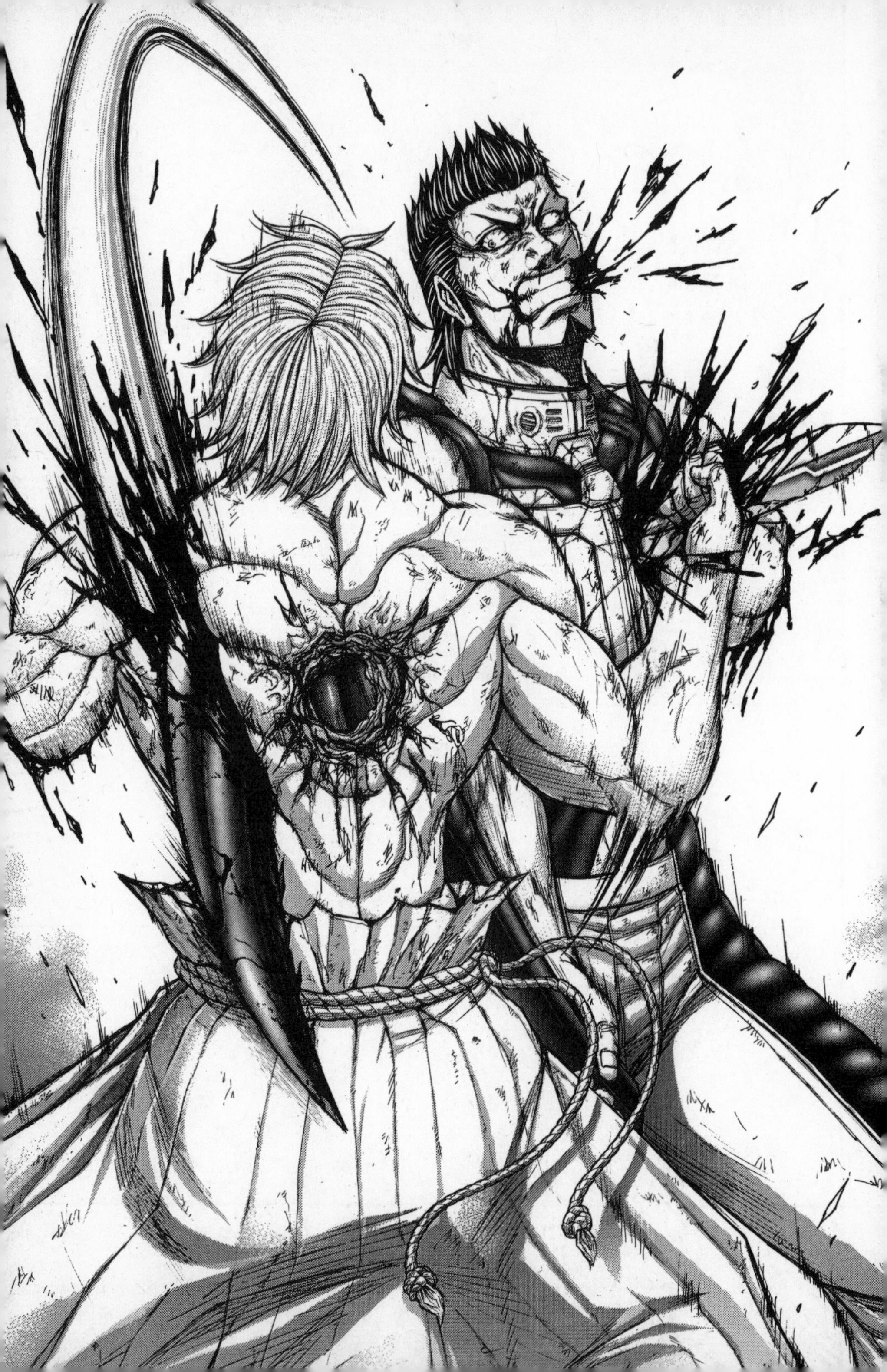

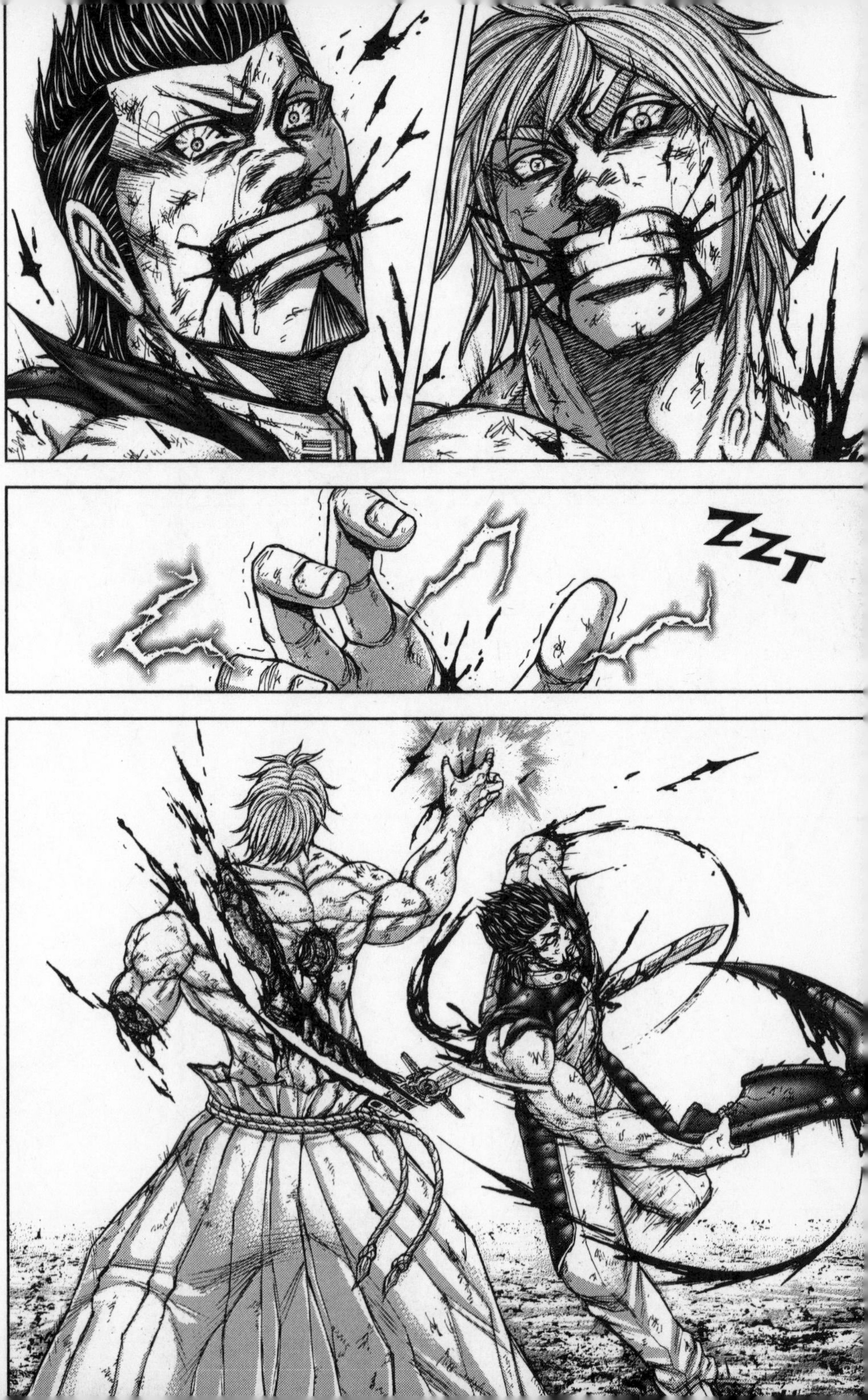
ZZZT

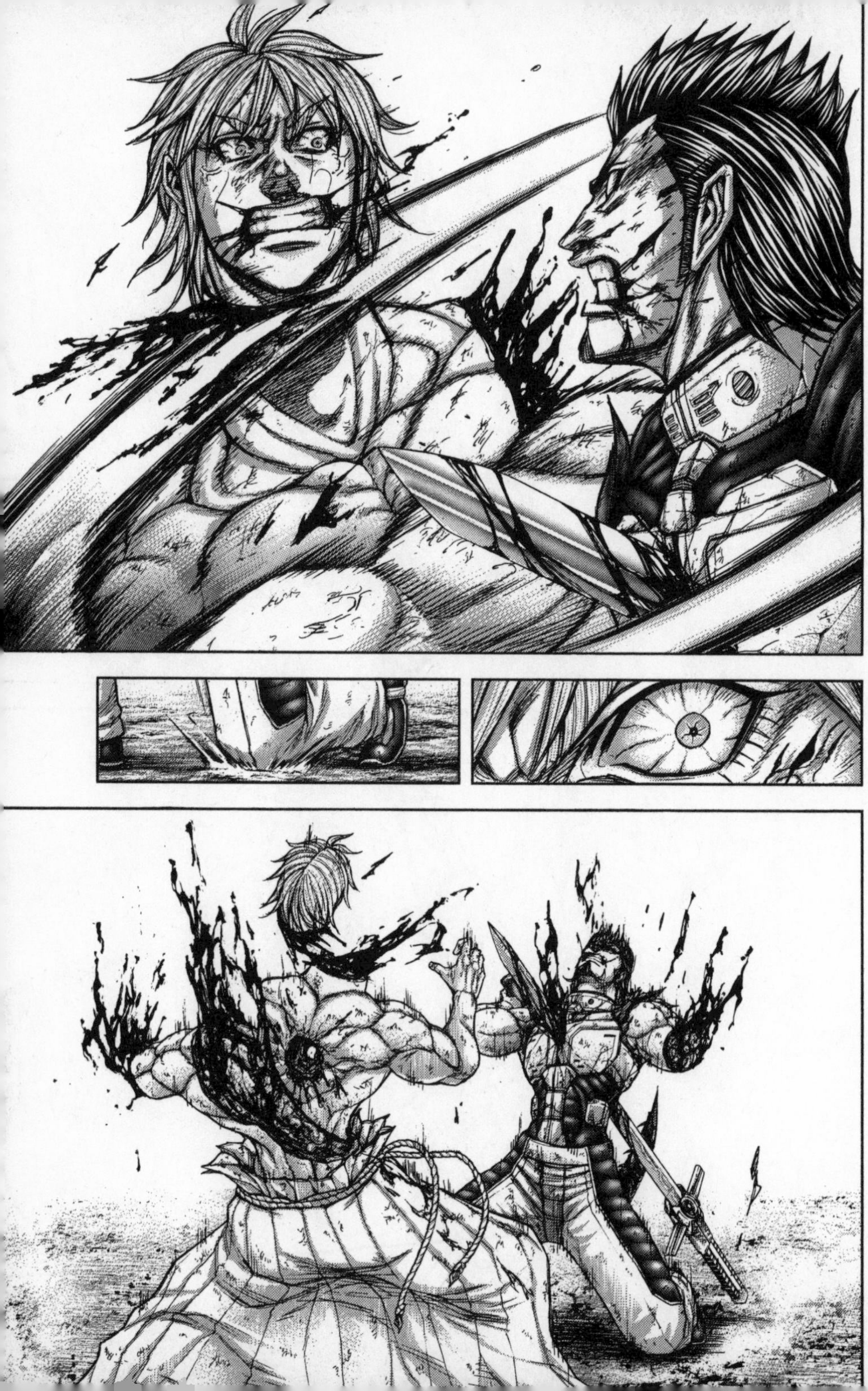

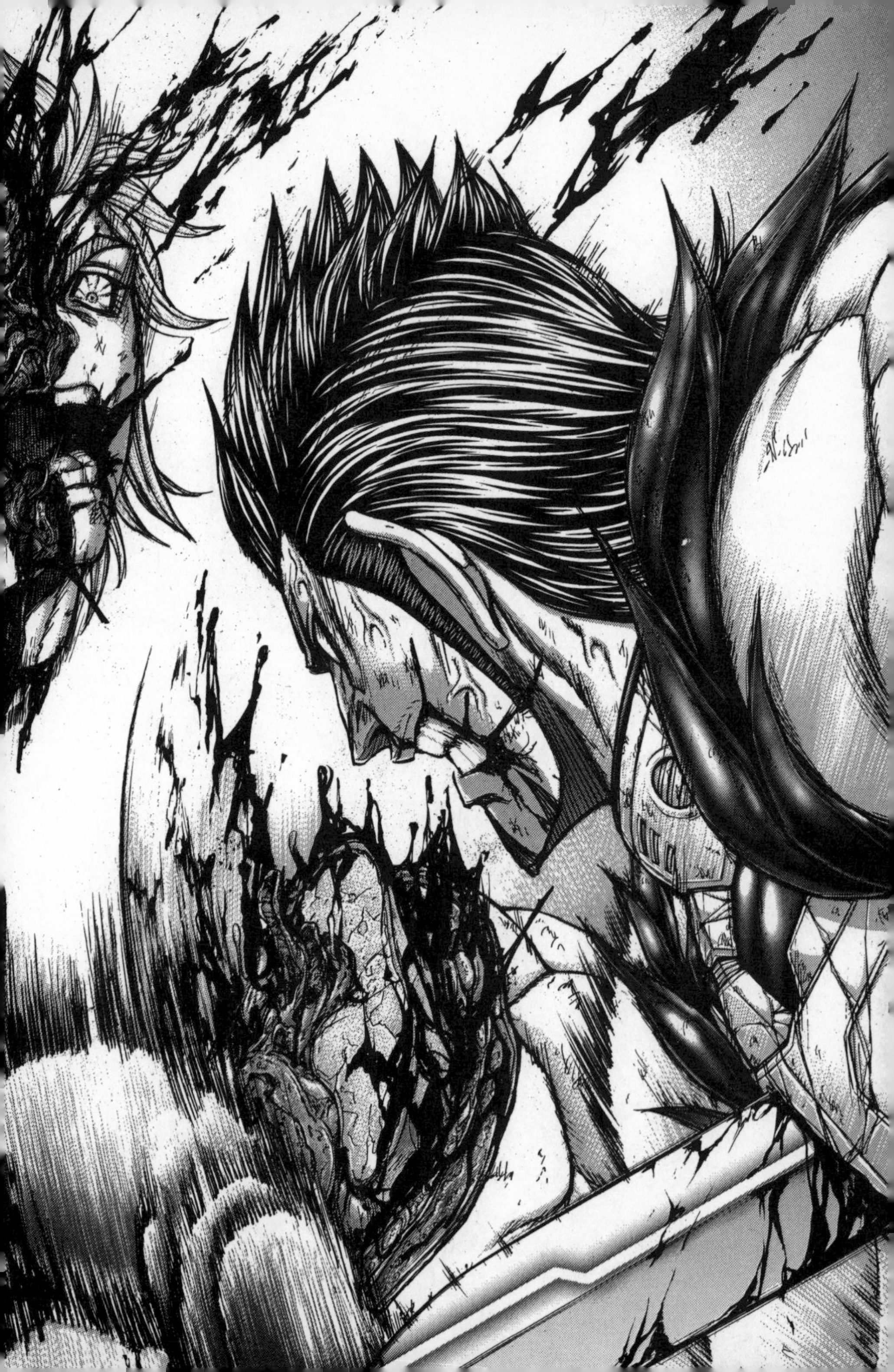

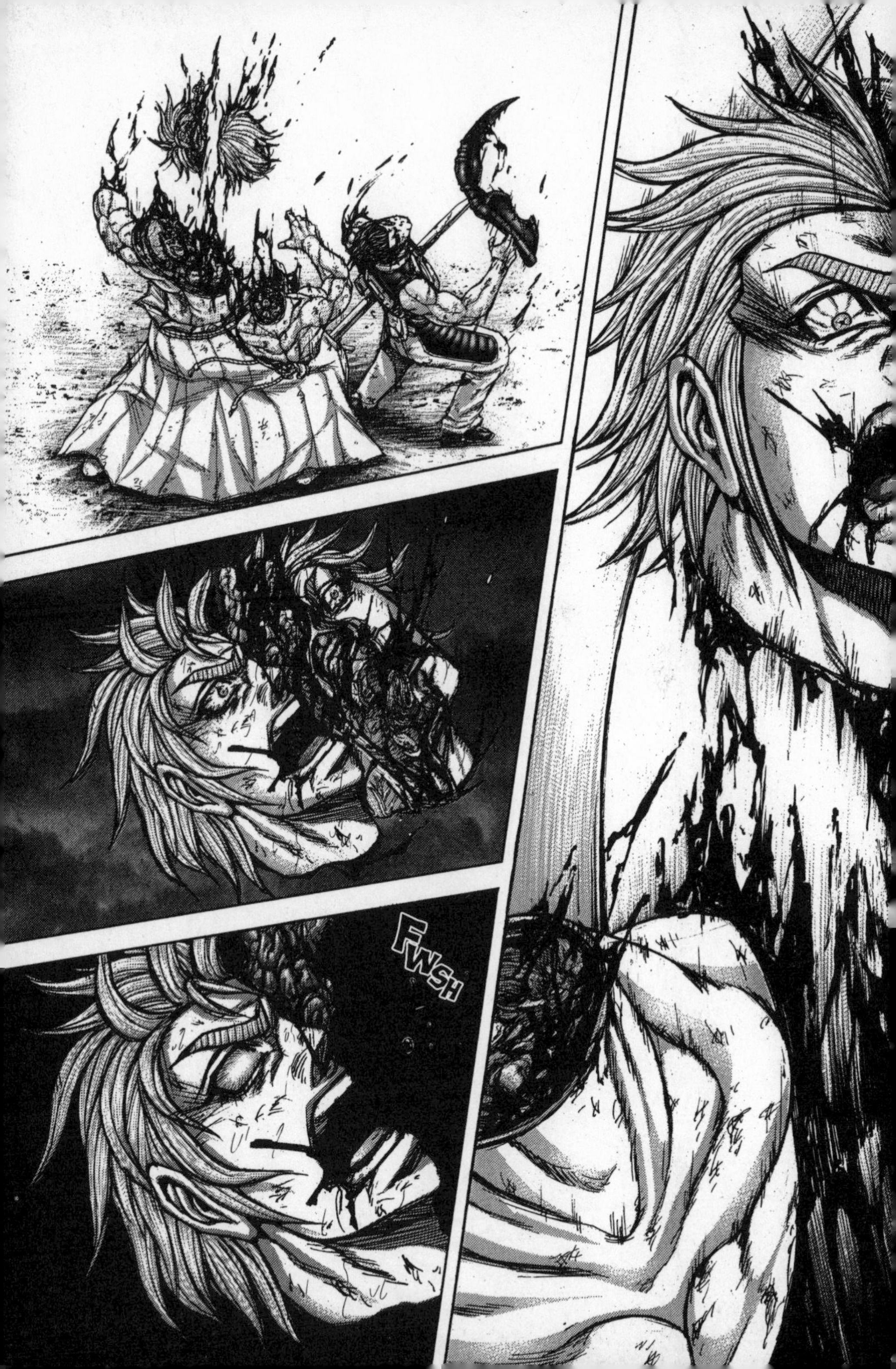
FWSH

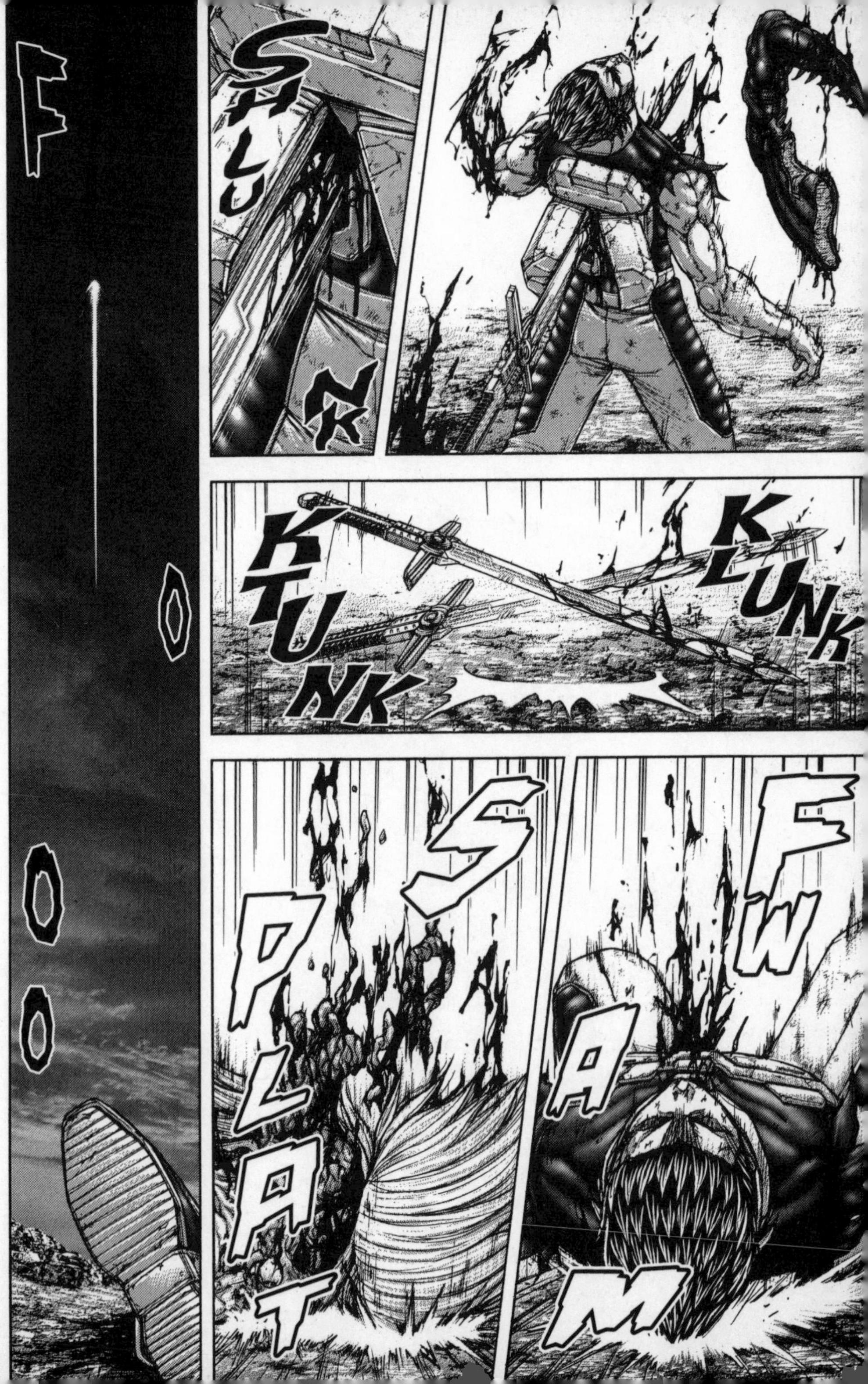
SHLUNK
KLUNK
KLUNK
FWAM
SPLAT
FOOOO

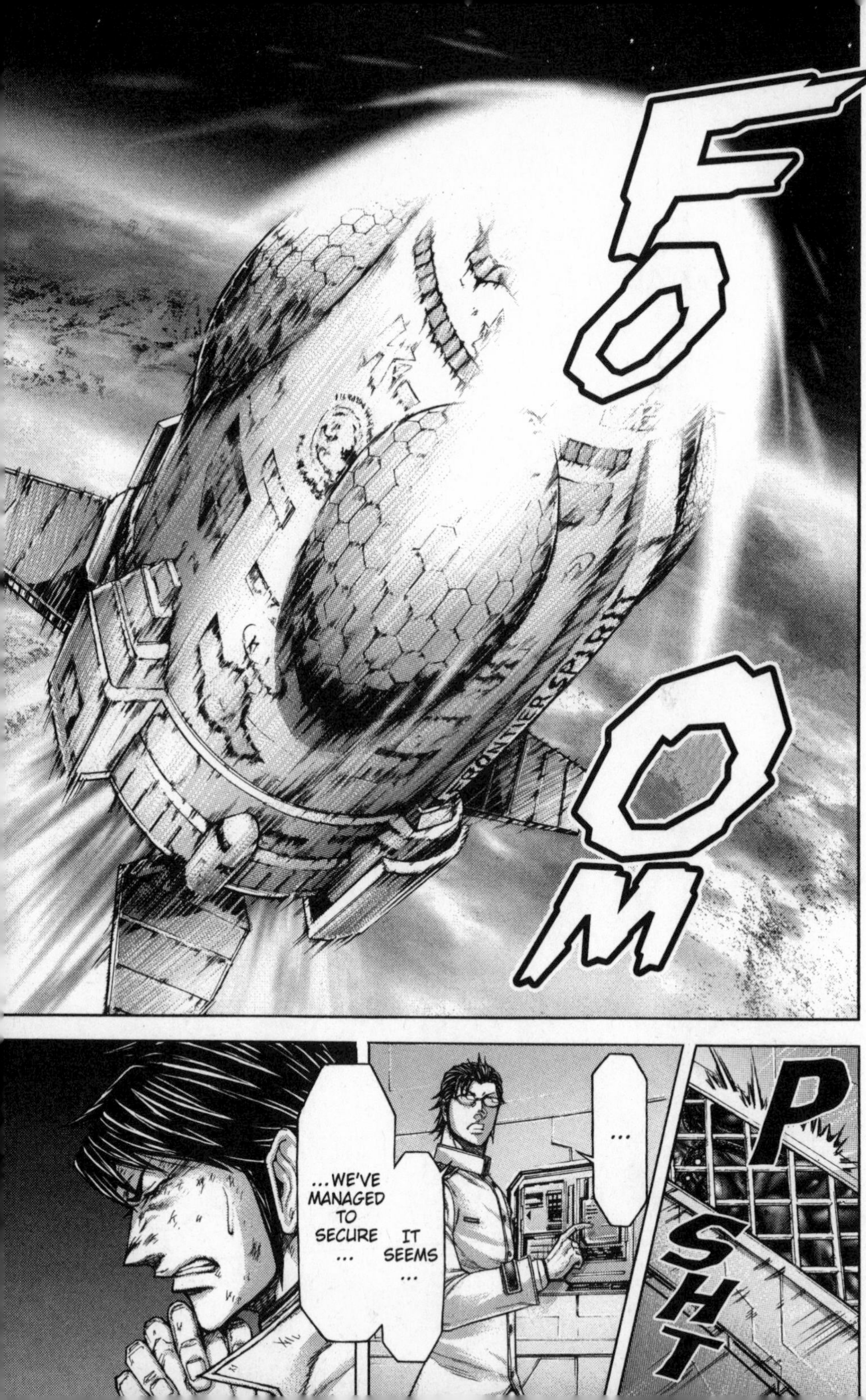
FOOM
PSHT
...
...WE'VE MANAGED TO SECURE ... IT SEEMS ...

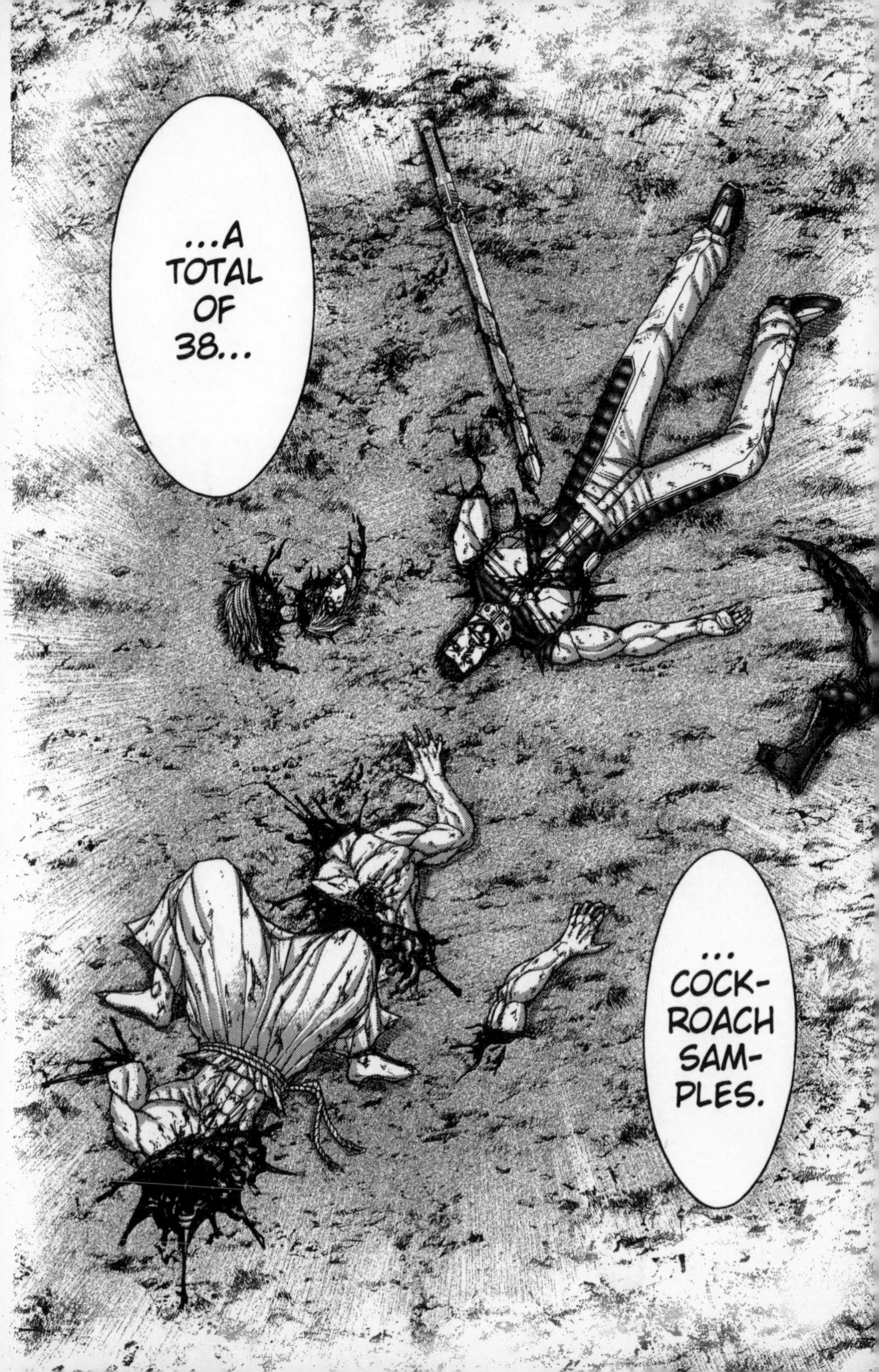
...A TOTAL OF 38...
...COCK-ROACH SAM-PLES.

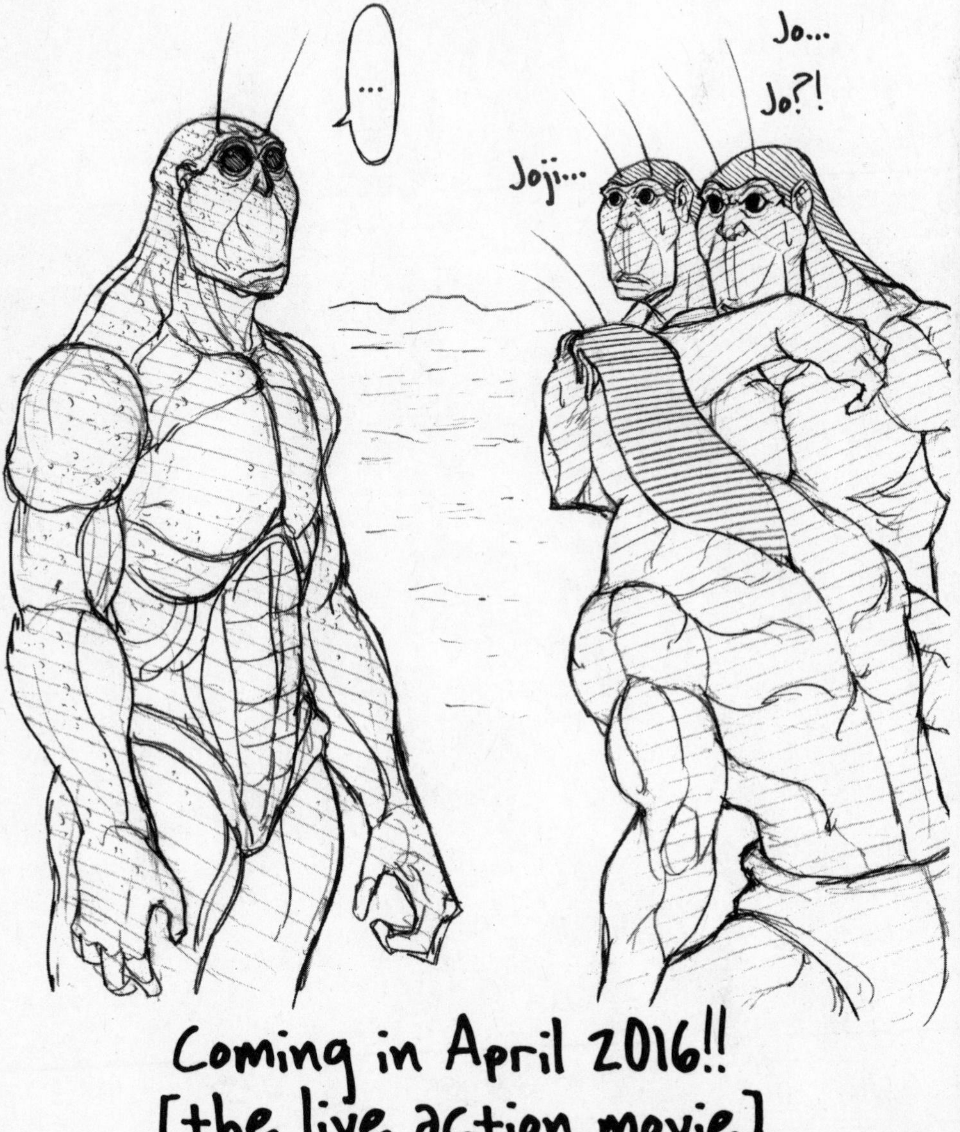
Jo...
Jo?!
Joji...
...

Coming in April 2016!!
[the live action movie]

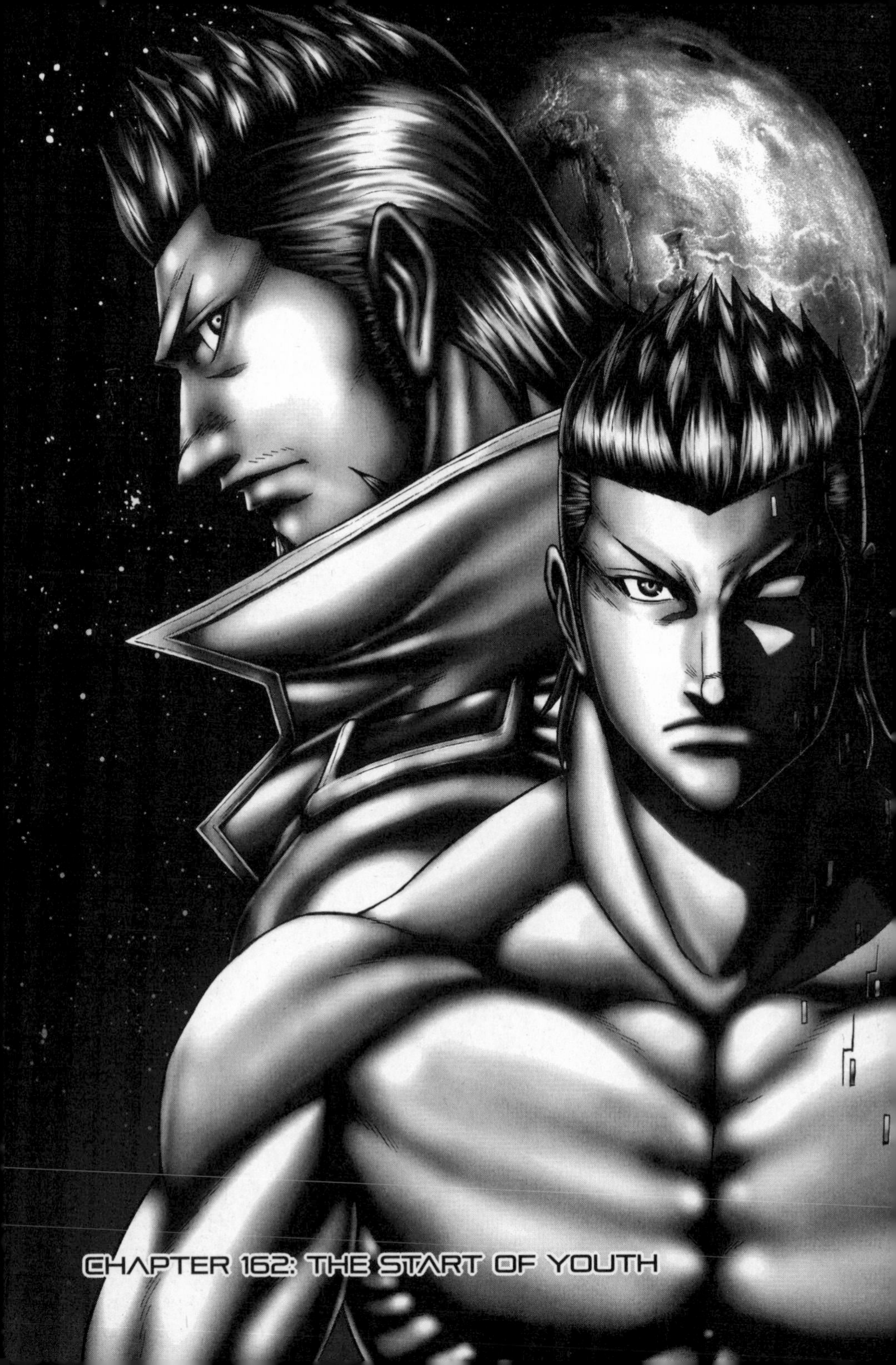
CHAPTER 162: THE START OF YOUTH

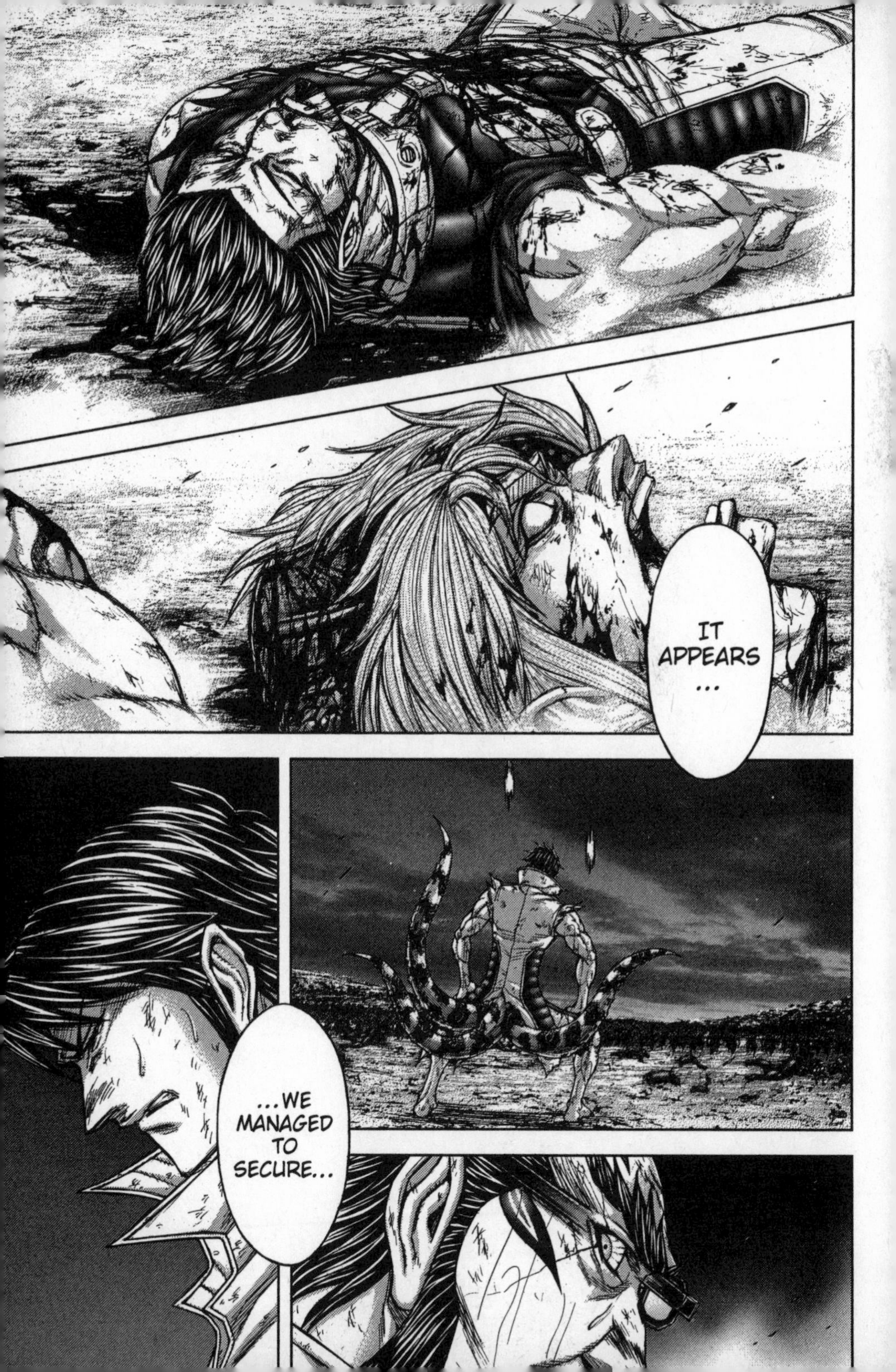
IT APPEARS ...
...WE MANAGED TO SECURE...

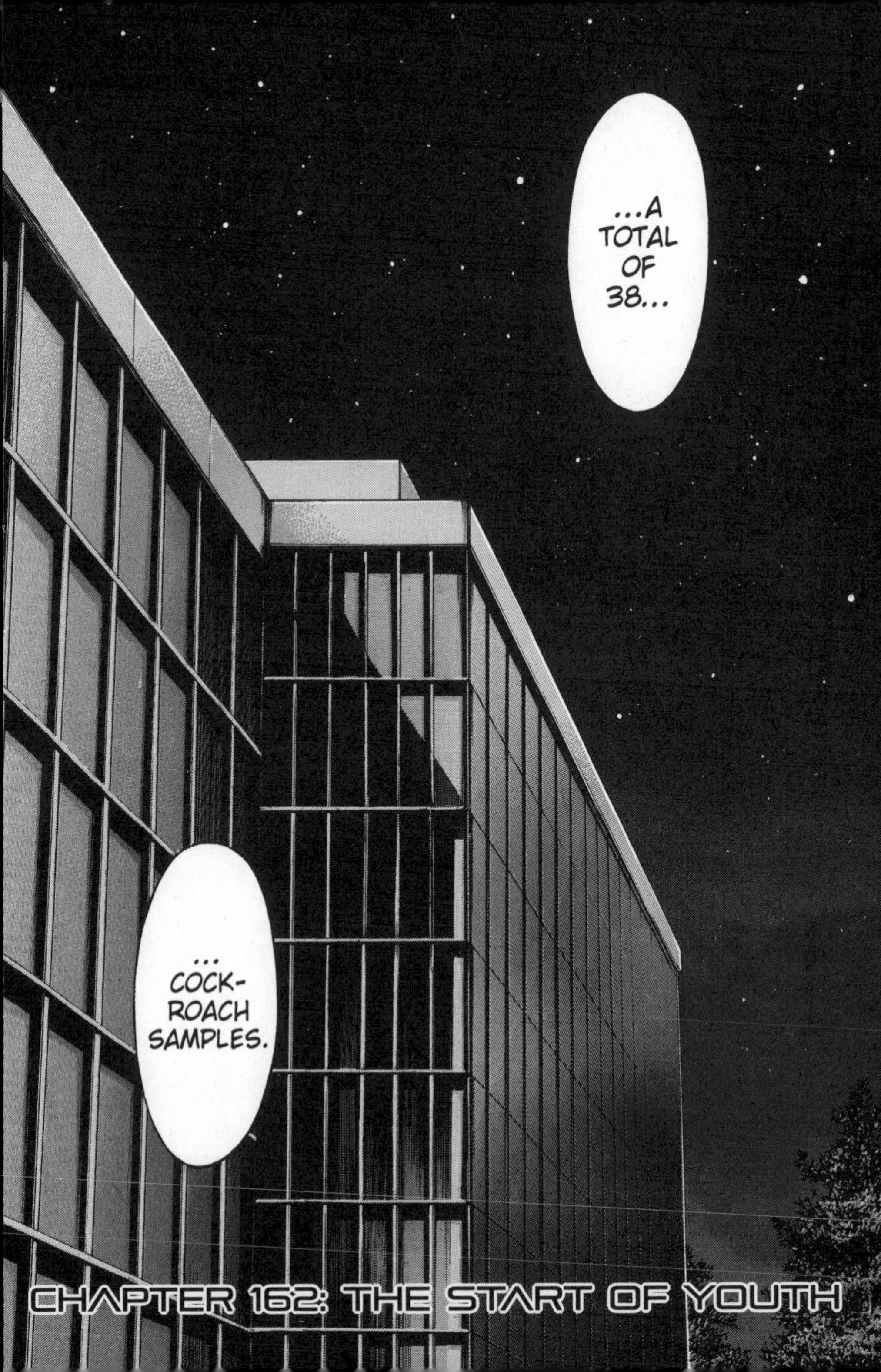
...A TOTAL OF 38...
... COCK-ROACH SAMPLES.
CHAPTER 162: THE START OF YOUTH

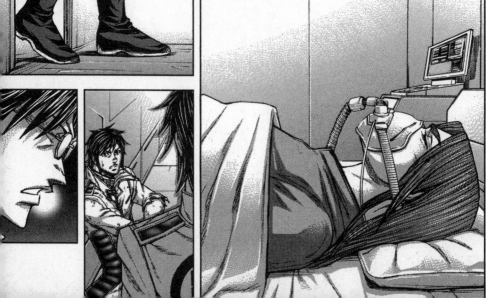

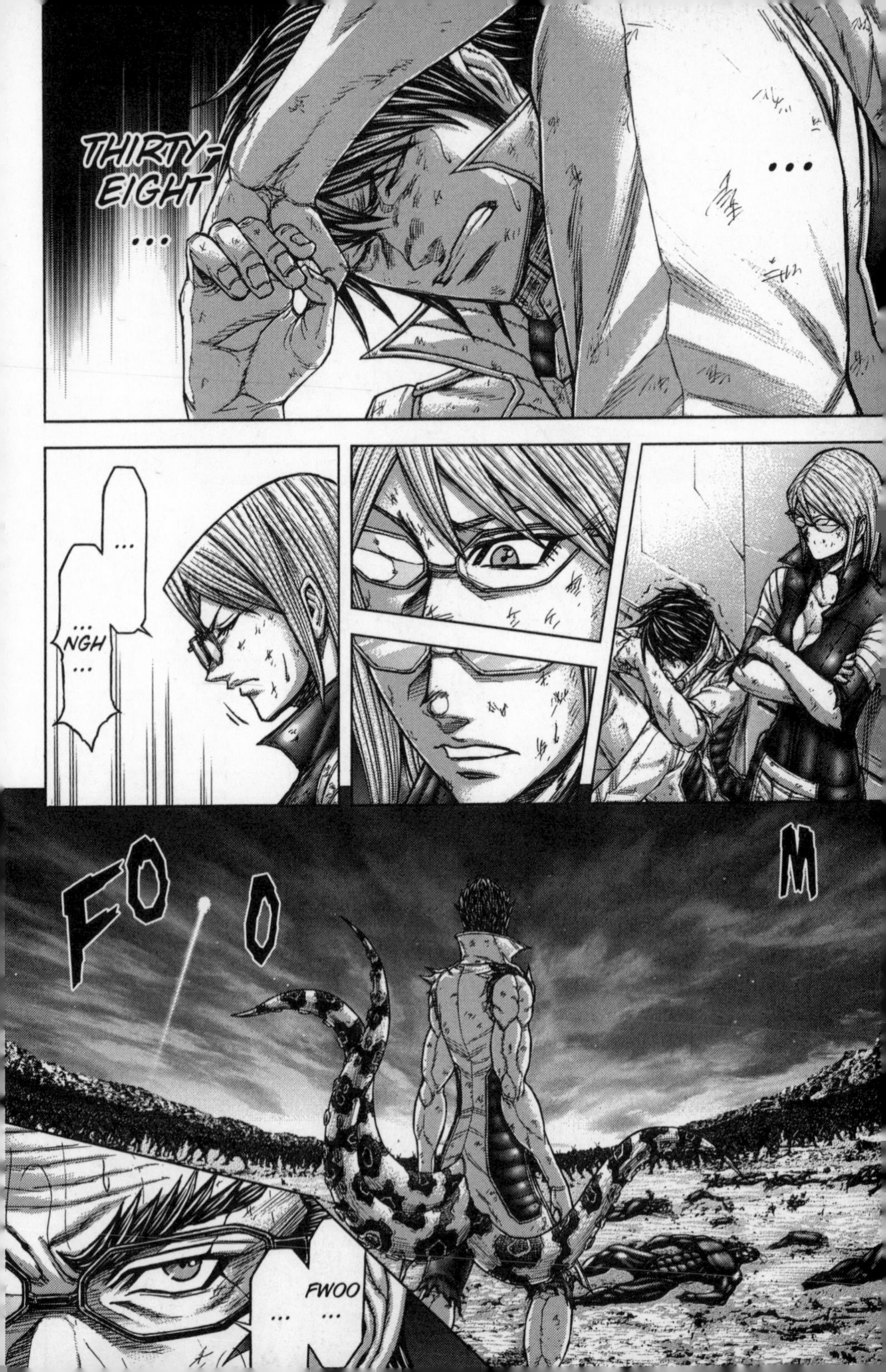
...
THIRTY-EIGHT
...
...
... NGH ...
FO O M
FWOO
... ...

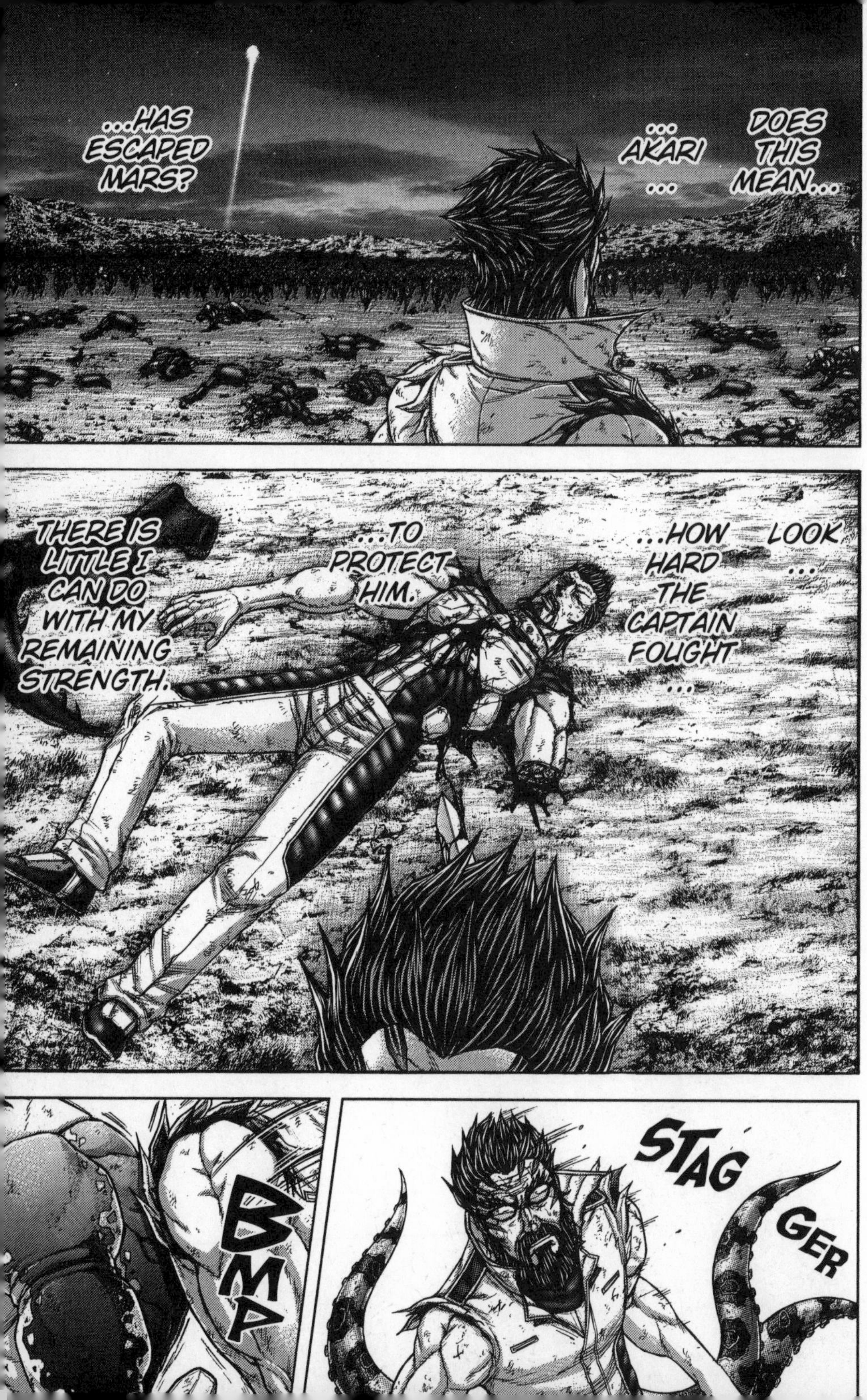
DOES THIS MEAN...
...AKARI...
...HAS ESCAPED MARS?
LOOK...
...HOW HARD THE CAPTAIN FOUGHT...
...TO PROTECT HIM.
THERE IS LITTLE I CAN DO WITH MY REMAINING STRENGTH.
STAGGER
BMP

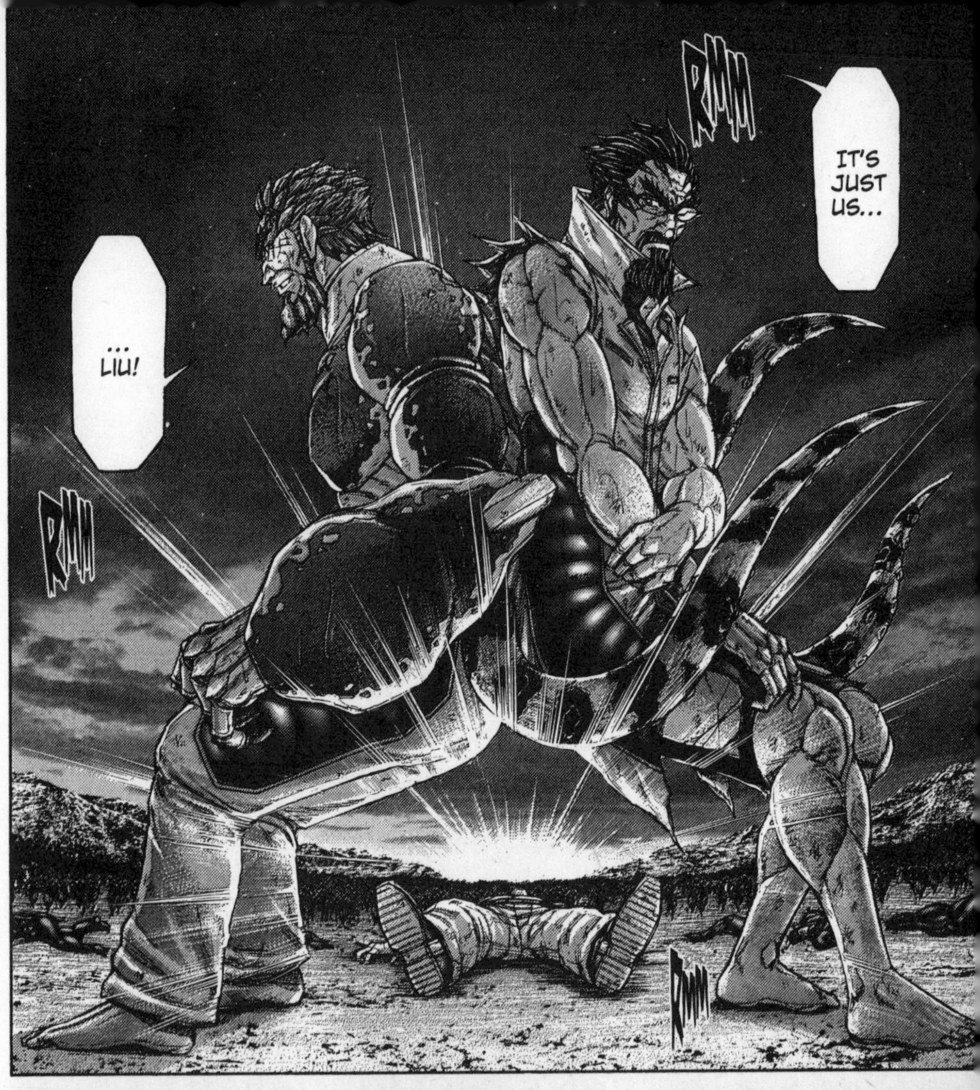
RMM
IT'S JUST US...
...LIU!
RMM
RMM

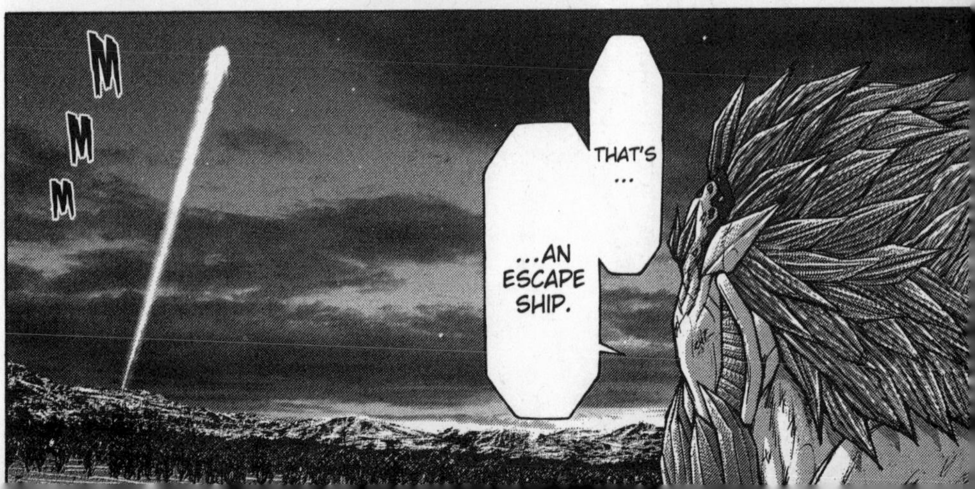
THAT'S ...
...AN ESCAPE SHIP.
M M M

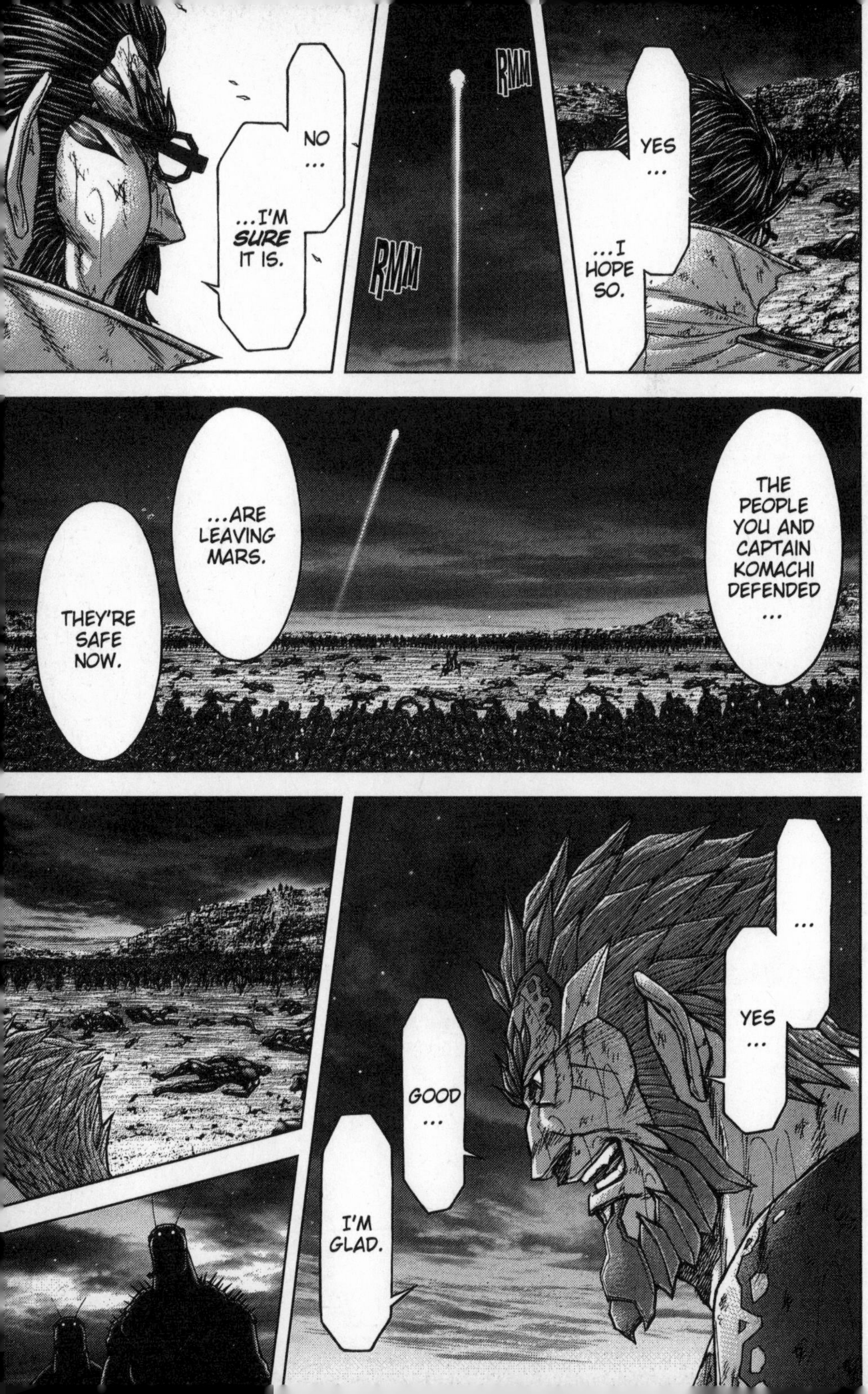
YES ...
...I HOPE SO.
RMM
RMM
NO ...
...I'M *SURE* IT IS.
THE PEOPLE YOU AND CAPTAIN KOMACHI DEFENDED ...
...ARE LEAVING MARS.
THEY'RE SAFE NOW.
...
YES ...
GOOD ...
I'M GLAD.

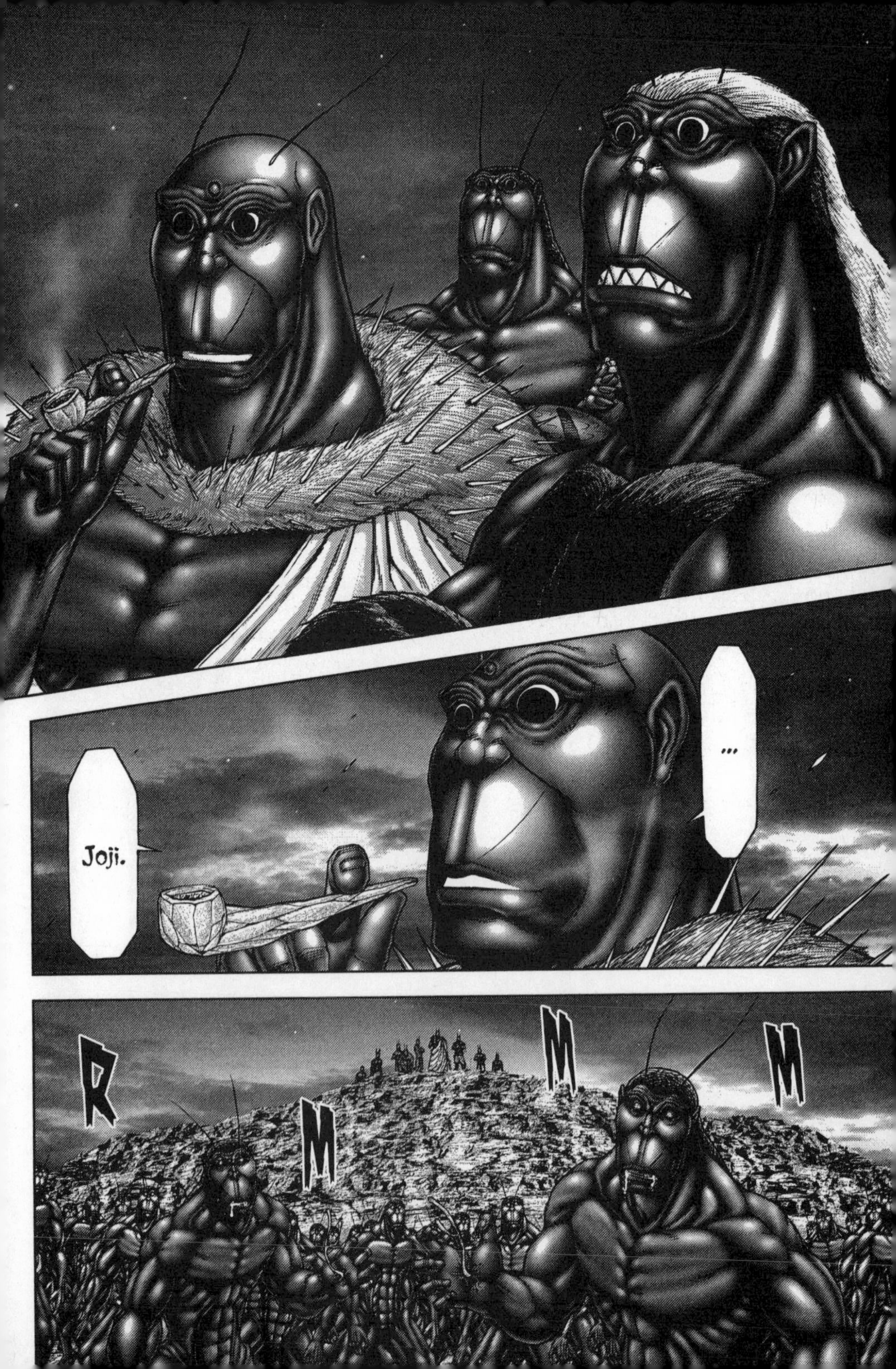
...
Joji.
R
M
M
M

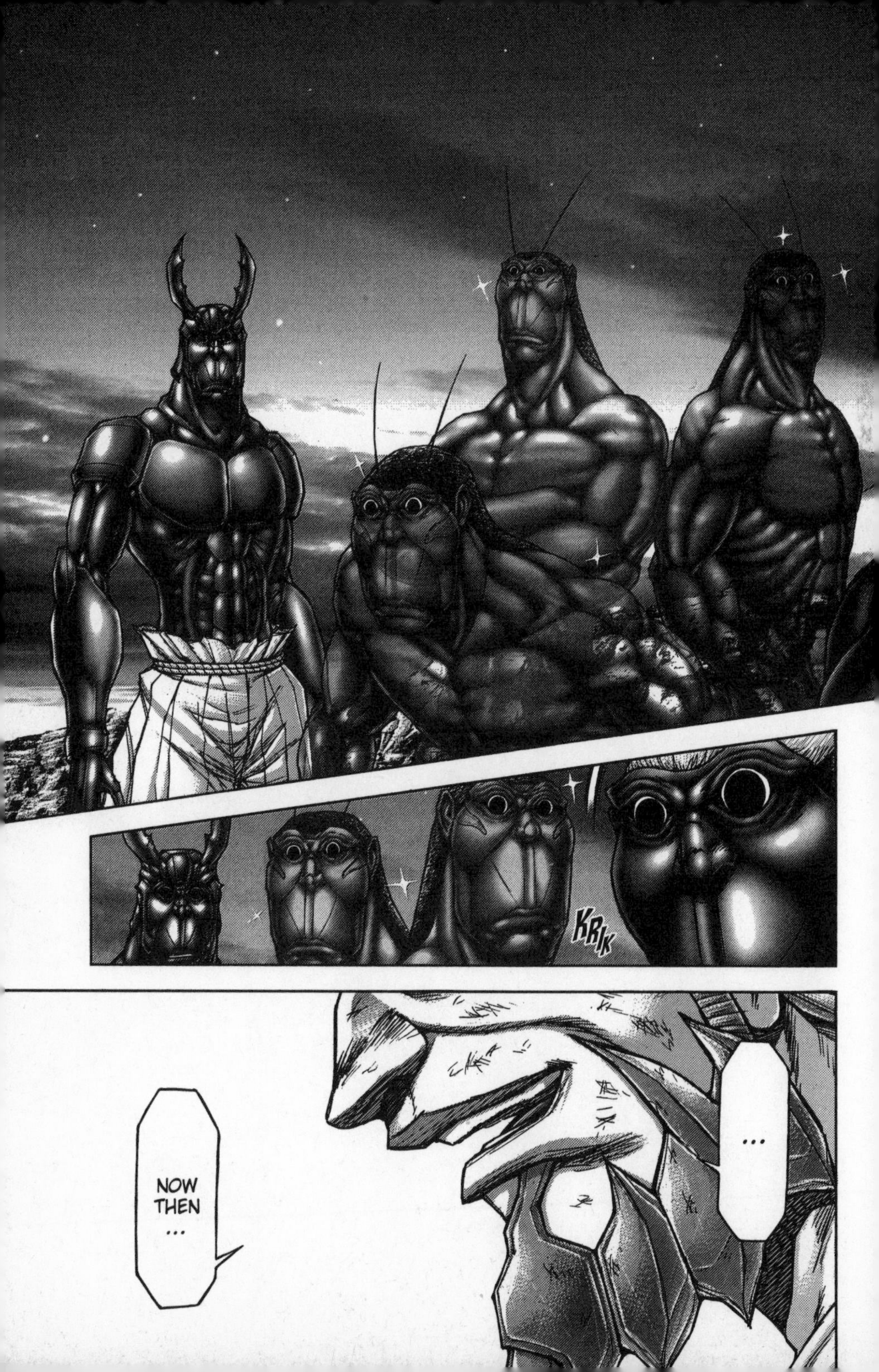
KRIK
...
NOW THEN ...

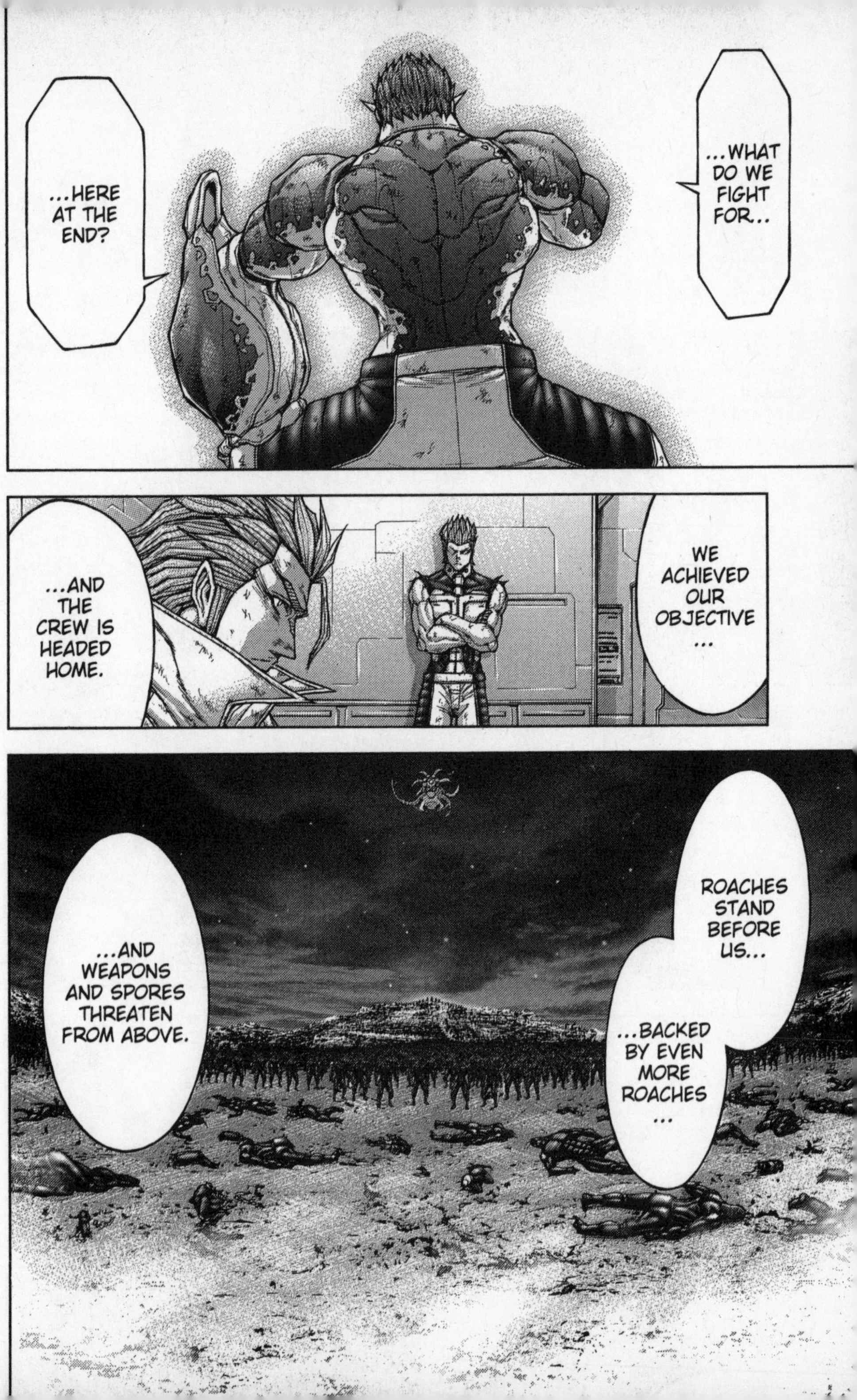
...WHAT DO WE FIGHT FOR...
...HERE AT THE END?
WE ACHIEVED OUR OBJECTIVE ...
...AND THE CREW IS HEADED HOME.
ROACHES STAND BEFORE US...
...BACKED BY EVEN MORE ROACHES ...
...AND WEAPONS AND SPORES THREATEN FROM ABOVE.

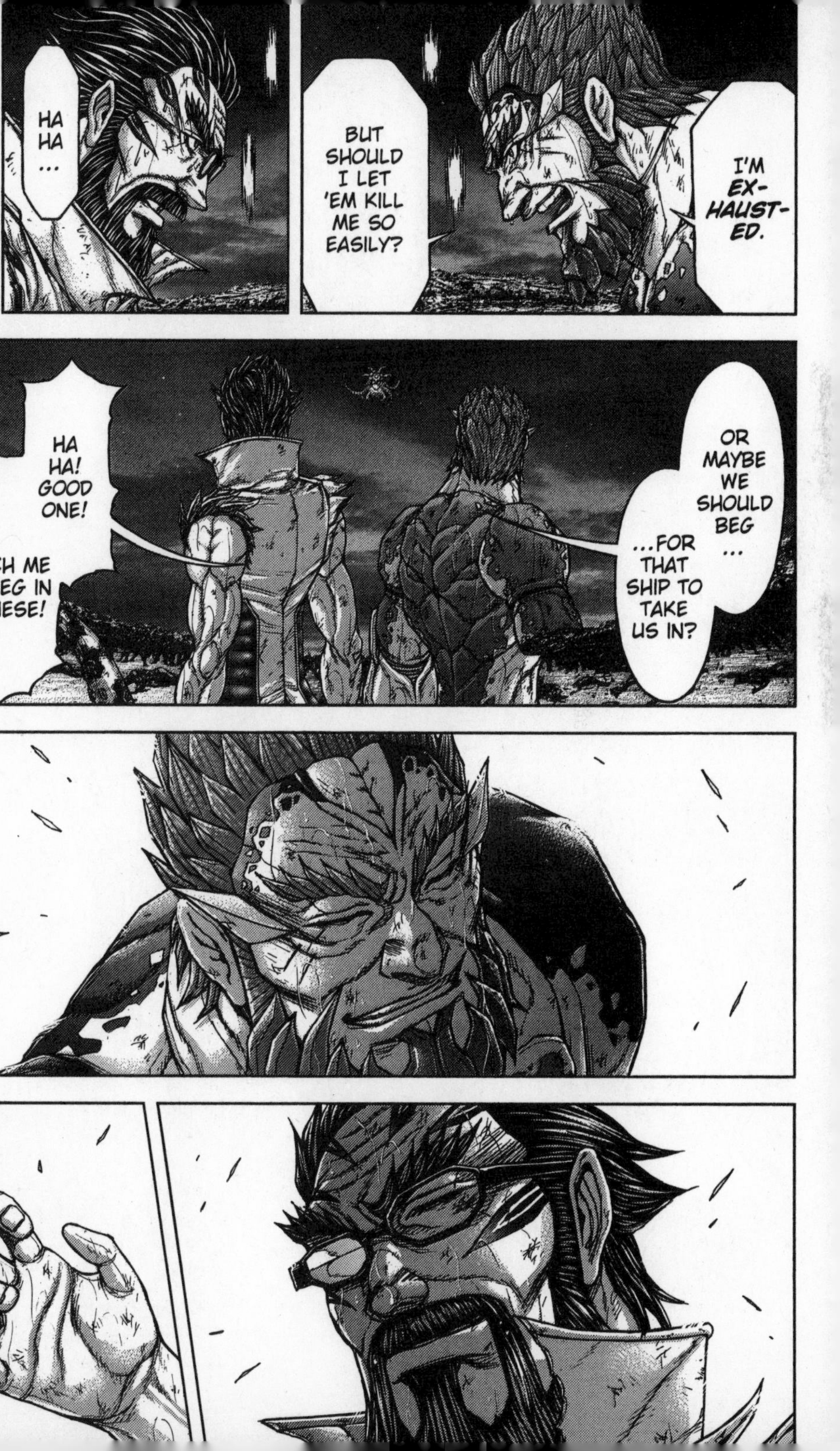
I'M EX-HAUSTED.
BUT SHOULD I LET 'EM KILL ME SO EASILY?
HA HA ...
OR MAYBE WE SHOULD BEG ...
...FOR THAT SHIP TO TAKE US IN?
HA HA! GOOD ONE!
TEACH ME TO BEG IN CHINESE!

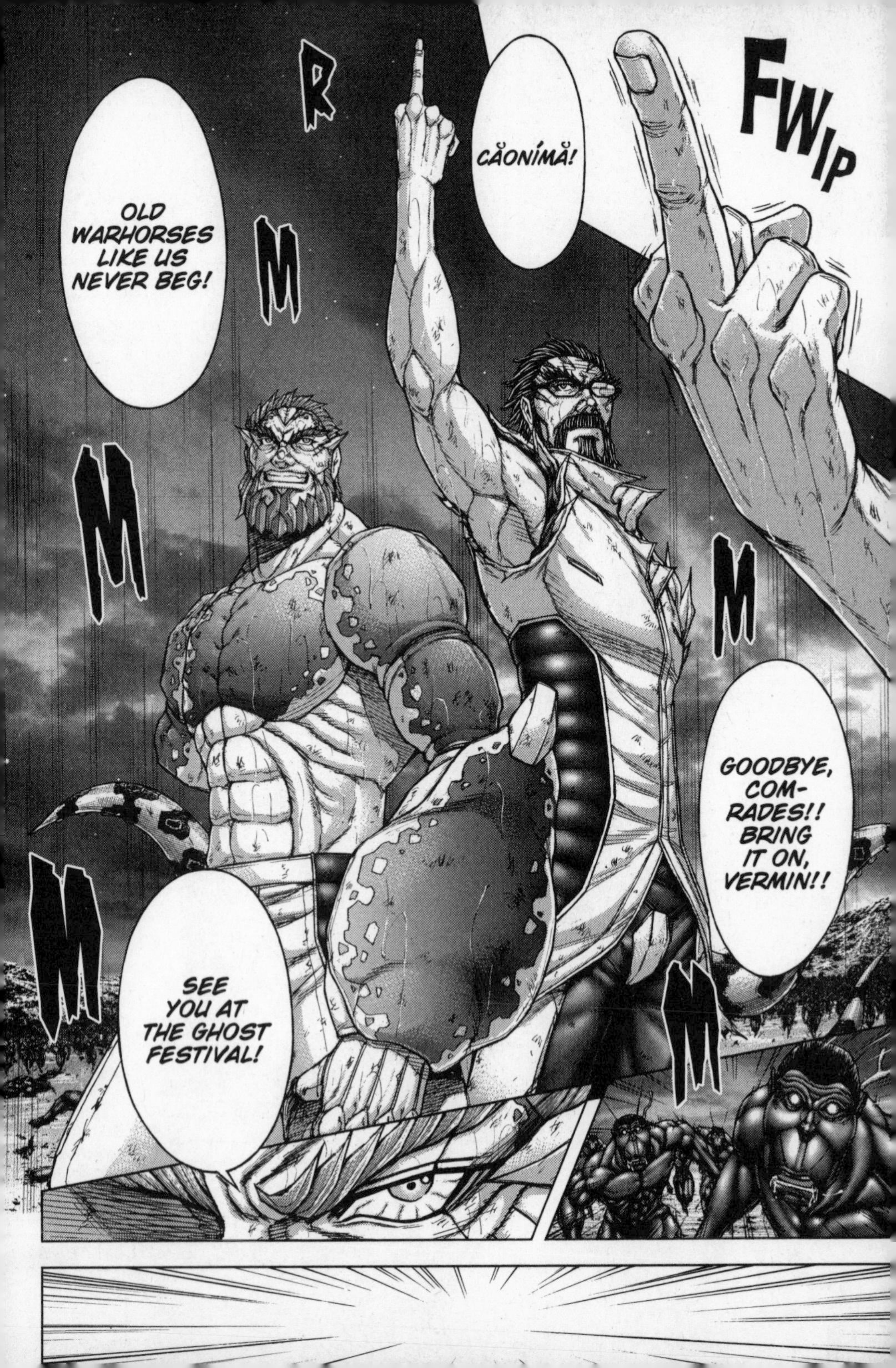
FWIP
CǍONÍMǍ!
R
OLD WARHORSES LIKE US NEVER BEG!
M
M
M
M
M
GOODBYE, COMRADES!! BRING IT ON, VERMIN!!
SEE YOU AT THE GHOST FESTIVAL!

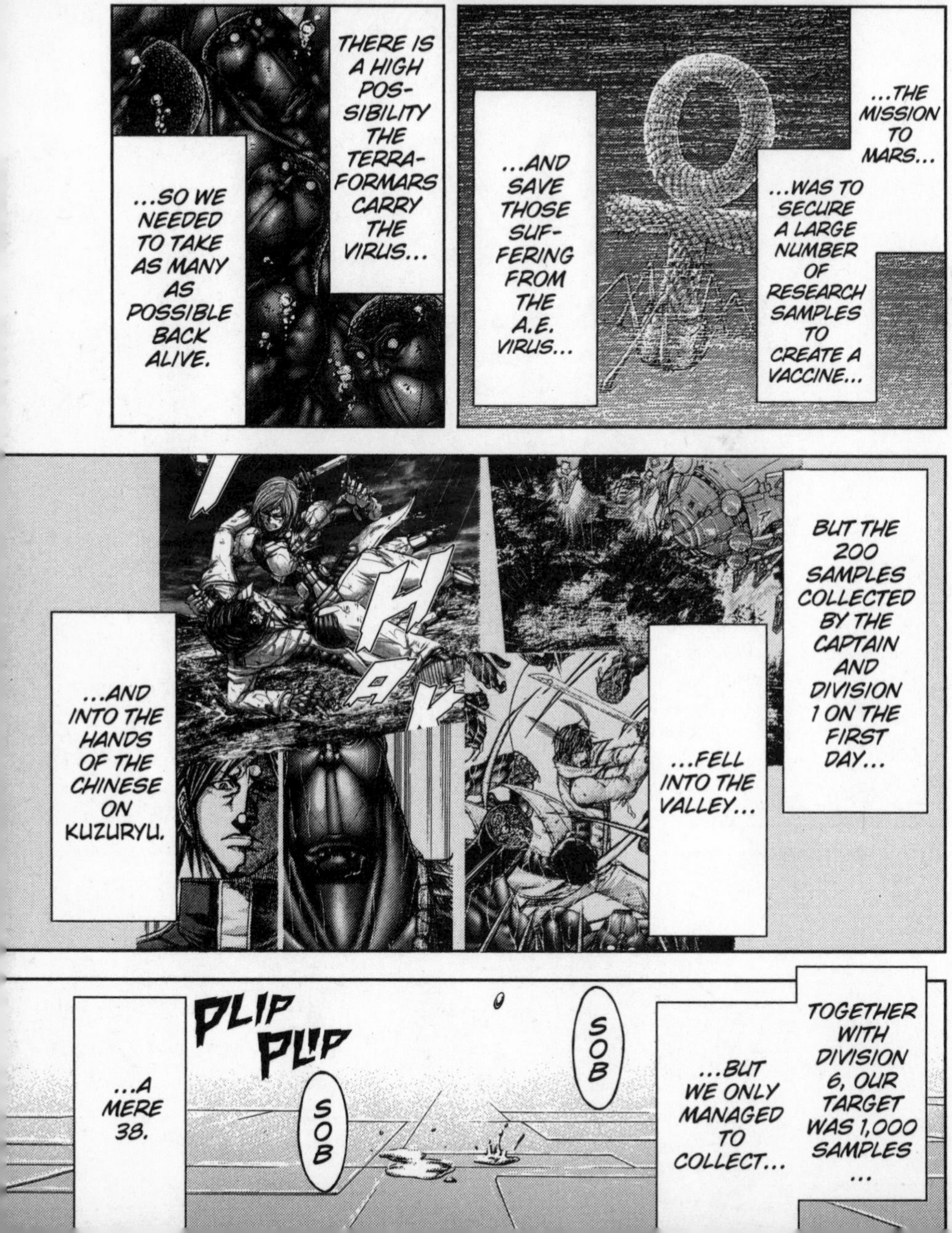
...THE MISSION TO MARS...
...WAS TO SECURE A LARGE NUMBER OF RESEARCH SAMPLES TO CREATE A VACCINE...
...AND SAVE THOSE SUFFERING FROM THE A.E. VIRUS...
THERE IS A HIGH POSSIBILITY THE TERRAFORMARS CARRY THE VIRUS...
...SO WE NEEDED TO TAKE AS MANY AS POSSIBLE BACK ALIVE.
BUT THE 200 SAMPLES COLLECTED BY THE CAPTAIN AND DIVISION 1 ON THE FIRST DAY...
...FELL INTO THE VALLEY...
...AND INTO THE HANDS OF THE CHINESE ON KUZURYU.
TOGETHER WITH DIVISION 6, OUR TARGET WAS 1,000 SAMPLES...
...BUT WE ONLY MANAGED TO COLLECT...
SOB
SOB
PLIP PLIP
...A MERE 38.

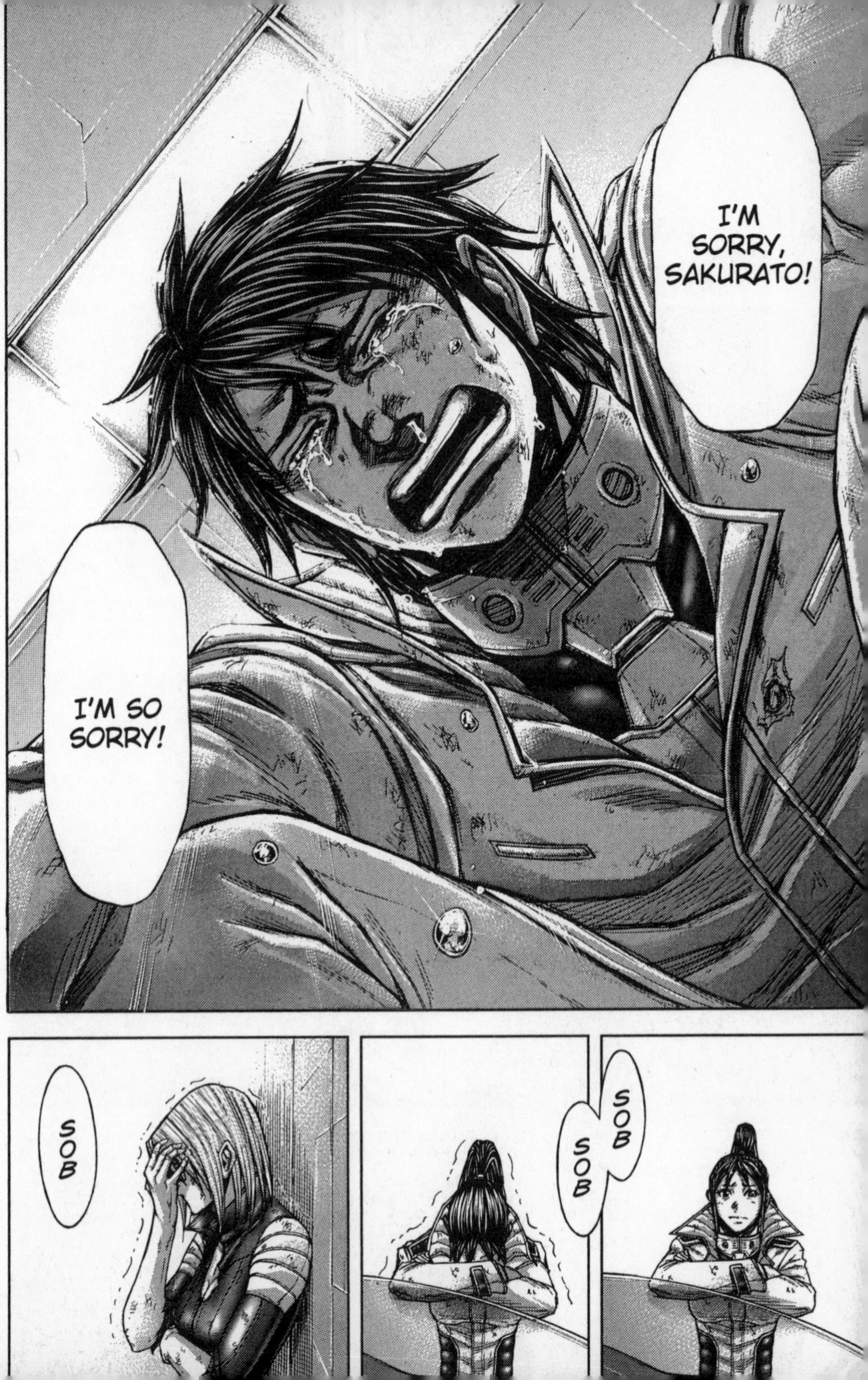
I'M SORRY, SAKURATO!
I'M SO SORRY!
SOB SOB
SOB

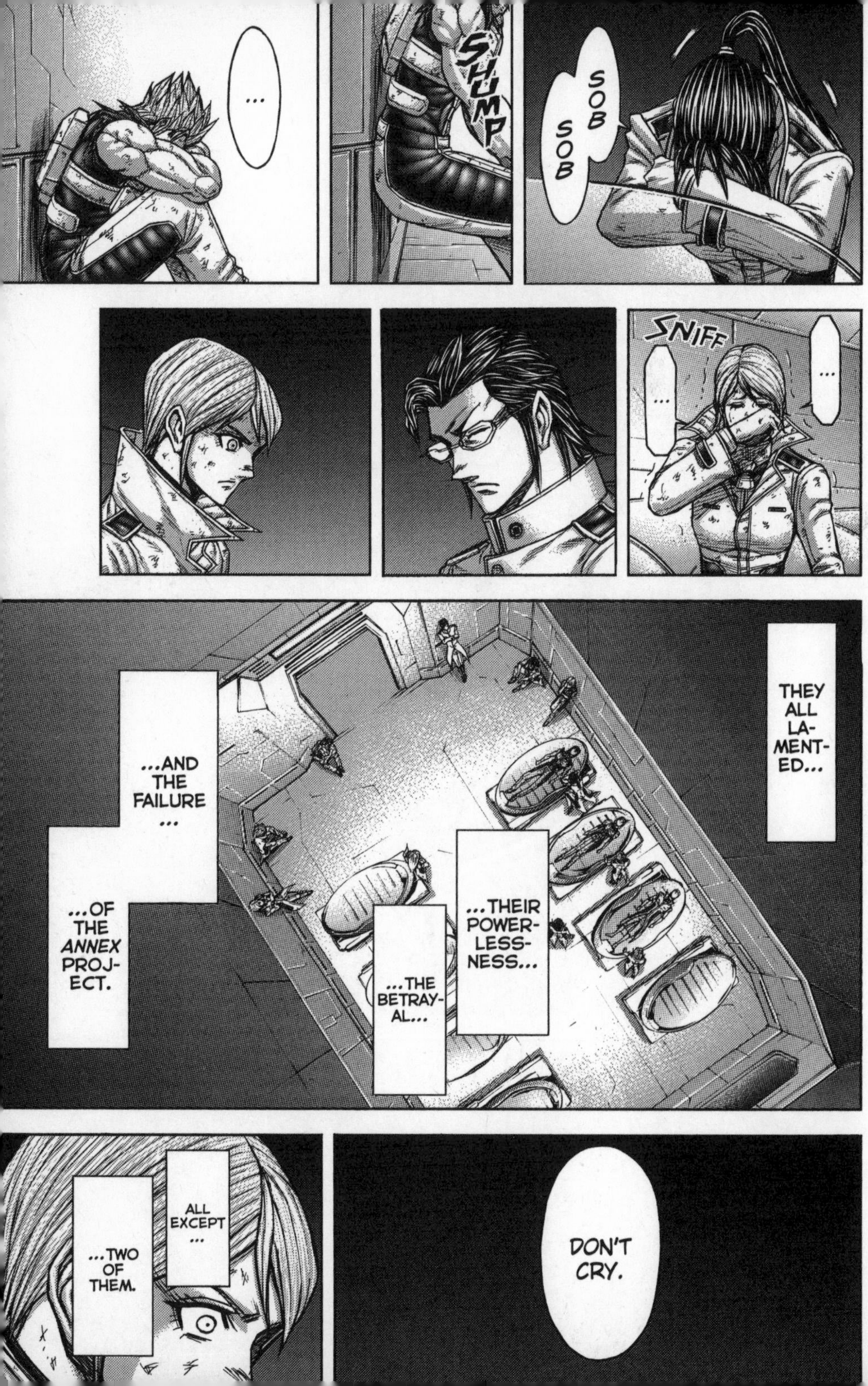
SOB SOB
SHUMP
...
SNIFF
...
...
THEY ALL LAMENTED...
...THEIR POWERLESSNESS...
...THE BETRAYAL...
...AND THE FAILURE...
...OF THE ANNEX PROJECT.
DON'T CRY.
ALL EXCEPT...
...TWO OF THEM.

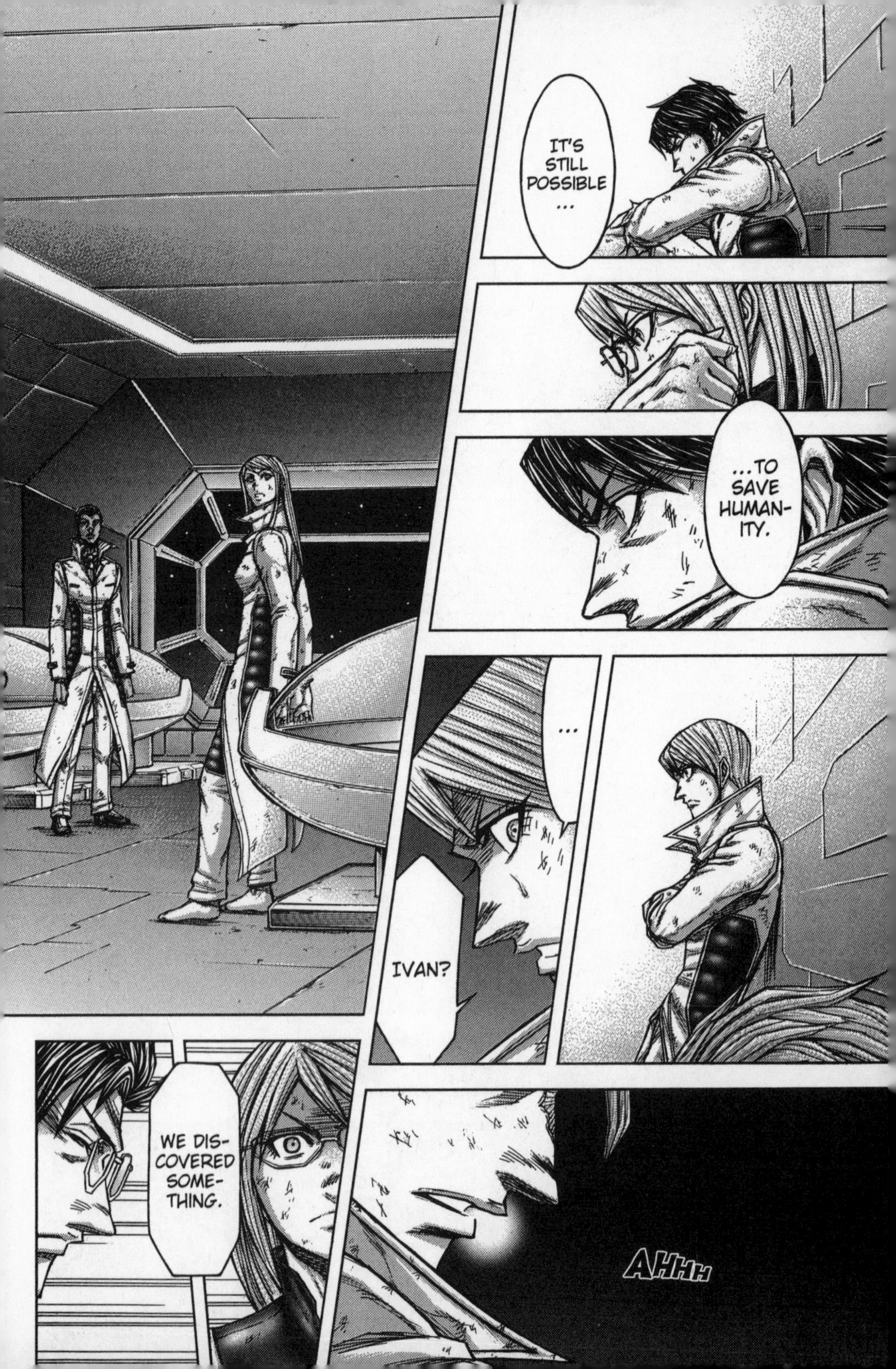

IT'S STILL POSSIBLE...
...TO SAVE HUMAN-ITY.
...
IVAN?
AHHH
WE DIS-COVERED SOME-THING.

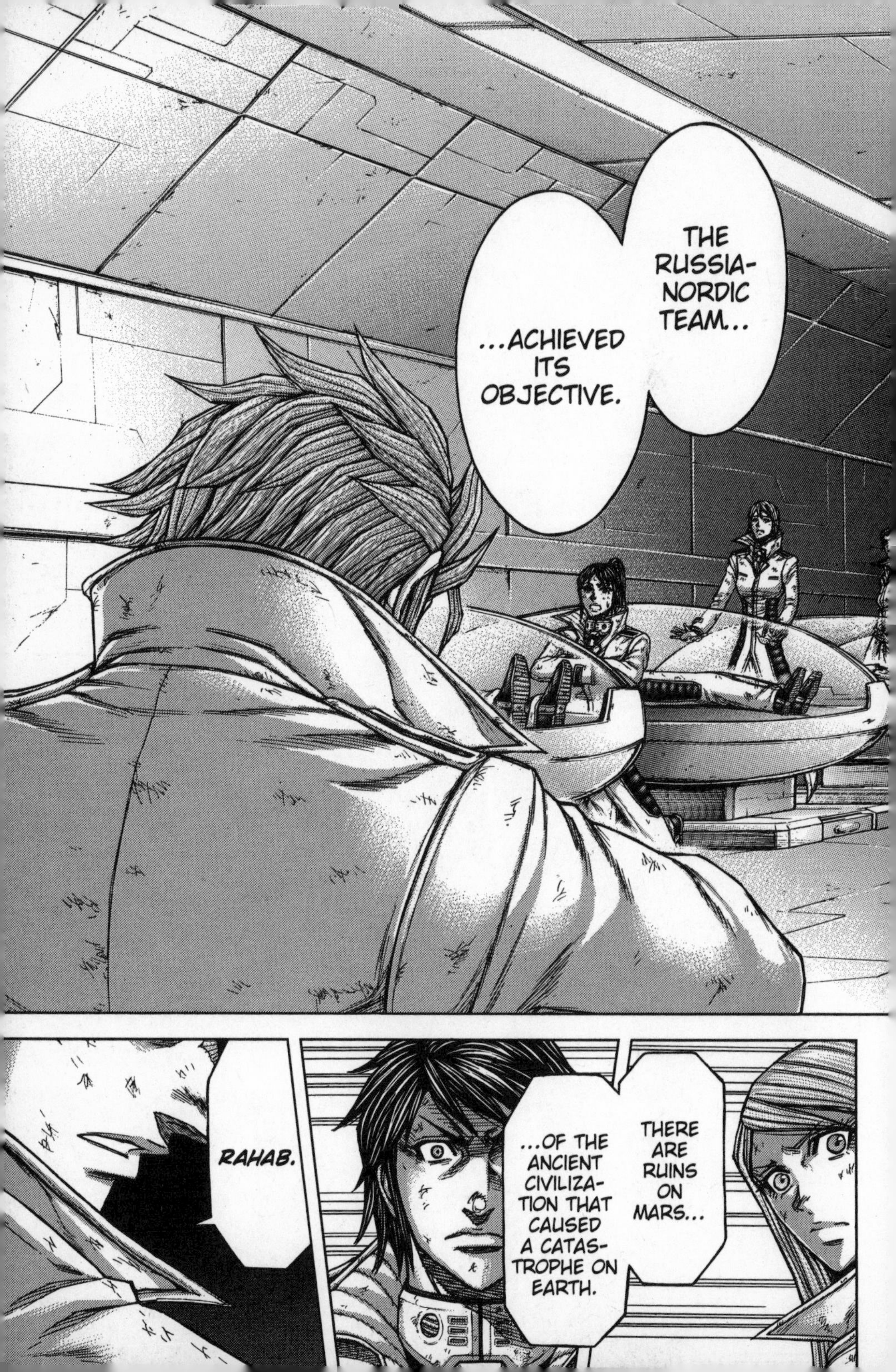
THE RUSSIA-NORDIC TEAM...
...ACHIEVED ITS OBJECTIVE.
THERE ARE RUINS ON MARS...
...OF THE ANCIENT CIVILIZATION THAT CAUSED A CATASTROPHE ON EARTH.
RAHAB.

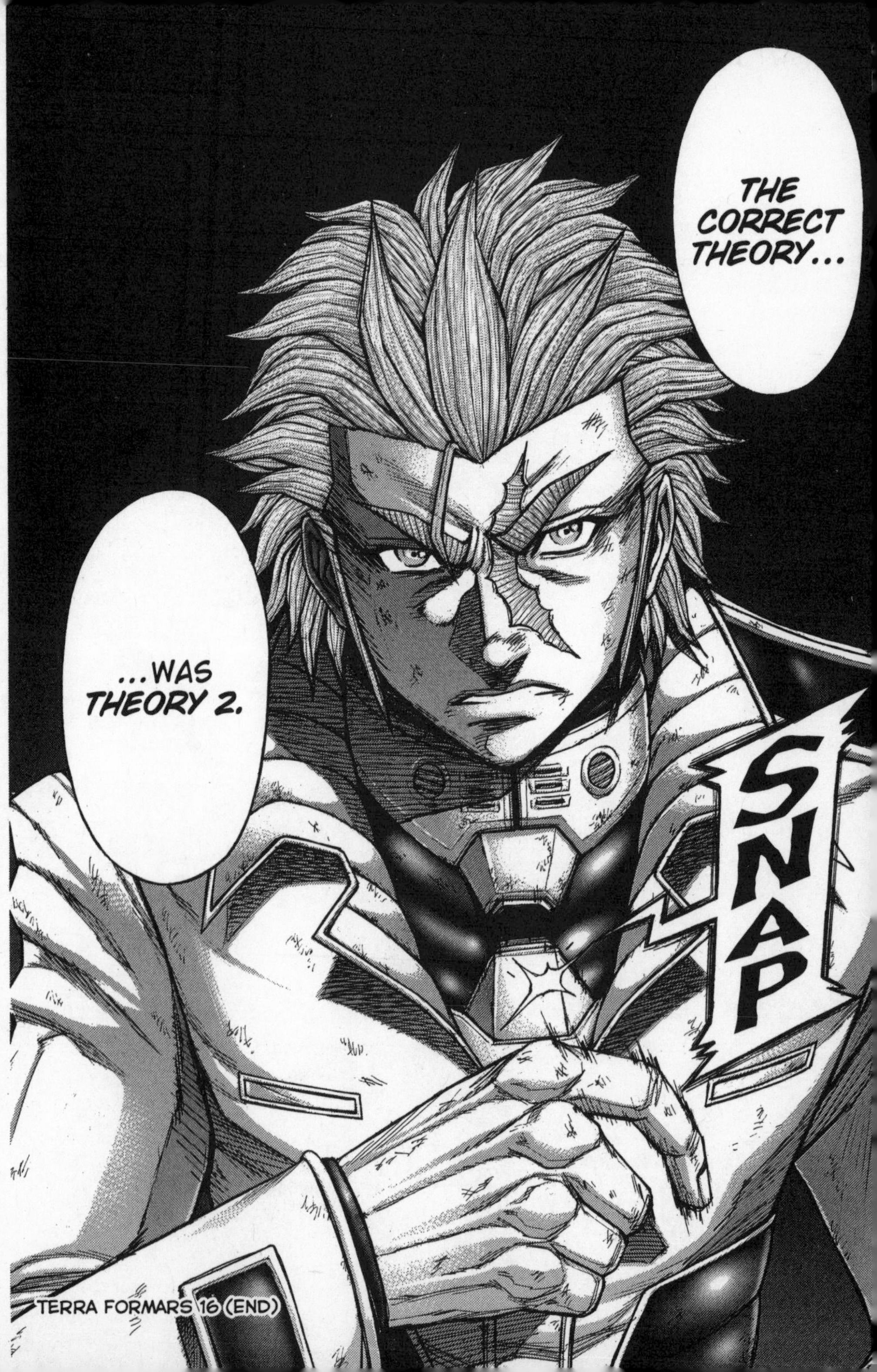
THE CORRECT THEORY...
SNAP
...WAS THEORY 2.
TERRA FORMARS 16 (END)